The Selected Letters
of
W. E. Henley

Henley as a young man *c*. 1880

The Selected Letters
of
W.E. Henley

Edited by
Damian Atkinson

Ashgate

Aldershot • Burlington USA • Singapore • Sydney

Published by

Ashgate Publishing Ltd
Gower House, Croft Road,
Aldershot, Hampshire GU11 3HR
England

Ashgate Publishing Company
131 Main Street
Burlington, Vermont 05401–5600
USA

Ashgate website: http://www.ashgate.com

ISBN 1 84014 634 6

British Library Cataloguing-in-Publication Data
Henley, W.E. (William Ernest)
    The Selected Letters of W.E. Henley
    1. Henley, W.E. (William Ernest)—Correspondence. I. Title. II. Atkinson,
Damian
    821.8   1003396333

US Library of Congress Cataloging-in-Publication Data
Henley, William Ernest, 1849–1903
    [Correspondence. Selections]
    The Selected Letters of W.E. Henley / edited by Damian Atkinson
        p.   cm.   (The Nineteenth Century)
        Includes bibliographical references (p.   ) and index.
    1. Henley, William Ernest, 1849–1903—Correspondence. 2. Authors, English—
19th century—Correspondence. 3. Lexicographers—Great Britain—
Correspondence. 4. Editors—Great Britain—Correspondence. 5. Critics—Great
Britain—Correspondence. I. Atkinson, Damian. II. Title. III. Series: Nineteenth
Century (Aldershot, England)
    PR4784.A4 19998   99–50906
    828.809–dc21   CIP

This volume is printed on acid-free paper.

Printed and bound by Athenaeum Press, Ltd.,
Gateshead, Tyne & Wear.

Contents

The Nineteenth Century
General Editors' Preface

The aim of this series is to reflect, develop and extend the great burgeoning of interest in the nineteenth century that has been an inevitable feature of recent decades, as that former epoch has come more sharply into focus as a locus for our understanding, not only of the past but of the contours of our modernity. Though it is dedicated principally to the publication of original monographs and symposia in literature, history, cultural analysis, and associated fields, there will be a salient role for reprints of significant texts from, or about the period. Our overarching policy is to address the spectrum of nineteenth-century studies without exception, achieving the widest scope in chronology, approach and range of concern. This, we believe, distinguishes our project from comparable ones, and means, for example, that in the relevant areas of scholarship we both recognize and cut innovatively across such parameters as those suggested by the designations 'Romantic' and 'Victorian'. We welcome new ideas, while valuing tradition. It is hoped that the world which predates yet so forcibly predicts and engages our own will emerge in parts, as a whole, and in the lively currents of debate and change that are so manifest an aspect of its intellectual, artistic and social landscape.

Vincent Newey
Joanne Shattock
University of Leicester

List of Plates

Acknowledgements

Many people and institutions have contributed to this edition. I must first thank all those who gave me permission to publish Henley letters and they are listed below:

The Beinecke Rare Book and Manuscript Library, Yale; Berg Collection of English and American Literature, the New York Public Library, Astor, Lenox and Tilden Foundations; the Bodleian Library; the British Library; Brander Matthews Papers, Rare Book and Manuscript Library, Columbia University, New York; Manuscript Department, William R. Perkins Library, Duke University; Mitchell Library, Glasgow City Libraries and Archives; Special Collections Department, Glasgow University; Houghton Library, Harvard University; Department of Manuscripts, The Huntington Library, San Marino, California; Brotherton Collection, Leeds University Library; Library of Congress, Washington D.C.; John Murray (Publishers) Ltd.; the Trustees of the National Library of Scotland; Musée Rodin, Paris; the Warden and Fellows of New College, Oxford; Fales Library, New York University; Pierpont Morgan Library, New York; Picture Library, National Portrait Gallery, London; Norman Colbeck Manuscript Collection, Special Collection, University of British Columbia Library; H. G. Wells Archives, University of Illinois Library at Urbana-Champaign; University of London Library; Department of Rare Books and Special Collections, University of Rochester Library; the Kipling papers, University of Sussex Library; and the Harry Ransom Humanities Research Center, the University of Texas at Austin.

Particular mention must be made of two institutions, the Beinecke Rare Book and Manuscript Library, Yale University, and the Pierpont Morgan Library, New York, who between them are the major repositories of Henley material. Without their excellent help and understanding over the years this selection would not have been possible. Mention must also be made of the great help received from the staff at the National Library of Scotland, the Newspaper Library at Colindale, and the Bodleian Library, Oxford.

I have to thank Eric Quayle for permission to include a letter to Clement K. Shorter, Anna Fleming for a letter to Anna Boyle and Elizabeth Hawkins for a letter to Wilfrid Blunt.

Permission to publish photographs is gratefully acknowledged to Mark Samuels Lasner; Anna Fleming; the Fellows of Jesus College, Cambridge; the Beinecke Rare Book and Manuscript Library; the Bodleian Library, and the National Portrait Gallery.

Thanks are also due to members of the Henley family: Eric and Jean Martin for their help and hospitality, Anthony Kersting for permission to publish the Henley letters, and the late Audrey Hunt (*née* Henley), who welcomed me as a member of the family. Eric Ratcliffe has provided me with much help with the early life of Henley and Brian Louis Pearce with the vagaries of Henley's early

addresses in London. Especial mention must be made of the late Doranna
Mitchell whose wonderful hospitality, knowledge of Henley (her mother
nursed Anna Henley in her final years) and boundless enthusiasm urged me on.
It is a regret that she did not live to see the result. However, I am grateful to her
daughter, Anna Fleming, who has continued in the same vein as her mother. I
am indebted to Elizabeth Dionne, of Vancouver, British Columbia, for helping
me with the copyright of the Henley estate, and to Paul Chipchase for help with
some footnote problems. Grateful thanks are also due to the following at St
Edmund Hall, Oxford: Nicholas Cronk, Deborah Eaton, Christopher Wells, and
Renée Williams for her translations of the letters to Rodin. Thanks are also due
to Peter McDonald, of St Hugh's College, Oxford, and Linda K. Hughes,
Texas Christian University. Ernest Mehew's unique knowledge of Robert
Louis Stevenson and his relationship with Henley has helped me in dating
some letters and solving footnote problems, and I offer him my grateful thanks.
I am also greatly indebted to him for his thorough reading of the manuscript
and any faults remaining are purely mine.

Throughout the main development of my research I must thank Margaret
Shepherd for her enduring help, understanding and support. My editor, Joanne
Shattock, has lived with Henley on and off since 1983 and I cannot thank her
enough for all that she has done. Thanks are also due to Ruth Peters and the
editorial staff at Ashgate for their guidance and sufferance, and also to my
anonymous indexer. Finally my thanks to my wife Ann, who has had to put up
with the intrusion of Henley into her life.

Autumn 1999   Damian Atkinson

Introduction

In a letter to the novelist R. Murray Gilchrist in January 1901 the fifty-one year old Henley remarked that 'I am a kind of walking imposture. I look well, but have wretched health. I talk bravely, & do nothing. I cannot hope nor believe that the New Century has much in the way of work in hand for me.' To a great extent this was true for Henley had made his mark as an editor and poet in the 1880s and 1890s. He had talked bravely and done much.

Henley's literary career was marked by four journal editorships: *London* (1878-79), the *Magazine of Art* (1881-86), the *Scots* (later *National*) *Observer* (1889-94), and the *New Review* (1895-97). As an aspiring journalist and hopeful poet, having published his 'In Hospital' verse sequence in 1875, he and Robert Louis Stevenson, together with George Saintsbury and Andrew Lang, were the main contributors to Glasgow Brown's weekly Conservative *London*. Other contributors were the novelist Grant Allen and the journalist James Runciman. This short-lived journal, one of a multitude of similar Victorian journals, gave Henley a good introduction to the day-to-day workings of a weekly journal. Stevenson's wife Fanny gives a picture of *London* under Henley's editorship:

> Mr. Henley was performing prodigies to keep it afloat. His own salary was small and the limited funds at his disposal allowed him to pay next to nothing to contributors. Both his and my husband's friends helped so far as they could, but a weekly publication made too heavy a drain on their good-nature. It often happened that an entire number of *London* was written by Mr. Henley and my husband alone... The circulation of *London* was extremely small...
>
> There were occasions when the journal presented the odd appearance of being almost wholly composed of verses. This occurred when the too sanguine editor found himself disappointed and had to make up his pages at the very moment of going to press. Verses filled space more readily than prose, and were easier to do; in such emergencies poem after poem would be dashed off by Mr. Henley and my husband until the blanks were filled. 'Hurry, my lad,' Mr. Henley would shout; 'only six more lines now!' My husband would scratch off the six lines, hand them to the printer's devil, who stood waiting with outstretched hand, and the situation was saved for another week.[1]

Much of Henley's *London* contributions were unsigned poems in the French style, best exemplified by Austin Dobson, and they included many to his future wife Anna Boyle. Henley and Dobson corresponded from then until Henley's

---

[1] 'Prefatory Note', in *The Letters of Robert Louis Stevenson*, Tusitala Edition (1923-24), *1*, 216-17.

death, with Henley often seeking help and encouragement from Dobson on his poetry and some of his editorial projects. Saintsbury later remarked that 'we made things hum'. Today *London* is remembered for the first appearance of Stevenson's stories which became the *New Arabian Nights* (1882).

Henley's early life, with his battle against tuberculosis, is now well documented and his first strong friendship, to the East End coffee-house owner Harry Nichols in the 1870s is reflected in his masculine and descriptive letters to him from Margate and Edinburgh. Contact with Nichols seems to have been lost once Henley became involved with *London* and married Anna Boyle. Stevenson had now supplanted Nichols.

The friendship with Stevenson was a turning point in Henley's life and career, and introduced him to the lawyer Charles Baxter and the art critic Sidney Colvin. Henley, although a strongly opinionated thinker and forceful talker, needed the approval of a mentor as well as a friend. The friendship, at first boyish and light-hearted as seen in the letters ('Dear Lad', 'Dear Boy'), developed into a major literary friendship with the collaboration on four unsuccessful plays. Henley was the dominant force in the collaboration as he believed that their fortune could be made. He writes of ideas for further plays and operas and of his attempts to seek performances. To some extent his persistence in wanting to revitalise British drama was an underlying cause of dissatisfaction in their relationship. Stevenson's marriage in 1880 to Fanny Osbourne was not welcomed by Henley, nor indeed by other friends, as he saw an interference in their friendship by the forceful Fanny. Despite this the friendship between the Henleys and the Stevensons prospered. In May 1884 Fanny turned to Henley for help when Stevenson was ill in France and he arranged for his own doctor to visit Stevenson. Throughout the late summer of 1884, after the matinée production of their play *Deacon Brodie* in London, Henley was visiting the Stevensons in Bournemouth where the two men worked hard on their plays. Henley's enthusiasm for the plays was supported by Fanny until she realised that her husband's success and skills lay in prose and she later resented Henley's persistence. Henley's letters of this period are frequent, often long, and full of literary news and ideas. Henley acted as Stevenson's unpaid literary agent when Stevenson was abroad and was instrumental in the publication of *Treasure Island* (1883) and *A Child's Garden of Verses* (1885), as well as the transfer of Stevenson's publishers from Kegan Paul to Chatto and Windus.

In November 1881 Henley, with the help of his friend Sidney Colvin, then Slade Professor of Fine Art at Cambridge, had become editor of Cassell's *Magazine of Art*, a rather staid monthly given to supporting the Royal Academy and English art. It is rather ironic that Henley gained the position at the same time as he was scathingly attacked by Ruskin in the October *Nineteenth Century* for his comparison of Millet with Michelangelo in his *Twenty Etchings and Woodcuts* (1881). Over the next five years Henley revitalised the journal introducing new blood and broadening its coverage of art. Edmund Gosse, Andrew Lang, Austin Dobson, Kate Greenaway, the drama critic William Archer, Robert Louis Stevenson and his cousins Katharine de Mattos and Robert ('Bob') Alan Mowbray Stevenson were among those who wrote for Henley. It was Henley who suggested to Bob Stevenson that he become an art critic rather than a painter and Henley was delighted when this happened. Henley included in the *Magazine of Art*, needlework and poetry, American and Japanese art, praised the Brabizon painters, introduced the English reading public to the merits of Rodin, and supported Whistler. Henley had met Rodin in 1881 and became his foremost admirer and championed him in the *Magazine of Art* and was later awarded by Rodin making his bust. The two men had much in common and corresponded until Henley's death. Whistler and Henley became friends and Whistler produced a lithograph of Henley but was not satisfied and pulled only six copies. The major portrait he promised did not materialise. Two of the existing contributors to the *Magazine of Art* were the Catholic literary couple Wilfrid and Alice Meynell, who were experienced writers and editors and introduced Henley to a new circle of friends. Wilfrid became godfather to Henley's daughter Margaret Emma in 1888. The young art historian and critic Julia Cartwright was given every encouragement but unfortunately no correspondence has been found.

Henley's strong opinions on art and literature ensured that his contributors' work was as he wanted it and he edited it to conform to his rigorous standards. His constant battle with the orthodoxy of his publishers led to his resignation in October 1886. After this the magazine began to revert to its former dullness and conservatism while Henley engaged in freelance journalism and the production of his *A Book of Verses* (1888). Not long after its publication he became consulting editor to the *Art Journal* for a period.

The Stevensons had left for America in August 1887 and the correspondence between the two men continued in the usual style until Henley's letter of 9 March 1888. In this letter, which he marked 'Private and Confidential', he remarked that Fanny's story 'The Nixie' was based on the story by Stevenson's cousin Katherine de Mattos and this was taken by Stevenson as an unwarranted attack on his wife. Henley believed that Katharine's signature should have appeared with Fanny's. Neither side would give way and the bitterness lasted until the end of both lives. Charles Baxter acted as intermediary, but he could not reconcile the two men, although the correspondence did restart later but not in the same friendly way. A full account, with the letters from both sides and those of Charles Baxter, is published in *The Letters of Robert Louis Stevenson*, vol 6 (1995), edited by Bradford A. Booth and Ernest Mehew.

One of Henley's influential Edinburgh friends was the wealthy art collector Hamilton Bruce who undoubtedly managed to have Henley commissioned to write the preface to the Edinburgh *Memorial Catalogue of the French and Dutch Loan Collection* (1888) and the notes to *A Century of Artists* (1889). Bruce, together with Charles Baxter, Walter Blaikie the printer and later Chairman of T. and A. Constable, and the lawyer and financier Robert Fitzroy Bell, appointed Henley editor of their weekly *Scots Observer* in December 1888. This venture had started in November 1888 but it needed a strong editorial hand and Henley was to rule over it for nearly five and a half years.

Henley, now aged forty, took control with his first issue of 19 January 1889 and quickly stamped his authority on the contents. The journal was already Tory and imperialist in outlook and Henley ensured that this aspect was even stronger. He now had the greatest editorial freedom of his career and used it accordingly. Among his contributors was the young scholar Charles Whibley, whom Henley had met while working for Cassells. Whibley became a minor replacement for Stevenson in Henley's affections and also acted as second-in-command on the journal. The relationship can be traced in the letters to Whibley where Henley is constantly badgering the lethargic Whibley for copy, taking him to task for failing to achieve deadlines and discussing ideas for the paper.

Henley's editorship is not only marked by his strident literary and political views but also by his clique of young writers including Kipling, Arthur Morrison, Gilbert Parker, Yeats, Barrie, Kenneth Grahame, the novelist H. B. Marriott Watson, the journalist G. W. Steevens, Harry Cust (later editor of the *Pall Mall Gazette*), the politican George Wyndham and Wells. It must be stressed that although Henley published Alice Meynell, the poetess 'Graham R. Tomson' (later to write as Rosamund Marriott Watson), Katharine Tynan, Katharine de Mattos and E. Nesbit, they were not among the *Modern Men of the Scots Observer* (1890) and *Twenty Modern Men from the National Observer* (1891). Henley's restaurant dinners for his 'Observers' at Solferino's were for men only. Henley's advocacy of promising writers is best demonstrated by Wells and *The Time Machine*. Wells was encouraged to continue writing the story after preliminary chapters had appeared in the *National Observer* and the final version appeared later under Henley's editorship in the *New Review*, with the book being dedicated to Henley. The Realist novelist Arthur Morrison was encouraged to publish his stories of the East End of London in the *National Observer* which later became *Tales of Mean Streets*.

The letters of this period are rich in descriptions of the work he was engaged in as an editor. He harried Gladstone and the Liberals, supported the Tory party, damned Parnell over Home Rule for Ireland, attacked the concept of the 'limited edition' of Ruskin, published Kipling's 'Cleared' which was an attack on the Parnell Commission, asked his contributors for more and yet more copy, and praised young writers. In 1890 Whibley involved Henley indirectly in an argument in the paper over the morals of Oscar Wilde's *The Picture of Dorian Gray*. 'Why go grubbing in muck heaps?' asks Whibley, setting the tone of the criticism as a personal attack. A correspondence between Wilde and the journal on the morals of art and writing was closed by the editor after a few weeks, but it demonstrated the tough, rigid views of the *National Observer*. In April 1895 the *National Observer* published a leader in support of the Marquis of Queensberry and urging a second trial.

Unfortunately Henley had never been too concerned with the business side of journalism, what was written and how it was written was of paramount importance to him, style was more important than popularity, and the *Scots Observer*, planned as a northern rival to the London journals, was forced to change its name in November 1890 to the *National Observer* in order to survive. As a last resort to counteract falling circulation it moved to London in 1892, but was finally sold by Fitzroy Bell in March 1894. Henley's third editorship, although a literary success, had failed commercially. As the editorship was drawing to a close Henley suffered the bitterest blow of his life with the death of his daughter from meningitis in February 1894. He never fully recovered.

During his editorship he had continued his literary interests and published an introduction to *Sir Henry Raeburn: a Selection from his Portraits* (1890), *Views and Reviews: Literature* (1891), and his successful poetical anthology *Lyra Heroica* (1892). He had also begun work on the seven volume *Slang* (1890-1904) with John S. Farmer and taken on the general editorship of the multivolume *Tudor Translations*, a project which was completed after his death by Whibley. Henley continued to write poetry and in 1893 he published *London Voluntaries* which included his jingoistic poem 'The Song of the Sword', dedicated to Kipling. This was a trite, bombastic poem which counterbalanced his evocative and lyrical descriptions of London in the verses which gave the book its title. In 1894 he began, with the Scot T. F. Henderson, an edition of Burns, which became a definitive edition for some years despite the severe criticism Henley's terminal essay received in Scotland for the treatment of Burns as a man and poet. Many of Henley's letters to Lord Windsor and Lord Rosebery deal with the progress of this work. With Whibley he published *A Book of English Prose* in 1894. His editorship of a major series, *English Classics*, managed only five titles.

By November 1894 Henley was preparing to take over the editorship of the monthly *New Review* which had been acquired by some of his friends, including the publisher William Heinemann and George Wyndham. It was to be a vehicle for Henley's editorial talents, but after the first year it was controlled by Wyndham and the editorial board with Henley as nominal editor. In spite of failing health, Henley spent much of his time working on his other, and to him, more important interests: his uncompleted edition of *Byron*, the final volumes of *Burns*, and the anthology *English Lyrics* with Charles Whibley. His editorship is marked by the publication of *The Time Machine*, Arthur Morrison's *A Child of the Jago*, Conrad's *Nigger of the 'Narcissus'*, and under protest Henry James's *What Masie Knew*. He also included work by Paul Verlaine and Paul Valéry, and increased the journal's literary content. The work of the old *Observer* days continued, though not with the strident impetuosity of old. Falling circulation and financial problems not unconnected with the serious political stand of the *New Review* and Henley's continued failing health forced him to resign in December 1897.

Henley's remaining years were spent on various literary works, notably editions of Fielding, Smollett and Hazlitt, the jingoistic Boer War verses *For England's Sake* (1901), the lyrical *Hawthorn and Lavender* (1901) and his second collection of *Views and Reviews* (1902). Henley had one final literary outburst with his 'assassin' *Pall Mall Magazine* article on Stevenson in December 1901. He used his review of Graham Balfour's biography of Stevenson to attack the myth of Stevenson 'this Seraph in Chocolate, this barley-sugar effigy of a real man', and it appears to be a jealous attempt to down grade Stevenson. Henley was an embittered man: he no longer had Stevenson in his life, his daughter was dead, and his clan of aspiring young writers had dispersed to make their own way in life. He was no longer the 'Viking Chief'. The Stevenson followers rounded on Henley, as the Burns followers had done earlier, but Henley would not retract.

The opinions expressed in his letter to Gilchrist in 1901 were mainly true, the 'New Century' offered him little, the attitudes towards literary expression were changing and he was not part of that change. His ardent politics were not in vogue and he was still a Victorian and no longer at the helm.

Letter selection and editorial principles

The present edition is a selection of some two hundred and fifty letters selected from over 2,300 letters known to exist. The main holdings of Henley letters are the Beinecke Rare Book and Manuscript Library at Yale, and the Pierpont Morgan Library, New York. These two important holdings comprise well over half the known letters and are well represented in this selection. A few letters in private hands are represented, though the extent of private holdings is not accurately known. The Beinecke holdings are the majority of those to Stevenson, some one hundred and eighty, together with over one hundred and fifty to their mutual friends Charles Baxter and Sidney Colvin. Later letters are to Henley's publisher Alfred Nutt, one hundred and five to the Edinburgh art collector R. T. Hamilton Bruce, and thirty to the financier and lawyer Fitzroy Bell. The Pierpont Morgan has well over eight hundred letters including those to Henley's future wife Anna Boyle, his collaborator John S. Farmer on the *Dictionary of Slang*, Lord Windsor, and nearly six hundred letters to Charles Whibley. The National Library of Scotland holds forty letters to Lord Rosebery concerning Henley's work on Robert Burns, and seventy-nine letters mainly to the publisher Blackwood and those to Stevenson relating to the quarrel. London University holds sixty-eight letters to Austin Dobson. There are sixty-three letters to H. G. Wells at the University of Illinois at Urbana-Champaign. Other important collections are the fifty-five letters at the Huntington Library most of which are the previously published letters to Harry Nichols. The few letters to J. M. Barrie, a lifelong friend, are at the University of British Columbia. Henley encouraged many young writers, apart from Wells, among them the novelists Arthur Morrison, Bernard Capes and Murray Gilchrist. The majority of the letters to Morrison are at the University of Rochester with some in private hands. Letters to Bernard Capes are at New York University and those to Murray Gilchrist at Pierpont Morgan Library. Henley's correspondence with his publisher William Heinemann is at the Houghton Library as are his letters to the artist William Rothenstein. The

University of Texas hold letters to the essayist and poet Alice Meynell together with letters from James Nichol Dunn, Henley's managing editor on the *Scots* and *National Observer*. Letters to Heinemann's partner Sydney Pawling are at the University of Virginia. Over one hundred letters, including those to the publishers Macmillan and the dramatic critic William Archer are at the British Library. Henley's letters to his friend the sculptor Auguste Rodin are at the Musée Rodin, Paris. Only one letter and a telegram to Kipling have been found and they are at Sussex University. It is surprising that no letters appear to survive to his collaborator on *Burns* T. F. Henderson who also wrote Henley's entry for the *Dictionary of National Biography*. Only one letter has been found to a member of his family other than his future wife and that is to Edward John Henley, his actor brother.

Few letters to Henley exist, the majority being those from Stevenson which are published in *The Letters of Robert Louis Stevenson*. In a letter to the writer H. D. Lowry, Henley writes: 'I destroy most letters that come to me' (Henley to Lowry, 6 August 1899, Fales Library, New York University). The Pierpont Morgan Library holds the majority of the remaining letters to Henley, including some from Rodin and T. E. Brown. Unfortunately there are only two from Farmer to Henley. Any letters from Fitzroy Bell concerning the selling of the *National Observer* would have made interesting reading as Henley was embittered towards Bell and totally distraught at the illness and death of his only child Margaret. A letter of condolence from Oscar Wilde on the death of Henley's mother is published by Connell. It is regretted that only one letter appears to have survived from the diligent Whibley who collected Henley's letters in six volumes. Family letters seem not to have survived. Letters received relating to his notorious article on Stevenson in the *Pall Mall Magazine* have also not survived which is probably not surprising as he was bitterly attacked for his views on his dead friend and collaborator. Some letters to Henley are published in the letters of Kipling, Wells,[2] and as previously mentioned, Stevenson. Letters to Henley from Fanny Stevenson are at Yale.

The selection of the letters has been difficult. The intention was to sample, as far as possible, the life of Henley, both literary and otherwise, and present, through the letters, a truer portrait of the man. The selection has been divided into the four major stages of his life, starting with his early years as an aspiring young poet and journalist, together with his meeting with Robert Louis Stevenson, his courtship of his future wife Anna Boyle and his short-lived editorship of the weekly *London*. The second section is his editorship of the *Magazine of Art*, the third his most influential period as editor of the *Scots Observer*, later the *National Observer*, and the *New Review*, and lastly his final years of failing health and literary editorships. Each section has a short biographical introduction followed by the letters.

An editor of letters is always conscious of the problem of presenting a

[2] *The Letters of Rudyard Kipling*, ed. Thomas Pinney (1990-) and *The Correspondence of H. G. Wells*, 4 vols, ed. David C. Smith (1998).

readable text without losing the immediacy of the writer's word and this leads to a compromise between the text of the original letter and a presentable yet accurate printed copy. In editing Henley's letters I have, I hope, been careful to include as much of his style of presentation without encumbering the reader with a host of minor orthographic detail which would hinder clarity and flow of thought.

The layout of the letters has been standardised. Each letter is headed by the recipient's name, followed by the date as standardised or a conjectural date within square brackets. Immediately beneath this is the source of the text with a note of any previous publication or major quotation. The position of the address is to the right irrespective of its original position and a printed or embossed address is signified by italics.

The text of the letter is standardised in paragraphs and postscripts are retained with prescripts placed after the closure, except where a letter is marked 'Private' or 'Confidential'. Henley's spelling has been retained throughout, as has his punctuation except where clarity demands an alteration or insertion. Henley's handwriting varies with age and health and is often very difficult or impossible to read. T. E. Brown writing to Henley in 1891 comments: 'Are you feeling stronger? Do you mind my telling you that your handwriting shows signs of nervous trouble, begins, in fact to be frequently illegible? (9 May 1891, Pierpont Morgan). This, unfortunately, was often the case. Cancelled passages are silently excised unless they are of importance and illegible words are indicated as empty square brackets. False starts have been omitted and words inserted by Henley have been silently included. A few omitted words are supplied in square brackets. Henley made frequent use of the ampersand and this has been retained; his occasional use of an underlined initial uppercase letter has been replaced by an italicised letter. Underlined words or phrases have been replaced by italics. Henley overused the dash and this has been retained. Titles of books and plays have been italicised and other titles are in single quotation marks. Henley frequently used contractions such as ''em' and ''tis' and these have been retained. A letter in French (with Henley's mistakes included) is followed by a translation. Quotations have been identified where possible and Henley did not always have a good memory for them.

Henley rarely failed to date his letters though when he did so he often wrote the day of the week rather than a date, thus making it difficult to date accurately. His letters to Baxter and Whibley often have the date recorded by the recipient. The closing of the letters has been centralised irrespective of the original position. Henley often used the closure 'Ever Affectionately Yours' which he also abbreviated as 'E. A. Y.'

Sources of Letters, Abbreviations and Short Titles

Archer	Lieut.-Colonel C, Archer. *William Archer: Life, Work and Friendships* (1931).
Baxter Letters	*R.L.S.: Stevenson's Letters to Charles Baxter*, ed. DeLancey Ferguson and Marshall Waingrow (New Haven and London, 1956).
Berg	Henry W. and Albert A. Berg Collection, New York Public Library.
BL	British Library, London.
Brotherton	The Brotherton Library, Leeds University.
Burns	*The Poetry of Robert Burns*. Centenary edition, ed. W. E. Henley and T. F. Henderson, 4 vols (Edinburgh, 1896-97).
Champneys	*Memoirs and Correspondence of Coventry Patmore*, ed. B. Champneys, 2 vols (1900, 1901).
Cohen	Edward H. Cohen, 'Uncollected Early Poems by William Ernest Henley,' *Bulletin of the New York Public Library*, 79, No. 3, Spring 1976, 297-314.
Connell	John Connell [J. H. Robertson], *W. E. Henley* (1949).
Columbia	University of British Columbia.
Columbia Univ	Columbia University, New York.
Congress	Library of Congress, Washington DC.
Duke	William R. Perkins Library, Duke University.
Fales	The Fales Library, New York University.
Glasgow	Glasgow University Library.
Glines	Elsa F. Glines, '"My Dear Miss Page" and "Demon Harry": some early letters of William Ernest Henley,' *Huntington Library Quarterly*, 49, November 1986, 325-51.
Goldman	Martin Goldman, *Lister Ward* (Bristol and Boston, 1987).
Haggard	Sir H. Rider Haggard, *The Days of My Life: An Autobiography*, 2 vols (1926).
Hallam	J. S. Hallam, 'Some Early Letters and Verses of W. E. Henley,' *Blackwood's Magazine,* September 1943, 200-209.
Harvard	Houghton Library, Harvard University.
Hayward	The Library, California State University, Hayward, California.
Huntington	The Huntington Library, San Marino, California.
Illinois	The Library, University of Illinois at Urbana-Champaign.

London	University of London Library.
Lucas	E. V. Lucas, *The Colvins and their Friends* (1928).
Mackenzie	Norman and Jean MacKenzie, *The Time Traveller: The Life of H. G. Wells* (1973).
Meynell	Viola Meynell, *Alice Meynell: A Memoir* (1929).
Mitchell	The Mitchell Library, Glasgow.
Morgan	Pierpont Morgan Library, New York.
Murray	Archives of the publisher John Murray, London.
Paris	Musée Rodin, Paris.
New College	New College, Oxford.
Payen-Payne	*Some Letters of William Ernest Henley*, ed. V. Payen-Payne (Privately Printed, Chelsea, 1933).
Princeton	Princeton University Library.
Quarrel	Edward H. Cohen, *The Henley-Stevenson Quarrel* (Gainesville Florida, 1974).
RLF	Royal Literary Fund.
Rochester	University of Rochester Library.
Ross	*Robert Ross: Friend of Friends*, ed. Margery Ross (1952).
Stevenson Letters	*The Letters of Robert Louis Stevenson*, ed. Bradford A. Booth and Ernest Mehew, 8 vols (New Haven and London, 1994-95).
Sussex	University of Sussex Library.
Texas	The Harry Ransom Humanities Research Center, University of Texas at Austin.
Virginia	University of Virginia Library.
Williamson	Kennedy Williamson, *W. E. Henley: A Memoir* (1930).
Works	*The Works of W. E. Henley*, 7 vols (1908).
Yale	The Beinecke Rare Book and Manuscript Library, Yale University Library.

Private holdings

Fleming	Mrs Anna Fleming.
Meynell	Meynell family library.
Quayle	Mr Eric Quayle.

Chronology: William Ernest Henley
1849-1903

1849	23 August WEH born at 47 Eastgate Street, Gloucester, son of William Henley, printer, bookbinder and picture frame maker and Emma Morgan.
1851	Anthony Warton Henley born 1 August at 47 Eastgate Street, Gloucester.
1854	Attended school at Suffolk House, Gloucester, which later moved to Newark House, Gloucester.
1856	Nigel Felix Henley born?
1857	Joseph Warton Henley born 18 August at Lower Barton Street, Gloucester.
1860	Edward John Henley born 17 August at Russell House, Stroud Road, Gloucester.
1861	Entered the Crypt Grammar School, Gloucester, in August. The Manx poet, Thomas Edward Brown, Headmaster (1 August 1861- 15 October 1863).
1863	'Left Midsummer, 1863. Returned Christmas 1864. Left Christmas 1865. Returned Michaelmas, 1866' (*Crypt School Register*). His schooling was interrupted by tuberculosis of the left leg.
1867	WEH leaves the Crypt and goes to London.
1868	His father dies aged forty-two on 8 February. 16 June enters St Bartholomew's Hospital, London, for treatment of TB. His left leg amputated below the knee probably at this time.
1869	8 April discharged from hospital. At 11 Bateman's Buildings, Soho Square, London by July.
1870	Living at 17 Richmond Terrace, Shepherds Bush, London, by March/April. Writes for the weekly *Period* which publishes his 'Bohemian Ballads'. By August is living at 11 Holland Road, Notting Hill. Meets Harry Nichols.
1872	Moves to 3 Victoria Terrace, Marine Terrace, Margate, for his health
1873	Enters the Royal Sea-Bathing Infirmary, Margate, in late February. Arrives in Edinburgh 23 August and enters the Edinburgh Infirmary for treatment on his right foot under Lister. His foot saved.
1874	Meets his future wife Hannah Johnson Boyle (called Anna), sister of Captain Edward Mackie Boyle, a fellow patient.
1875	Introduced to RLS by Leslie Stephen on 12 February at Edinburgh Infirmary. Writes his poem 'Invictus'. Leaves the

Infirmary in April and moves to 45 George Street, Edinburgh. Moves to 4 Straiton Place, Portobello, Edinburgh, in May. His 'Hospital Outlines: Sketches and Portraits' published in the *Cornhill Magazine*, July. His poem 'Morning' published in *Macmillan's Magazine*, August, and his ten poem 'Notes on the Firth' in the October issue.

1876   January/February moves to 19 Balfour Street, Leith Walk, Edinburgh. Contributes at least nine entries to the ninth edition of the *Encyclopaedia Britannica*. Moves to 19 Bristo Place, Edinburgh, in May. He is sacked from the *Encyclopaedia Britannica* for his article on Christopher Columbus. WEH and Anna engaged on 6 December.

1877   WEH, with RLS, is a major contributor to Glasgow Brown's weekly *London*. He stays at Brown's address, 21 Park Side, Albert Gate, London, in August and finally settles at 11 Adelaide Terrace, Adelaide Road, Shepherds Bush, in October. WEH edits *London* from December. Contributes to the *Saturday Review*.

1878   22 January marries Anna Boyle at St Mary's Roman Catholic Chapel, Broughton Street, Edinburgh. Charles Baxter is one of the witnesses. By end of June they are living at 12 Wilton Villas, Uxbridge Road, Shepherds Bush. WEH and RLS start writing the play *Deacon Brodie*. At the end of December the Henleys are at 4 Earls Terrace, Devonport Road, Shepherds Bush.

1879   In January RLS and WEH work on *Deacon Brodie* at Swanston Cottage, Lothianburn, Edinburgh. Last issue of *London* 5 April 1879. Contributes book and drama reviews, and poetry to the *Academy*, *Athenaeum*, *Vanity Fair*, *Manchester Guardian*, *Belgravia* and the *Pall Mall Gazette* among others. Visits Dieppe in March. By 11 April the Henleys are at 36 Loftus Road, Shepherds Bush. They are at 1 The Parade, Goldhawk Road, Shepherds Bush, by the end of October. Anna has a stillborn child in December.

1880   By June the Henleys are at 51 Richmond Gardens, Shepherds Bush. Acts as RLS's unpaid agent. Contributes to T. H. Ward's *The English Poets*.

1881   RLS dedicates his *Virginibus Puerisque* to WEH. In August he meets Rodin in London and they become friends. Acts as witness at Bob Stevenson's wedding 27 August. Publishes his *Jean-François Millet. Twenty Etchings and Woodcuts*. Ruskin attacks WEH's view that Millet was an artist in the mould of Michelangelo. From 1 November WEH becomes editor of the *Magazine of Art* at a salary of £300 per annum for three and a half hours per day. Anna has a miscarriage.

1882   Sells RLS's *New Arabian Nights* to Chatto and Windus. WEH in Bradford for the first performance of *Deacon Brodie* at Pullan's Theatre in December.

1883   Elected to the Savile Club. Reviews *Treasure Island*. Has small unspecified operation.

1884   In January visits RLS and Fanny in Hyères with Baxter. In May, with Baxter, takes control of the treatment of RLS's serious illness sending Dr. Mennell to Hyères. Visits RLS in Bournemouth and collaborates with him on the plays *Beau Austin* and *Admiral Guinea*. By November the Henleys are at 18 Camden Gardens, Shepherds Bush. *Deacon Brodie* staged at Prince's Theatre, London, on 2 July.

1885   WEH and RLS collaborate on their play *Macaire*. *Magazine of Art* salary reduced to £240 pa. Resigns as music critic of the *Saturday Review*.

1886   The Henleys visit Paris in August. WEH sits for his bust and introduces RLS to Rodin. Resigns from the *Magazine of Art* in the late summer or early autumn. Appointed consulting editor for the *Art Journal*.

1887   Visits RLS in Bournemouth in March and late June. WEH's only play *Mephisto* performed (unsuccessfully under the pseudonym Byron McGuiness) at the Royalty Theatre, London, on 14 June, with Edward Henley in the lead. RLS and Fanny leave for America in August. *Deacon Brodie* performed in America. The Henleys move to 1 Merton Place, High Road, Chiswick, in mid-October.

1888   WEH's letter of 9 March to RLS accusing Fanny of plagiarism in publishing under her own name a story based on an earlier one by Katharine de Mattos's precipitates the quarrel and estrangement between them. Baxter acts as mediator. WEH's *A Book of Verses* published in May. WEH and Anna's only child, Margaret Emma, born 4 September. His mother dies 25 October. RLS writes in memoriam verse. WEH becomes editor of the weekly *Scots Observer* in Edinburgh. WEH and Andrew Lang publish their *Pictures at Play or Dialogues of the Galleries by Two Art-Critics*. Produces the text to the *Memorial Catalogue of the French and Dutch Loan Collection* exhibition at Edinburgh, 1886. Stays with Hamilton Bruce in December.

1889   Publishes his first number of the *Scots Observer* on 19 January. Visits St Andrews in mid-January. The Henleys move to 11 Howard Place, Edinburgh, in April. Publishes Kipling's 'Barrack-Room Ballads'. Visits Lake Windermere in July. Rents Ivy Lodge, Levenhall, Musselburgh, as a second home. WEH visits London in October. Produces *A*

	Century of Artists. A Memorial of the Glasgow International Exhibition, 1888.
1890	WEH's *Views and Reviews: Literature* published. He provides the introduction and notes for *Sir Henry Raeburn.* WEH begins his collaboration with John S. Farmer on *Slang.* Stays with Charles Whibley in London. Rents Seaforth, Levenhall, Musselburgh, in place of Ivy Lodge. *Scots Observer* publishes damning review of Wilde's *The Picture of Dorian Gray. Beau Austin* performed at the Haymarket Theatre, London, 3 November. *Scots Observer* becomes the *National Observer* on 22 November and is also published in London. Publishes Yeats's 'The Lake Isle of Innisfree' 13 December.
1891	Begins work on the poetry anthology *Lyra Heroica.* Visits London in March. Spends most of May and June at Musselburgh. The *National Observer* survives financial crisis. *Lyra Heroica* published in October. Visits St Andrews in early December.
1892	WEH's *The Song of the Sword and Other Verses* published in April. Spends May at Musselburgh. The *National Observer* moves to London. Begins the *Tudor Translations.* WEH lives at 1 Great College Street, Westminster. Starts collaboration with Charles Whibley on *A Book of English Prose.* The Henleys settle at Ashburton Lodge, Addiscombe, Surrey. Holidays at Musselburgh in September.
1893	The *National Observer* again in financial trouble. Holidays in Eastbourne in April. Awarded LL.D of St Andrews University, 6 April. October in Musselburgh. Margaret ill in November.
1894	Fitzroy Bell decides to sell the *National Observer.* Margaret Henley dies of meningitis 11 February. WEH publishes H. G. Wells. He resigns the editorship of the *National Observer* on its sale in March. Moves to 3 James Street Mansions, Buckingham Gate, London, 22 March. Disagreement with Bell over financial settlement. The Henleys move to 9 The Terrace, Barnes in May. *A Book of English Prose* published. WEH becomes editor of the monthly *New Review.* Is commissioned to produce an edition of Burns with T. F. Henderson. RLS dies on 3 December.
1895	His first *New Review* published in January. Starts work on the short-lived *English Classics* series for Methuen. Publishes Wells's *The Time Machine* in the *New Review.* Visits Deal in May. WEH becomes an unsuccessful candidate for the Professorship of Rhetoric and English Literature at Edinburgh University. Edits *A London Garland.* Fails to become Poet

	Laureate. Starts work on an edition of *Byron* for Heinemann.
1896	Moves to Stanley Lodge, Muswell Hill. Vol. I of *Burns* published.
1897	Takes a holiday in Sussex in February. Remaining three volumes of *Burns* published. WEH publishes Conrad's *The Nigger of the 'Narcissus'* in the *New Review*. Holiday in Brighton. WEH's anthology *English Lyrics* published. T. E. Brown dies. *Admiral Guinea* performed 29 November at the Avenue Theatre, London. Resigns from the *New Review* in December.
1898	*Poems* published in January. Stays at The Ivy, Burwash, Sussex, late April — early May. Awarded Civil List pension of £225. He has an operation for piles. Writes thirteen quatorzains to William Nicholson's *London Types*. Stays at The Fishery, Wheathamstead, Herts, in July. Collaborates with George Wyndham on *The Poetry of Wilfrid Blunt*. Stays in Seaford, Sussex, with Anna, in late September and October. His actor brother Edward dies at Lake Placid, New York, on 16 October. WEH has another operation.
1899	The Henleys move to St George's Lodge, Chesswood Road, Worthing. Contributes regular column to the monthly *Pall Mall Magazine*. His fiftieth birthday, 23 August. Contributes his 'Hawthorn and Lavender' verses to the *North American Review*, November 1899 to September 1901. Edits the *Works of Tobias Smollett*, 1899-1901.
1900	Bob Stevenson dies 18 April. Co-edits the *Collected Poems of T. E. Brown*. Publishes his war poetry *For England's Sake*. Starts work on an edition of Shakespeare which is completed after his death by Walter Raleigh. William Nicholson paints his portrait.
1901	Nicholson's portrait exhibited in London. His *Hawthorn and Lavender* published. Contributes seven articles to the *Sphere* between November 1901 and March 1902. The Henleys take a flat at 19 Albert Mansions, Battersea. Return to Worthing in December. WEH contributes his controversial 'assassin' essay on RLS to the December *Pall Mall Magazine*.
1902	Most of February spent in Battersea. Spends last ten days of March in Battersea. Moves to Heather Brae, Maybury Hill, Woking. Severely shaken while attempting to board a train on 26 March. Introductions to the *Complete Works of Henry Fielding* and *Collected Works of William Hazlitt*. Rides in Alfred Harmsworth's car. Publishes *Views and Reviews: II Art*. Starts work on *A Song of Speed*.
1903	*A Song of Speed* published. Dies 11 July and is cremated at Woking and buried at Cockayne Hatley with his daughter.

1. The Early Years: 1870-81

William Ernest Henley was born on 23 August 1849 at 47 Eastgate Street, Gloucester, the eldest of five sons of William Henley (1826-68), and Emma Morgan (1828-88). William Henley senior was born in Cheltenham and was listed as a bookseller in *Hunt's Cheltenham Directory, 1847*. By the time of William Ernest Henley's birth two years later he was in the same business in Gloucester. No record of his marriage to Emma Morgan, a Cheltenham girl, has been found but there is a suggestion of a previous marriage on 5 November 1844 to a Sarah Cox in Cheltenham.

Henley senior and his family were constantly on the move in Gloucester, a practice mirrored by young Henley in his early journalistic career in London. Henley's early education was at Suffolk House, Gloucester, and later Newark House, Gloucester. On leaving this school Henley went to the Crypt Grammar School, which had been founded in 1539. Here he was lucky to fall under the influence of Thomas Edward Brown, the Manx poet, who was Headmaster 1861-63. During this brief period Henley gained his first and lasting love of literature, a love that was to lead him to a life of a man of letters and the editorial chair of two major journals of the 1890s.

Henley suffered from tuberculosis in both legs and had his left leg amputated below the knee, but the date is uncertain. After leaving school in 1867 he went to London to try his luck as a journalist. He entered St Bartholomew's Hospital in June 1868 and left uncured in April 1869, though it is most probable that his left leg was amputated. Unfortunately there is no hospital record for this period.

He managed to contribute some verses to the short-lived weekly *The Period* and also to the *Belgravia*. He aspired to being a poet and wrote to men of fame and influence, Swinburne and the publisher John Murray III being the two known examples. It was during his stay in London that he met Harry Nichols, a coffee-house keeper in the Commercial Road, who introduced him to the Bohemian life of East London. The closeness of the friendship and style of life can be gauged from the surviving letters to Nichols. They seem to have had a fairly intimate relationship based on drink, smoking, and the music hall. Here, too, he met a Miss Page, with whom he corresponded for a short period in the early 1870s though nothing is known about her. A stay in Margate at the Royal Sea-Bathing Infirmary in 1873 failed to halt the tuberculosis and he went to the Royal Infirmary in Edinburgh in August 1873 to seek the help of Joseph Lister. There has been speculation as to how Henley was able to obtain an introduction to Lister at the Edinburgh Infirmary and how he was able to pay for his stay. Richard B. Fisher, in his *Joseph Lister 1827-1912* (1977), strongly suggests that Henley was recommended to Lister by 'a Lady in the South of England of very considerable influence in London Society'. In view of Henley's Bohemian way of life in east London it is very unlikely that he would be in contact with anyone of such standing. Nevertheless, the possibility exists that he may have met such a person while at Margate Sea-Bathing Infirmary. Henley, himself, would seem to refute any suggestion of patronage in a letter to J. M. Barrie for he says that he 'had heard of Lister & Listerism, & went to Edinburgh, as a sort of forlorn hope, on the chance of saving my foot' (28 May 1888). A stay of twenty-two months was to be the turning point of his life and launch him firmly into the world of letters. Lister saved his right leg. Henley immersed himself in self-education, making up for the time lost at school due to illness. He read French, German, Portuguese and Italian and wrote verses. Here he wrote what was arguably his best poetry and certainly his best known, the 'In Hospital' sequence, a collection of verses describing his experiences in a Victorian hospital. Leslie Stephen introduced Robert Louis Stevenson to Henley in February 1875.

Here, too, Henley met his future wife, Anna: his growing love for her and his desire to marry, against opposition from her parents, are clear in his love letters. How could a penniless journalist hope to marry and to marry a Catholic at that? But they did marry in January 1878 and Henley never regretted it though he was later to lament the marriages of two of his friends, Stevenson and Kipling. What was right for him was not right for them.

After his discharge from Edinburgh Infirmary he managed to find employment writing entries for the ninth edition of the *Encyclopaedia Britannica*, but he was sacked for incompetence after writing an article on Christopher Columbus.

Through his friendship with Stevenson Henley was introduced to a small but influential Edinburgh literary and financial coterie, which included the lawyer Charles Baxter, later to play an important role in the quarrel between Stevenson and Henley, and the art critic Sidney Colvin. These friendships later helped Henley with literary contacts. Stevenson's university friend Robert Glasgow Brown founded and funded the weekly journal *London* with Henley and Stevenson being the main contributors. This was an exciting time for Henley and he eventually became the editor in 1877 living in London. As the friendship with Stevenson progressed they began to collaborate on plays, the first being *Deacon Brodie* and their letters are full of plots and ideas with Henley being the more enthusiastic, whereas Stevenson was the more realistic. Henley was still writing verse but he was generally unsuccessful in publication apart from the poems he printed in *London*, many of them being 'fillers'. In 1879 he was asked to contribute some selections and comments to T. H. Ward's *The English Poets*. After the closure of *London* in April 1879 Henley continued to contribute book reviews to many of the major journals, including the *Athenaeum, Academy, Saturday Review* and the *Pall Mall Gazette*.

Henley's great interest in art led to his meeting Rodin in 1881 in London and there began a friendship that lasted until Henley's death. He recognised the genius of the sculptor and championed his cause in England. In the same year Henley published his first work on art, *Jean-François Millet. Twenty Etchings and Woodcuts*. Henley's interest in, and knowledge of, art led to his being appointed as editor of the *Magazine of Art* from November 1881.

To A. C. Swinburne,[1] 20/70 [March-May 1870]
ALS: Berg. Published Cohen.

                                17 Richmond Gardens, Shepherds Bush, W. [London]
Sir,
   In addressing you without being in anywise known to you, I am conscious that I commit both a fault and a breach of etiquette. Perhaps, however, after the lecture of this letter you will be good enough to pardon both of these and receive in good faith the apology that I offer you with all the assurance of sincerity and necessity.
   It is impossible for me to explain the purpose wherewith I venture to write to you, without running the risk of being considered *un peu egoiste* by talking of myself. However, I shall take the liberty of sparing you as much troublesome detail as possible and commence at once by telling you that, not yet twenty-one years of age, I find myself as trouble-scared and as unfit to struggle with life as a soldier after a Beresina and a new Russian retreat.[2] The terrible misfortunes through which I have passed — I will detail them to you fully if such be your future desire — have obliged me to take the only career left open to me, the only one I am bound also to say that, troubles apart, I should have chosen, the career of letters. I have attempted this alone and unaided with success both encouraging and discouraging at once. I have been connected with a certain satirical journal, whose untimely decease put an end to the first connection I had formed, and in this I was allowed to say pretty much what I thought without any fear of evil consequences arising from an outburst of British *begueulisme*. The eight 'copies of verse' forming a series of 'Bohemian Ballads'[3] were indeed but the commencement of a design I had formed of

---

[1] WFH's early attempts at poetry owe much to his reading of Swinburne.
[2] The French army retreated across the river Beresina in Russia after being defeated in November 1812 during the Napoleonic war.
[3] WEH had been writing for the *Period*, a small London weekly which ran from 30 October 1869 to 26 February 1870 with a new series from 14 May 1870 to 18 February 1871. It was edited by the writer, engraver and publisher Henry Vizetelly (1820-94), who first published Zola in England. Vizetelly was a co-founder of the *Illustrated London News* in 1842. WEH's eight 'Bohemian Ballads' were published in the *Period* between 18 December 1869 and 26 February 1870.

delineating the lights and shadows of the *Vie de Boheme* of Henri Murger:[4] the paper stopped, however, as I have already had the honour of telling you and elsewhere I have been so unsuccessful that but for a certain blind love for, and confused idea of the glorious beauty of Art, I should perhaps have pitched away ink and pen and learnt to sew nethersocks or their modern equivalents to procure myself the luxuries of life which are verily, ill as I am, necessities to me.

I do not think I have failed for lack of power: (literary variety is, doubtless, so well known to you that you will pardon, I hope, this seeming conceit) I rather choose to believe that I have failed through my peculiar education. Knowing scarcely enough Latin to stumble through an Ilyhphallic of Cattulus, I have thrown myself body and soul into French sentiment and art as represented by Balzac and Alfred de Musset.[6] Ill and alone I have mused and dreamed over their words until a reproduction, an invitation, a corresponding vein of though had become almost second nature with me. One English author only has exercised a power over me perhaps — nay certainly — superior to theirs: and such is the passionate admiration I entertain for the writings of this last that I can give you no greater proof of my embarrassment than by confessing to you that I have only been able to become possessed of two of his books; viz the *Poems and Ballads* and the *Atlanta in Calydon*.[7]

It is perhaps this peculiar vein of reading and expression that is one of the causes of my want of success: and certainly this why I venture to apply for counsel to a man whose position as an artist is so high that my poor tribute of admiration, though it be sincere, cannot add one whit to his glory though it may reflect some credit on my own taste. I have been of such length in my explanations that I fear I have wearied you — if indeed you have read thus far — and with this thought I hasten to the real end of my letter in order to bring it to a speedy conclusion.

I ask then permission to submit to you for your consideration a poem that I have at present in my desk. I do this because, without friends or advisers of any kind, almost alone in the world in fact, I am unable to form any judgement as to my own productions: A boy of twenty, if he possesses any critical faculty, is quite unable to exercise it on his own works. And furthermore I beg of you, should you judge it to have any merit, to help me with the advice and encouragement I so sorely need. If by introduction & counsel you could aid me to make a creditable appearance in the pages of any review or magazine wherewith you may be connected, believe me that the sweetest reflection of all to me would be that I had won my spurs under the conduct of a leader whose notice would be my pride as his works have been my delight.

---

[4] The French writer Henri Murger (1822-61) author of *Scènes de la Vie de Bohème* (Paris 1851).
[6] The French poet, playwright and novelist Alfred de Mussett (1810-57).
[7] *Poems and Ballads* (1866) and *Atlanta in Calydon. A Tragedy* (1865).

I am at present very ill and this letter to you stands in the position of a forlorn hope. Written with the hope of interesting you, you will pardon me the faults of composition, the wearisome detail, the expression of admiration in which I have indulged. Believe me, Sir, that I have written with perfect sincerity, and that, knowing the many applications of the same sort men of genius are pestered withal, I am sorry to find myself obliged to rank with the other privates in the ragged regiment of literature. That I have had no choice, however, you may know by the knowledge of my position, by, the peculiar nature of the poem itself and by the account of the circumstances under which it was written which I shall not fail to send you with it should you incline to its perusal. In a worse position that that of Chatterton[8] I appeal to you for counsel: it is for you to say whether in doing this I have done well.

I am, Sir,
Yours most obediently,
W. E. Henley

A. C. Swinburne Esquire.

[8] The poet Thomas Chatterton (1752-70), who in despair at the lack of success of his poetry, killed himself.

To John Murray,[1] [?May 1870]
ALS: Murray

17 Richmond Terrace, Shepherds Bush

Dear Sir,
   You have been kind enough to assist me in many ways with counsel and material,[2] several times, and therefore I am emboldened to apply to you once more for assistance, at a period when I need it more that I have ever done before, precarious as my existence hitherto has been.
   After a great deal of trouble, the *Period*, the journal to which I was in the habit of contributing, has started a second series, the first having dropped by reason of a series of misfortunes, and the Editor reclaims my services. I have been very ill in fact I have not left the house for nearly three months, as much

[1] John Murray III (1808-92), grandson of the founder of the publishing firm. He took control of the firm on the death of his father in 1842.
[2] This was not the first letter from WEH to Murray. In an earlier letter (5 January 1869, John Murray Archives) WEH writes: 'The trifles you were so kind as to read have so many faults notably those of hasty composition and non-revision that I should have certainly been ashamed to place them in your hands: they were written for my own amusement and for that of — to quote a sarcastic writer in the *Daily News* — "admiring female relatives".'

on account of poverty as ill health — and I find my[self] exceedingly ill-placed for the collection of those subjects necessary for the subject-matter of a funeral to be as caustic & high class as possible. I am, therefore, straining every nerve to get together a sum which shall enable me to appear once more in London, since country air seems neither beneficial to my body nor to my mind. And it is to this end, that I make so bold as to ask help of you. Believe me, that nothing but the very strongest necessity for immediate action on my part, would make me write thus to you: and that had I no hope of success, I should not presume to ask aid for a fruitless undertaking. However, that I have done so, is entirely owing to the fact of your having helped me unbeknown to you, several times before. I have only to beg you to consider this note as I have marked upon the envelope and to request an answer of you at your earliest convenience and I have done.

I am, Sir,
Yours most obediently,
W. E. Henley.

Jno. Murray Esquire.

Harry Nichols,[1] **[October 1872]**
ALS: Huntington

3 Victoria Terrace, Marine Terrace, Margate[2]

My son,
    Here's no end of a letter to thee. I have nothing particular to say, but I doubt not I shall manage to fill four quartos, for all that. The sky is heavy with rain: the sea is grey and desolate: there is a bold & bitter wind afoot. Decidedly I am for in-doors this afternoon! — I feel just now a strong objection to any conversation with Dr. Alun respecting the Italian verbs; & I have no book to dip into and no money to exchange for Irish, *Hot*; while I am sick of the very name of tobacco. Can you blame me that I write to you?
    Margate is empty. The terrace is deserted: the bathing-machines have retired

---

[1] Harry Nichols (1840/41-?) kept a coffee-house at 11 Crombies Row, Commercial Road, Whitechapel, London, which by 1881 had become 329 Commercial Road East, although Nichols had moved by then. Here WEH and Nichols spent many hours in talk and drink. This was WEH's first close friendship.
[2] Presumably WEH moved here from Richmond Terrace, though it is far from certain as the location and chronology of his early lodgings can not be fully established. He moved to Margate in an attempt to save his right foot from amputation due to tuberculosis of the bone. Subsequently he entered the Royal Sea-Bathing Infirmary, Margate, in late February 1873 and left in August for Edinburgh. He gave his address as 19 Portland Road, Notting Hill, on entry to the Edinburgh Royal Infirmary.

into private life: the basket chairs are laid up in ordinary. The strict, but meritorious, Matrons have sought the domestic hearth: the idiotic, but not altogether objectionable, misses have started — I hope! — for heaven: the itinerant minstrels have departed — I trust! — for the opposite extremity of creation. There are but a few nurse-maids, & no flymen to flirt with them: these latter being occupied with getting up their strength against next season. The lodging-house keepers have nought to do but hunt for those peculiar 'Gentlemen in Brown'[3] whom Nature has apparently intended to reside in Furnished Apartments. Encouraged by the near approach of perfect rest, the very donkies have taken heart of grace, and are rebellious: for did I not march an antient jackass on the sands this morning, who bore upon the back of him an infant? at whose legs were firmly planted in the sand, at whose jaw the proprietor of him tugged & wrenched in vain, and at whose hind-quarters the male & female to whose charge the infant freight might be laid, were making vigorous manual application? — Margate is empty, my son, & such little scenes are a consequence.

Among the doves, soiled & smirchless, who have long since flown elsewhither, my sweet Unknown must, alas! be numbered. I was inconsolable, as you may well believe, for several days, during which I finished her Cycle of Songs,[4] & made several important discoveries concerning Irish Whiskey.

Irish Whiskey, otherwise Potheen, otherwise Fenian, is a fluid possessed of extraordinary properties. I shall not stop to communicate any other than this; Taken Hot, with Sugar & a thin shaving of Lemon-peel, it encourages, in him who imbibes, a tendency to stand for many hours over a bar, while it imparts to him an unusual facility of agreeable & audacious speech. I can vouch for this, which is indeed a result of long & patient observation on my part. Miss Crump is of the same opinion.

Miss Crump — Mary Ellen — hath 19 years, a rich brown skin, a spare but hugable shape, & the brightest, clearest, honestest black eyes in the world. She & I are excellent friends. We amuse each other dreadfully. She flirts, & coquettes, & smiles, & looks disdain, & delight, *en coulisse*, and full front: while I — well! — I do my best to credit my dear Balzac. *Certes*, I don't think that anyone has talked to Miss Crump as *I* have talked: I say all that comes into my head, and it amuses us both: I don't believe she understands one half of it, but she likes it none the worse for *that*. From certain indications, I am sometimes inclined to believe   when I consider things *en fat* — that she would have no objection to fall in with my views: the pity of it is that she is honest. If she were not! — my imagination refuses to paint the probabilities. Yours may be more audacious.

King John is very bad: a terrible skin-wound across the shoulders.[5] As he

---

[3] Bedbugs.
[4] The history of this cycle is vague though some poems have been identified; see Cohen.
[5] A fellow patient later referred to as 'Majesty'.

has nobody to take care of him, I amuse myself by dressing it for him (*this is a secret: you will see why.*): much against his will. I am so cool & dexterous over it, that I believe I should have made a good surgeon. It is not exactly what I should like; but — *on fait ce qu'on peut!* — If your French will carry you triumphant through that phrase, you will find that Life is summed up in it.

You will receive, in a day or two, the *Professor at the Breakfast Table*:[6] a sort of sequel to our old friend, the *Autocrat* of that Ilk. It is very good, though not so good as its predecessor; a little lecture-room-ified but still very readable, and full of science made easy: the sort of matter your soul delighteth it. Read it carefully, & you will not regret.

I had a very kind letter from Cadman[7] the other day. He regrets that you don't visit him oftener: (this *entre nous*). I have had, too, wild billets from Felix:[8] and an astonishing romance, *Les Liaisons Dangereuses*,[9] of which more in my next. Also several severely enthusiastic epistolary trumpet-blasts from Jim.[10] I wrote to Tom Hallam[11] some time ago: the address was a *chef-d'oeuvre* of orthography: the villain has not yet answered me. His condition, I take it, may be summed up in one (French) word: *Basé!*

Have you got a spare crown to dispose of? — I suffer much from impecuniosity — the old ailment! And I owe my respected landlady a few shillings. If you have, overcome your dislike to letter-writing so far as to P.O.O. me to that amount.

I am wonderfully better: must not walk, though, yet! — My love to Lawrence.[12] — Yours, old man,

W.E.H.

---

[6] The American medical professor and writer Oliver Wendell Holmes (1809-94), author of *The Professor at the Breakfast-Table* (1860) and *The Autocrat at the Breakfast-Table* (1858).
[7] One of many unidentified friends and acquaintances.
[8] Another unidentified friend.
[9] A novel by Pierre [Ambrose François] Choderlos de Laclos (1714-1803), French general and novelist, published in 1782.
[10] James Runciman (1852-91), schoolteacher in the East End of London and later journalist and writer. He worked mainly for the weekly journal *Vanity Fair* and the *St James's Gazette*. He and WEH eventually quarrelled.
[11] Thomas Hallam (?1849-1932), relation of Nichols and a schoolteacher. At this time he had started his teaching career at Waltham Abbey Board School after training at The British and Foreign School Society, Borough Road, London.
[12] Another friend.

To Miss Page,[1] 16 March 1873
ALS: Hayward. Published in Glines, 340-41.

Royal Sea-Bathing Infirmary, Margate

Dear Miss Page,

My conscience has oftimes smitten me sore for my unpardonable neglect of you which I am at a loss either to explain or to excuse. I have been many times on the point of writing, but some trifle has always occurred to defer the good action, or I needed no less a stimulus than your kind letter to oblige me to instant & practical repentance. Accordingly, I sent you, on Friday last, a packet of *MSS*. — & to-day, Sunday, after having yawned my head off, I feel that I can't do better than pay my debt to you: which I does.

I am really seriously ill. That is to say, my right & only foot is in a parlous state of disease. I do not think it will need amputation; in fact I am doubtful whether a simple incision will be required: but it is bad, & many months must elapse before it can be to me half so useful as you knew it. Where these months will be passed, I have really no idea: here, I suppose, or in the workhouse; but certainly not in Bohemia, nor in any adjacent regions.

I have been an inmate of this admirable institution some three weeks. I am very uncomfortable: as yet I have a good straw bed, plenty of sheets & blankets, and as much milk & meat as is good for me; also a nice young person, of the severest virtue, to wake me in the mornings. I smoke a good deal, read a little, write not much, play occasional Whist & Euchre, & see the surgeon once a week. I have sent Pegasus out to grass,[2] abandoned the imbibition of deleterious mixtures, & forgotten the black eyes that caused me (at least a month ago) so much sorrow, anxiety, & lyrical agitation. The past is dead & buried, the Present is not altogether discouraging, & the Future is of no consequence nor interest to me. Ought I not to be happy?

I should be, I think, if I were turfed: but I don't see any chance of that desirable consummation just yet. So I must e'en make the best of that bad bargain, my life, a while longer. Till the end, then, as I am, I shall be. Healthy, isn't it?

You will be surprised to hear that, short as has been my sojourn, I enjoy a most villainous reputation here. With such a character as mine, the least I could do, if I wished to act up to it, would be to seduce all the nurses on the establishment. As, however, such is not my desire, I have formed, solely with the idea of rehabilitating my reputation, an Anti-Female League, under my own

[1] Miss Page has not been identified but it seems she and her family were well known to WEH who corresponded with her between 1870 and 1873. She appears to have had a brother Frank. There is a similarity of content in WEH's letters to both Miss Page and Nichols but his approach to Nichols is more masculine and personal.

[2] Abandoned writing poetry.

presidency, the members of which bind themselves by fearful oaths never to look kindly on woman more, & never to miss an opportunity of telling the truth (in other words, of spreading ill) of her. I regret to say that my efforts in the cause of the idea have hitherto met with but scant success, my following being divided as to how far the principle should be carried out, while the womankind do their best, by abstraction of creature comforts, to compel the enlightened back to darkness. But I don't despair.

I am sorry to say they have been but badly off at home of late. The address is 19 Portland Rd. Notting Hill.[3] You must make your own excuses.

I rejoice greatly for Fid's success: he has the ball at his foot now, & I hope he'll keep it. Give Frank my blessing & tell him that, if he wishes to retain my regard, he must altogether abandon the society of everything in petticoats, his relatives excepted. My kindest regards to Papa & Mama, & I do hope Papa will soon hit the mark. My most distinguished compliments to yourself & the Chief Justice: we shall no doubt meet again someday. Till then, farewell!

W.E.H.

P.S. — Miss Turner! Uh, but! Return *MS.* when you have read & admired & don't fail to criticize. I enclose the Valentine I was fool enough to waste on — but no matter! It is good!

---

[3] According to the 1871 census a commission agent Mr Baynes and his family were living there. *Kelly's Post Office Directory* for 1873 shows a William Pilling, tailor, as resident. WEH's mother and brothers were living here.

To Harry Nichols, 18 April 1873
ALS: Huntington. Part published in Hallam, 203.

                                    Royal Sea-Bathing Infirmary, Margate
I ought to have replied to you ere this, old man, to have acknowledged your kindness with the promptitude it deserves. But the fact is, I have been so elated during the last few days with the unwanted chinking of silver, that I have not been able even to smoke steadily. I thank you indeed for your goodness & loving kindness, which have relieved me from a very nasty state of things: from a more abject impecuniosity than I ever remember to have undergone. To you then be all thanks! — If I *can* do anything for you, command me, my emperor, for I'm yours to the shoe-string.

I don't suppose I shall write you a very lively letter; for it is raining, & I have just been prayed over for upwards of ten minutes: which circumstances would, I think be sufficient to excuse even absolute flatness, staleness, &

unprofitableness.[1] It is a sorrowful business for me, my boy, this morning prayers. I sit among the crowd, dreaming vaguely of far other matters: of yourself, perhaps — of my beloved London, of the girl who might have been so much to me & who is so little: & our esteemed pastor is all while babbling monotonously of — you know the cant of his clique? — And presently the hymn wakes me, & I sit & shudder at the horrible cacophony; for piety & harmony, my boy are by no means synonymous. And then follows another specimen of ministerial faith & eloquence, which completes my frustration: till, when we emerge, I feel as abject & spiritless a thing as an onanist of ten years' practise. I am afraid I am one of the wicked, an irreclaimable scoundrel, my son! — For I am beginning to hate with a mortal unquenchable hatred the whole superstructure that ecclesiasticism has builded on the teaching of the Son of Man. I enclose you an extract from Shelley, which will, in some sort, explain my sentiments. I am not quite so far gone yet, but I am getting rapidly on that way. I expect another doing shortly: in the wards. The weather has delivered me into his hand: there is no escape.

(Interval of ten minutes: Mrs Jones)[2]

The ten minutes in question have expanded into fifty: I have had a satisfactory interview with Mrs. J. & I dodged the chaplain; consequently I feel much better. A little lotion now, & I should be right as a trivet.

I have heard of Mr. Arthur Creighton:[3] in fact, I know all about him. But I have not heard that he shines as a composer. I don't know that it is much use to send him any of my songs: but however, I shall post you the Song-Cycle I told you of. You can — & will, I hope! — read it yourself; & if any of the numbers please him he is welcome to try his hand upon them. I must, however, hear the setting before the public is so honoured. Writing a song, my boy, is not an easy art, whatever you may think to the contrary: & rather than anything of my begetting should appear coupled to such rot as Claribel[4] was wont to engender, they should all remain unheard till the end of time.

Majesty is tolerably well — as well, that is to say, as he is ever likely to be, without attendance & good grub. But horrid poor! I shall see him to-morrow & will then give him your message. But as he is mediating a journey to London, it is more than possible that you will soon have the honour of entertaining his Kingship in person. If you do, I adjure you, think of his anxious mother, & don't pour too much Irish into his manly guts. He has enormous capacities for

[1] 'How weary, stale, flat, and unprofitable / Seem to me all the uses of this world!' *Hamlet*, I. ii. 33-4.
[2] Mrs Jones may have been the Almoner.
[3] Probably the composer Arthur W. Creighton.
[4] Pseudonym of Charlotte Alington Barnard (1830-69), ballad writer and poet.

consumption, but he lushes then, by instinct, till he cannot even fart. So pray be careful!

Excellent good is very excellent Shakespearean English: but it is *not* modern grammar.

I had intended to say something about my life here, but, on second thoughts, it will come better from my very lips over a pipe & some 'Hirish 'ot. I shall content myself with observing that it goes on with a sameness & facility that are absolutely demoralising. I suffer much from want of books; all these that I have with me having been sucked dry long ago. And I find composition quite an impossibility. I have not written a line since Valentine's Eve, when I engendered the lyric which you will find on the last page: it is not bad. I seem quite worked out: no energy, no will, no guts: since Molly Crump turned me up for good and all. If I ever write again, it will be something very different to all that I have hitherto done. All that I now do, is to absorb sun & sea-air: my verses will be none the worse for *their* presence, eh?

Apropos of the said Molly, as I foretold you, she has never been to see me, & I do not fancy she will ever come. She belongs already to the past, & though I have suffered much, though I shall suffer yet, I am wearing regret every day. I suppose I ought to confess that she was wiser than I, & that what has happened is the best for both of us. Also to own that I was thoroughly licked! — How is this? — She is just nineteen, not witty, not learned in books or the world: & I — well you know *me*! — And yet if I had been a schoolboy in the hands of a woman of forty, I could not have been more perfectly *flambé*! — However, I have bought & paid for my experience: I doubt not that it will serve me. I intend making another attempt presently. You shall be advised how I fare: in due course.

Have you heard *Fleur de Leys* yet?[5] Are you going to do the *Wandering Jew*?[6] Did you watch that lying version of the arch-liar *Charles I*?[7] Are you going for *Eugene Aram*?[8] — I am glad you don't get tight so often: I shall make a man of you yet. As for your helps, to parody Artemus,[9] helps is a poison:

[5] A three act *opéra-bouffe* by Henry Brougham Farnie (?1837-89) with music from the opera of the same name by Leo Delibes (1836-91), had its first English performance on Saturday 5 April 1873 at the Philharmonic Theatre, London, and closed on 14 June 1873.

[6] A romantic drama by Leopold David Lewis (1828-90), opened on Monday 14 April 1873 at the Royal Adelphi Theatre, London, and closed on 1 October 1873.

[7] A play by William Gorman Wills (1828-91), which opened on 28 September 1872 and closed on 28 September 1873.

[8] *The Fate of Eugene Aram*, a play by Wills, opened on 19 April 1873 at the Lyceum Theatre, London, and closed on 20 June 1873.

[9] Artemus Ward, pen-name of the American journalist and humorist Charles Farrar Browne (1834-67). He was editor of the New York *Vanity Fair* and later a contributor to *Punch*.

however, if you don't deprive too many of them of their *virtue*, you will do well in course of time. I will report on Osbourne.[10] A double health to thee!

Thine ever,
W.E.H.

A Valentine

=1=

Up, my Song! — Unfold me thy wings
Brilliant & broad as a marvellous bird's;
Feed thee with fancies of exquisite things,
Robe thee in raiment of passionate words:
Forget for a while that thy master weeps
The glad sweet thing that may hardly be;
Seek me the spot where my Lady sleeps,
And bear her a message from Love & me.

=2=

Breathe me a sigh in her innocent ear,
Look me a smile in her bright bland eyes;
A sigh & a smile, & a word & a tear
For the dream that lives & the hope that dies;
Lay me a kiss on her flower-like lips,
And tell her that long as our blood shall beat,
Our life lives to be laid at her feet.

W. E. H.

---

[10] Presumably another friend.

To Harry Nichols, 18 December 1873
ALS: Huntington. Part published in Hallam, 204-5, Connell, 52-3, and in Goldman, 86-8.

Reserved Ward B, Royal Infirmary, Edinburgh[1]

Fiend!

I have been for some time minded to write to ye, in spite of the devilishly characteristic silence with which you have darkened my last letter. But I wanted to tell you something good, so I waited. And now it is too late, for the present, to write happy tidings so that I must, if I would write at all, speak of things as they are and (of course!) ought not to be.

I ought to describe my first operation, that you may the better understand the second, that of last Sunday: to do this I must tell you that when Professor Lister was at Glasgow, a man was brought in to him with his foot nearly severed over the instep, *in front of the ankle*, by a circular saw. Instead of taking the foot off, the Professor conceived the idea of trying to heal the wound & oblige the severed parts to grow together. He did so with complete success; & this inspired him with the theory out of which came the operation, for disease of the *tarsus*, that he has performed on me & four other unfortunates with satisfactory results in every case: not excepting, I hope, my own.

There was a long cut across the foot, from ankle to ankle, dividing vessels, tendons & everything, & laying open the affected bone, which in its turn was scooped out (gouge and pliers), so that a large triangular cavity was the result, the apex of which pointed to the toes. This cavity was filled with strips of lint in carbolic oil; changed, first of all, every four hours, then every eight hours, then twice a day, then once a day: the leg itself being bandaged into a long iron splint, & the foot pulled out so as to expose every part of the internal surface of the cavity to the action of the oil. In this position it was left to granulate (granulations are the most elementary form of tissue: flesh in embryo, in fact); the Professor intending, when the whole surface should be completely covered with granulations, to bring the lips of the wound together & leave them to unite & heal. It was this last operation that I expected to have to announce to you; &,

---

[1] WEH arrived at the Edinburgh Infirmary on 24 August 1873 in the hope that his right foot might be saved by the surgeon Joseph Lister (1827-1912). In a letter to Harry Nichols WEH writes: 'I have passed through deep waters since I last writ to you; here's the inventory. Wednesday, Aug. 20 — I set off from Wapping. Thursday 21 — I am somewhat sea-sick. Friday Aug 23. — I landed at Leith; train it to Edinburgh, cab it hither; arrive with exactly 10½ pence ...' (September 1873, Huntington Library). Lister was Professor of Clinical Surgery at Edinburgh, 1869-77. Richard B. Fisher, in his *Joseph Lister 1872-1912* (1977), 207, suggests that WEH was introduced to Lister by a lady whom he identifies as Lady Churchill. How WEH would have come to know her, if he did, is not known. WEH's first extant letter to J. M. Barrie of 28 May 1888 seems to refute this suggestion (see p. 176). WEH is described as single and a writer in the hospital register, but the duration of his stay and the nature and treatment of his illness are not noted.

of course, I ain't able to do so.

I fully expected, when I was borne to the Theatre, on Sunday last, (in a long basket, like poultry!) to return with my foot replaced & fixed up for healing; for Mr. Lister had almost notified as much to me once or twice during the week. When I came to my senses, however, I was in no way surprized to find that a lot more bone had been removed, & that I was as far from the Second Act as ever. I have seen my foot since then, & I can assure you, Mephisto mine, that the aspect of it is not calculated to put me in spirits, or to give me any higher opinion of my wretched self than the tolerably cynical one I have already.

Nevertheless, I am informed on good authority that I am 'a good case' & that Mr. Lister is confident of being able to save my foot. He is a great surgeon my boy! — Antiseptic surgery — his theory & practise — will have to fight its way, to fight for life indeed, & it will be long ere it is generally adopted. But already I think I am justified in saying that, next to the use of anaesthetics, it is the most beneficent discovery of the century. Joseph Lister is an Englishman, & (whether he save my foot, or no) we may rejoice therefore. The conceit of these bloody Scotsmen 'unmitigated', as Delaney used to say!)[2] is something atrocious.

I am well enough off for books: especially French books. If you want to know anything about Baudelaire's *Fleurs du Mal*[3] I can tell you that, in my opinion, they are real flowers: no artful *pastiche* of some clever *fleuriste*, but genuine flowers, lustrous & metallic of leaf, strange and violent of odour; poison-flowers, flowers from the Devil's hot-house, perhaps — real for all that. Gautier's *Émaux & Camés*,[4] too, are about the best society verses I have ever read. If, however, you want to read a *Book* (s.c.), try George Eliot's *Middlemarch*;[5] & when you have another woman, remember, wonder & admire that the Poor Thing that lifts her chemise for you, is of the same sex as Dorothy Brooke[6] & her creator. Hats off! when you speak of George Eliot; tho' the *Saturday*[7] does patronize her. One of her *Books* (s.c.) old pal, is worth a hundred times than all the flippant stuff that ever came out of Southampton St.[8] — After which, as it's time to go to bed (8/15 p.m.) I'll shut up for the night.

---

[2] A mutual friend.
[3] Charles Baudelaire's *Les Fleurs du Mal* was published in 1857 and consisted of one hundred and one poems.
[4] Théophile Gautier (1811-72), French poet, novelist and journalist. His *Émaux & Camées*, a collection of poems, was published in 1852.
[5] George Eliot's novel was published 1771-72.
[6] Dorothea Brooke, the main character of *Middlemarch,* is an intelligent idealist who makes an unhappy first marriage but finally finds fulfilment in her second.
[7] *The Saturday Review of Politics, Literature, Science and Art,* a weekly, 1856-1938, to which WEH later contributed.
[8] Southampton Street contained many printers and booksellers.

19 December 1873

I have read over my letter to you, old man, & find it dull: I suppose you will do the same. I decided on flattering your physiological instincts with descriptions of the operation; & fear I haven't succeeded as I ought. Perhaps you'll pitch these sheets unread into the drawer, light up that ineffable pipe (for the forty-seventh time), swear at the matches, or the bacca, or the dhudeen[9] itself, enwrap your manly form in the celebrated blanket — all things to all men, the mantle of Lagardère & the Grecian Bend[10] — fling yourself on the immortal sofa, & curl yourself into one of those wicked sleeps, where you dreamed of the mischief you woke to do. — or is all that sort of thing part of a dead & buried past? — Are your habits completely changed? Have you ceased to sacrifice at the shrine of Aphrodite of the Pavement? to pour libations of Irish 'Ot to the Dionysos of the Private Bar? Are you become a Good Templar?[11] Are you determined to make a fortune & retire to a suburban cottage, or a pleasant roadside pull, where are horses & pigs & pigeons & cabbages & roses & onions, & a spade & a harbour (not a sea-port) & a garden-hat? — Or — most terrible of all! — have you taken unto yourself a wife? whom you will one day introduce to me with the usual apology of my acquaintances: She is not *your* sort, you know, *but* — ? This last idea has recurred to me many times. I should not be sorry if it were true; for I think too much of you to care to see you wasting your life in solitary selfishness; which — after all your excuses, is practically where you are going.

I don't know whether we shall ever meet again. We have been already long divided, & the old associations, the old links that bound us are broken, the old thoughts we may have had in common are vanished: who knows? As in Henri Murger's pleasant melancholy rhyme: '*Et Musette qui n'est plus elle, disait que je n'etais plus moi.*'[12] — I am saying all this in the old dreamy sort of way, uttering half-truths, may-be, or only cynical falsehoods: appreciations that may be clear, or that are distorted & untrue: doing a prose '*My Pipe*',[13] in fact! And while I am writing, the spirit of the old time is strong within me, & I feel that, if I could be transported to 11 Crombie's Row, I should sit down opposite to

---

[9] The Irish name for a short clay pipe.

[10] Henri de Lagardère is the main character in the novel *Le Bossu, Aventures de Cape et d'Epée* (Bruxelles, 1857) by the French writer Paul Corentin Féval (1817-87). The Grecian Bend was a form of stoop in walking and appears to have been an affectation assumed by some women *c.* 1869-80. It was also the title of a song written and arranged by Bella Moore.

[11] An American association of total abstainers introduced into England in 1868.

[12] Marcel's poem, chapter XXIII, in Henri Murger's *Scènes de la Vie de Bohème*. The book was the basis of Puccini's opera *La Bohème.*

[13] WEH submitted some 'Tobacco' poems to *Macmillan's Magazine* in September 1875 but they were rejected. They were subsequently published in *Lyra Nicotiana: Poems and Verses concerning Tobacco*, ed. W. G. Hutchinson (1898). It would seem, therefore, that WEH had written at least one such poem before this letter.

you, & swear at, & lecture you, just as I used. — This sounds sentimental; you *may* laugh at it; but it's true.

I might have made you laugh over some of the people I have met; but I am tired of writing about them. I might have told you of the real love that I have found & that I have felt constrained (Thus Conscience doth make cowards of us all!)[14] to compel within strictly Platonic limits; but it would not be fair to her. I might have — no, never mind! — I have writ as I have, suppressing all personalities, poverty, *ennuis*, etc., & I hope you'll be grateful enough to send me a wee word in return.

Yours, old pal,
W. E. Henley

[14] *Hamlet*, III. i. 83.

To Harry Nichols, 17 May 1874
ALS: Huntington. Part published in Connell, 54-5, and in Goldman, 125-7.

Private Ward, Royal Infirmary, [Edinburgh]

Encourageons le vice! — Laziness incarnate, a letter to you: Tho' you are all that's bad, & my conscience would easily forgive me if I took no more notice of you. Do try & repent, & send me a scrawl, if it's only three lines thereof. Half a loaf is better than no parsnips; a stitch in time saves two in the bush: — need I say more?

I want to do business with you. Anthony[1] is etching on copper, like another Marc Antonius,[2] & turning out some of the most admirable little transcripts of nature you ever saw: leafy nooks of English paysage that would rejoice your Cockney soul, & make you shed tears & do justice (for once) to your h's. The price of each is 10/: let me send you four. I am sure you will be grateful for the chance. If I were home, you know me well enough to know you would probably get them for nothing. But I'm not at home, & they are very very poor, so you would be doing us a good turn & yourself a kindness to take them, either thro' me, or directly from 19 Portland Road, Notting Hill, London W. — Do shake off your blasted laziness for doing for doing right, your cussid inaptitude for active virtue, & either write to me, or go & get the four subjects, & see all the others, large and small.

Now for myself: I need not say I am excessively poor, still less need have I

[1] Anthony Warton Henley (1851-1914), artist brother of WEH, specialised in landscapes.
[2] The Venetian engraver Marcantonio Raimondi (*c.*1480-*c.* 1534), famous for his engravings of Raphael's work.

to declare myself excessively dull. If it were not for sounds of feline ecstasy in the corridors at night, & amorous cawings & twitterings from the crows & sparrows in the quad, I should hardly guess it was May. *I* don't feel like it at all. I have no will to read, & less to write: the songs & sonnets I vent occasionally are almost Baudelairian in their bitter fixity of *ennui*. I have no belongings nor illusions; for, thanks to the privacy of the little ward upstairs, you have no longer the advantage of me in any knowledge whatever. My foot is slowly getting well: at all events, it is absolutely painless: but my stomach is horribly deranged — the Dream of Constipation possesses me, & I form a striking contrast to that Tartar god of Diarrhoea Heine talks of,[3] who purchased, in one day, for his own sole use, no less than Six Thousand *Pots de Chambre*. And my head suffers, too: as you may believe. Altogether, tho' I look excellent well (the women here find me very handsome!). I am anything but satisfied with myself. What I shall be fit for when I get the bullet goodness only knows.

I have been degraded to the ground floor since last I wrote: *autres pays, autres mœurs*. It is a small mis-shapen room, low-ceiled & flag-floored, & the walls are a dirty-buff-brown. There are two beds in it, two chairs, two or three worn out rickety tables and stools; with an illumination & a sheaf of hymns hang on the plaster; the sun never shines farther into it than the extreme edge of my bed — in fact it never looks cheery save in the light that gladdens everything — however dull & dreary inherently, the pleasant intelligent blaze of a good hearty *Fire*.

I am close to the window, & thro' it, I can see the grass-plot in the quad, the sweet sun shining on the daisies & dandelions, chasing the shadows slowly from point to point, along the walls & windows , & flashings on the skylights, like the amiable tyrant he is: — I can see the quick bright sparrows fighting over the crumbs I throw them: the corpulent crows waddling about, breast high in grass, after belated worms, the hospital terrier, a jolly, ugly lively kindly dog with the most intelligent tail I ever saw, larking about with his friends, barking at the birds, & flying (in fun) after the cats, who come to sun themselves & snooze on the window-sills after their nocturnal philanderings. I can also see the whole body of nurses & probationers go to dinner & tea, & return, singly & in squads: but this is a negative advantage, because of Miss Webb.[4]

Miss Webb is young & fair & English, with the sort of skin you like to fancy you are kissing. She is short, & would be very well built, if she were not *quite* so stout. Her walk is provocative & irritating in the extreme: from her footfall,

[3] 'The diarrhoea of Tartar folklore, which tells in horrible droll fashion how this grim belly-aching *kakodaimon* one day bought six thousand pots for his own use and thus made the potter a rich man.' Heine's *Lutetia*, 1. Teil, section xxxiii (Paris, 20 April 1841), quoted by S. S. Prawer in his *Heine's Jewish Comedy: a Study of His Portraits of Jews and Judaism* (Oxford, 1983), 662. The German poet Heinrich Heine (1797-1856) was an early influence on WEH.
[4] Louisa Webb (b. ?1851) had come from Gloucester where she had worked in St Lucy's Hospital and spent ten months at the Royal Infirmary, Edinburgh, before eventually going to South Africa.

you can tell that the other end of her leg is satisfactorily heavy also. Miss Webb is the plague of my life: I have made all sorts of attempts to get acquainted with her: if she came once, I say, twisting my moustache, she would certainly come again. — But she won't come once; & this is why I say to myself with a sigh: 'Oh, Miss Webb!', why I dream of her in all sorts of improper conjunctures; why I confess I would give all I am worth in this world, my artificial leg included, once with my lips to divide those beautiful breasts, once with my body to open those adorable legs, once with my etc. etc. etc. — Oh, Miss Webb! — ... I am resolved to write her some verses in my best, most exquisite vein — epileptic anapaests, sonorous iambics, tinkling trochees: declare my passion, or bust in the attempt.

My own sweet Mistress has left the Institution, so that I've all in my favour. I swear to love her for ever; & I'm already seriously meditating an infidelity. Such is life. *Ainsi va le monde!* — My own nurse is neither old nor ill-favoured; I am teaching her French. Between me & the Night-nurse, a robust young person with wonderful eyebrows, there is much palaver, amorous on my side, disdainful on hers. If only I had another leg! — Nick, old pal, there was a real 'un lost to the world, when I was spoiled; I regret it, for the sake of all the women on earth.

Talking of Don Juan, when I return, I shall have much to tell you of that great ideal figure. If I don't write, it is that I don't know enough yet myself, to do it properly. Meanwhile, I should advise you to go & hear Faure sing the serenade under Zerlina's window,[5] as soon as you can. It will do you good, & prepare you for the intelligence of my lecture on the character....Why, oh why, do we trouble & debauchery ourselves with Verdi, when there is the exquisite heaven of Mozart's melody to fly to & stay in for ever & ever? — It's a licker. When I see Miss Webb, I seem to hear the music of the *Così fan Tutti* — love, & laughter, blue skies, & bluer seas, glad sunshine & happy starlight. — Oh, Miss Webb!

Apropos de bottes, the Russian poet Pouchkine has said: 'What affirms the superiority of the hand over the foot, is the fact that the foot conducts to *Something*, while the hand leads to *Nothing*.'[6]

I have read out the Library here: they have nothing to send me now but garbage, or trash, or history. I am in despair. I seldom or never read English: why, I don't know, for Spenser & Shakespeare are always at my elbow. Alas! That it should satisfy my conscience to know they *are* there! As for Swinburne, I don't think I should care to read even his new book.[7] I have got over my old fancy for him: he never wrote but one true line in his life: — 'All the world is bitter as a tzar' — & that is only true at certain stages of impecuniosity,

---

[5] Mozart's opera *Don Giovanni* (1787). The French baritone Jean-Baptiste Faure (1830-1914) sang the part of Don Giovanni.

[6] The Russian poet Alexander Sergeevich Pushkin (1799-1837).

[7] It may be that WEH had finished with Swinburne rather than a reference to a particular book.

temperature, & luxury.

I shall send you in a day or two a couple of chapters of translation from Taine's *Pyrenses*:[8] I think you will like them....Did Hallam send you my last letter, as I bade him? For certain reasons you wot of, you need not show him this one....Do you ever see Delaney? He seems to have given up writing to me altogether: why, I don't know. And the young man with name of indecent-suggestiveness? *Comment va-t-il?*...If you are troubled with secondaries, Iodine of Potass (five grains, thrice a day) & a fly blister will put you right.....I am wearying for a little cold mutton & pickles, for a tune on the piano, for a sniff of the smoke & sawdust of a bar, for a taste of Irish 'Ot — When shall we, eh? — Till we do, 'Arry of my soul, I bid thee 'Ail! — or rather, Farewell.

There she frisks across the quad — Adorable wagtail, kiss — Alas she's gone. Oh, Miss Webb!

W.E.H.

[*Added by WEH at the top of the letter*] Remember me to Uncle Ben.[9] When he hears me play *Outward Bound* he'll feel it![10]

[8] *Voyage aux eaux des Pyrénées* (1855), a literary guidebook by the French philosopher and critic Hippolyte Taine (1828-93).
[9] Presumably a mutual friend.
[10] Although there are several titles for the period the most likely is *The Outward Bound Gallop* (1863) for piano by J. W. Williams.

To Harry Nichols, [Early January 1875]
ALS: Huntington

4 Private Ward, [Royal Infirmary, Edinburgh.]
To the hinimitable 'Arry,

These!

Thanks for the quid! As somebody says in Shakespeare, in fact — 'For this relief much thanks!'[1] Be good enough, in some sober interval, if such ever occur, to do the correct & proper thing by our mutual friend Hall, for his contribution to our necessities. Tell him too, that if he could post me say two decent cigars, I would smoke 'em religiously, such an article not existing (apparently) in these pairts. Which is a great pity: or, in the language of the Himmortal — "Tis true, 'tis pity, & pity 'tis true.'[2] A-hem.

I am progressing fairly, & fully intend to take advantage one of these days of that there month's invite transmitted to me thro' the Inferior Demon employed in

[1] *Hamlet*, I. ii. 8.
[2] 'That he's mad, 'tis true: 'tis true 'tis pity; / And pity 'tis 'tis true. A foolish figure!' *Hamlet*, II. ii. 97-8.

your bureau. Expect to be astonished, when I do come. Expect also to be improved, admonished, reformed. Make up your great mind to abandon drinking & whoring, which are your two pet virtues, & to take to vices of an opposite complexion. I myself am quite changed. I wear a nightcap, & I read the *Saturday* religiously & well. I do suppose that I shall presently develop into a more respectable character than even Saint Nicholas; or, Nichols, whichever you will. I am not altogether sure, mind you, that supposing you commit the crime of putting me in the way of a plump, shapely, smooth, juicy lively female nudity, I should be man enough, or rather angel enough, to shut my eyes, and put my hands in my pockets. No, no, 'Arry of my soul! We are all of us mortal & with little weaknesses — especially some of us! And my resolution would certainly not take me to such an icy heighty of refrainment as that. But except that, I know of nought that can shake, much less subdue my infinite goodness. I am not ashamed to own my weaknesses: I do so here, that when I arrive at 345 Commercial Road, [I find] you, inspired & drinking. I spare you the epigram dancing thro' my brains *à ce propos*, but *Beware*!

Been to see Hirvin' in 'Amlet?[3] — Of course; but you don't like him 'alf so well as Fechter?[4] Of course, again. If you did, 'twere pity. And *The Merry Wives*? — With your dearly beloved Phelps[5] — 'an old barrel, with a crick in his back & a bad cold,' as Jim describes him to me. And have you heard *Girofle Girofla*?[6] And did you do much in Harvé?[7] And how about the fascinating Amy's display of 'light flesh & corrupt blood',[8] as Venus. And what is the last dirt Leybourne's[9] spiritual posturins [*sic*] have evolved for an admiring public? And — but what's the good of asking questions of one that goes to sleep at the Opera, & is better up to a carving-knife than a pen?

The new year has been as yet, if I may use the expression to one so fastidious on the score of language, some what of the snotty-nosedest. I

[3] Henry Irving played the title role in *Hamlet* at the Lyceum Theatre, London, from 31 October 1874 to 19 June 1875. Henry Irving (John Henry Brodribb) (1838-1905), knighted 1895.

[4] Charles Fechter (1824-79) played *Hamlet* at the Princess's Theatre, London, on 2 June 1872.

[5] Samuel Phelps (1804-78) played Sir John Falstaff in *The Merry Wives of Windsor* at the Gaiety Theatre, London, from 19 December 1874 to 13 February 1875.

[6] *Girofle Girofla*, an operetta by Alexandre Charles Lecocq (1832-1918), opened at the Philharmonic Theatre, London, on 3 October 1874 and closed on 11 January 1875.

[7] I have not been able to identify this.

[8] *King Henry IV. II*, II. iv. 291-2. The actress Amy Sheridan (?1839-78) appeared as Venus in the three-act opera *Ixion-Rewheel'd* by F. C. Burnand, which opened at the Opera Comique, London, on 21 November 1874 and closed on 16 January 1875. She was manageress of the Opera Comique Theatre, Strand, London, 2 November 1874 to 28 March 1875. Francis Cowley Burnand (1836-1917), writer of operettas and translator of French farces. Editor of the weekly illustrated *Punch* 1880-1906. Knighted 1902.

[9] George Leybourne (1842-84), theatre proprietor, singer, comedian and actor. He was the lessee of the East London Theatre, Whitechapel Road, Stepney, from 31 August 1873 to 26 April 1874.

snuffled the old one out in a shroud of a dirty pocket-hanky, & the New 'un is coated in the same fabric. To drop metaphor, I have had a bad cold, only just beginning to return to the devil whence it came. But I 'ope that sort of thing's all over. Can't write much. 'It ain't no bottle', as you would say. Nothing to be done till I am exhaled hence. But then — Higher up, Sane! I may get out a volume this year; Jim is working like the old 'un to that end — God bless him for it! Tho' I am not altogether sure that he deserves it for his interest in such stuff as I produce. But presently I'll be among the prose; then, look out!

Enclose two newspaper slips for your amusement & instruction. Read, mark, learn & inwardly digest them both, particularly the wee one. With which, & all blessings, injunctions to keep out of Worship St.[10], & warnings against strange flesh.

Adieu.

W.E.H.

[*Added by WEH at the top of the letter*] If you want a laugh, buy [?Tedkiel].

[10] Worship Street runs between City Road and Shoreditch High Street, London. It was an area frequented by prostitutes.

To Robert Louis Stevenson,[1] 14 March 1875
ALS: Yale

                                Surgical Ward 4 Private, Royal Infirmary, Edinburgh

My dear Stevenson,

When I disclaimed the need of your London address, I had forgot the possibilities enclosed.[2] My excuse for troubling you with them is manifold: you

[1] Leslie Stephen took RLS to meet WEH on 12 February 1875. In a letter to Mrs Sitwell RLS describes this first meeting:

> Yesterday, Leslie Stephen, who was down here to lecture, called on me and took me to see a poor fellow, a bit of a poet who writes for him, and who has been eighteen months in our Infirmary and may be, for all I know, eighteen months more. It was very sad to see him there, in a little room with two beds, and a couple of sick children in the other bed; ...Stephen and I sat on a couple of chairs and the poor fellow sat up in bed, with his hair and beard all tangled, and talked as cheerfully as if he had been in a King's Palace, or the great King's Palace of the blue air. He has taught himself two languages since he has been lying there. I shall try to be of use to him' (*Stevenson Letters*, 2, 116-19).

Leslie Stephen (1832-1904), editor of the *Cornhill Magazine,* 1871-82, was the first editor of the *Dictionary of National Biography*, 1882-91. Knighted in 1902.
[2] The enclosure was the series of verses giving WEH's impressions of his stay in the Infirmary.

have taken great interest in the series, which I am anxious to get done with; the two subjects are quite congenial to you; & I really want your pencil-marks. I shall not ask you to write about them. Pencil the *MS.* as you are wont to do, and post it to me as quickly as you can.

I hope you won't forget Van Laun.[3] His address is 48 Lancaster Rd. If you can do a little blasphemy on his hearth-rug, for my sake do not hesitate to commit yourself.

The weather continues binding.

Always Yours.
W. E. Henley

R. L. Stevenson Esqu.

PS. — I hope you will not think of showing these crudities to anyone who knows what's what. If you do, there will be matter for a bloody single combat when next you cross my path.

In asking for the *Romancero*, name the Brockhaus (Leipzig) Edition.[4] I don't know that there is any other, but this will 'mak sicker'.

They were subsequently published as 'Hospital Outlines: Sketches and Portraits,' *Cornhill Magazine*, July 1875. WEH was paid £9.9.0 for them (WEH to Harry Nichols, 18 May 1875, Huntington).
[3] RLS was in London en route to France. Henri Van Laun (1820-96), French author and teacher of French. T. E. Brown, in a letter to WEH, said he would write to Van Laun, 'whose conversation, would, I think amuse, and perhaps cheer you' (Brown to WEH, 17 September 1873, Pierpont Morgan).
[4] Heine's *Romancero*, first published 1851, was written during his long final illness when he produced some of his finest poetry.

To Robert Louis Stevenson, 15 April 1874[5]
ALS: Yale

Surgical Ward 4 Private, Royal Infirmary, Edinburgh
My dear Stevenson,

Yet a wee while & it will not be possible to see me in the Infirmary; I leave that desirable place of residence on Saturday next[1] — *D.V.* of course. I go to pass a few days in George St., thence to Portobello,[2] where I hope to see you (if you never find your way into such an aristocratic *locale* as George St.) & renew those interesting discussions you wot of. I am not cured, but there is a

[1] 17 April.
[2] From 45 George Street to 4 Straiton Place, Portobello, Edinburgh.

chance that the sea-side will cure me; if it don't — ! 'Why then lament therefor'.[3] I have struggled up so far as the Forked Hill with one wooden leg, it shall go hard — or rather, I shall find it comparatively easy to get a little further with two. Which is logic.

You were a true prophet! The Sonnets have been accepted & rejected (vice versa, I meant!); the history of all that is too long to write, I will keep it for our first pipe. The upshot of it all is, that they are to appear in the June number of our orange coloured Mag.[4] Such is life! Baxter,[5] who has been exceedingly good to me, was quite excited when I told him the good news after the bad. I have already fingered the stumpy, so my interest in them has expired; but I shall want your help over the proofs, & I fancy I shall have either to omit one or two types, which I am unwilling to do, or to introduce one or two fresh ones, which I am anxious to do. If you should see the Able-Editor ere you quit the smoke, be so good as to mention this to him, & if he is restive, coax him.

I write to you without having the remotest conception of your whereabouts. Some day, I suppose, you will turn up again: which day the Lord send soon! — When he does, you will find a lot of Rondeaux & Lieder to cut at, to butcher into excellence. All the tobacco songs are done; Baxter is much pleased with them; I laid them aside, not unmindful of Mrs. Burns & the ballad —'Robin gied this one an awfu' brushin!' I haven't done any prose; but I really am going to rewrite Quevedo[6] as soon as I get out. I am ashamed to make this confession, to which I ought to add another — that my German hath rusted of late; your Heine is no good after twenty lines — but Man is Far from Perfect.

But I hope *you* have been a-working. Some day, when you are a particularly great novelist, the English Balzac *par exemp!*, I mean to write an essay proving that Burns, like W. Shakespeare, was really possessed of prophetical powers, & that when he wrote the line 'We'll a' be proud o' Robin',[7] he had in his mind's eye a certain distinguished young Advocate of this place & time.[8] But this is of course dependent on your ability to write dialogue & to drop the Ego in your expositions. I hope you are there by this time — or at all events a little

---

[3] *King Henry IV. ii*, V. iii. 105.

[4] July, not June.

[5] Charles Baxter (1848-1919), an Edinburgh lawyer, Writer to the Signet (W.S.) and close friend of both RLS and WEH. He and RLS knew each other at Edinburgh University and formed a close friendship which later was supplemented when he acted as RLS's legal and business adviser. He was a true friend to both men and managed to remain so during their later bitter quarrel when he acted as an intermediary.

[6] Francisco Gomez de Quevedo y Villegas (1580-1645), Spanish writer and poet.

[7] Last line, verse four, of Burns's 'There was a lad'.

[8] RLS was called to the Scottish Bar on 16 July 1875, two days after being admitted to the Faculty of Advocates. RLS had studied engineering at Edinburgh University as he was expected to become an engineer like his father, Thomas Stevenson (1818-87), the well-known lighthouse and harbour engineer. RLS eventually gave up his studies and agreed to qualify as a lawyer to safeguard his future while he took up writing.

nearer than you were. So shall the name of Stevenson ('with a *we*, my Lord'!)[9] become illustrious otherwise than in connection with the shaping of brass & the shaping of Iron — dear to the readers of Mudie,[10] & a romantic & beautiful fact to all nice girls uncorrupted of Mathematics & with a taste for strong emotions & good stories.

This is an awfu' long letter; but I can't help writing it. It is a law of my depraved nature to cover with ink-marks all the blank paper I may come in contact with. But the infliction is over. When I have recommended you warmly to take the underground to New Cross some evening & to put Pollaky[11] on to the trail of the infamous Van Laun, if you fail to find him otherwise, I shall have done enough to satisfy my disgusting instinct & more than enough to weary you. Having achieved the which, I bid you fare well — 'long as thou canst *fare well*!' I will write my address to you as soon as I know it.

A vous toujours,
W. E. Henley

R .L. Stevenson Esquire.

[9] Mr Weller in *Pickwick Papers*, ch. 34.
[10] Mudie's Circulating Library was founded in 1842 by Charles Edward Mudie (1818-90). A bookseller's son, he opened a lending library in Bloomsbury and another later in Oxford Street.
[11] An inquiry agent, Ignatius Paul Pollaky, of 13 Paddington Green, London.

To Harry Nichols, 1 November 1875
ALS: Huntington. Part published in Hallam, 208, and in Connell, 78-9.

4 Straiton Place, Portobello by Edinburgh

How are you, Old 'Un? D — d cold, ain't it? I have to sit with my toes (such as are left of 'em) in the fender simply to keep life from freezing up. I am beginning to sympathize with the North Pole, & to conclude that the Artic Expedition will not be such fun after all.

But this is by the way. The real thing is, How are you? And the Missus?[1] And the little Stranger? — For I suppose there is one! I never was good at dates, so that if my enquires are a little premature, you must forgive me, & go on to the next.

I am a free man yet. But oh! the difficulty I have had to keep so! — I narrowly escaped an action for B. of P., or something of that sort. When I consider that it is all over & my letters burnt, I feel inclined to believe in a Special Providence — a mood that is but rare with yours truly.

[1] Harry Nichols married Rebecca Lowdell at Christ Church, Spitalfields, London, on 26 January 1875.

The Muses smile on me now & then, but blast them! they pay but ill. However I hope you did your old pal the honour of reading his 'Orspital Outlines (*Cornhill*, July, 1875) & the Notes on the Firth that he signed in the October number of *Macmillan's*.[2]

There is a second lot of Hospital stuff to come, but I doubt it will never see the light till the author is one with the dark. I have called it *Lazarus*[3] — not without memories of Heine; but it is good. Yes, I can lay my 'and upon my 'art, my 'Arry, & say it is good. If it should ever appear, I will not fail to give you the tip, that you may get it & read it. If I am departed when it bursts into the public's ken, you will read it all the same, I suppose, but then it won't so much matter to me.

Anthony is with me. Just returned from the Highlands, where he has painted four pictures & etched two plates. Will you invest? Proofs 10/- each — and worth it. The colour is really remarkably good. He finished last week a little picture of Brunstane Burn, with all the autumn tints in it, that I think would fetch you.

The most remarkable thing that has yet come out of the States is certainly Walt Whitman's book. *The Leaves of Grass* [4] is worth getting, my Nicholas — particularly if you could get the unexpurgated edition, which I fancy you could, thro' Chatto & Windus.[5] Such a book! Such tremendous nonsense, side by side with such superb manliness of thought, such magnificent hope & faith, such extreme beauty of expression. It is emphatically a new Gospel, & one that is maybe destined to replace altogether our four old friends — fast dropping to the deuce now, poor creturs! If anyone abuses Walt Whitman in your hearing, hit him on the nose, & tell him he is an ass.

Not much else to say. We shall perhaps go to Edinburgh to pass the winter; in which case I will advise you of our whereabouts. I feel rather ashamed to tell you that my foot is not yet *quite* well. That it will be a cure, I have not the slightest doubt.

Give my kind regards to Mrs. Nichols. I suppose you are an authority on the 'Whitechapel Tragedy'.[6] Did you know Wainright? I hope to hear all about it some day. Till then, my Nichols, Farewell,

---

[2] 'Notes on the Firth', *Macmillan's Magazine*, October 1875. This was a series of ten poems, six of which were republished in WEH's *Works*.

[3] This was WEH's second series of hospital poems and he was obviously influenced by Heine's *The Book of Lazarus* (1845).

[4] Whitman's *Leaves of Grass* was first published in 1855. WEH is probably referring to the 1867 edition which was substantially larger and contained apparent vulgarity and reference to homosexuality. This would be the 'unexpurgated edition'.

[5] The publishers.

[6] *The Times* of 28 October 1875 reported that a Henry Wainwright had been charged with the murder of Harriet Lane on 11 September 1874 in Whitechapel, London. He was sentenced to death on 1 December.

Always Yours,
W. E. Henley

[*Added by WEH at the top of the letter*] We are both of us getting old, Harry! I am Six & Twenty past & I have altogether given up Bohemianism. I would marry without a pang. And you! — You are older than I.

To Anna Boyle,[1] **5 February 1876**
ALS: Morgan

19 Balfour St., Leith Walk, Edinburgh
What is the meaning of that title, The book of H—?[2] Let me tell you a fairy story, & then you will know (I hope) as much as I.

'Once upon a time (you see how properly it begins), once upon a time, there was a Fairy Prince, who was certainly the most unfortunate in the world. So luckless was he, that he could do nothing that turned out other than ill. If he got into an omnibus, old maids gave him tracts. If he went to a tea-party, he fell in love with the wrong people. If he wrote articles for a journal (there were both articles & journals at that time in Fairyland) the journal smashed or the editor would not pay. He had, I believe, some talent for this sort of thing & for the making of verses; but even in this he was unfortunate & chose the wrong side. So that while a few, a very few, held him to be a genius, the rest of the world, a tolerably large world, were firmly persuaded that he was a fool.

So my prince went on, sorrowfully enough; for he was very very lame, and poor as prince could be. And at last he got so far as to conclude that Life in general was a mistake, & that his own life in particular was the greatest mistake of all. In which I (now) think that he was wrong; tho' certainly, at the time, he had apparently every reason for such a conclusion.

Lameness, dreadful & abominable, at last brought my prince to a gray city somewhere in the north of fairyland. Doctors wanted to cut off his unfortunate foot (his foot was the most unfortunate part of him) but he would not give his consent. So they put him to bed in a great place full of other unfortunates, & there they left him. And my prince, sorely tried but valiant to the end, took more than ever to the writing of songs. Which probably saved his life; a life that he would in no wise lose after a certain occurrence had shown him how precious, with all its drawbacks, it really was.

[1] Hannah Johnson Boyle (1855-1925), called Anna. She first met WEH when she visited her brother Captain Edward Mackie Boyle (1840-1919), a seaman, who was in the next bed to WEH in the Infirmary, Edinburgh. Edward Boyle passed his Second Mate's Certificate in 1862 and passed as Captain on 16 April 1868 at South Shields. He gained his own command, the *Wentbridge*, the same year. His final ship was the *Java* which worked the Liverpool to New York run in 1870. He was admitted to the Infirmary on 2 March 1874 but there is no record of his treatment nor his discharge date. He married Annie Frow but the date has not been found.
[2] The Book of Hannah (WEH to Anna Boyle, Wednesday [early 1876], Pierpont Morgan).

He had lain in the great house of misfortune for six weary months, during which time he had amused himself by a very serious flirtation with a certain person whom he met there. This affair had grown to be a bore to him, when he was removed from the great room where he had lain to another & smaller where he found a man with a beard: also a prince — a Sailor Prince. With him he talked, & they played cards (My prince was but a poor mortal after all!) & told stories, & beguiled the time in various ways. And one day, the Sailor Prince, who was fond of his relatives but mortally hated his brother-in-law,, produced a portrait (painted of course on the finest ivory by a great magician in the West, & richly set with diamonds of an extraordinary size) & tossed it over to my prince, saying to him; "This is my sister, the Princess H—. What do you think of her?" — And my prince looked at the portrait, & knew at once that thitherto his life & all in it had been an immense mistake; for his heart swelled within him, & he got quite uncomfortable, & something (also his heart, no doubt!) said; "This is She — at last!" And when soon afterwards he looked upon her gracious self, he sorrowed greatly, for he felt that, with his ties & in his situation, tho' the thing was certain & She, & only She, had in her hands for him the keys of Life & Love, he had no more chance of winning her than he had of replacing the Man in the Moon, or of writing a poem that would sell.

Miserable indeed he was. As a first step, the instant he could, he tried to free himself from the other, that he might not be faithless even in thought to the sweet lady of his dream. But he did not succeed, & when he looked on the one for whom he lived, as now & then he did, & compared her with the Destiny that seemed his, he grew sadder & more reckless than ever, & Life seemed a greater & more painful mistake than ever in the old time, before he had seen the face that revealed to him its value.

So he wrote away his sorrow. In songs so full of her that they were all of her, yet tinged withal with such a despairing cynicism that they seem less of her than of the poorest & wildest of women.[3] And at last a day came when he was released from his prison & sent into the world. Not lone & friendless, for She took him in, & gave him meat & wine, &, what was more precious than all, the sight of her own sweet face. And the tone of her songs changed; & when he left her house & went to live by his beloved sea, he had made some that were nearer to her & worthier her thought. Full of love, but laden with farewell: strenuous with desire, but forlorn with regret & hopeless resignation. These she took of him, & these she read. She told him she liked "some of them", & he felt glad that she had not said which.

---

[3] Many of these verses were published in the weekly journal *London*, during WEH's editorship 1878-79. For details of this journal, see WEH's letters of 27 November 1876 to Charles Baxter and 15 December 1876 to Anna Boyle.

He saw but little of her, for she was a wandering princess, & was often away. But whenever he did see her, her felt another & a better man. A remorse came on him for the life he was leading, a determination, constantly broken & as constantly renewed, to live a worthier life. And evermore the thought "How should I win her? And would she listen if I won?" An evening on the rocks, full of the quiet gold of sunset, of the far tide & the shining sands: a gray summer afternoon, first by the sea, then in his own little room: these were not much, yet enough. After the last; after the sail away into the golden summer day, & return thro' a mystic dusk, when his hand was first blessed with the touch of her yellow hair; my prince was resolved, & the end came.

But she was away, wandering in the West again; & all he could do was to write to her. Ah, the story of those letters! — The glad thought they would please; the utter despair when he found there was One that — But I cannot go on. I shall only say that My Prince, as he saluted the sunset — for your dear sake, my Love! — believed her utterly lost, never expected to see her more.

She came, however, & again & again. And when she went wandering once more, my Prince had written her a letter, & told her all he hoped, & out of the distance she answered & told *him*, that he was a goose.

So it seemed good to the Prince, no longer the most Unfortunate, but surely the luckiest of Princes, in Fairyland or other, that he ought to try & show his appreciation of such conduct. So he determined to make a book, & to call that Book, the Book of So & So. Into it he put many songs; none were good enough, but they were true; & he said "So, if I die, at least I shall have done all I could towards her immortality! — Let us on, or finish!" — And he on'd!'

Here my story ends. Whether my Prince married his Princess in the end, & whether they had many children & lived happy ever afterwards, as princes & princesses used to do, I know not. I hope they did, but I am by no means certain. All I know is, That (from a source that need not now be farther particularised) I possess an *MS*. — authentic — of the Book in question, which Book, coming down to the eve of the last of the Princess's Wanderings, I am just now endeavouring to redact. It contains some five & thirty songs. None of them are very good; some of them are very bad; but I do not think that, as a whole, it would be displeasing to you. If you would like a copy, say so, & send the *MS*. I last gave you, packed nicely, to Mr. Jas. Runciman, 12 Laurie Grove, New Cross, London SE, & you shall see what you shall see. But you must first promise, on your word of honour, not to show what you see to anyone, or you will perhaps see nothing at all.

I am now out of breath with my story, which is a very good story very badly told that I have none to go on with. I am beside horrible cold. I will finish this to morrow. Sunday, my dear Miss Boyle, is the happiest day in the week; for, if I do nothing else, I am pretty sure to write to you. And you know what that means. I have a deal to tell you, but I mustn't fill any more paper, or you would not read me. And so, *bon soir!*

6 February 1875 [1876]

A Sabbath morning, gray & misty, vibrant with sound-waves from many bells, with instincts of sunshine. Let me complete my letter. I was very glad to hear that you were teaching Nigel[4] the machine. I *hope* he will learn them all, the mower especially; also as much knitting & sewing as is possible. It is very much to Edward's[5] interest to do this, for I am convinced that Nigel has sown his wild oats, & would be, with encouragement & opportunity, a most valuable servant to him. If you can & will help in this, I need not say how grateful I shall be. Once taught, I shall be free of all responsibility, & so much more at liberty to look after myself. I ought not perhaps to mention it, but Nigel knows how much I am indebted to you, & I am quite certain that if you refuse confidence in him, you will not have made a bad outlay.

I tried my best the other night to produce a form of Report. I cannot flatter myself that I succeeded. If, however, I had that one the Howe Company gave you I am pretty sure I should be able to make one. I hear that William Wemyss[6] is back from Liverpool, so that it is not probable I shall have any opportunity of serving you in this way. If you think I can, I need not say that you have only to command me. In mentioning this I am perhaps treading on forbidden ground. You can notice it or not, as you think fit.

As yet my attempts to procure regular employment have failed. It seems that, to get work as press-corrector, I need a practical acquaintance with typography. If it be possible to get this, I shall get it. Of course I shall have to go into a printing office, & work (I suppose) as a compositor for a time. This will be nasty enough, but my hope is so strong that I should not hesitate over anything ten times as disagreeable. Meantime, I am trying to redact my two books & reading (fitfully) the Portuguese grammar. I hope, by the time you return, if May is to see you back among us, to have got the two ready, to have read Faust, to know my Portuguese, & to have gone far in the study of the Portuguese dialects. As yet, however, everything is very uncertain. Only one thing is sure, that the dream you know of grows dearer to me every day, & that I hope the end will justify me & teach me that I have not lived in vain.

I was glad to get Brown's[7] letter back, for it is very precious to me. What he

---

[4] WEH's brother Nigel Felix Henley (?1856-?).

[5] Edward Boyle.

[6] William Wemyss Kennedy, unsatisfactory husband of Anna's sister Margaret Mackie Boyle (?1844-86). They had married in 1860 but separated in 1875 with the divorce in 1881. She later married Archibald Nichol McAlpine, a lecturer in Botany. WEH's poem 'I.M. Margaritae Sororis (1886)' is dedicated to her.

[7] Thomas Edward Brown (1830-97), schoolmaster and Manx poet. After a double first at Christ Church, Oxford, he became a Fellow of Oriel in 1854. He was ordained the following year and returned to his old school in the Isle of Man. On his marriage in 1858 he became Vice-Principal of King Edward's College until 1861. Brown was Headmaster of the Crypt School, Gloucester, (1861-63) when WEH was a pupil. He then became Second Master at Clifton College, Bristol

says therein is so beautiful & benignantly said, & is so true, that it must never be forgotten. Of course, because I have used certain words now & then for which there is no authority, you must not conclude that I write bad English. I believe my English, these occasional blots apart, to be better than that of most men. For the vulgarity, I promise you that you nor he shall henceforth have reason to complain of me on that score. The two Romances[8] he speaks of are neither of them very favourite work, & one is to boot perhaps the most utterly blackguard piece of verse in English. I wrote it in the Infirmary during one of my worst periods; it has been praised by a poet (not Swinburne);[9] I shall probably burn it. Meanwhile, I insist that its value is really greater than the one Brown sets upon it.

I will try & send you Mrs. B[10] (& possibly her husband) next week, in my next letter in fact. If his portrait be a success I shall introduce it in the Infirmary cycle. I have not yet sent to Glasgow, for I have no copy to send, Jim having neglected to return me the best & most correct of all. Should I send yours & Mrs. K's?[11]

I hope you had an hour's pleasant reading out of Bret Harte.[12] He is an exceedingly clever man. His descriptions are not overloaded with detail, but eminently *suggestive*; try the moonlight (or dawn, is it?) in the *Rose of Tuolumne*[13] & see what a beautiful impression it leaves behind. Then much of his dialogue is simply as right as it can be; he has that faculty, the most difficult of all, of finding the word for the minute....I hope you will read *Daniel Deronda*,[14] George Eliot's new book. I am promised it soon, with the Book of H —. A dreadful falling off!

If you want to laugh, see *Black-Eyed Susan* at the Duke's in Holborn.[15] It is the jolliest burlesque ever written. Anthony's etchings are not a success so far; the Academy never takes etchings, engravings, or anything of the sort;[16] we

---

until 1893. Brown took a great interest in the literary career of his old pupil and the two corresponded until Brown's death. In 1930 the Crypt School named one of its Houses in his honour, as it did for WEH.

[8] These have not been identified.

[9] RLS.

[10] WEH completed a sequence of twenty-two poems called *Men and Women* (*MSS.* now at the Pierpont Morgan). Two of the poems were included in the final version of the 'In Hospital' series. The second poem, 'Apparition', is WEH's well-known portrait of RLS. The portrait of 'Mrs. B' is probably that of Anna's mother. WEH's title is from Robert Browning's *Men and Women*, a series of fifty-one poems published in 1855.

[11] Two of the *Men and Women* sequence. 'Mrs. K' is Mrs. Margaret Mackie Kennedy.

[12] (Francis) Bret Harte (1836-1902), American writer.

[13] 'The Rose of Tuolumne' in his *Tales of the Argonauts, and Other Sketches* (Boston, 1875).

[14] George Eliot's *Daniel Deronda* (1876).

[15] *Black-Eyed Susan: or all in the Downs*, a play by Douglas William Jerrold (1803-57) at the Duke's Theatre, Holborn, London. It opened on 8 January 1876 and closed on 25 February 1876.

[16] Royal Scottish Academy, The Mound, Edinburgh.

shall send them to London. I don't know much about Boyle's portrait, but we will see presently.

We have had no more accidents, & so the house is not ensured. Next week, I shall have to use a pockethandkerchief I stole in July last year, — or go without. Anthony is bashful, & won't look after a laundress, so I must desecrate my one relic.

Always Yours,

W. E. Henley

[*Added by WEH at the top of the letter*] The stocking does very well, but it is much too short. Make the next, say five or six inches longer. Two will be enough. Unless the F.P. comes and wisks you off. I trust you may make me some more when these are worn out. I have not yet received the second sock, & the first is already a thing of the past.

PS. — I am praying daily to Saint Valentine. As yet he is the hardest saint in the calendar; he will whisper me nothing.

To Robert Louis Stevenson, 25 April 1876
ALS: Yale

[19 Balfour Street, Leith Walk, Edinburgh]

My dear Robert Louis,

I have received a very satisfactory letter from Brown.[1] He wishes me to work off some Stock-Exchange types;[2] I have promised to try, but unless you collect some information about them while you are in town, I shall be considerably fogged.

Try & see the Missus while you are in town.[3] She is but poorly, & seems excessively low-spirited. A.T., A.R.S.B., W. 'Caricature'[4] — which was blazing ill done, procured me the compliments of my superiors. I have worked

---

[1] Robert Glasgow Brown (d. 1878) was one of RLS's friends at Edinburgh University. With others they founded *The Edinburgh University Magazine*, January 1871-April 1871. He was editor of *Vanity Fair*, 1875-76.

[2] In a letter to Mrs Sitwell RLS writes: 'Also, I am writing about City men, at £4 a scurrility (*Stevenson Letters*, 2, 176). They have not been identified but were possibly for *Vanity Fair*.

[3] WEH's widowed mother (his father died of apoplexy at the Berkeley Arms Hotel, Berkeley, Gloucestershire, on 8 February 1868) was living at 3 Adelaide Terrace, Adelaide Road, Shepherds Bush West.

[4] WEH was working on the ninth edition of the *Encyclopaedia Britannica* (1875-89). I have managed to identify nine articles by him.

off old Castillejo[5] since. I am to do the Cenci,[6] but as yet have no material for Congreve,[7] but our dear little friend (him of the Dicky) had petitioned to be allowed to reveal him to the B.P., & I was left lamenting. But I have asked for Charles of Orleans & Alain Chartier,[8] & suppose I shall have them. I suppose I may rely on your help; they will be wanted shortly. I need not say that if you will be reconciled (& there is no obstacle in the way but your own very poor pride), I shall abandon the Roundel & Ballad Gent to you; with enthusiasm.

In the *Biographie Universelle*[9] Alain Chartier (signed Vallet de Vireville) is credited with the invention of the 'Rondeau declinatif'. What the devil is a 'Rondeau declinatif'?

I beg of you to call upon Baynes[10] while you are in town. I have found out the secret history of your Burns,[11] & entirely exonerate the Professor from blame. I will tell you more when you return. Meanwhile, you must consider this letter as strictly confidential. If I can only induce you to do this, I feel assured that you will do well, & that coins & good work will be the issue. By the way, you will have your revenge (I promise you!), when you read the substitute. To judge by it, your father's explanation was the true one. But of this anon!

Amusez-vous bien.

Always Yours,
W. E. Henley

R. L. Stevenson Esq.
I hope you have seen Rossi.[12]

[5] The Spanish poet Cristobel de Castillejo (1494-1550).
[6] Shelley's verse tragedy in five acts (1819).
[7] William Congreve (1670-1729), dramatist. The *EB* article is unsigned.
[8] In a letter to RLS WEH writes that: 'I finished C. d. 'O yesterday' (?May 1876, Yale). His work was not used. Charles, duc d'Orleans (1394-1465), the last major French courtly poet. Alain Chartier (c.1385-c.1435), French poet and writer.
[9] *Biographie universelle ancienne et moderne* (*Biographie Michaud*), a dictionary of biography, first published in Paris, 1811-28.
[10] Thomas Spencer Baynes (1823-87), scholar. Professor of Logic, Metaphysics and English Literature at St Andrews University, from 1864. He was supervising editor of the ninth edition of the *Encyclopaedia Britannica*, 1873-87.
[11] RLS's article on Burns had been rejected by the *Encyclopaedia Britannica*. It was assumed that Baynes had not read the article and one of his staff together with Charles Black decided that it was not acceptable and rejected it. Baynes reluctantly accepted this view.
[12] Ernesto Rossi (1829-96), Italian actor. He played the title roles in *Hamlet*, *Lear*, and *Romeo and Juliet*, at the Drury Lane Theatre, London, from 19 April 1876 to 11 June 1876.

To Charles Baxter, [27 November 1876]
ALS: Yale

[19 Bristo Place, Edinburgh]

My dear Charles,

If you consider that the Literary articles are in the charge of yours truly & of R.L.S. in person,[1] you will not need any answer to your question. Nevertheless, it is possible that Jim[2] may be of use to Brown in some way or other, so you can make them known to each other.

I will write a line on Saturday. This is just to answer yours. We are all hoping soon to see you.

Yours always,
W.E.H.

[1] Glasgow Brown had decided to publish a weekly journal to be called *London: The Conservative Weekly Journal of Politics, Finance, Society and the Arts*. The first issue was on Saturday 3 February 1877, published from 281, Strand, London, W.C., price 6d. The final issue was on 5 April 1879. See also WEH's letter of 15 December 1876 to Anna Boyle.
[2] Runciman.

To Charles Baxter, 6 December 1876
ALS: Yale

19 Bristo Place, Edinburgh

My dear Charles,

Your letter enchanted us both, for of course I disregarded your injunctions & showed it to Stevenson. As long as you are such a 'd—d good writist' (I need not say whose the phrase) you needn't be afraid of professional people, tho' you *may* be permitted to entertain some scruples about putting them to the blush.

I've only read one number of the Rougon-Macquart set,[1] & that was not so repulsive — not *quite* so repulsive, that is, — as your *Curée*. Your description, my Charles, has stayed my appetite, & I feel rather glad the book has not yet arrived. Of course you are right about it. Only I dissent from one at least of your conclusions. Zola is *not* a patriot; only a partizan! — He is a Republican, & provided he can resolve the Empire into its original elements of *merde*, mind, clap-juice, & stale Champaigne, it matters little to him how far he begrimes his country & fouls his own hands. Country is nothing in these cases; '*la vraie patrie c'est l'Idée!*' — I want to hit that man in the eye with a turd, &

[1] Emile Zola's main work was *Les Rougon-Macquart*, a series of twenty volumes depicting the life of the Second French Empire. They were published between 1871 and 1893. *La Curée*, the book read by Baxter, was published in 1872.

if I can't do it without stinking, *eh bien, va pour le crottement*!

Only unfortunately Zola can write, & write d—d well. He is a disciple of Gustave Flaubert,[2] of course, & not so great an artist as his master. His talent is wider, I suppose, but he has produced no book like *Madame Bovary*. As for the obsession of impurity you experienced over *La Curée*, I got the same feeling from the *Salammbo* of the master. So I understand it.

Try to get *Thérèse Raquin*,[3] while you are in town. Roques in High Holborn, Dulau in Soho Square, Rolandi in Berners St., Jeffs in the Burlington,[4] — any one of them will have it.

I shall be very glad to see you again for more reasons than one. I want to consult you professionally. And (this is apart from all other considerations) for God his sake don't spend all your coins.

I hope you've seen Jim & Brown. I shall expect to hear largely about them.

I go to my work thro' the High St., & regularly as the morning cometh I pasture my eyes upon the lovely spectacle of the Scottish Bar, hastening to its toil, the fire of honest industry in it's eye, the smile of superior intelligence on its lip, — clean shaven, & rosy & fresh from its morning tub & the chaste embraces of it's highly respectable spouse! Oh, my brethren, how sweet & joyful a thing it is to be an Advocate! He it is whom my soul loveth, & in his sight I am as the young roe — as the young roe on the mountain of Bether![5] (*NB*. This is *not* pederastic).

Thine ever,
W. E. Henley

[2] Gustave Flaubert's first novel, *Madame Bovary*, was published in 1857. *Salammbo*, a novel of ancient Carthage, was published in 1862.
[3] Zola's *Thérèse Raquin* was published in 1867.
[4] Pierre Alex Roques, French bookseller and stationer, 51 High Holborn, London; F. Rolandi, 20 Berners Street, off Tottenham Court Road; A. B. Dulau & Co., 37 Soho Square; W. Jeffs, 15 Burlington Arcade, Piccadilly.
[5] *Song of Sol.* 2. 17. AV.
'Until the day break, and the shadows flee away, turn, my beloved, and be thou like a roe or a young hart upon the mountains of Bether.'

To Anna Boyle, 11 December 1876
ALS: Yale

[19 Bristo Place, Edinburgh]

That's something like a letter, Nance! — That's the sort of thing I've been wanting from you ever since I've began to write to you. Now I've once tasted blood, now the ice is broken (what a thick, thick ice it was, & what a deal of hammering it has taken, to be sure!), I shan't be satisfied with anything else. In this respect, I mean to be most despotic — a perfect tyrant! So mind, if you like my letters, you will write me just such others as this, or — but you'll see!

I only mislike one bit in it; that you passed the chapel, but didn't feel good enough to go in. That, I think, is not a right feeling; not the feeling I should have had. I never leave, but I am a league above the best in the world, & infinitely more fit to pray than ever I am at any other when [sic]. Now, if you feel exactly the contrary, it is surely my fault, & I wouldn't have you lose your faith for anything on earth. Why, it is calculated to make me rather miserable. Don't you think so?

Had it not been for the rest of your letter, I wouldn't have been quite so gay & free as I am. But that was enough to compensate me for all my troubles. And again, I say, you must always write to me.

I'd a letter from Clifton this morning.[1] Brown thinks Columbus 'not brilliant', but useful & saleable. What will he say when I tell him that it [was] rejected because of its general flippancy & lightmindedness? It is curious how different people regard a piece of work. R.L.S. goes thro' it at a gasp, as he would thro' a novel; Stephen thinks it satisfactory as to style, & well & clearly told as to story; T.E.B. opines that it's useful & saleable; Adam Black[2] would have 'regarded its appearance as a calamity'. I wonder what Jim & the Jenkins[3] will say! I must have the sheets lined with muslin, or it will fall to pieces. I am resolved that everybody I know shall read it; & then I'll give it to you. [rest of letter missing].

[Added by WEH at the top of the letter] Send me two or three stamps, my pet! I haven't one. I won't say anything to the Missus, but I won't tell her anything more. I'll tell you.

[1] Brown remarked that he thought the article was also 'a little heavy' (T. E. Brown to WEH, 9 December 1876, Pierpont Morgan). WEH had lost his position on the *Encyclopaedia Britannica*. In a letter to Harry Nichols WEH writes: 'I have left the *E.B.* Columbus bitched me up. I wrote a stunning article, & they sacked me for incompetence' (31 December 1876, Huntington).
[2] Adam Black (1784-1874) founder of the firm of A. and C. Black, Edinburgh, publishers of the *Encyclopaedia Britannica*.
[3] Henry Charles Fleeming Jenkin (1833-85) was Professor of Engineering at Edinburgh University 1868-85. Here he met and became a good friend of RLS. His wife, Anne (d. 1921), was an amateur actress of some note. The Jenkins often staged plays at home with their friends taking part.

To Anna Boyle, 15 December 1876
ALS: Morgan

[19 Bristo Place, Edinburgh]

I doubt not, my dearest Love, that you are wroth with me for not having written you ere this. But I am sure you will pardon me, if you haven't done so already when you hear what sort of life I have been leading. I have been living ever since last Tuesday evening in other men's rooms & eleemosynary dinners & lunches, at hotels & in cabs, & I think the ultimate issue will be satisfactory.

Brown turned up after all. He came in the afternoon, & we had a talk. Then I received Archibald Constable,[1] who promised to make interest with Blackwood[2] for me, & who offered to print me a dozen copies of Columbus. Then I went & dined in George St., where I remained all night. Next morning I lunched at the Palace Hotel, & spent the afternoon in talk with Brown. In the evening the whole band dined at Simpson's,[3] & there, after dinner R.L.S., Brown & I mapped out the paper, settled length, divisions, type & paper, & came to some understanding as to what it's politics & principles should be. I slept again in George St., & Brown having gone down to Dumbartonshire, I came home for half an hour, found no letter from you, & went away to lunch in Heriot Row.[4] Then we drove to Ferrier's who is still abed,[5] & who was very glad to see us. Then I went to Princes St. Finally I drove again to Heriot Row, had some dinner, & afterwards arranged the rough notes of prospectus of our journal. And then I came home, went to bed, & didn't wake till nine this morning.

Brown is expected in George St. at half past two, about which time my graceful & slender form will probably be seen descending from a cab somewhere by the new buildings. We are to meet for a final consultation, & he is to leave to night for Town. As he is the most promiscuous person in the whole world, it remains to be seen whether he will keep his part of the bargain. I don't much think he will, but we shall see.

The Journal is to be called *London*,[6] & will (at my suggestion) make a strong private bid for the support, direct or indirect, of Lord Beaconsfield, whose organ it ought to be. This gained, the whole country party-squires with land & beeves, apoplectic rectors, respectable country lawyers with gray whiskers & large shirt fronts — become our subscribers, & we float at once into a large circulation, perfectly independent of London favour. This is *my* proposal, & if it could be acted on, would probably make Brown's fortune. Whether it will be so or no remains to be seen.

---

[1] Archibald Constable was the grandson of the founder of the publishing firm. He formed a new company in 1890 and retired in 1893.

[2] John Blackwood (1818-79), son of the founder of the publishing firm of William Blackwood. He was editor of *Blackwood's Magazine*, May 1845 to October 1879.

[3] St Colme Street, the home of Sir Walter Grindlay Simpson, Bt (1853-98), son of the well-known gynaecologist and obstetrician Sir James Young Simpson, Bt (1811-70), pioneer of chloroform. Walter Simpson was a close friend of RLS.

[4] 17 Heriot Row was the home of RLS.

[5] James Walter Ferrier (1851-83), fellow student and close friend of RLS and a friend of WEH and Baxter. He was a contributor to *London*.

[6] This was the first journal that WEH was directly involved in as a full-time writer and, later, as editor. Brown's early interest waned rather quickly. Benjamin Disraeli, twice Conservative Prime Minister, was created Earl of Beaconsfield in 1876.

The journal is to be divided into four parts[7] — St. Stephens (political), Capel Court (financial), Mayfair (social), & Bohemia (artistic); with two subdivisions; The Whispering Gallery — rumours, gossip, scandals, — & the novel. I rather think that this will need some modification; but we shall see. These names, & the devices attached to each, as yet are mine. I am inclined to believe that Vanity Fair (a suggestion of Brown's) will take better & be more comprehensive than Mayfair; & I feel sure that Bohemia will have to be sacrificed.

If peace be certain, the journal is an accomplished fact. The first number should appear four weeks hence at latest. Our chief care now is to get up a stock of advertisements which will render the cost of publication as little a drain on the capital as may be, & make the journal to some extent self supporting. And for awhile all that we can do is to direct our energies to the production of a good specimen number, with prospectus. The preparation of this latter will probably devolve on R.L.S. & me.

Altogether the scheme looks well, my pet of pets, & I don't see at all why I shouldn't make some money by it. If I were in a decent state of health & hadn't the hope I have, I would at once go to London on the strength of it, & feel pretty confident as to the results.

All this is *confidential*. You are not to tell *any-body*. Wait until we appear, & then perhaps you shall talk. But these are mysteries that are not for the common ear. It is not fitting that they should be admitted behind the scenes, so mind & hold your tongue.

I have had to send the watch to a watchmaker. He says that the gent who last repaired it put in some of the machinery upside down, & made sure of the rest too tight, & some of it too loose. An ingenuous person, this! — I am to have it back today.

C.B. is still most unwell. He will probably winter in Algiers.[8]

During all this, I did my best to keep sober, for somebody's sake. I did not *quite* succeed, but I was more successful than I ever dared to hope. So I hope you will be pleased with me, & give me a good loving kiss when next we meet for my reward & as a slight token of affection & esteem.

---

[7] *London* was divided into six sections:

    I. St. Stephens — political news.
    II. Capel Court — financial news.
    III. Feuilleton — short stories and serialised novels.
    IV. The Whispering Gallery — 'rumours, gossip, scandals'.
    V. Vanity Fair — society news.
    VI. Bohemia — the arts, mainly literature.

[8] In a letter to Anna WEH writes: 'C.B.' s [Baxter's] right lung is slightly affected. He will leave Edinburgh for Algiers (via *Glasgow*) in a few days.' Later in the same letter WEH writes that Baxter's parents 'won't let him go to Africa' (17 December 1876, Pierpont Morgan).

The Missus seems in a poor way. You mind & make her see a *good* dentist at once, & make her take tonics and as much good fortifying grub as possible. I asked her yesterday how long the academician[9] was to stay; & she told me, two or three weeks. I laughed secretly & subtly, & had a vision of a picnic in the back shop at an earlier date than we anticipated. But she told me after all that her term of travel was doubtful, entirely depended on such arrangements as might be made. Mind you keep me posted, my darling! — It has more than once occurred to me that this visit may end in your own transfer to London. If there is any hint of that you must object strongly; decline, in fact, to be bamboozled in any such wise. If we once say goodbye, there is no knowing what may happen. I am directing my energies to make a stay in Edinburgh or at farthest in Glasgow, & you must help me. If you went to London, I should have to follow you, & they would win without an effort, Dear Love of my Heart, for it would kill me.[10]

I will write to you again on Sunday, so that you may expect a letter on Monday morning. I hope by that time to have heard from you, & to have something nice to say to you about your own letter. You mustn't be angry with *me* for not writing. You know by this time that I would if I could. How many times I've thought of you I needn't say. I have dreamed myself to sleep with you every night, & have been more glad in the dreaming than I can tell.

I hear that you've had more neuralgia.[11] I feel very very angry with you, for I know it's all your own wilfulness that you've to thank for it. If I hear any more of it, I won't write to you for ever so long, & I know you'll feel *that*. So beware!

The time of half sheets is over. We went to a shop for paper to map out the journal upon, & I persuaded C.B. to purchase me some note paper & envelopes. These are the flower of their respective packets, so be grateful.

And now Goodbye! I wish I were coming over to morrow, to see & hear & take you again in my arms. But you know the vanity of wishing, my sweet! — I cannot come, but I shall think of you, — of that you may be sure! — & I shall pray for another *tête-à-tête* as soon as may be. How jolly they are, ain't they? When we *are* married, we shall have something to talk about after all. I am lame & poor & all that sort of thing, but few couples have ever had a better

---

[9] Marianne Mackie (Molly) Boyle (b. 1853), Anna's elder sister, was studying singing at the Royal Academy of Music, London. She was lodging at 113 Victoria Street, London. She married the landscape painter William Mcbride or MacBride (1855-1913) on 10 December 1885.

[10] The Boyles were Roman Catholics. Marriage between Catholics and non-Catholics was rare and subject to strict conditions, e.g. that any issue were to be brought up as Catholics. In a letter to Anna WEH writes: 'I do not think that we shall ever marry with your people's consent .... Those who love you will seek, for your sake, to make you retract your word, & we shall have no encouragement saving from ourselves' (10 December 1876, Pierpont Morgan).

[11] Anna suffered with neuralgia throughout her life.

time of it sweethearting than we. It is only a prophesy of the happier time that is coming, Dear Love! — Only that! — At least *I* think so.

I *must* stop, for I'm in an awful hurry. I kiss your dear mouth, *you know how*. GoodXbye. Think of me a little sometimes, & write to me as soon as you can.

Your Will.

To Anna Boyle, 23 February 1877
ALS: Yale

[19 Bristo Place, Edinburgh]

My dearest Nancy must not be disappointed, if she only gets the briefest of notes. She set herself the example.

London is a very fair number, but so riddled with printers' errors as to be almost ludicrous.

R.L.S. is responsible for 'An Old Song', which Brown has hacked & hewn disgracefully & somewhat stupidly, for the Paris Bourse, & for the 'Book of the Week'.[1] I take the Prince of Wales, Legros, Longfellow, A Morality, the two Echoes, Rhoda Broughton, & all Mudie but the two last.[2] Mind you tell no one. If you do, you shall find out who's who yourself.

I sent you *Truth*[3] this afternoon. *Black Spirits & White*[4] went to Mrs. K. on Tuesday. It's a shame not to have sent them.

I got the books all right this morning. You might have waited. I would have brought them home to-morrow. But perhaps you don't mean to come. If I don't get a letter to-morrow, or this evening, *I won't write all next week.*

So beware! I kiss you ten thousand times — my love, my Nancy!

Your Will.

---

[1] RLS's short story 'An Old Song' was not republished until 1892. The other two have not been reprinted. The 'Book of the Week' was a review of *Russia* by Sir David Mackenzie Wallace.

[2] WEH's contributions were: 'The Prince of Wales (leader)', 'M. Alphonse Legros', 'Lady Novelists: Rhoda Broughton', 'Longfellow and the sea', 'A Morality (poem)', 'Mudie's (book reviews)', and 'Echoes (poems)'. The poems were very much 'fillers'.

[3] A weekly journal edited by the journalist and politician Henry du Pré Labouchere (1831-1912), which ran from 4 January 1877 to 27 December 1957. After various attempts to enter Parliament (with one year as an MP, 1867) Labouchere finally became MP for Northampton in 1880 until 1905. In *Truth* he supported the Liberals and vigorously attacked fraudulent businesses which brought him many enemies and libel actions.

[4] A novel by Frances Eleanor Trollope (?1834-1913) published in 1877. She was a sister-in-law of the novelist Anthony Trollope.

To Charles Baxter, 25 August 1877
ALS: Yale

21 Park Side, Albert Gate, [London] S.W.[1]

My dear Charles,

I managed to get our Editor away (to Trouville, I think) last night. He is a veritable wreck. But I hope he'll pull through.

I am located in his rooms; in charge of copy & proofs. I am rather impressed with the greatness of my position, & am extremely dubious as to capacity. But I shall do my best. If the 31st *London* is not as good as the others,[2] you will know what to attribute it to, & whom.

I shall send you some lists of subscribers. And I will try & make up a whole set for you. Do what you can. We need it. Our publisher is an ass — a sumph.[3] It is to his ridiculous apathy that the decrease in advts is owing; entirely. Also a decrease in the circulation. He has been discharged, & a new & younger man comes in his room on Monday.[4] We hope much of this one. God grant that our hopes be not disappointed!

There *is* money (between you & me). How much I know not. But we don't yet know whether life or death is to be our portion.

Payn will give us his novel.[5] But not until February. Meantime, we are thinking of translating Gaboriau's *Crime d'Orcival*.[6] What think you?

I had intended to do some 'In & Outs,' but R.G.B. has taken his key with him, & the family retires at ten p.m. So that unless I make a night of it in St. James's Park, I don't see how it's to be done.[7]

I've seen Stephen, who has given me introductions to *Saturday Review* & *Pall Mall Gazette*. I've dined with Payn. I've sent £20 to R.L.S. (between you and me). And I hear that Ruskin is much pleased with Anthony's work,[8] & that

[1] Brown's residence.
[2] The issue of 25 August 1877.
[3] George Edmund Shepherd.
[4] Frederick Evans took over on Monday 27 August.
[5] James Payn (1830-98), *By Proxy* (1878). He was editor of *Chambers's Journal* 1859-74. From 1874 to 1896 he was a reader for Smith, Elder and Co., publishers of the *Cornhill Magazine* of which he was editor 1883-96. He was a prolific and popular novelist. His novel was reviewed in *London*, 4 May 1878.
[6] Emile Gaboriau (1832-73), French crime novelist. His *Crime d'Orcival* was published in 1867. A translation possibly by RLS and WEH was published in *London* in thirty-seven weekly instalments from 22 September 1877 to 1 June 1878.
[7] 'In and Out of London', within the 'Vanity Fair' section. For example; see 'In and Out of London. The Moore and Burgess Minstrels', *London*, 1 September 1877. They were playing at St James's Hall, hence WEH's reference to St James's Park.
[8] In a letter to WEH (12 July 1877, Pierpont Morgan) Leslie Stephen writes that he is going on holiday to Wakehead Hotel, Coniston, Ambleside, and: 'I shall be a neighbour of Mr. Ruskin's with whom I have some acquaintance. If you could send me any drawing of your brother's [Anthony] I might be able to show it to that genius & his opinion, if encouraging, might be worth something.'

Ruskin's adopted nephew,[9] a landscapist of some note, is enthusiastic about it. Nevertheless, I feel dubious & repressed.

I shall stay at least three weeks longer. Write to me if you can. If all goes well, when next you press my hand, it will be the hand of a Benedict[10] & a brother.

May I salute Mrs. Baxter? If I may, I will. Can you send me a Whisper or two?[11] Or an article of some sort? Do, if you can.

Yours always,
W. E. Henley

[9] The painter Joseph Arthur Severn (1842-1931) had married Ruskin's niece, Joanna. In a letter to his future wife, Julia Prinsep Duckworth, Leslie Stephen remarked that Arthur Severn had commented that one of Anthony Henley's paintings 'was good enough to be exhibited at the Dudley Gallery, where he [Severn] is an authority and if I [Stephen] would send it in he would look after it' (18 August 1877, Berg Collection, NYPL).

[10] That is, WEH would be married. The reference is to Benedick, a bachelor of long standing, who finally marries, in *Much Ado About Nothing*. In a letter to Anna (Saturday [25 August 1877], in private hands) WEH writes: 'My idea is this; to give Brown 3 weeks holiday, & then to bring him back for a week. During that time I should run over to Ireland, & — you know what. Then I should return to London — with you?'

[11] For the 'Whispering Gallery'.

To Anna Boyle, 1 September 1877
ALS: Fleming

[21 Park Side, Albert Gate, London, S.W.][1]

I am glad to have heard from my darling even tho' the letter contains such ill news.

But why did you not say more? I am half-mad & wholly miserable at the thought of it. Do write & tell me why it cannot be managed as we wished. Explain it in full, for I ought to know.

I cannot do without you, Dear Love, & if you hold me off longer it will be good for neither of us. Wife of my heart, you *must* be mine at once, or the world is over for me. I need your hand in mine to make life tolerable & liveable. Why must you delay to achieve the fruition of that love which has made you what you are?

[1] WEH was still at Brown's address but his movements were uncertain. Kennedy Williamson states that WEH's first home in London was at 7 Oaklands Road, Shepherds Bush, where he lived with his mother and brothers, but there is no direct evidence to support this. According to Williamson the family moved to two houses in Adelaide Road, Shepherds Bush. However, WEH's mother was at 3 Adelaide Terrace, Adelaide Road, in April 1876. WEH was at 11 Adelaide Road by November 1877 (WEH to J. Winter Jones, 29 November 1877, BL).

For God's sake write soon.

Always & only yours,
W. E. Henley

The current *Contemporary* contains a bitter attack on the new weeklies[2] —
London among the number. I am referred to as 'the scribbler who gives himself
airs of pedantry on the strength of being able to spell through Gautier's *Historie
du Romantisme*'.[3] Let. I am at once amused & saddened by it. I don't know
whether we shall take notice of it.[4] I've seen the *Saturday*.[5] I'm to do 'Life in
Hospital' for him.[6]

[*Added by WEH at the top of the letter*] I sent you *London* yesterday I hope you
have it. A kiss, Dear Soul, on that mouth that is all the world to me. God bless
you. Write soon.

[2] R. W. Buchanan's unsigned 'Signs of the Times (no.1): the Newest Thing in Journalism,'
Contemporary Review, September 1877. Robert (Williams) Buchanan (1841-1901), poet,
novelist, playwright and critic. His best novel is *God and the Man* (1881), a study of hatred. He
achieved notoriety with an attack on the Pre-Raphaelites in the *Contemporary Review* of
October 1871.
[3] Published in 1874.
[4] Dismissive notice was taken, though only briefly; in 'The Magazines,' *London*, 8 September
1877.
[5] Walter Herries Pollock (1850-1926), journalist, sub-editor and later editor (1833-94) of the
Saturday Review. WEH referred to him as 'Wollock'.
[6] WEH's unsigned 'Convalescence,' *Saturday Review*, 6 October 1877. This is WEH's only
other comment in print on his experience in hospital. He writes not of the harsh reality as in his
verse, but of the pseudo-pleasure that can be felt in the pain of recovery. He sees convalescence
as a weary period as strength returns to the moving body after a period of inactivity. The whole
process is 'a trying period both for nurses and patients, especially after severe illnesses. It is an
uninteresting, unsympathetic, and uncomfortable probation, and severely tests the temper,
patience, and endurance of the victims of disease and the victims of invalids.'

To Robert Louis Stevenson, 14 December 1877
ALS: Yale

11 Adelaide Road, Shepherds Bush, W.
My dear Lewis,[1]
   I should have writ to you last week, but I was too busy & had besides a hell
of a cold. It is a bit better, but it's left me as weak as water, & a disposition to
see the world in gray which is truly indomitable.

[1] RLS's second name was originally 'Lewis' but he changed it to 'Louis' when he was about
eighteen. WEH always regarded this as an affectation and often used 'Lewis'. In 1878 RLS
wrote to him 'Robert Louis, mind, not Lewis, (*Stevenson Letters*, 2, 254).

The brutal & licentious sent for me last week, & asked me, in his absence to take charge of the proofs. This is tantamount to editing the paper, as I suppose you know. But he is obliged to finesse over everything. I am to receive a pound a week for the work. But finesse again steps in & shuffles the cards; so far from having a weekly pound, I've not yet received my last week's screw. As the b. & l. has flown to the contonong, it's doubtful when I shall get it. As before he fled, he contrived to quarrel violently with Runciman, & entirely to sever the connection between them, it's still more doubtful what he really wishes to be at. My own opinion is that his disease has degraded him so much that he doesn't know what he's doing; that in fact he's maliciously & tyrannically mad. I don't think he'll ever return. I'm afraid he's too far gone. In quarrelling with Runciman, moreover, he has laid up a store for a tremendous 'difficulty'. Jim is a good fellow, as you know — but he thinks Brown has been damnably insolent to him, & insolence is a thing he never takes from anyone. He dreams fervidly of horsewhips & the manly fist. And of other engines too less lethal but in finality more dangerous. So that Brown will have his hands full. I must say that, ill as he is — & he's at death's door — I can hardly find it in my heart to pity him. I've not got any animosity for I don't bear ill-will long to anyone. But such interest as I take in him, which is rather kindly on the whole, is purely intellectual & scientific.

You men spoiled me, Lewis, & that is the truth. I believed that everybody was like you. And oh! what a dreadful mistake I made! After all, it's comforting enough in its way, the reflections that one's friends are good men, & that one is not all unworthy of them. Don't you think so?

As for me, I'm trying to play my game as cautiously & as honourably as may be. I have determined, if its possible, to marry in January.[2] To that end I may need your help — or rather Simpson's thro' you, — to the extent of a loan of £50, to be repaid by instalments within the year. That will clear me of all my debts, & enable me & my dear one to start with a good deal less of encumbrance than falls to the lot of most. I am tolerably sure of getting work, & more even than I can do. I don't think, modesty apart that I am the worst journalist before the public, & I've good friends & true who'll help me with introductions, & back up my own work. I've averaged 11 1/3 cols. a week for the last nine numbers; & you know it hasn't been all bad. How long it will last is another pair of sleeves. Not long, I fancy, unless I marry. This dreadful loneliness is killing me. For, my dear lad, I'm as lonely as you, & my mind & brain are not nearly as yours. I cannot & will not live much longer like it. If I fail (but I shall not fail) I mean to return to my old haunts & my oldest friends. We have known each other, Lewis of my heart, but a little while, as time goes; & yet how much you have been to me! My life seems to date from that moment when Stephen brought you into the darkened room in the old Infirmary. The

[2] WEH and Anna were married at St Mary's Roman Catholic Chapel, Broughton Street, Edinburgh, on 22 January 1878. The witnesses were Anne Jenkin and Charles Baxter.

love that has filled my life was only a dear & impossible dream then, & but for your help & counsel & companionship would never have been other. Truly in revisiting these glimpses of this London moon,[3] tho' I worked & hungered & suffered under it not so long syne, I seem & am a stranger in a strange land. I think that my wife & I will be happy enough in our little way. But I don't think we ought to live here. I have laid out my life to exault & complete her life; but glad as I shall make her — & I know I have that in me that makes women glad & good — I think she nor I will ever consider this great hateful selfish London our home. To live here a little is to understand Arcadia.

Let us have lambs & merry milkmaids & cockcrowing & mown meadows & shepherds piping on a hill! Frieze is your only wear. Augusta & Phyllis are a long chalk better than Miss Blank & Misses Niminy & Piminy. This is *not* journalism, tho' it reads like it. So mind.

London is a vile hole, & the theatres are its worst corners. Saw *La Cigale* the other evening.[4] Good play in the original, particularly for an actress of the Chaumont's genius[5] — I say genius advisedly. Farren, 'the English Chaumont',[6] is a dancing cad, with neat feet, immense hodgenishness, & the voice of a cheap jack. She played damned bad — yet this morning her manager advertises that the 'first act shows her command of pathos' (which in an inverse sense is certainly true) & that 'her *physical attributes*' are fitter for the part than those of the Chaumont!! thereby. There's more of it. And yet John Hollingshead's an intelligent man. Isn't it lamentable, grandsire? I've not yet seen a bit of good acting since I've been in town.

Over there in Paris, our own great man has been playing *Othello & Hamlet.*[7] He has not been entirely successful, of course, for he doesn't happen to be a Frenchman. The critics have not yet settled, it would seem, whether he or Rossi is the better Othello. I've not seen what Sarcey[8] says, but really, after that, my faith in French dramatic criticism has received a certain shock. But he's had his moments, the good man that he is. He plays a piece called *La Morte Civile.*[9] The house is thin, indifferent, conversationally given. 'Suddenly Tommaso goes in for one of his dying scenes. Some interval elapsed after the curtain fell before the audience ventured to applaud. Then they recalled Salvini repeatedly,

---

[3] 'Revisits thus the glimpses of the moon' *Hamlet*, I. iv. 53.
[4] *La Cigale*, adapted from the French by John Hollingshead, was at the Gaiety Theatre, London, from 10 December 1877 to 30 March 1878. John Hollingshead (1827-1904), author, journalist and theatre manager. He founded the Gaiety Theatre, London, in 1868, and was the inventor of the matinée performance.
[5] The French actress Céline Chaumont (1848-1926) had played the main role in the last performance in Paris in October.
[6] Nellie (Ellen) Farren (1848-1904), actress.
[7] The Italian actor Tommaso Salvini (1829-1916) was touring with his own company.
[8] Francisque Sarcey (1827-99), well-known French drama critic who wrote for the daily newspaper *Le Temps*.
[9] *La Morte Civile*, a play by the Italian dramatist Paolo Giacometti (1816-82).

but — strangest tribute of all to the impression produced — they still linger about their places, unwilling to leave, the women sobbing & the men very pale.' Throw up your hat, my Son! And drain (with me in spirit) a bumper of health to him. I copy from the *D.T.*[10] — an eyewitness. I've sent the cutting to Queen Anne.[11]

I've heard a little from Bob.[12] Anthony's had a touch of rheumatic fever. Palizzi[13] is very much pleased with him.

Before the brutal & licentious left, I arranged with him about settlement with Katharine[14] & James Walter.[15] I regret to say that he's not paid Katharine (£5..2..6 for seven numbers), & I suppose he hasn't yet paid J.W. either. It's not my fault, for I went as far with him, as under existing circumstances, I could. Teddy,[16] I'm happy to say, is not pipped. A bad, a very bad cold & a hard whatshisname. But you can send the watch, in spite of that. My own's in pawn, so are the spoons I'd bought for my marriage.

And now how are you? What are you doing? They tell me that you are being handed over to the Philistines — that they are searching among for young ladies to mate with you in the bonds of wedlock. Is it true? I'm afraid it is. I do not kid you, for I know you ever so much wiser than I, & in these cases a man's stout heart is his best friend and truest counsellor. But write to me as soon as you conveniently can. Your letters do me good. Try to send me back Austin Dobson's[17] first vol., which I want my mother to read. Would you like Locker's

---

[10] 'The French Crisis', *Daily Telegraph*, 14 December 1877.

[11] A nickname for Anne Jenkin.

[12] Robert Alan Mowbray Stevenson (1847-1900). A cousin of RLS, he became an artist after leaving Cambridge University, studying in Antwerp and Paris. He later exhibited at the Royal Academy. He turned to writing on the advice of WEH, working for various newspapers and journals, including the *Magazine of Art* and the *National Observer* both under WEH. From 1888 to 1892 he was Professor of Fine Art at University College, Liverpool. He was also the art critic of the *Pall Mall Gazette*, 1893-99.

[13] The Italian artist Filippo Palizzi (1818-99) who appears in a photograph with Bob Stevenson and Anthony Henley, among others, taken at Grez-Sur-Loing near Paris. It is reproduced in Will Hicok Low's *A Chronicle of Friendships 1873-1900* (1908).

[14] Katharine Elizabeth Alan de Mattos (1851-1939), sister of Bob Stevenson. She had married William Sydney de Mattos on 25 June 1874 but the marriage soon ran into difficulties and she eventually left him.

[15] Ferrier.

[16] WEH's wayward brother, the actor Edward John Henley (1860-98).

[17] Henry Austin Dobson (1840-1921), poet and writer on 18th century literature, worked at the Board of Trade. He and WEH later formed a firm friendship through their common interest in French poetry and its imitation and they corresponded from 1878 until WEH's death. WEH often consulted Dobson about his own poetry. Here WEH may be referring to Dobson's first publication *A Valentine* (1865).

London Lyrics[18] in return? They will please you mightily. How did you like my quatrains?[19] I am very proud of them? Axiom: 'No person of intelligence ever perused *Émaux et Camés*, without profit.'

Tell me, tell me Shepherd,[20] if I'm to write a review of anything ('a bright & pleasant little paper', say) in January.[21] I hope I am. While I've command of a journal, an orgin so to speak, that horgin is always at the service of those I love.

How is Baxter married, or the married Baxter?[22] Has Simpson returned to Edinburgh? Have you seen the living Jenkin? Has Queen Anne deserted us, & gone over to the recreant Irving? If you can find time to answer some of these questions, do so. If not, you may retire hup, & hold converse with the Immensities there.

God bless you. My mother sends her kindest love.

Yours always,

W.E.H.

Good news from Paris? I thought about Paris a little when I heard Woodhull.[23]

[*Added by WEH at top of the letter*] This of Brown had better be held privy & confidential.

---

[18] Frederick Locker, *London Lyrics* (1857). WEH may be referring to the 1876 edition. Frederick Locker, later Locker-Lampson (1821-1895), poet and writer.

[19] The unsigned 'The Cathedral Close,' *London*, 8 December 1877. This poem is not included in his *Works*.

[20] In a letter to Baxter (*Stevenson Letters, 2,* 207) RLS uses a line from the glee 'Ye Shepherds, tell me' by Joseph Mazzinghi (1765-1844).

[21] Probably WEH's unsigned six line review of RLS's 'The Sire de Malétroit's Door,' *London*, 12 January 1878.

[22] Charles Baxter was married to Grace Louisa Stewart on 24 July 1877.

[23] Mrs. Victoria Claflin Woodhull (1838-1927), an American advocate of sexual morality. WEH's unsigned article, 'In and Out of London: Mrs. Victoria Claflin Woodhull at the St. James's Hall,' appeared in *London*, 8 December 1877.

To W. H. Brett,[1] **22 February 1878**
ALS: Yale

11 Adelaide Rd., Shepherds Bush, W.

Dear Sir,

You do me much honour in asking an opinion of me concerning your verse. I shall give you one with all frankness — promising, simply, that it is merely [   ], & in no wise to be regarded as authoritative

I think, to begin with, that you have a great deal too much facility, & that you are apt to fall into a mistake that, however common to the young rhythmists, is none the less to be violently & steadily eschewed: the mistake, that is, of being content with mere fluency, & of disdaining the higher needs of verse. Verse, as verse, is valueless utterly unless it is well made, and it is not usually well made without the expenditure of a great deal of thought & consideration. This much you do not seem to me to give. You write a great deal & correct, I should fancy very little indeed. Your verse therefore shows too-frequent signs of a looseness, a laxity, a slovenliness of fancy & of craftmanship, that are greatly to be deprecated. I shall not now enter on the question of whether you may happen to have in you aught that is worth saying. I shall contend myself with pointing out that whatever & however it may be, you have yet to learn how to say it. When you are a little further advanced in skill, in the art of making verses, we will perhaps consider the other. Meanwhile if you wish to win consideration of any sort, you must *soigner* your style, & learn to know affectation from originality: weakness from violence, good stuff from bad.

I hardly think, if you will allow me to say so, that you are fortunate in your choice of models. Your last copy of verse, for instance, seemed to me an imitation of an imitation of a poet who is perhaps of all poets the one to be most carefully avoided by a young writer who is not quite strong enough to stand on his own base. You are fluent & facile, enough, sometimes even graceful in a kind of way; but you lack force, you lack precision, the quality of definiteness, & you do not seem to have much knowledge of words except as metrical feet or as rhymes. I have written much verse in my time, & do not think that I have been wise in doing so; but my experience has been quite the same as your own. As you are beginning, so did I begin. I ran away after inspiration, rhythmic drunkenness, what you will; & I was a nuisance to everyone who came near me. I date the beginning of my own return to sanity

---

[1] William Howard Brett (1846-1918), American librarian. From 1874 to 1884 he worked for the Cobb and Andrews Book Store, Cleveland, Ohio, where he made its reputation as the best informed bookshop of the city. He was Dean of the Library school of Western Reserve from 1894 until his death. As a librarian he produced the *Cumulative Index* which later became the *Reader's Guide to Periodical Literature*. He was President of the American Library Association, 1896-97.

from the time when I came to see that the old artists, the great wordsmen, were the best. Whatever I have since written (if you will pardon my egotism) has been written under their guidance, & if any of it be good at all, it is because I have, in a manner, exampled myself with them, & have cultivated as well as I could my intelligence of their more imitable qualities.

This what I should like you also to do. Have you ever heard of Théophile Gautier? That incomparable stylist was wont to the last to study his dictionary. If it paid him to do so, surely we may do the same. Avoid contemporary verse as much as you may — above all the verse of journalists & magazine writers; & if you read Tennyson, read him only as a master of phrase & diction, & by way of comparing him, from that point of view, with Wordsworth & Milton. These two men you may read always — particularly the latter. If to these you add Chaucer & Burns, & write as little & polish as much as you can for a twelve month, you will be a great deal more considerable than you are.

What you want, in fact, is to draw from the antique. Let Milton and Chaucer be your critique, & do you draw from them — read & analyse them, that is — as much as you can. Presently you may enter the life class, & then, you know, you can begin to paint pictures; but not till then.

I return your Valentine. Frankly, I am not surprised at its rejection. It is very crude indeed. But if you care to try & follow the advice I have presumed to give you, you will do so much better by this time next year, that you will wonder how you could have tolerated it at all.

I have not much time for letter-writing, & none at all for the periphrases of delicacy. Pray forgive me if I have hurt you very much. I know that most of that I have said will jar a great deal. But I have had too much good from the application of the rod myself, to shrink from administering it when I think it is necessary. I shall be glad to see anything you may have to send me; but I shall be still more glad to hear that you have taken my advice. If I have taught you anything of the value of reticence, restraint, sobriety, I shall congratulate myself a good deal.

Faithfully Yours,
W. E. Henley

Mr. W. H. Brett.

To Austin Dobson, 6 June 1878
ALS: London. Part published in Connell, 82-3

11 Adelaide Rd, Shepherds Bush, W.
My dear Sir,
I hope you don't very *much object* to parodies.[1] I really couldn't help it.
I am vexed about the 'Ballade of Names'.[2] I think I will go off, and leave the field to you. I am sure the world will be obliged to me.
I have read thro Miss Robinson's *Handfull*.[3] She is really a most pleasing young person. I do like your selections ('Le Roi est Mort' & 'Apollo's Garden'[4] are they not? I've mislaid your letter & don't remember certainly), but I think her little 'Pastoral' I will not say the best, but the most promising of all.

Faithfully Yours,
W. E. Henley

Austin Dobson Esq.

The Chant Royal won't come, I'm glad to say.[5]

[1] WEH's parody of Dobson's, 'The Beggars,' *Evening Hours*, May 1876, appeared unsigned as 'The Prodigals. (Ballade: after Mr. Austin Dobson) Dedicated to Mr Chaplin, M.P., Mr Richard Power, M.P., and the two hundred and twenty-three who followed them,' *London*, 8 June 1878. Mr Chaplin proposed the motion that the House of Commons adjourn as usual for Derby Day. The motion was carried with ninety-five against.
[2] Dobson's 'A Ballade of Names' written in 1878 but not published until 1923; see *The Complete Works of Austin Dobson*, ed. Alban Dobson (1923).
[3] Agnes Mary Francis Robinson (later Darmesteter, later Duclaux) (1857-1944), writer and translator of French literary works. Her *A Handful of Honeysuckle* was published in 1878.
[4] 'In Apollo's Garden.'
[5] The Chant Royal is an extended version of the French Ballade containing five verses, each of eleven lines with an envoi of four or five lines. The Ballade has three verses, each of eight or ten lines with an envoi of five lines. In a letter to Dobson, WEH writes: 'I've velleities of Chant Royalism, I'm sorry to say' (WEH to Austin Dobson, 31 May 1878, University of London).

To Charles Baxter, Saturday [16 August 1879]
ALS: Yale. Part published in *Stevenson Letters*, *3*, 4-5.

36 Loftus Road, Shepherds Bush, W.[1]
I am very sorry to hear of your mother's death, my dear Charles.[2] It is one of

[1] The Henleys had moved here by 11 April 1879 (WEH to Austin Dobson, Good Friday 1879, London University).
[2] Mrs Mary Baxter died on 11 August 1879.

those unhappy things that come to all of us but that is none the less tolerable for all that. I was in some measure prepared for it, for Louis told me he feared that such a loss would soon come upon you. It has come sooner than I thought. Be assured, my friend, that you have all the sympathy my wife and I, who love you, can give.

I sent off the letter. Bob's address is *chez* Leopold, Cernay-la-Ville, Seine-et-Oise. I hope that it was not in writing to you that he omitted his address. He is capable of having done so, I know. Indeed he's capable of anything in that way. I wonder what he'll say to Louis's journey.[3] He would be capable of pursuit, I think. I bless God that he hasn't the money. Louis and he are best apart: particularly under the present circumstances and in the present complication.

Colvin[4] and I saw him off, my dear Charles, and I don't think we were very happy. He promised he wouldn't go any farther than New York, so that, whether he does any good or not, I hardly think he'll do any harm. I couldn't say no to his going nor Colvin either; and difficult as it is to see what end he could gain, it was still more difficult to make him see as we saw. After all, it was his duty, and to have done it will comfort and cheer him a great deal. That is the main thing. They may never meet, but I know he'll be the happier for the step he has taken, and that is enough. When we see him again he will be better and stronger than ever. I hoped she would be brave and generous enough to have given him up: — to have shown herself worthy of him by putting herself out of his way for ever. But she's not, and there's an end on't. So far as I can see, the one thing to be feared for him is that he may be induced to go to Monterey,[5] and there get mixed up once more in the miserable life of alarms and lies and intrigues that he led in Paris.[6] If he don't do that, I not much fear for him. It will end in a book, I expect, and in a happier way of life. If it come to the worst, my boy, we shall lose the best friend man ever had: but it won't. And we may keep our pistols in our pockets.

How are you? I am well. Why do you never write? You've much more time than I have. I wish I were in Edinburgh. As I live I regret that I left it. It is the

[3] RLS had met the American Fanny Osbourne, *née* Van de Grift, (1840-1914) in Grez-Sur-Loing, near Paris, in the late summer of 1876. He was immediately attracted to the estranged wife of the ne'er-do-well Samuel Osbourne. In August 1879 RLS set off to America in pursuit of Fanny. She was divorced from her husband in December 1879 and married RLS on 19 May 1880 in San Francisco. His friends, especially WEH and Colvin, were strongly opposed to the marriage and hoped he would return unmarried from America.

[4] Sidney Colvin (1845-1927), art and literary critic. Slade Professor of Fine Art, Cambridge University, 1873-85. He was also Director of the Fitzwilliam Museum, Cambridge, 1876-84. From 1884 to 1912 he was Keeper of Prints and Drawings at the British Museum. In 1903 he married Mrs Frances Sitwell, whom he had known for more than thirty years and whose husband had died in 1894. He was knighted in 1911. He and WEH met through RLS. Like RLS he was a member of the Savile Club having been elected in 1869.

[5] Where Fanny was living.

[6] RLS and Fanny had lived together in Paris.

Holy City of Memory — a Mecca of the past. *Allons*! God bless us all! We have lived somewhat, and we have loved. If we do but take each other's hands with pleasure in the years to come, we need ask no more. I think we shall. Don't you? This is sentiment, I know, and sentiment between a venal journalist and a kind of family lawyer is — ah well! Be it so! It's a comfort all the same.

I've meant writing to you since some time. I've a serious *Histoire de la Prostitution*[7] — a book full of curious & unpublishable facts. Would you like it? 'Tis in eight volumes — the common French octavos; & it is worth reading. Let me know; & I'll send it.

Have you a Molière?[8] If not that in the *Grands Ecrivains* series is the only one possible.

I've a little work; for *P.M.G.* & *Athenaeum*. In the latter of these I'm responsible (this Saturday, I think) for notices of Charles Lever & *Madame Bonaparte*.[9] But *je suis pauvre comme toujours*. There ain't enough for me to do.

Write *by return; if possible*, about the book. If yes, it shall come by hand.

Yours, dear lad,
W.E.H.

[*Added by WEH at the top of the letter*] Anthony is working *very well*, but selling not. He's not here, but I know he'd send his love if he were.

---

[7] *Histoire de la prostitution chez tous les peuples du monde depuis l'antiquite la plus reculée jusqu'a nos jours par Pierre Dufor* 8 vols. (Brussels, 1861).
[8] Jean-Baptiste Poquelin (1622-73), known as Molière, French dramatist.
[9] Charles (James) Lever (1806-72), prolific Irish novelist whose novels of military and Irish life were highly popular. WEH did not review him. However, he did review Eugene L. Didier's *The Life and Letters of Madame Bonaparte*, *Athenaeum*, 16 August 1879.

To T. H. Ward,[1] 15 September 1879
ALS: Texas

36 Loftus Rd, Shepherds Bush, W.

Dear Sir,

Many thanks for your letter. I esteem it an honour to have been asked to take part in your project, & will do my best with Butler for you.[2] He is not a

---

[1] Thomas Humphry Ward (1845-1926), journalist, editor and writer. He graduated in 1868 from Brasenose, Oxford, and became a Fellow in 1870. On his marriage in 1872 to Mary Augusta Arnold, better known as the novelist Mrs. Humphry Ward (1851-1920), he resigned his Fellowship. He joined *The Times* in 1881 becoming a leader writer and later the art critic.
[2] Ward was editing a collection of English verse from Chaucer to the turn of the second half of the nineteenth century published as *The English Poets: Selections with Critical Introductions by Various Writers and a General Introduction by Matthew Arnold.*, 4 vols (1880). WEH

favourite of mine, but perhaps I shall do him better justice than if he were.

You ask me to name the poets, or the period of poetry with which I am most familiar. I am afraid that I can hardly give you a very satisfactory answer. The poets I should like to speak of & to select from are Burns & Scott — particularly the latter. If you could allow me one or the other — or both — of these, I should do them for you very willingly. Outside of these I have no predilections — or none I could advance with any show of reason, unless it be those for the makers of society verse & the writers of songs in general.

I assume that Herrick is already in hand;[3] had he not been so I should have been glad of him. Apart, however, for the poets of whom I have spoken, I should be glad to have any work allotted to me. What ever it be, I will do it to the best of my ability.

Very Faithfully Yours,
W. E. Henley

T. H. Ward Esq.

contributed the following signed selections: Samuel Butler (1613-80), Robert Henryson (?1424-?1506), John Byrom (1692-1763) and Charles Kingsley.
[3] The poet Robert Herrick (1591-1674).

To Sidney Colvin, 2 January 1880

ALS: Yale. Part published in Lucas, 116-7[1] and *Stevenson Letters*, *3*, 40-1.

1 The Parade, Shepherds Bush, London, W.[2]

My dear Colvin,

I wrote you a note yesterday. I write again in the hope that another may find you ere you return.

I know no more of Runciman's doings than yesterday.[3] I hope, however, all will go well; I think it will. The right of excision I have reserved.

Write by all means. If you've not sent what you had written, send it. Don't defer expostulation because he's ill.[4] On the contrary. It is absolutely necessary that he should be brought to see that England & a quiet life are what he wants & must have if he means to make — I won't say a reputation — but money by literature. We shall pass off all he's done, but I won't answer for much more. Come back he must, & that soon. Married or unmarried — *je m'en fiche*. If we can't have our Louis without the rice, we must have him with it.

[1] Most of this letter was published by Lucas but he omitted WEH's strong views on RLS, no doubt to avoid tarnishing the image.
[2] The Henleys were living here by December 1879 (WEH to Baxter, 3 December 1879, Yale).
[3] Runciman was trying to have RLS's *The Amateur Emigrant*, his account of his journey to America, serialised in *Good Words*. RLS had originally sent the manuscript to Colvin.
[4] RLS.

I don't believe that our letters (I've not yet written, being too blasphemously given towards California & Californian things to trust myself) will have any effect at all in diverting him from his project. He has gone too far to retract; he has acted & gushed & excited himself too nearly into the heroic spirit to be asked to forbear his point. All we can hope to do is to make him get through his work quickly & come back quickly.

The threat of disinheriting is unhappily of little use to anyone. If aught had been wanted to hasten on the marriage, that threat would have filled the gap. I don't know whether father or son is nearer lunacy. There isn't much to choose.[5]

I shall try & write to-morrow, though I don't quite know what to say. I am hopeful as far as Louis himself is concerned — very hopeful. As regards the other actors, I am not hopeful at all. You may expect that Louis will resent our criticisms of the last three works; I know he will. But I think it right he should get them; et avec, a confident expression of hope for the future, & as confident a prediction that Monterey and he will never produce anything worth a damn.

You are too rough on the *Egoist*.[6] I read over my *Athenaeum* article yesterday (first time since Cambridge) & stand by it. You push my theory too far (pardon my vanity, Colvin! The book is as good & not as bad as you say. It is an attempt at Art by an elderly apprentice of genius. It is the material for a perfect comedy — not of intrigue; d—n intrigue; intrigue is not comic — but of character — the Missing Link between Art & Nonsense. An inorganic *Misanthrope*.[7] Do you know the French for jelly-fish? Then Meredith, *c'est Molière-méduse*. The devil will surely damn him hot & deep. I hate & admire him. Won't you try an article on *The Egoist* somewhere? Surely you could get *The Times* & three columns to do it in? How I wish — how I wish you would! I withdraw 'ripe & sound' from my *Athenaeum* note. *The Egoist* is rotten-ripe, & only sound by reason of complete syphilisation. How far do I differ from you after all? Faith, I don't know. I think that we should everywhere agree — everywhere but on the question of dialogue. I'm to do a fourth *Egoist*,[8] & will re-peruse. Then we'll see.

Try & see the Bob. When you return you will look upon the face of one who has read 'Fine Arts,' by Professor Colvin.[9] I swear it.

---

[5] RLS's parents were violently opposed to his journey to America to join Fanny.
[6] WEH's review of Meredith's *The Egoist* in the *Athenaeum*, 1 November 1879. WEH was an admirer of Meredith's work and to quote John Lane: 'From that period the tide turned in favour of Mr. Meredith's works, and no one can doubt that Mr. Henley's brilliant criticisms, which won the praise of James Thomson, did much to open the eyes of critics and reader alike' (John Lane in his 'George Meredith and his Reviewers 1849-1899. A Bibliography', vi, in Richard Le Gallienne's *George Meredith: Some Characteristics*, 1890).
[7] Molière's comedy *Le Misanthrope*, produced in 1666.
[8] This review appeared in the *Teacher*, 14 February 1880 (see WEH's letter of 31 January 1890 to John Lane) and is noted in Lane's bibliography. WEH wrote two more reviews one in the *Pall Mall Gazette*, 3 November 1879 and the other in the *Academy*, 22 November 1879.
[9] 'Fine Arts,' *Encyclopaedia Britannica*, 9th ed. (1879).

I dine with Lang to-night.[10] Let me see you soon. I won't detain you long, & I'll try to do my best (in return) to see you often. Don't imagine you are going to effuse wisdom at the cost of me. I look upon you for the vacation as partly beholden to me, & I shall worry you as much as ever I can.

No more plays from the infamous Greenwood. He did his *Falcon* for himself.[11] I earned last month a matter of £20 from *P.M.G.* I'd have had half as much again but for the editorialism & that sort of thing.

The Deacon's got as far as 'O hevving of hevvings that I were a good man!'[12] It looks nice in print. Read H. James's *Confidence.*[13] It will console you for much in G. Meredith's *Egoist*. There's a hartist if you like.

Yours ever,
W .E. Henley

[10]Andrew Lang (1844-1912), writer, poet and Greek scholar.
[11] A review of Tennyson's play *The Falcon, Pall Mall Gazette*, 31 December 1879. Frederick Greenwood (1830-1909), journalist and co-founder and editor of *The Pall Mall Gazette*, 1865-80. In 1880 Greenwood founded the *St James's Gazette* and was editor until 1888.
[12] RLS had produced a draft of the play by 1869 and it was not until WEH saw it that the idea of collaboration occurred. A copyright edition was printed December 1879-January 1880. A revised edition was printed for private circulation in 1888. The first published edition was in 1892 in *Three Plays By W. E. Henley and R. L. Stevenson.* Throughout their collaboration WEH was the prime mover believing that their fortunes would be made but RLS was not so naive and the plays were not successful.
[13] Henry James, *Confidence* (1879). The American novelist and critic had made visits to Europe and finally settled in London from 1876 until 1896. He then moved to Rye in Sussex and became a British subject in 1916.

To Robert Louis Stevenson, 20 January 1880
ALS: Yale

1 The Parade, Shepherds Bush W.
Hurray, my Louis! Compliments, congratulations, love, best wishes, etcettery! I am very glad, thou art very glad, he is very glad, we are very glad, & so on! Make haste & get married & come home & live happy ever afterwards.[1] That is all we ask.

I think it's like your d—d impudence to complain of me as a correspondent. I've written about 3 letters to your one. I wrote to you last to Monterey — a slasher.[2] It has been put out of date & made impertinent by circumstances. I suppose you'll never forgive me.

[1] This contrasts very strongly with his views expressed to Colvin in his letter of 2 January 1880.
[2] WEH must have written in November 1879 as RLS replied to him on 11 December 1879 (*Stevenson Letters*, 2, 35-7).

There's no news, except that my hospital experiences won't do for *Cornhill*. Any more than for *Nineteenth Century*. 'Too long & too minute,' says Stephen; & no doubt he's right. My only comfort is in the reflection that they are a damned sight better than the *Emigrant*.[3] I wish you were here to help me redact them.

Herewith, *registered*, I send a copy of the *Deacon*. Be good enough not to let it get abroad. I will write further about it presently; when I know the law of copyright. I've been trying to arrange a scheme for you to employ your leisure on in the States, but as yet I've failed. You must please take care of the *Deacon*, not let him out into the world, unless I tell you, or it's safe to do so. The modern dramatist is a hungry hound, & would have him in a twinkling. It's not a bad play as you'll see, & would be a godsend to most playwrights. Don't show it to *anybody*, till you hear from me further about it.

Which you shall do by the next mail. Anna's love & mine.

Yours ever,
W.E.H.

Take care of yourself, & don't despond *il n'y a vraiment pas de quoi*.

---

[3] In a letter to RLS WEH writes: 'The *Emigrant* is feeble, dull, pretentious; & if you saw it now, you'd wither & cower over it' (12 February 1880, Yale).

To Robert Louis Stevenson, 23 March 1880
ALS: Yale

                                          1 The Parade, Shepherds Bush W.
My dear Louis,

I got your two last letters to-day: one by first post this morning, the other at noon. God bless you for your good news of yourself. I wish (of course its no use) but I wish you had been married right away. It could have done no harm, & would have probably done great good. However, it's only got to be some other time. The sooner the better. You always were a most steep person in the way of kindness to other people; & I think that perhaps you're a little too steep in that way now & show too much respect for this person & too much consideration for that, & too much unselfishness to the other. Anyhow, I wish you were married & on your way home. In my way I'm as selfish as you are, & I want you back bitterly. So do we all. I'm afraid that, as for money-making goes you've taken up unpromising quarters. However, here's to you, dear lad, and with all my heart! Only, mind! — The sooner the better!

The *Deacon* ain't so promising as once he were. Warner has no influence with Gooch[1] & Gooch — absolutely unlettered — is mad for sensation, *clous*, extraordinary effects, & is buying French melodramas like fun. However, we have arranged a reading to him; & next Sunday, if he's *de retour* from Paris, the trick will be done. The worst of it is that we come a little late. That accursed Irving, on whose grave may the jackass bog for ever & ever, has really done us no end of harm. Had he but given us an answer, yes or no, within three months, the *Deacon* would now have been a popular play. As it is, we may have to wait some months. I'm not at all sure that I shall close with Gooch unless there's a good prospect of our getting out the thing within a reasonable time. I think of the Adelphi (with Clayton & Taylor)[2] as possible & even probable. The theatre's in a bad *déveine*, & I believe the proprietors — who are penny-ice people named Gatti[3] — would go for us.

As to the production in America, we must make sure of how the law stands ere we attempt it.[4] If your actor's an honest fellow, I don't know that there will be any harm in showing him the thing. But I'll see. Presently I'll send you a copy for him; together with the new first scene & the last scenes also (as Warner has shaped them), & a copy of the bulk of the play, with the excisions agreed upon. Herewith (as we're on the subject of copyright) an extract from the *Daily News*,[5] which gives me strange thoughts about the *Duke's Heart*.[6] I'm afraid we must make the play first, or that you must so write the story as to hide its dramatic potentialities pretty carefully. But of that anon.

All right about *Hester*.[7] I'm not sure but I'll change the opening, & I feel pretty certain that Scene 11 will be Hester, Dorothy & Roger. Meantime, do you try & let me have the rest (II, III, & IV) in detail. I don't want much; only the lie of the thing — that, however, I must have. Have no fear as to the results. I told Warner about it, & he was much fetched. I think he believes in us. His constant cry is 'Why didn't you do better? You've done so well that you ought to have done better. You've done so well that you may do, anything.' He says we are capable of doing the biggest thing ever done since W.S. And so on. On

[1] The actor Charles Warner (1846-1909). Walter Gooch, sometime manager of the Princess's Theatre, London.
[2] The actor-manager John Clayton (1843-88) and the actor James Goulde Taylor (?1837-1904).
[3] Agostino and Stefano Gatti were the proprietors from 29 September 1878 to 28 September 1885.
[4] To obtain copyright in America before 1891 a book had to have its title deposited in Washington, be published in Great Britain and America with a deposit copy within ten days in America and within two months in Great Britain. Failure to do this would enable the book to be pirated in America as the Americans considered a book protected only in its country of publication.
[5] 'The Theatres,' *Daily News*, 22 March 1880. A paragraph discussing the authorised adaptation of a foreign play from the author's own novel for the stage while another author is writing a play based on the original novel.
[6] This may have been the projected play *The King's Heart*.
[7] The projected play *Hester Noble's Mistake; or a Word from Cromwell*. WEH also refers to it as *Esther Noble* and *Cromwell*. RLS and WEH had discussed it in January 1879 at Swanston.

the other hand, he is certainly an actor.

Warner thought Moore a gorgeous part; I think I'll teach that actor, he told me of, to make a Badger[8] that'll make their hair curl! As for George S.,[9] I expect it'll be Edward John Henley's first creation. If he's up to it, I certainly mean to consider the question.

Apart from this, I've no news. I've read Jenkin's play[10] — or rather, I've read a part of it. The Jenkin is very much on the spot in idea & intention; the possibilities of the thing are infinite; but it's as bald as my backside. I should like to try & rewrite it — or rather write it in. Anthony's painted a picter pronounced by Legros[11] to be fit for the Grosvenor. He's going to try & paint one or two more of the same pattern. My Mother has been very ill; she is better now. She sends her love & blessing. So does my wife, who's very well indeed. So do we all. If you'd only think out the scenario of *Hester* — *rien que le scénario*! I'd far rather have it than a first draft! — I would bless ye, bless ye, dear kind gentleman, while there's breath in my body. So I wull, wulln't I?

Do try & get the scenario, dear lad! I'm doing nothing particular, & want it bad. Not the draft — only the bald program of character & scenes.

We are to settle about the *Emigrant* to-morrow. News by next mail, therefore. Your stern parent has not said a word about the *Deacon*. Colvin sends an *Athenaeum* with a par. in it by yours truly.[12] Read my letters carefully, I mean all I say; especially all that relates to business. I can sell, or get sold, all you do. *Voilà*.

Colvin sent me on your last — the letter descriptive of life as it is to you. How I wish I could but drop down at 608 Bush St,[13] chuck your little hatchet out of the window, & work you off on the spree — as you used to walk me off in Edinburgh's historic streets. Never mind! Here's a good letter, with glad tidings of good things! You're a poor correspondent & don't deserve it. On to page 1 [*rest of letter missing*].

---

[8] The robber Humphrey Moore in Brodie's gang.

[9] George Smith, another member of the gang.

[10] Jenkin's privately printed play *Griselda* was published posthumously in his *Papers Literary, Scientific, etc* (London and Edinburgh, 1887).

[11] The French artist Alphonse Legros (1837-1911) had moved to London in 1863, and was Professor of Etching at the Slade School, 1876-92. WEH had written an essay on Legros in the London *University Magazine*, February 1880.

[12] WEH's unsigned review of Theodore Tharp's *The Sword of Damocles* in the *Athenaeum*, 20 March 1880.

[13] RLS's long newsy letter of 18 January 1880 from San Francisco (*Stevenson Letters*, 3, 45-8). RLS had described how chopped wood and broke coal for his fire with 'his little hatchet'.

To Charles Baxter, Wednesday [?November 1880]
ALS: Yale

51 Richmond Gardens, Shepherds Bush, W.[1]
I've been a-meaning to write this long time, my boy, but I've never managed to make my meaning clear; even to myself; till now. Last night, however, I received the two facts of your message. I am greatly obliged for them. They fit me, & I have 'em on. I have had 'em on all morning — & all morning, I need hardly say, I have been beset with bawdy thoughts & impure imaginings. *Voilà.* I am grateful all the same; as, for the rest, without any telling from me, you know.

And I am more grateful still for the service you have rendered us over the shop.[2] I don't know much about it; but I am given to understand that you've been kindness itself. As is your nature to. The next time I see you I'll promise to be fou wi'ye (forgive the pedantry) by way of thanks. And if there's any other way in which I can render unto Baxter those thanks which are Baxter's, why I'd thank you to trot it out, & give the honour of a name.

I am bloody poor, & have no prospects. Except the very gloomy one of having a little to do for *Truth.*[3] Don't scorn me when I tell you that, gloomy as it is, I am glad to command it. The new *P.M.G.* & I do not agree.[4] I don't know why; except it be that I am *au fond*, (more Scotch, you see!) a duffer. At present, I am mainly busied upon a new immortal work, destined to revive the tarnished glories of the British Stage, & which I have as much chance of producing as if I were an inmate of Colney Hatch — the local Morningside.[5] Of that anon.

Simpson gave me strange accounts of your attitude towards the Emigrant's Bride.[6] I wish they had been incredible as well as strange; but, as you know, I

---

[1] The Henleys had moved here by 15 June (WEH to RLS, 15 June 1880, Yale).
[2] This may be a reference to 1 Goldhawk Road, Shepherds Bush. According to Williamson WEH and Anna moved there after their wedding in 1878, where they lived over a grocer's shop. However, this has not been confirmed.
[3] Any contributions made by WEH have not been identified.
[4] George Smith (1824-1901), proprietor, and co-founder with Greenwood of the *P.M.G.*, had given the paper to his son-in-law Henry Yates Thompson (1838-1928). As the political sympathies changed from Tory to Liberal Greenwood resigned and John Morley (1838-1923) became editor in May 1880. He was previously editor of the *Fortnightly Review*, 1867-82. He was editor of the English Men of Letters series and also wrote a fine biography of Gladstone. He entered Parliament in 1883 as Liberal MP for Newcastle, becoming Chief Secretary for Ireland, 1886 and 1892, and Secretary of State for India 1905. In 1908 he was created 1st Viscount Morley of Blackburn.
[5] Colney Hatch was a nearby lunatic asylum. Morningside was a lunatic asylum in Edinburgh.
[6] RLS and Fanny, now reconciled with his parents, spent the winter of 1880-81 at the health resort of Davos, Switzerland.

can believe anything of you. Was it you, by the way, who sent me *Fraser*, per Douglas & Foulis?[7] Or was it the Baronet?[8] Whoever it was, much thanks to him. Mr. Thomson[9] is poorer than I've ever known him.

Our kindest regards to Mrs. Baxter. And more to that beautiful Broadwood of yours. I am learning some Beethoven specially for its sake; & when I come north, which I hope to do again ere I die, you shall judge of the effect. I wish you'd wade in on your own account. It makes me wild to think of that lovely piano a mere futility & the good pianist who might be a mere potentialist. I don't know whose is the more prevented & unnatural destiny, yours or the instruments.

Write when you can. We are friends enough to keep silence & inflect neglect, & letters are not much after all. But write when you can, all the same.

Affectionately Yours,
W.E.H.

[7] This was a reference to RLS's, 'The Old Pacific Capital,' *Fraser's Magazine*, November 1880. Douglas and Foulis, booksellers, 9 Castle Street, Edinburgh.
[8] Simpson.
[9] RLS was in poor health after his illness in America. Baxter and RLS had created the comic characters Johnson (or Johnstone) and Thomson and often referred to them and their drunken adventures in their letters. They also addressed each other by these names. RLS and Baxter later brought WEH into the saga under the name of 'J. Jackson'. WEH had visited the Stevensons while they were staying in London before they left for France en route for Davos on 19 October.

To Robert Louis Stevenson, Tuesday [15 March 1881][1]
ALS: Yale

51 Richmond Gardings [*sic*], Shepherds Bush, W.
I was glad, indeed, of your letter, my dear lad. And I hasten to say so. I shan't write much, having fish to fry that won't bear keeping. Sprats — sprats; & be d—d to them but. But fish, & therefore saleable.

About Henry James. I think you look at him too loftily: as from a Pizgah, where honest plain idiots like myself can't follow. And I think you do not do the man full justice in another respect. You don't, or won't see that he's perfectly sincere — that he's not a humbug & a liar like W.M.T.[2] but that he speaks out as much of the better as is visible to him. The excellence of his workmanship, too, appears to have made you forget that he is passing through a certain stage of development, & not yet himself. I am much mistaken if that's

[1] Dated from internal evidence: see note 23 below. This is in reply to RLS's letter from Davos of late February or early March (*Stevenson Letters*, 3, 159-60).
[2] The novelist William Makepeace Thackeray.

not so, at all events: but I may be in error, so I won't push it. As regards the cynicism — *voyons, voyons*! James is a child of a miserable & cynical age — the age of Balzac, Turguenieff, Zola, Flaubert, Thackeray, the Goncourt people;[3] & he writes as his epoch bids him. He is not heroic, I grant; & he likes to treat of failures. But I don't find him cynical, & I don't find that he leaves a bad taste in the mouth. On the contrary, he is, to any thinking, a good deal too dispassionate & too full of amenity. *Washington Square*[4] is unhappily enough in its way, but look how revoltingly discomforting it might — & would — have been if any one of the gents I've named above had done it. To me, it's merely a piece of pure prose — conceived, constructed, executed by a man who is prose incarnate. As the man is exceedingly good tempered, & as the man's work is irreproachable of its kind, I am uncommon glad to know both the one & the other. The common place is not my game, as you know; but of such quintessence of the commonplace as *Washington Square* — clear of bad temper, clear of cruelty & of malice, free from vileness — I shall welcome as many as come right heartily.

'Fizzle' *is* too strong;[5] but that H.J. was ever looked upon as 'an open air stand-up man' by anybody but yourself, I never heard. All the same, his work has the human quality in it; & that is just now a rare enough commodity to make me grateful for it when I happen to see it.

I haven't read the *Reminiscences*.[6] I wish I had. Colvin promised 'em, but he seems too busy to do anything but overwork himself, just now, & I haven't yet seen his promise realised. Soon I shall, no doubt, & then I'll communicate. Meanwhile, I've seen extracts, & they don't, to me, seem calculated to better the old boy's reputation, either for good sense or good feeling. I thank God that his work is what we know, or the howl about him would be just now loud — loud, my boy, & the condemnation pretty general. I can't help suspecting that the book will modify the best men's judgements not a little, & that his biography will resolve itself into a study of an abnormal egoism, as intense & almost as savage as George Meredith's, & with a twist in it, of melancholia & of Hypochondriasis, that makes it monstrous — like a distorted oak, tortured by storms — & gives it something of a fantastic & grotesque quality, which is lacking in the other. Egoism for egoism, I prefer the egoism of Dickens; it was more generous & kindly in itself, & infinitely more beneficent in its action. I suppose I am wrong, but I can't help it.

And this mention of Carlyle's extraordinary contempt for all the world that wasn't sib to him, brings me to a very curious reflection. Have you not

---

[3] The Russian novelist Ivan Sergeevich Turgenev (1818-83). The brothers Edmond Goncourt (1822-96) and Jules de Goncourt (1830-70), French writers.

[4] Henry James, *Washington Square*, 2 vols (1881).

[5] In his letter RLS had called James 'a mere club fizzle' but then acknowledged that 'fizzle perhaps too strong' on representations from Fanny.

[6] Thomas Carlyle's *Reminiscences*, ed. J. A. Froude, 2 vols (1881). Carlyle had died on 4 February 1881.

observed that, consistent with the 'honourable catholicity' you noted in Swinburne 'tother day, & which is apparently the aim & object of every writing person in these times, there is to be seen in action a passion for depreciation as well? We are all of us inclined to make most damnably light of each other. I come for cash, I know; and so are many others I could name. The human is to be generous, & even exquisite in print; & *de vive voix*, the exact reverse. In both these ways, & by both these means, the critic proves his superiority — his peculiar & unquestionable superiority; & he is happy. I don't believe I am, myself, so violently carried away from grace as most men; for there's something canine in me, & I take a pleasure in the recognition of superiorities. But oh! Louis, if it were not so, how bloody ill natured & right I could be! I am going to gibbet William Black for his *Sunshine*;[7] very shortly. And if my temper doesn't sweeten between this hence & then, the poor intense letters man will catch it.

You will like Saintsbury's *Dryden*.[8] Four-fifths of it are damn good — as good as I want to read. The other fifth, Dryden as a dramatist, is not good at all. I am sorry for this because I had to fall foul of Saintsbury for his drama games in the *Primer of French Literature*;[9] & I shan't be honest if I don't fall foul of him again. I think I must content to be dishonest for the nonce, rather than blow about the drama any more. It looks so much as if you thought that you only knew anything at all about it! By the way, I believe that you and I and Fleeming Jenkin are the only three men in England who do; but it doesn't do to say so — either in print or *de vive voix*. All this to the contrary, Saintsbury's damn instructive & sensible on many points, & I feel sure that you'll read him with the greatest pleasure.

As regards the Swinburne article,[10] we praised it piecemeal. I read the Rizpah page, & refrained from the rest; you read the rest, & refrained from the Rizpah page. *Voilà*. Only you've been luckier than I, for you carried away with you matters for gratitude & an honourable kindliness; while as for me I got nothing but stuff for wrath & scorn. Thus was it ever.

What in the world put it into your head to write to Morley, you dear & generous & delightful jackass, you? Did you really expect that a Roman-

---

[7] WEH's review, if there was one, of Black's *Sunrise: a Story of these Times* (1881), has not been found. William Black (1841-98), Scottish novelist and journalist. He moved to London in 1864 where he worked for various newspapers and journals before becoming assistant editor of the *Daily News* in 1870.

[8] George Saintsbury, *Dryden*, English Men of Letters series (1881). George Edward Bateman Saintsbury (1845-1933), writer and major literary critic. He was Professor of Rhetoric and English Literature at Edinburgh University, 1895-1915. He wrote for WEH in *London* and later became a prolific reviewer for the major journals.

[9] This review by WEH has not been found.

[10] Swinburne's 'Tennyson and Musset', *Fortnightly Review*, February 1881. Swinburne was full of praise for Tennyson's poem 'Rizaph'.

Brummagen[11] cove like him was going back on his opinion for a mere Sentimental Journalist like you? God bless you all the same. I wouldn't have let you do it if I had fully understood your little game; but since it's done, why God bless the gent as done it. I should like to know what he said, if you don't mind telling me, for the wretch is an able wretch in his way (I wish I were as half as able, d—n him!), & it might be useful to me. As he sacked me without a word of warning or advice, I'm not ashamed to confess myself curious in the matter. I can hardly think it was my prose — altogether my prose at any rate. I believe it was my opinions; & my manners. These communistic people are greatly afflicted with personal dignity; & for a capacity of universal dogmatism commend me to your professional anarchist! — Are these remarks unworthy? Bon! then I withdraw them. But I was, & am, very sore; & from the attack of dry-rot which I owe to the Able bird in question, from the demoralisation consequent on his proceedings, I haven't yet recovered. So my spitefulness is explicable, if it's also inexcusable.

When's your 'Pepys' a-coming out?[12] Soon, I hope. And what news is there to hand of *Virginibus Puerisque*?[13] What says the diplomatic Kegan?[14] Answer, answer, for information there is none.

I think my Berlioz (on which I ought to be hard at work this minute) will be readable enough.[15] But long articles are not my game at all. *Et puis*, I am a stupid cove, & know not whether I do well or ill. I may have at the mags. like fun, but it's beating the air, & nothing else, dear lad. I have had a fair offer at letters, & — somehow or other — I have failed. That I shall succeed I haven't the faintest hope. What I am doing now, & what I expect to have to do while I live, is for bread & cheese & onions. I am like Falstaff's boy: — 'I would give all my hopes of fame for a pot of ale & solvency.'[16] I have discovered Beethoven, & the rest may go hang. What says C. Sly Esq? 'Come, madame wife, sit by my side, & let the world slide. *We shall ne'er be younger.*'[17] Isn't that sound philosophy? It's mine — at least for the moment; & I defy Morley, with all his logic, to prove that I'm not wiser than he is. Perhaps the play will come off one of these years; but *après*? I answer myself with the reflection that Teddy is going to be a good actor & that Anthony's landscapes are getting, year by year, to be more & more like *Art*, with a great A. They are partly my creations, & — for the moment, at least! — I am content. Insolvency is not a

---

[11] 'Roman-Brummagen' refers to Morley's friendship with the Liberal politician Joseph Chamberlain (1836-1914) of Birmingham. Brum is a colloquialism for Birmingham.

[12] RLS's 'Samuel Pepys', *Cornhill Magazine*, July 1881.

[13] RLS's collection of essays *Virginibus Puerisque and Other Papers* which had a dedication in letter form to WEH was published in April 1881.

[14] The publisher Charles Kegan Paul (1828-1902) had published RLS's *Inland Voyage* and *Travels with a Donkey*. WEH refers to him as the 'Keg'.

[15] His 'Hector Berlioz: a biography', *Cornhill Magazine*, July 1881.

[16] 'I would give all my fame for a pot of ale, and safety.' *Henry V*, III. ii. 13.

[17] Christopher Sly in *The Taming of the Shrew*, Introd. ii. 141-2

pleasant state; & just now I am quite too insolvent to be thought about with composure. But I'd rather be stone-broke than such a ghastly caricature of greatness than Meredith, or such a beautiful expression of the Ridiculously clever as Gosse,[18] or such a monstrous abortion of success as Zola. All for the moment, mind you! What I shall think the day after to-morrow is, as R.L.S. would say (that bright & pleasant creature, R.L.S. — Do you know him?) 'another pair of sleeves'. For the present, there are some thousands of ideas, by J. L.[sic] Beethoven, to be read; & that's enough.

· Symonds[19] must be a curious bird. I should like to see you two together a good deal. And I should enjoy a talk about him horrid. When is one to be expected? He's at it again, like a good 'un, too, in the current *Cornhill*.[20] Foregad, these fellows [make] such affection out of everything. Their mothers must have bred them in a place like Abbotsford:[21] among French jewellery, & in the wake of Bulwer Lytton.[22]

M. Strogoff was produced last night.[23] A great success; but Warner cut his hand horribly in the fight, in the last scene. Ted seems to have done capitally. The great Byron was very nice to him. Warner was bereft of a good deal of blood, & fainted largely. Ted says that he (Ted) was the only one who kept cool, & that he it was who sent for the doctor, & directed the others, who were all off their heads, to ligature the wrist & keep out the fingers of the injured hand. But if this is true or not I don't know. If true it is, Warner ought to be grateful. How the devil they came to be playing with a cutting knife I can't say. But they were, & it pierced the actor's hand, at the palm, almost through, cutting a tendon, & making a very nasty hole. I [*rest of letter missing*].

[18] Edmund William Gosse (1849-1928), writer, critic and poet. Knighted 1925. He worked at the British Museum, 1867-75, and then at the Board of Trade, 1875-1904. From 1904 until 1914 he was Librarian at the House of Lords. WEH was never very keen on Gosse and referred to him as Becky Sharp after the unscrupulous character in Thackeray's *Vanity Fair*.

[19] John Addington Symonds (1840-93), writer, critic, poet and Italian art historian. He suffered from tuberculosis and settled in Davos Platz, Switzerland, to recover his health. He and RLS had become friends.

[20] Symonds's 'Autumn Wanderings', *Cornhill Magazine*, March 1881.

[21] Sir Walter Scott's home near Melrose, Scotland.

[22] Edward George Earle Bulwer-Lytton (1803-73), novelist, playwright and politician. He edited the *New Monthly Magazine* from 1831 to 1833 and published the first of his historical novels, *The Last Days of Pompeii*, in 1834. He also wrote novels of science fiction and spiritualism. Knighted in 1837, he was created Baron Lytton in 1866.

[23] *Michael Strogoff*, a play adapted from the French, by Henry James Byron (1834-84), which opened at the Adelphi Theatre, London, on 14 March 1881and closed on 8 July 1881.

To Charles Baxter, 21 April 1881
ALS: Yale

51 Richmond Gardens, Shepherds Bush, W.

My dear Charles,

I send you *Truth*, as usual. You will be pained, I am sure, by the Lab's reflection on the Earl.[1] It is a terrible thing to be wholly compact of villainous prose, & to have no imagination but the libeller's & the stockbroker's. Isn't it? However, I suppose the poor wretch can't help himself. He writes according to his lights; & as he is rather proud of them, though they are mere bawdy-house night-lights, I suppose he is, in his miserable little way, respectable. I am bound to say that, after reading, I despise him, brains & heart, more bitterly than ever. In one sense the little beast is humorous: i.e., when he assumes & works the high moral tone. Think of the high moral tone of a professional libeller, who old does wax & from whose weary limbs honour has been cudgelled utterly! Think of the mean-mouthedness of a dashing Cyprian![2] He reminds me of the lady Louis knew & went in unto, & whose sentiment of decency obliged her to refuse to perform the act of intromission for him.

It is very pleasant to note the manner of most of the journals in speaking of the old boy. The *D.N.* has done him justice at last,[3] or nearly justice as you could expect, & far more nearly than I hoped. The continental prints, too, are very loud & proper indeed. Altogether, I am content. Among the people the feeling seems deep & strong. The Earl's genius was not an English genius at all, but the admiration & interest & confidence he inspired have proved to me, very curiously, the fact, which. I had always suspected, that the English people, bourgeois & thick-witted as it is, can be touched home *through its imagination* not less surely than through its breeches pocket. It is a mistake to suppose that the masses loved the old man for his pluck & conduct of affairs, & cleverness in debate; they did not hate him for these qualities, it's true, but if he has died the most popular man of his time, if he has seemed for an instant to make the world imperfect in his loss, it was that he had produced a profound imaginative impression on his fellows. He had fascinated them as a good artist fascinates his public; he was mysterious & wonderful & unique to them. In five years hence, with health & strength, he would have been the arbiter of Europe, & the most popular minister at home we have known in history.

Another jolly thing to see is that all the old reproaches — of trickery, hollowness, charlatanism, insincerity — have been wiped away, & that the man

---

[1] The Earl of Beaconsfield (Disraeli) died on 20 April 1881. An assessment of him as politician and statesman was published in *Truth*, 21 April 1881, written by Henry du Pré Labouchere. Lord Beaconsfield is attacked for his personal ambition and disregard for his fellow men.
[2] A prostitute.
[3] 'Death of the Earl of Beaconsfield' and 'Memoir', *Daily News*, 20 April 1881. The *Daily News* was a Liberal paper.

stands fuller for a true patriot & an earnest & determined statesman. To the souls that find expression in Labouchere — the souls of mud & muddery & meat only — he will always be what he was, & he will seem ignoble to them because he is incomprehensible. But the mass of the public has heart, & it is the mass of the public that one has to look to; & with these, he has come to be known for his true self.

What a career it was! Napoleon's own is, in a certain sense, less wonderful. The most surprising, I suppose, in history. And doesn't it prove, my dear Charles, the absolute veracity of Balzac's theory of life & morals & society! Think of Rastignac & De Marsay,[4] & you think of Benjamin D. Only his life surpasses in romance anything the Comédie can show. It is cast on Balzac's lines from first to last, but it is as much greater than Balzac's as the potentialities of truth are greater than those of the imagination: as the story of the Czar's murder, for instance, than the story of Ferragus. On this question there is no end to say, & this morning I don't seem able to say anything at all. So I'll write no more; & only add that Balzac is nearer Shakespeare every year, & that I am proud to think that you & I & Louis didn't wait for death to do our seeing & honouring, but were men enough to begin long ago, & to go on in the right way ever after.

Write to me when you can; & tell me why you haven't written before. — If it is that you have lapsed, & are ashamed, I shall be doubly angry. Anna will be in Edinburgh next week, & of course you'll see her. Next week, too, I hope she'll be home. I am beginning to find solitude a bore. I've got the proof of Berlioz: £19..19 worth. And the cheque, too; to-night I shall have just 5/- left. Get the first number of *Our Times*;[5] & read, for me, the Millais Gallery, French Gallery, & Painter-Etchers, the 'Roméo et Juliette', & *Mick. Strogoff*, Modjeska, & Booth's Shylock — the last, a good deal cut.[6] I've seen no proofs, & don't know what it's all like. The Keg hasn't thought fit to send me *Virginibus Puerisque*, so I haven't seen the dedication.[7] They tell me it's very

---

[4] Characters in Balzac's *Comédie Humaine*, a series of ninety-one novels written between 1827 and 1847.

[5] A short lived monthly which ran from May to June 1881.

[6] *Our Times*, May 1881. In a letter to Colvin (17 April 1881, Yale) WEH writes:

> I have done a lot for *Our Times* including a notice of the Millais Gallery, which I wonder how you'll like. I had to take up the Fine Arts at the last moment, as Gosse deserted; & I did the Millais lot, the Painter-Etcher, & the French Gallery. Of these notices I have just seen a revise (so-called) reeking with errors. The *Romeo & Juilette* & the theatres I didn't see in proof, & I shudder to think what they will turn out to be. If I'd had them, I wouldn't have minded, but I haven't. I was writing with difficulty when I did them, & got very clotted & congested; And I thought with joy of proofs, & the corrections & improvements I'd be able to make. Unhappily, I have been deceived.

[7] The dedication was in the form of a letter addressed to WEH, part of which refers to their relationship:

nice, & I'm surprised to find that it hasn't added one cubit to my stature.[8] Will you have Berlioz? or won't you? The frame's making, but chips are wanted ere we can send. Hob appears to have sold the *Meadows* (£13),[9] but the coins haven't yet turned up. Do write, there's a good fellow.

Yours affectionately,
W.E.H.

These papers are like milestones on the wayside of my life; and as I look back in memory, there is hardly a stage of that distance but I see you present with advice, reproof, or praise. Meanwhile, many things have changed, you and I among the rest; but I hope that our sympathy, founded on the love of our art, and nourished by mutual assistance, shall survive these little revolutions undiminished, and, with God's help, unite us to the end.

[8] 'Which of you by taking thought can add one cubit unto his stature?' *Matt.* 6.1
[9] Anthony Henley's painting.

To Robert Louis Stevenson, 23 April 1881
ALS: Yale

51 Richmond Gardens, Shepherds Bush, W.

This is only a kind of hail, my dear lad. You'd have had it before, if I had but known where you were.[1] This morning the Charles sent me your address, & I hasten to make some kind of use of it.

People tell me the Dedication is a fact. But I haven't seen it with these eyes, & am half-inclined to doubt the good fortune still. Colvin says, you ordered a copy to be sent to me. The Wily Keg has very subtly omitted to do so.[2] I suppose that presently I shall hear from him. When I do, you shall hear from me. Or, if I see it in any other way. I am too poor to purchase, of course, or I'd have done so long ago.

You are advertised in *Athenaeum* at length.[3] I send the page herewith. I've seen no reviews, though I suppose there have been many. I see so few journals! I doubt not that all will be good.

My old master, Brown, whose letters I used to show you, has written an admirable book of *Fo'c'stle Yarns*. I've reviewed it for MacColl;[4] but MacColl

[1] RLS was in Paris after his stay in Davos.
[2] RLS replied: 'If you have not had my book, which has been out for weeks, it is the fault of the nefarious Kegan, for whom there is no place hot enough in hell. On this occasion, however, I believe, it is more likely a clerk who is in fault than Keg himself...' (*Stevenson Letters*, 3, 173).
[3] An advertisement for *Virginibus Puerisque* appeared in the *Athenaeum* of 23 April 1881.
[4] WEH's unsigned review of T. E. Brown's *Fo'c's'le Yarns* (1881) in the *Athenaeum*, 7 May 1881. Norman MacColl (1843-1904), journalist and editor of the *Athenaeum*, 1871-1900.

thinks my review 'an extravagant panegyric', & I shall most likely write no more for him over it. Of course, he's wrong. But I note that he has no confidence in my judgement; & that vexes me a good deal. The man who does most of his poetry is an *A*ss,[5] & writes stuff about Browning & Swinburne that is really preposterous. But it passes unquestioned; while I have only to say that a new man's a good man, & a new book by him real literature, to be accused of panegyric. I think it will end by my retiring to an estate in the country, & bidding journalism go hang itself in its own tripes. I'm afraid, too, that it's all your fault. I was a dullard when you found me, & I could have followed the bell-wether then with anyone. You taught me to think for myself, & to speak in the name of my own conscience & heart. And Lo! I am what I am. Why didn't you leave me ignorant & anserine & happy? I could have earned a living if you had. Now, I am a man who likes what's good in Art, & above all what is great, & who cannot stand what's bad or small or most peculiar; & I owe my tradesmen. It's *Bouvard & Pécuchet* o'er again.[6] I am B. & P., & I ought to stick to my desk, & leave the higher life to the higher men. Come, undo your work, ye bitch! Fork out the gross of quills & a copying table; & let me work out my destiny.

The old man's death has impressed me a great deal. Twas a wonderful life; & a heart & brain not less wonderful. I think a good man, too; & I am a man of an abundant & shining sincerity. In some ways, his personality is more interesting. A king of men, truly. His eminence was and is a splendid proof that in the English constitution one great element is Imagination. It's all very well to say that the English saw a self-made man in Dizzy, & admired his pluck, & his resolution, & his artfulness. The truth is, that he had touched them like great art, & to the same purpose & extent. He got to their heart through their imaginations, & back to their intelligence through their emotions. Could he have lived 5 years longer, with health & brain & energy still active & ardent; he would have died the most popular minister we ever had. As it is, he has had to die the most popular man merely. I feel a sense of personal loss; Charles tells me that his is the same; & indeed, it is the same with most of us, I think — the Rads & dogmatists & doctrinaires excepted, of course. With him the *A*rtistic type & element & spirit evanish from English politics; & we fall into the slough of pure grocerism — grocerism, that's to say, that would be pure but for a leaven of doctrinairism & professorism & intellectualism generally. Such is life! The biggest man & the biggest Force in England — the England of Clive & Cromwell, & Shakespeare & Nelson, & Chatham & Fox & Marlborough — is an Ideal Banker. The Union Jack is a pocket-handkerchief full of shavings; & the Empire's heart is a Parish Pump. *Vive la Verity*! — —

[5] (Walter) Theodore Watts-Dunton (1832-1914), poet, writer and critic, was a close friend of the poet Swinburne and lived with him from 1879 until his death in 1909. He added Dunton to his name in 1896. He was a regular reviewer for the *Athenaeum*.
[6] Flaubert's unfinished novel published posthumously in 1881.

I perceive that I'm running on somehow. *Allons!* Since I'm in for it, I'll be in to the throat. Jenkin came in just where you see these — — dashes. He sends you his love. He had his last proofs in his pocket, & is a happy man. Of *Griselda*, I mean. A damn good play it is. I think we could beat it, if we set ourselves to do so; but only in the writing. I am no end pleased with it. And Jenkin has every right to be proud of it. — — He tells me, by the way, that Froude[7] has a pecuniary interest in the *Reminiscences*, all the profits of which are his, & which he sent to the printers while the old man lay a-dying. It's awkward for Froude, isn't it? At the same time, dear lad, I am not with those who want a man's work to be dished & sauced before the public is let sit down to it. It's a bad plan & a bad principle. Comes, I suppose, of general mienmouthedness & falseness; part of our general scheme of Insincerity. Carlyle hasn't improved himself in men's hearts by the enormous peevishness of his Egoism, it's true; but what then? If we care for him at all, we are more or less interested in him in any state; & the *Reminiscences* are, in a certain sense, as valuable & as personal as the *Frederick* itself.[8] I think somehow that I did not say a very foolish thing when I said that, in the end, the final portrait of Carlyle would prove to be a study in Hypochondriasis. It's a pity we can't take our sage with his onions all about him, & that the instant he's found imperfect, we all want to try & cease caring for him. Respectability has been the ruin of us, dear lad; and a little villainous company would do us no end of good. We expect our heroes to have no vices & not much sex; & if they have either one or the other, they are heroic no more, they cease to be examples, Mr. Smiles couldn't possibly put them into a book.[9] *Actum est.* It's all over with 'em! An odd thing, isn't it? Out of the religion of Christ has come the cult of the Respectable; Respectability is one of the last forms of Christianity — a heel on the dying dolphin, a shape of the falling Proteus. Christ was the aboriginal of those who live in squares, only copulate among watch-pockets, or would rather die than use 'bloody' as an expletive! Of course respectability is very well in its way; but I don't see that it has anything in common with aesthetics; & I think the two should be kept apart — even on the Walls of the *A*cademy, even on the shelves of Mudie. Art, however, is no longer a matter of personal expression. It's a question of supply & demand — a commercial question, flushed over with a [*pages 9-12 of the letter missing*].

[*page 13*] hand on the style; for I got no proofs excepting 'Fine Arts',[10] & — as

---

[7] James Anthony Froude (1818-94), historian and editor of *Fraser's Magazine*, 1860-74, was Carlyle's literary executor. His publishing of the *Reminiscences* caused an outcry because of its frankness.

[8] Thomas Carlyle, *The History of Frederick II of Prussia called Frederick the Great*, 6 vols (1858-65).

[9] Samuel Smiles (1812-1904), writer, surgeon and journalist, who wrote on political and social reform. He published biographies with an emphasis on moral character but is remembered for his very popular *Self-help* (1859) which preached thrift and general self-improvement.

[10] *Our Times.*

I made sure of getting them, & over pressed for time — I left the stuff a good deal rougher than I ought. As regards other matters, I've 19 pp. of 'Hector Berlioz' in proof for the *Cornhill*. All the coins are gone of course; but I'm £20 out of debt in comparison with what I was ere I got 'em. The article's only biography & not very good at that, I think. It would have been far better as it stood at first; in 30 pp. or so. But Stephen wouldn't, & he was doubtlessly right from his own point of view. As it is, I think it's readable; and that's all.

I have been a widower these four weeks, & expect to be so for a fortnight yet. The Châtelaine's[11] away north. She needed rest & change a good deal. She asked more than once after you; but news of you I'd none to give. Runciman's away to Messina; a pallid wreck. Rest & change or a madhouse was the word & he preferred the first alternative to the second.

How are you? What a dog of a correspondent it is! I can't believe in this weakness of yours human as you are. Particularly as there's the Secretary,[12] who loves me well, owes me one for a doggie eased of worms, & who, she said, is always ready to assist. Do try & get up a little Christian sentiment: enough to enable you to tell how you are, & what are your intentions as regards 'location', & so forth. (*Location* is of course a touch of local colour; not without a humorous intent). It's terrible writing to you. It's like writing to the Post-Master General! I feel, when I post to you, as if I were slipping a letter into the mysterious vastiness within the Lion's Mouth. Fie on't! O fie! And you a literary man, too! By the way, Payn says you have been talking of him (very nicely, he thinks) as a man keen for his price. What's this new Morality of yours? That the only hire we labourers ought to think worthy of us is the wage of Truth? I agree with you; but — alas! Alas the day! We are the children of a corrupt civilisation, & the servants of an *A*rt that is only another name for Profit; & what can we do?

I wrote to Colvin awhile ago;[13] a long letter, meant for you as well as for him. And I was agreeably surprised to find that you had cut Davos, & were loafing around in Paris. Next week my game is J-F. Millet; I would I'd coins, & I'd come & hunt for his works, & see you at the same time. By the way, our scheme for producing *Deacon B.* in the provinces has fallen through; the drammy is now in the hands of Coghlan,[14] who will probably wash them of it as soon as possible.

[11] WEH often referred to Anna as the Châtelaine.
[12] Fanny Stevenson to whom RLS had dictated his letter to WEH.
[13] 17 April 1881.
[14] Charles Francis Coghlan (1848-99), actor, manager, and playwright. Born in Paris, he worked in London and in America, where he toured with the famous English actress Lillie Langtry (1852-1929) from 1887 to 1890 and where he eventually died.

My love to you both. Try & get up a fit of ink & paper if it's only two lines long.

Affectionately Yours, Dear Louis,
W.E.H.

To Charles Baxter, Thursday 26 May 1881
ALS: Yale. Published in *Stevenson Letters*, *3*, 183-4.

[51 Richmond Gardens, Shepherds Bush, W.]

My dear Charles,

I want to say that I've seen a good deal of Louis,[1] & that he is in a very curious state. I saw him examined by a friendly doctor — Z. Mennell[2] — & I've no fear for his lungs. If he lives sagely, & avoids colds, & can indulge in climates, he is right.

For the moment, though, his nerves are all to pieces. He is more the Spoiled Child than it is possible to say. And, for the time being, it will be well for you, *& for his father & mother*, to receive him with open arms, make no references to coins, & take all the care you can of him.

He & I exchanged a few words on the subject of coins. I told him you were a little annoyed, & he was very remorseful. Nothing's more evident than that he is tolerably irresponsible, & that his hosts have taken every conceivable advantage of him. But, all the same, when he told me of his feeling, I laughed at it & told him he was an idiot to think of money at all. And this I believe to be, for the moment, the proper thing to do. He is curiously excitable & unstrung; emotion is always excessive with him; & any provocation to sentiment ought steadily to be avoided.

What I hope, therefore, is this: that you'll make no change of any sort in your manner to him but you'll content yourself for the moment with being better & more charming than ever; & that you'll see your way to advising *père et mère* to be the same, to avoid reproaches & regrets like poison, to ask no account of past days, & to make life at Braemar[3] as quiet, as healthy, as uneventful, as studious for him as they possibly can. When he comes south again, you may speak, & speak boldly enough; for then his *morale* & his nerves will be all the stronger & all the better, & he'll probably be tolerably responsible.

[1] RLS and Fanny who had been staying in Paris arrived in London shortly after Wednesday 18 May and after a week went to Scotland.
[2] WEH's doctor Dr. Zebulon Mennell, M.R.C.S., L.S.A. (1851-1911), of Oxford House, 31 Shepherd's Bush Road, London. Mennell had served as a medical officer in Venezuela and West Africa. WEH often referred to him as 'the Pirate'.
[3] RLS and Fanny spent the summer with his parents first at Pitlochry and then at Braemar.

And, another thing : — be as kind & as nice to Mrs. Louis as ever you can. I have seen much of her, & I have modified a good deal. I like her some, & I can't help pitying her much. My wife's feeling is the same. So don't let us have any more of your abominable Baxterisms, my boy, or I shall lecture you.

I fear it's a mistake, but if it be one it's an irreparable; & we must strive with all our hearts & minds — with all our hearts especially — to make the best of it.

They are a couple of Babes in the Wood. *Voilà. C'est pas plus malin que ça.* And, for the life of us, we can't venture for the moment on whipping their bottoms, & sending them to bed. Presently, when the male Babe is more himself, things will change, & we shall be better pleased. Meanwhile, *Zut!*

I see, too, that the male Babe is the principal; & that it's to him only that we must look for governance. She is indolent, unpractical, quite feckless; & if he doesn't introduce order, order will never be introduced at all.

I could say more if you had been here; but I haven't & I must say what I can. Of course it's all between ourselves. Make what use you can of it.

Is there a chance of seeing you? Has Brown turned up?[4] I am desperately hard up; so is Anthony. Write soon. I've been expecting a letter every day this week, & am fearful of sending this one off, lest it cross you on your way south.

Louis has some Berlioz for you.

The Châtelaine sends her love to both of you.

Yours ever,
W.E.H.

[4] Presumably Horatio Robert Forbes Brown (1854-1926), historian of Venice and friend of RLS and Symonds.

To Robert Louis Stevenson, 14 June 1881
ALS: Yale

51 Richmond Gardens, Shepherds Bush, W.

My dear Louis,

I send you herewith, per register post, the scraps of the drammy.[1] I want you to read them through, & give me your opinion about them.[2] And I want you to take care of them, as I've no second copy. And to send them back soon — soon — soon; with a long letter (for which I beg the Secretary[3] on my bended knees!), telling me bluntly what's your views.

[1] A draft of WEH's play *Husband and Wife* which appears later to have been retitled *Old Glory*. No manuscript has been found.
[2] RLS did so in positive terms at great length in his next letter. See *Stevenson Letters*, *3*, 191-3.
[3] Fanny Stevenson.

There is enough, I think, to enable you to understand the drift of the thing, & the way in which I've seen it for the stage. I've not corrected anything, nor tried to rewrite any part. I send it with all its imperfections on its head. Be patient with it, & if it's worth combing out, the crunch if you please. And soon — soon.

I don't know what to think of it myself. There are times when I'm mighty cock-a-hoop about it, & ready to back it at long odds against anything on the stage. There are others when I wouldn't refuse two bob for the whole billing. At the worst I am ready to take my oath that there are right scenes & right drama in it. Am I wrong? Or is my despondency ill placed? It's for you to judge.

I would I could be with you, to point out the novelty of certain parts: — of the prologue, for instance, of which I feel pretty sure. In a week we might talk it into shape. But I'm here in Shepherds Bush, & you're there in Pershire; & I can do nothing but agonise & ruminate, & be the pitiful dullard I am.

I don't want any scenes of conspiracy, mind. The emotional interest is the one; & if they want more sensation than they get in the last act, they must go elsewhere for it.

I have done nothing since you left, but ruminate like an ox, & read G. Byron. He is the gent for my money just now. I prefer him to Swinburne, strange as it may seem; & to Tennyson likewise. If I do him for the *Athenaeum*,[4] I will send you the article. I have also read *Barry Lyndon*,[5] which I admire, but do not like. It confirms my theory of Thackeray: as the original Stupid Man — narrow, spiteful, illiberal, unintelligent; a London Clubster with a genius for prose & the prose imagination in perfection. I have much to say on the subject, & will likely return to it.[6] I've also read *Martin Chuzzlewit*.[7] *Voilà de l'imagination, mon fils!* The death of old Anthony, & the murder, & all that follows it to the capture & suicide, are magnificent. Why should those devils of hell cross the Channel to fawn on old Hugo,[8] when they've stuff like that *chez eux*? Construe me that. I've also read (& bought) the cheap edition of *Travels with a Donkey*,[9] by one, R. L. Stevenson. A charming booklet it is. If you see the author, tell him that I was right about it having been through a second edition, inasmuch as the present is called 'the third'. It's a delightful work, Sir! Colvin affects to think that there's too much ashplant & goad in it; but that's my eye.

[4] WEH's unsigned review of Matthew Arnold's edition of *The Poetry of Byron, Athenaeum*, 25 June 1881.

[5] Thackeray's *The Memoirs of Barry Lyndon, Esq* (1856).

[6] WEH's unsigned review of *Extracts from the Works of W. M. Thackeray, Athenaeum*, 12 November 1881.

[7] Dickens's *The Life and Adventures of Martin Chuzzlewit* (1843-44).

[8] Victor(-Marie) Hugo (1802-85), French poet, novelist and playwright.

[9] The third edition of *Travels with a Donkey in the Cevennes* (1881). It was first published in 1879.

It confirmed me fully of the *Emigrant*. I could have done the *Emigrant*; I couldn't the *Donkey*, not to be made a postmaster. The one's art, the other's journalism. *Voilà*.

Colvin, by the way, is well pleased with my Millet,[10] & thinks that I ought to do a book on 1830.[11] Says I'm the gent for it & would do it well. I'm mighty proud, but I don't know. Said Colvin abuses you for remaining dumb, but supposes that it's because you're happy. And is therefore content.

Bob & I heard Gluck's *Orpheus*[12] very ill done on Saturday. It fetched us down to the ground. A critic in the *Daily News* — a blood-relation of the Wollock's, I'm sure! — is pleased to note the 'occasional dramatic power'[13] of the work! Think of that! — It's as if I said 'the occasional dramatic power' of Sophocles. It's a most magnificent & surprising work, is *Orpheus* & it warms my heart to think of it. In certain ways Gluck seems to me to go higher than Beethoven himself. *Apropos de* Beethoven, we heard his *Egmont* overture, & his Seventh Symphony last night.[14] And the way in which he *écrasers* gents like Wagner (who is bloody clever, certainly) is a thing to see. 'A noble old man, Sir!' Next Monday[15] they give his *Coriolan* overture & the *Erocia*; & we are praying to God for the half-quid needful for a couple of seats. If we get it, I shall turn professing Christian, & pal on with curates. Richter[16] is a most gaudy conductor, & his Beethovenisms are all so many revelations. Unhappily, he is an ardent Wagnerite; & your professional Wagnerite doesn't, so far as I can find, admit anybody but Wagner & Beethoven. The consequence is that Richter hasn't played a bar of Gluck in England. Gluck, as you know, invented opera, & worked off Wagner's discovery a century or so ago, & that to infinite purpose. It follows that to be a good Wagnerite you must ignore Gluck; & you must also ignore Berlioz, who adored Gluck, invented the famous principle of *leit-motive*,[17] & taught Wagner the true meaning of the word 'instrumentalism'. I believe, too, that you must also believe in Schopenhauer,[18] hate all Jews, & go

---

[10] *Jean-François Millet. Twenty Etchings and Woodcuts, reproduced in fac-simile, and a biographical notice by William Ernest Henley* (1881). This appears to have been commissioned by the Fine Arts Society. WEH's views of Millet as in the mould of Michelangelo brought an attack from Ruskin in the *Nineteenth Century* for October 1881. Ruskin could 'not find any reason for publishing the book' and refers to the etchings as 'scrabbles'.

[11] WEH did not produce a book on 1830.

[12] Gluck's opera at the St James's Hall, 11 June 1881.

[13] 'Mr. Ganz's Orchestral Concerts', *Daily News*, 13 June 1881. The music critic of the *Daily News* from 1866 to 1886 was Henry John Lincoln (1814-1901).

[14] A concert at St James's Hall, London, on 13 June 1881.

[15] A concert at St James's Hall on 20 June 1881.

[16] The Austro-Hungarian conductor Hans Richter (1843-1916) was one of the first of the international conductors.

[17] The principle of a recurring theme in music.

[18] The German philosopher Arthur Schopenhauer (1788-1860) who developed the idea that in order to ease the suffering in the world Man must control his will and lesson the desire to reproduce.

in for Blue China & its accompaniment generally. But of that I'm not so sure.

How do you like the *Mémoires*?[19] And why did you not hand them over to C.B., as it was agreed & covenanted & determined, between us? If you lose 'em — well! no matter! But — ! no matter, I say. The *Souvenirs*[20] are disappointing but there's first-rate stuff in them, for all that.

Anthony has sold to the tune of £40, & expects to sell more. He is out of debt, & radiant with hope. My future is damn bad. I would sell it for two pence, & warrant it unsound, with the utmost freedom.

Chatto is out of town for a few days.[21] I shall see him about the *English Prose*[22] book as soon as ever he returns & I shall mention the *Slate*[23] as well; so get to work as soon as you like.

Is there any chance of a letter? I suppose not, or I'd ask you to tell me how you found our beloved Cockshott?[24] He has succeeded in persuading me of my own ineptitude in which I now believe as in the existence of a Deity. God bless him! He is a powerful creature. I've a long letter from him in my drawer, & I haven't energy to answer it. He is as irrepressible, & as indestructible, & as impervious, as the hero Punch. He was born to have the last word & the last blow, & to be always partly right. When I think of the number of absurdities to which I stand committed in his eyes — owing to an injudicious indulgence in epistolary argument with him — I feel that my self-respect is flown forever.

The Châtelaine sends her love to you both, & hopes you are all right, & that Mrs. Louis will write to her. Also Wogs.[25] My mother's dear love to you. She would have liked to see you bitterly. Write soon, & criticise me.

Yours, dear lad,
W. E. Henley

[19] Vicomte de Chateaubriand, *Mémoires d'outre-tombe*, 12 vols (Paris, 1849).
François-René, Vicomte de Chateaubriand (1768 1848), French novelist and writer.

[20] Chateaubriand's *Souvenirs d'Italie, d'Angleterre et d'Amérique, suivis de Morceaux divers de morale et de littérature*, 2 vols (Paris, 1815).

[21] Andrew Chatto (1840-1913) who together with his partner William Edward Windus (1838-1910) formed the publishing firm.

[22] Possibly a reference to a selection of English prose.

[23] *What was on the Slate* was a projected but unfinished novel by RLS and Fanny.

[24] RLS called Fleeming Jenkin 'Cockshot' in his essay 'Talk and Talkers' in the *Cornhill Magazine*, April 1882.

[25] RLS's dog Wogg, later known as Bogue.

To Austin Dobson, Tuesday [August/early September 1881]
ALS: London. Part published in Connell, 94.

51 Richmond Gardens, Shepherds Bush, W.

My dear Dobson,

Thank you no end. And Monkhouse likewise.[1] I am truly grateful to you both: more grateful than I can well say.

I am in doubt & difficulty about the matter all the same. The fact is, I want posh, the ready, the mopuses; & have some I must. To get some instantly, I am writing a Millet which I hope to put off on Stephen.[2] And to make this good enough for him I shall have to put into it all I can. It will be difficult, I imagine, to do a third, & not repeat from numbers one & two.

What I should like would be this: — that I should take the book in hand & *finish it at my own time*.[3] The I feel sure that I could do it creditably; whereas, just now, I do not feel sure of it at all. To do it well is the only thing I really care about; for the coins are far in the future (the date of publication being uncertain), and on them I don't care to speculate. Indeed, I can't afford to do so. I've been idle & unfit too long; & I must buckle to for stuff on the nail, or 'lie still' & be d—d to it.

The two anterior Millets[4] have determined me to take in Rousseau[5] as well. They are both good men; but I can say all I want to say of each in 40 pp. So *Rousseau & Millet* be it.

Do you think that this can be managed. I mean, do you think that Cundall[6] will give me the open order? And will you forgive me for referring so persistently to my own circumstances? I couldn't explain my position without doing so; or I would.

If Cundall will as I wish, I foresee good things. A *Delacroix*; a *Daumier & Gavarni*;[7] perhaps a *David & Ingres*. Who knows? To do the first two I am most resolutely inclined. 'Tis 1830 always; & on 1830 I must write, & I will.

I have got some Daumier. *Quel homme, et quel grand artiste*! I feel humble

---

[1] William Cosmo Monkhouse (1840-1901), poet and art critic. He worked at the Board of Trade as did Austin Dobson. He was a contributor to the *Magazine of Art* for many years and contributed over one hundred and thirty entries on artists to the *Dictionary of National Biography*.

[2] 'The early life of J.-F. Millet', *Cornhill*, March 1882.

[3] A projected, but unwritten, book on Millet. WEH did write 'A Note on Romanticism' for the *Memorial Catalogue of the French and Dutch Loan Collection* (Edinburgh, 1888). See WEH's letter to Hamilton Bruce, 6 October 1886.

[4] One was his *Jean-François Millet. Twenty Etchings and Woodcuts* but the other has not been found.

[5] The French painter Étienne-Pierre-Théodore Rousseau (1812-67).

[6] Joseph Cundall (1818-95), publisher and writer on art. He edited the *Illustrated Biographies of the Great Artists*, 39 vols (1879-91).

[7] Sulpice Guillaume Chevalier (1804-66), French caricaturist.

before him; as before Millet. What an article I ought to be able to Scribnerise[8] on him! Isn't it an odd thing that we should know so little of the heroes of 1830 as we do? There is in Berlioz the wherewithal to make a hundred greetings, for instance; there are a score of Scheffers & Delaroches[9] in Eugène Delacroix; & in Daumier — well! Daumier is, in many ways, a greater & truer artist than Victor Hugo. And 'tis only of late that Daumier & Delacroix & Berlioz have been notable in this country in any way.

I have a *Robert Macaire* article in hand.[10] I think it will be interesting.

I have done a feat in verse. I have translated, or rather blackguardised & imitated Villon's *Ballade par laquelle V. crye mercy à chascun*[11] into fairly correct & significant slang. It is totally unfit for print, of course; but the form is right, & the diction, if a little arbitrary, is passably cocknified. Shall I send it to you? I suppose it's a uniquity, isn't it? Or have you forestalled me? I am burning to essay the *Tout aux tavernes et aux filles*[12] also.

Let me know as soon as may be how the possibilities stand. And think of me as someone really grateful to you both.

Truly Yours,
W.E.H.

[8] WEH did not produce an article on Daumier for the American *Scribner's Monthly.*
[9] Ary Scheffer (1795-1858), Dutch painter and engraver.
[10] No such article has been found. The character Macaire appears in the French play *L'Auberge des Adrets* (1823) by Benjamin Antier and others, which was later adapted by RLS and WEH (see WEH to RLS, 2 January 1885, n. 3).
[11] Villon's ballade beginning 'A Chartreux et a Celestins ...' published in his *Le Testament* (Paris, 1489). WEH's version was published in *Recreations of the Rabelais Club* (1885-88), 6-7. WEH is listed as a member in the vols 1882-85 and 1885-88 but is not listed for 1880-81. The Club was founded by Walter Besant in 1879 to promote and discuss the work of Rabelais. It lasted until 1889.
[12] Villon's 'Ballade de bonne doctrine' ('Car ou soies porteur de bulles ...') in *Le Testament*. This was WEH's 'Villon's Straight Tip to all Cross Coves'.

To Charles Baxter, 8 October 1881
ALS: Yale

[51 Richmond Gardens, Shepherds Bush, W.]
My dear Charles,

We leave on Sunday night.[1] So you may expect me, photos & all, on Monday morning.

The good news is real. After 1*st* Nov. I am editor of the *Mag. of Art*,[2] & in

[1] For Edinburgh.
[2] The *Magazine of Art*, a monthly journal from 1878 to 1904, was published by Cassell, Petter, Galpin and Co. WEH was a surprising choice as he was against the staid orthodox view of art

receipt, for 3½ hours daily, of £300 a year.

I want you to get me some £30 till Christmas. You *must*. For if you don't, I'm bust.

Lots to tell you. Goodbye now, & don't fail to drink good luck to my new adventure, in a glass of the best when next you sit down to dinner.

Our kindest regards to Mrs. Baxter.

Yours ever,
W.E.H.

Ain't it fun? I can see you grinning as you read. And it's real, dear lad! I signed & sealed last night.

as propounded by the *M. of A*. The journal recognised art as being English rather than universal and rooted in the Royal Academy of Art.

After passing through the hands of Professor Eric Robertson, Mr. W. E. Henley became editor in 1881, when the magazine, now enlarged and its price increased to a shilling, assumed a position of authority, and succeeded in commanding, what it has since retained, the largest circulation of any art paper in the world (*Annual Index of Review of Reviews: Index to the Periodicals of the Past Year: List of Standard Photographs*, 1891, 108).

Henley *c*. 1885

Anna Henley, the Châtelaine

Margaret Emma Henley,
aged about three

Charles Baxter
(from *W.E. Henley* by John Connell, 1949)

Henry Austin Dobson

Bernard Capes

Arthur Morrison

2. The World of Art: 1881-88

Colvin was influential in Henley's appointment to the *Magazine of Art*. It was a position that Henley entered into with enthusiasm but it later turned sour as he constantly had to fight the rigidity of his publishers. During this period Henley increased the circulation of the magazine and introduced his readers to the art of Europe, America and Japan, together with articles on the arts in general. He published his old friend Sidney Colvin, Slade Professor of Fine Art at Cambridge, and introduced his readers to the criticism of Stevenson's cousin Robert Alan Mowbray Stevenson and the work of Rodin, who was to reward him with his bust in 1886. Tired of the constant battle for control of the art content of the magazine Henley resigned in the late summer or early autumn of 1886. The collaboration with Stevenson resulted in the first production of *Deacon Brodie* in Bradford in 1882 which is vividly described in a letter to Stevenson. Despite the onus of his editorial work Henley was acting as an unpaid agent for Stevenson and played a major part in the publication of *Treasure Island* in book form.

Henley and Baxter visited the Stevensons at Hyères in January 1884 and all seemed well, although RLS was seriously ill in Nice after their return. In May Fanny was appealing to Henley for help following RLS's severe haemorrhage which became a major concern for his close friends in England. Henley took charge and organised medical help with Baxter. RLS survived and later in the summer Henley was a constant visitor to the Stevensons in Bournemouth. At first both RLS and Fanny shared Henley's enthusiasm but later Fanny found the play writing of the two as too much pressure on her husband and this led to some resentment against Henley. Stevenson, too, was feeling the pressure of Henley's insistence that the plays were to make their fortune. *Deacon Brodie* was produced London in July 1884 and RLS and WEH were collaborating on their plays *Beau Austin* and *Admiral Guinea* which were completed later that year.

The following year RLS and WEH wrote their play *Macaire* which was not performed until 1900. In April 1885 WEH resigned as music critic of the *Saturday Review* though the reason has not been established.

In August 1886 the Henleys visited Paris where WEH sat for his bust and he introduced RLS to Rodin. After resigning from the *Magazine of Art* he acted as consulting editor of the *Art Journal* for a short period.

In 1887 WEH continued to visit the Stevensons in Bournemouth with ideas for plays. WEH's only play *Mephisto*, written under the pseudonym Byron McGuiness, was unsuccessfully produced in London in June with his brother Edward in the lead. WEH was asked by Hamilton Bruce to write the introduction to the *Memorial Catalogue of the Dutch and French Loan Collection* for the 1886 exhibition at Edinburgh.

1888 was to be a crucial year for Henley. The Stevensons had left for America the previous year and Henley was unemployed. He still did journalistic hack work but lacked the editorial chair suited to his talents. In a letter to Stevenson in March 1888 he remarked that Fanny had published a story under her own name which was based on a story by Stevenson's cousin, Katharine de Mattos. It was this letter which brought about the quarrel and final estrangement between the two old friends. RLS saw Henley as disloyal in the accusation and confirmed his view that Henley was a source of trouble to him. Neither would give way and the break was made, though they still corresponded occasionally but the intimacy of old was gone.

Henley's first book, *A Book of Verses*, was published in May and in September his only child, Margaret Emma, was born.

To Robert Louis Stevenson, 26 October 1881
ALS: Yale

                                        51 Richmond Gardens, Shepherds Bush, W.
My dear Louis,

I am awful sorry to hear of the cold. I trust in God it's but a little one. Take all the care of yourself you can, I beg & pray. Or we shall all be ill with thinking of you.

Now (for this must be but a scrawl; the truth this morning) for news. Stephen has sent me back the 'Shadow'.[1] Very glad to have read it, but doesn't think it quite suitable for the *Cornhill*. I hope to use it myself.

Next, I have fetched Gosse,[2] & I think he's mine. I am to see him to-morrow, & talk things over. Dobson, who saw my letter, says that if I am artful as that with all my contributors, I shall make a damn good editor. I wrote from my heart. *Voilà*.

Lang joins me; book & all, I hope; — but of that there's a slight doubt. Dobson & Monkhouse are body & breeches mine. Clifton Brown[3] (tell Symonds) has promised. The lively Fleaming [*sic*] is eager for the fray, & snuffs the battle from afar. Colvin is on of course. They promise me Blackmore

---

[1] A story by Fanny which WEH tried unsuccessfully to have published. It finally appeared as 'The Warlock's Shadow' in the *Belgravia*, March 1886.
[2] Gosse had written to WEH on 23 October 1881 (Pierpont Morgan) congratulating him on his appointment as editor of the *Magazine of Art*.
[3] T. E. Brown.

& Jefferies.[4] I can get at Kate Greenaway[5] when I will. Also at May Probyn[6] — who has been writing verses that Dobson says he'd be very proud to sign. You & your wife I have already. I can have heaps beside; but that's enough to start with. Don't you think so?

The Child Art is a good idea.[7] Think it over & develop it a little. *The Pilgrim's Progress* paper is to be of another series: 'Byways of Book Illustration'.[8] It will have Stackhouse's *Bible*,[9] Quarles[10] & the Dutch Emblematologists, Boydell's *Shakespeare*,[11] set for its companions. Get to work at it as soon as you receive the book, for the more I have in hand the better.

A certain Kate Lawson[12] has been suggested as a possible artist for your verses. She is good enough, but I shall try for Kate Greenaway. *Apropos de* both, send me your *Davos imprecations*[13] for Dobson. He wants to read 'em badly.

I asked Runciman to write for me. He refused. I incline to think he'll regret it. He is getting vainer than ever. I haven't time to give instances. But that's so.

I did little or nothing to *Diogenes*[14] in Edinburgh. Since I've returned I've done nothing but cut hither & thither, in search of contributors. To-day I'm fairly plastered. Runciman is crying out for a draft of the thing, which he's evidently funking heart & soul. Thanks to your supplies, I hope to send him one

[4] R(ichard) D(odderidge) Blackmore (1825-1900) author of *Lorna Doone* (1869). He did not write for WEH. Richard Jefferies (1848-87), journalist and novelist. His passion for nature runs through his novels his best probably being *Bevis, the Story of a Boy* (1882). He later published the autobiographical *The Story of My Heart* (1883) which caused a minor scandal with his views on the importance of nature in society. He was a contributor to the *Magazine of Art*.

[5] Kate Greenaway (1846-1901), one of the foremost illustrators of children's books. She was elected a member of the Institute of Painters in Water Colours in 1889. She did illustrate for the *Magazine of Art*.

[6] The artist and writer May Probyn (1856-1919).

[7] RLS appears to have proposed an 'Art in Youth' series in his letter of 20 October (*Stevenson Letters*, 3, 240) which was to have included *The Pilgrim's Progress*.

[8] Only three article in the series on books and their illustrations were written. RLS contributed two articles and Dobson the other.

[9] Presumably Thomas Stackhouse's *A New History of the Holy Bible, from the Beginning of the World to the Establishment of Christianity*, 2 vols (1737).

[10] The poet Francis Quarles (1592-1644), became famous for his *Emblems, Divine and Moral* (1635) with its symbolic illustrations.

[11] *A Catalogue of the Pictures, &c. In the Shakespeare Gallery* (1790) by the engraver John Boydell (1719-1804).

[12] Probably a Lady Kate Lawson who illustrated her *Highway and Homes of Japan* (1910) from her own photographs.

[13] *Casparides*, a series of eight lampoons against the frauds perpetuated by two Davos tradesmen. They were unpublished.

[14] RLS and WEH projected a contemporary satire called *Diogenes*. Two fragments were privately printed as *Diogenes in London* and *Diogenes at the Savile Club* and are reprinted in vol. 26, Vailima edition of Stevenson's *Works* (1923). The intention was to include, in the section about the Savile Club, humorous verses about leading figures of the day.

to-night or to-morrow.

All you send will do well. At all events for a basis. More when I've read it finally. As regards Colvin, right you are. As regards the others, remember that they are just now being kind to me, & that we mustn't be other than kind to them. Cruelty might cost me my staff, & my place in the Club.[15] So don't be frolicsome.

I have a splendid *motif* for Gladstone.[16] The others will come, I've no doubt. get the song of the medical men done, if you can. I've peppered Oscar most damnably.[17] I think the Prince de Galles will be a real hit. Baxter (d—n him) was completely bust by it. I suppose I'll leave your introduction & Savile description much as they are, so you may write 'em as you like. D—n Henry James,[18] & all his kind.

I saw your father; dined with him at Rothesay Place,[19] & am to have the book.[20] Insisted on the introduction of Pepys.[21] He loves the Canallettos I got for Charles; so I insisted on giving him two which I have by me. Nigel is framing them just now for him. I'd a great mind to tell him of your two Piranesis, but didn't as the framer is in the family, & it mightn't have looked well. Piranesi, by the way, fetched the Bart more than *I* could have believed. He ordered six on the spot. The lady Bart[22] is amusing enough, but I'd rather she were the wife to someone else. I saw Baynes, & told him to read your 'Pepys'. I were afinishing off the *E.B.* article for you; hope you'll get it. Shouldn't be surprised if I did. Also brought up the subject of J.W.F. in connection with a life of his sire for one of Blackwood's series,[23] & rather fancy I may have done that graceless dog (whom I love with all my heart) a good turn. I can write no more now. I am too played out. Love to both of you. Take care of yourselves, & write no more than is good for you.

Yours affectionately, dear lad,
W.E.H.

[A*dded by WEH at the top of the letter*] I am told to beware of Dr. Shaw.[24]

---

[15] WEH was elected a member of the Savile Club in 1883.

[16] The great Liberal statesman and four times Prime Minister.

[17] Oscar Wilde.

[18] Henry James was included in *Diogenes*.

[19] Baxter's house.

[20] RLS's collection of essays entitled *Familiar Studies of Men and Books* (1882).

[21] RLS's 'Samuel Pepys' in the *Cornhill Magazine*, July 1881. His father wanted it in *Familiar Studies*.

[22] Sir Walter Simpson had married Anne Fitzgerald Mackay (d. 1941), his long-time mistress, on 13 January 1881.

[23] Walter Ferrier's father James Frederick Ferrier (1808-64), Professor of Moral Philosophy and Political Economy, at St Andrews, from 1845 until his death.

[24] He has not been identified, although he may be someone to be included in *Diogenes*.

To Auguste Rodin,[1] **23 November 1881**
ALS: Musée Rodin

                                       51 Richmond Gardens, Shepherds Bush W.
Cher M. Rodin,
   Depuis que je vous ai vu, j'ai eu le bonheur d'être nommé rédacteur en chef
d'une revue mensuelle, *The Magazine of Art*, qui est assez répandue, et don't
les gravures sont assez bien en vue.
   J'ai l'idée de vous demander la permission de faire graver de vos choeses.
Est-ce que cela vous serait bien désagréable? Dans le cas où cela vous ferait
plaisir, j'aimerais bien publier la gravure du *St. Jean* — le buste seul, ou toute
la statue. Mais je m'en rapporte entièrement à vous, et je ferai ce que vous
voudrez.
   Je serai enchanté de publier des nouvelles de ce que vous faites, si vous
aurez la bonté de m'en faire parvenir. Je puis dire ceci: qu'en faisant cela vous
me rendrez un grand service en même temps que vous me ferez un grand
plaisir. Aussi, ne balancez pas, je vous en prie. Dites-moi ce que vous faites, et
je le redirai à mon public, avec ou sans fanfare, comme vous voudrez.
   J'ai encore un service à demander. Mon frère, qui est peintre, comme je
crois vous avoir dit, a vu chez moi l'épreuve du *St. Jean* que vous m'avez
donnée, et il en a resté tellement saisi que je ne peux pas m'empêcher de vous
en mendier encore une épreuve. Si, par bonheur, il vous en reste encore, je suis
sûr que vous m'en expédierez une; et je vous en remercie mille fois d'avance.
   J'espère que vous ne tarderez pas me donner de vous nouvelles, et de me
dire avec la franchise la plus parfaite ce que vous pensez sur mon idée de faire
graver le St. Jean. J'espère enfin que tout va bien, et que les grandes portes
don't nous avons causé un moment vont toujours, au fur et à mesure, a votre
gré. Avec ça, cher M. Rodin, je vous prie d'agréer l'assurance de mes
sentiments les plus respectueux. J'ai eu bien du plaisir à faire connaissance;
j'en aurai bien plus à vous être utile.

                         Bien à vous,
                         W. E. Henley

La statue de Legros est bien belle; sa médaille de Darwin me semble plus belle
encore. Je crois que c'est un peu à vous ce nous les devons. Vous pouvez en
être bien fier.

---

[1] WEH had been introduced to Rodin, who visited England in August 1881, by the French artist
Alphonse Legros and he became an ardent admirer and fearless supporter of Rodin. WEH
visited Paris in August 1886 to sit for his bust which is now in the National Portrait Gallery,
London, with a copy by Rodin as a memorial to WEH in the crypt of St Paul's Cathedral,
London.

[*Added by WEH at the top of the letter*] Je vous enverrai demain un numéro de la revue — — Il ne faut pas m'en vouloir trop si j'ai mal écrit; et si je me fais à peine comprendre. Le Français n'est pas facile à écrire — même pour les Français.

Translation

Dear M. Rodin,

Since I last saw you, I have had the good fortune to be appointed Editor-in-Chief of a monthly magazine called *The Magazine of Art* which sells quite well; its engravings are also quite well thought of.

I have a mind to ask your permission to reproduce some of your things. Would you find this terribly unpleasant ? If by any chance the idea appealed to you, I would like to publish your *St. Jean*, just the bust or the whole statue. But I will leave it to you entirely, and I'll do what you want.[2]

I will be delighted to publish news of what you are doing, if you are kind enough to let me know. All I can say is this : in so doing you'll do me a big favour as well as a great pleasure. So, do not hesitate, I beg of you. Tell me what you are up to, and I'll tell my readers, with as much or as little trumpeting as you wish.[3]

I have another favour to ask. My brother, who is a painter, as I think I have already told you, has seen in my house the copy of the *St. Jean* which you have given me; and he was so bowled over by it that I cannot stop myself from begging another copy. If, by a happy chance, you have some left, I feel sure that you will send me one ; I thank you a thousand times in advance.

I hope it won't be long before I have news of you, and have you tell me absolutely frankly how you feel about my idea about publishing an engraving of the *St. Jean*. I hope everything is going well, and that the great doors which we had briefly discussed together are still going, bit by bit, as you wish. With all that, dear M. Rodin, please accept the assurances of the respect I have for you. I have been very delighted to meet you, and will be even more so to be of service to you.

Yours ever,
W. E. Henley

Legros's statue is very beautiful; his medal of Darwin seems to me more

[2] The *St Jean*, which had been exhibited at the Royal Academy in 1882, was illustrated in WEH's 'Current Art', *Magazine of Art*, April 1883.
[3] Frederic V. Grunfeld, in his *Rodin: a Biography* (1988) comments: 'Beginning in 1882 the whole trajectory of Rodin's career could be charted more accurately in the pages of Henley's magazine than in the Paris press' (207).

beautiful still. I believe that we owe them a little to you, and you should feel very proud of that.

[*Added by WEH at the top of the letter*] To-morrow I'll send you a copy of the *Magazine*. Please do not hold it against me if I have written badly, and if I am barely understandable. French is not an easy language to write — not even for the French.

To Robert Louis Stevenson, [mid/late November 1881]
ALS: Yale

[51Richmond Gardens, Shepherds Bush, W.]
[*last 24 pages of a 28 page letter*]
scarce a single writer on our staff who can string two sentences together. If I hadn't *such* a light heart & *such* a thin pair of breeches, I'd give up the ghost to-morrow. As it is, I festinate slowly; I am full of amiability & modesty, & I am deferentially aggressive; I ask advice all round, & I sometimes take it; & I hope for better things. The world, I find, is very full of E.W.G's[1] — E.W.G's minus the intelligence, that is: & I think I have proved my capacity to deal with it, in the general & the particular both.

As regards the January issue, my first, I think it will do me good rather than ill with the firm. Everything I have done for it I have shown to Gell[2] — a delightful gent; laborious, patient, boyish, sweet; & everything I print will be marked, & seen by the partners in solemn conclave. Over one passage supplied by me Gell roared with laughter. I suffer under an American contributor, you must know — one Benjamin.[3] Benjamin is a devil of hell. How they discovered him I know not; but they believe in him mightily. When I first read the works of Benjamin I tore my hair & wept. The English of Benjamin is a kind of maniacally feeble Johnsonese:[4] a Johnsonese whose mind has gone through frigging. Not an organic phrase does it contain; not a sentence that will stand on its own feet; not a metaphor that will hold water. I at once sat down & rewrote Benjamin, & I am bound to say that I succeeded in making a man of him. By an inspiration, I was moved to send up the proof for approbation ere I dispatched it to the printer. The consequences were alarming. They wagged their heads; their face was grave & melancholy; they were alarmed; they couldn't think of such a thing. Benjamin they said, has the whole American press at his back; he would

---

[1] Gosse.
[2] Phillip Lylleton Gell (1852-1926), educational director of Cassells.
[3] Samuel Greene Benjamin (1837-1914), American writer, painter, and diplomat. He was the first American minister to Persia, 1883-85.
[4] WEH is referring to Samuel Johnson's ponderous style.

consider himself slighted if his style were so far improved; he would resent the slight in print, & so would all his friends; & good bye to our American circulation. I swore; but I tried again. And after a good deal of trouble I hit the golden mean. I did something for Benjamin after all. I sewed him on a button or two, I provided him with a brace, I wiped his nose, & tucked in his shirt at two or three holes behind; & I got him off my hands with credit. When the proof came back in page form, I was horrified to find that 19 lines were wanting. I waded in, & tried to write honestly. But it was no go. The demon of parody took possession of me. And the nineteen lines I wrote were true Benjamin. I took them up to Gell, & Gell shouted with laughter. 'The sentences are a little too straight & concise,' he said, 'but Benjamin won't know 'em from his own.' You may be sure that I rejoiced. If only I'd dared, to 'develop these traits', as Benjamin dares, I'd have done some Benjaminisms that would have killed Benjamin off at sight. But I didn't. As it is, I think you'll allow I've been tolerably cheeky.

The odd thing is that Benjamin is unknown outside Belle Sauvage Yard. Gosse, whose Americanism you know, swears positively that Benjamin invented himself (like a pill!), & that his influence is a myth, a matter for Lang or Max Muller.[5] A prime jest is that Benjamin — Little Benjamin, as Gell & I now call him — on being asked for copy, refused to write under 50 dols. Per article. A still primer jest is that they gave him all he asked: 'Like wealthy men that care not how they give':[6] So that Benjamin's bad Americanese is to the full as marketable as your good English. A consequence of this is misplaced generosity was that Benjamin sent in six articles at a burst — broke out into Benjaminese all over the shop, in fact. Three of these are yet on my hands. I purpose to get rid of them as quickly as I can. I need not add that I cherish the same intention, in a much higher state of development, with regard to their author.

I mentioned Lang just now. Did I tell you that the name by which he goes — when he's out of earshot of the speakers — is 'the Merry Andrew'? That's by the way. The facts are these. I wrote a formal letter to the Merry A., inviting him (as 'Dear Sir') to contribute some articles on Savage Art,[7] and on English pre-Raphaelitism. What does he do but write back to me as 'Damned Sir'? What does he go on to say that 'the art of savages principally consists in carving & gilding their behinds'? This precious epistle, addressed to 'The editor', was opened — as all letters so addressed are opened — at the central office, & there men looked at it as at a case of dynamite. Authority was

[5] Friedrich Max Müller (1823-1900), German born naturalised Briton. Taylorian Professor of Modern European Languages, Oxford University, 1854-68, and from 1868 until his death Professor of Comparative Philology at Oxford.
[6] Line 17 of Tennyson's poem 'Tithonus'.
[7] Lang had two articles in the *Magazine of Art* for March and April 1882.

fearfully hurt & fearfully scandalised. Such an insult to the house! Such a reflection on the magazine! Such an affront to the altar! — The consternation was universal, for the missive went from hand to hand to hand, from office to office; — spreading like a poison through the veins of the whole establishment. Till at last it got to Gell (who knows his Lang), who read it with yells of laughter, & — by explanations prompt & ingenious — succeeded in restoring the House to its accustomed equanimity.

I am curious to see if I shall be paid for my excess-matter in the January number. I am under agreement to contribute 3 pp. per month. I start by contributing some 6 pp. at least.[8] If they don't pay me my £3..3, I shall be a heavy loser. *Mais nous allons voir.*

As regards your own business, I suppose you will have heard that — as I expected — the *Essays* are a failure.[9] They decline the book through me, with every circumstance of respect, but they decline it. The fact is (between ourselves) that the new departure of which I trumpeted so loudly & clear, is my eye. It's not yet ready to come off, & I doubt if it ever will be. Cassell's is still Cassell's, & vast as their publishing arrangements are, they do not comprehend the issue of such books as yours. They feel they could not send it out as it deserves, nor circulate it in its proper sphere; & they prefer to have nothing to do with it. Gell (who only knew you anonymously; as the author of those Davos games in the *P.M.G.*)[10] behaved very charmingly about the matter, & volunteered to do all he could to put the matter to you in its proper light. I thought it best, however, that you should hear of it from me. The chances are, though, that you'll hear of it from me.

The *Songs of Innocence*[11] (as I can't help calling 'em) are another pair of sleeves. There you have 'em, & have 'em as you will. Of these they see the practicability, & it's odds but you & they will deal. They look on your verses, dear lad, as a new thing in child literature; & they are fully prepared, on certain conditions, to go for 'em through thick & thin, to regard them as the withal, not only of a passing success, but of an abiding popularity. The conditions are one in number. They have the good sense to see that they've nobody in their employ who can do the verses justice in the matter of illustration; and they have resolved, either to associate Caldecott[12] with you, or not to publish you at all. This I regard as sound policy & I'm delighted to think that they have been so wise about the thing. My great fear was that they would jump at the poems,

---

[8] Although there are no signed contributions by WEH in the January *Magazine of Art* he may have written 'The Hill Collection' and 'The Palmer Exhibition'.

[9] Presumably WEH had offered RLS's *Familiar Studies of Men and Books* to Cassells who refused it.

[10] Five unsigned articles about Switzerland in the *Pall Mall Gazette* during February and March 1881.

[11] RLS's *A Child's Garden of Verses* was eventually published by Longmans Green and Co. in 1885.

[12] The well-known children's book illustrator Randolph Caldecott (1846-86).

& hand 'em over to one of their own artists; & I cannot say how much pleased I am to find them resolved to do nothing of the kind, but to make the book the best in every way it can possibly be.

Matters are now at this pass, then. Colvin has the verses, & is to impose them upon Caldecott with all the weight of his influence & authority. He thinks that Caldecott will turn out of his way to oblige him, & that, deep in work as he says he is, he will probably prove to be not so deep but he can buckle to at the *Songs of Innocence.* Once we have his promise, your own action begins. You will add as much as you think fit to the *MS.*, & you will — or Colvin will for you — make a formal offer of the book to C., P., G., & Co., associating yourself with Caldecott, &, if possible naming a price. That done, the matter will be settled in two twos; & you'll be, I reckon, in a fair way of getting at the biggest public in existence, & of becoming a household oracle in the Universal Nursery.

Am I too sanguine? I don't think so. Everything depends on Caldecott & on Colvin. If Colvin works the oracle aright, he will nick his Caldecott exactly; & if Caldecott ain't a hass, he'll be only too grateful for such an opportunity — of a new departure & a steady & abiding popularity — as your verses give him. That's my way of looking at the business. I am bound to add that I think that Caldecott, if he's a human being, should not be unwilling to stretch a point to oblige me. I have never spoken to him in my life, but I've written more pleasantly & more steadily about him than I've written about anybody living[13] — yourself alone excepted.

While I am dealing with the subject, I may as well notify the fact that Greenaway — whose little book, *Mother Goose,*[14] is immensely popular — was sounded by Austin Dobson, & found to be impossible. She has had three years' work in hand, & doesn't know which way to turn.

Gosse's 'Buccaneers' is now with the printer.[15] I'll tell you about it when I've read the proof. I accepted it blindfold. The said Gosse has promised me a set of sculptures. I am afraid he is preposterously unsound; *mais que veux-tu?* I lunched with him last Saturday (at the Savile), and we had a very pleasant talk thereby. I confessed defeat over *Diogenes* (as I did to Colvin), & told him the cause of it. He was that stumped; as well he might be. I need hardly add that I told him that 'we had projected, among other details, a Savile Club that would have lifted the roof off the establishment'. Bowles[16] & Runciman, you see, are not to be depended on; & it's as well, in a matter of this sort, to get first one on. They may never gab; but, on the other hand, they may. If they do, we had

---

[13] 'Randolph Caldecott', *Art Journal*, April 1881.

[14] Kate Greenaway illustrated *Mother Goose: or, the Old Nursery Rhymes* (1881).

[15] Gosse's poem 'The Cruise of the Rover', *Magazine of Art*, October 1882.

[16] Thomas Gibson Bowles (1844-1922), politician and founding editor of *Vanity Fair*. RLS and WEH had hoped that *Diogenes* would be published in *Vanity Fair*.

disclosed our secret for ourselves. If they don't, we have done no harm, for we have said next to nothing. I ought to add that Colvin, when I confessed our crime, suddenly ceased from beaming, & was inclined to be angry with the pair of us. In no great while, however, he began to beam once more. So, as I suppose, we are forgiven.

Did I tell you Bowles's criticism of the *Modern Arabian Nights*?[17] I forget. Anyhow, here it is. 'These,' said our adleheaded nobleman, 'these are a set of fairly clever imitations of Society Tales, obviously the work of a writer who is not one of us, & knows nothing at all about Society.' — — — And this creature edits & irons a journal, & makes £3000 per annum by it! — Such, dear lad, is life. Gosse told me a delicious story about the said T.G.B., by the way, which some day I must try to tell you. Not this trip, however. I am feeling tired & must push on.

I am afraid that Mrs. Gosse[18] is not a great writer. Like her husband, she seems capable of a good deal of misplaced admiration. Still, I intend to ask her to go on writing. She will save me some trouble, & give me a chance of being nice to Gosse (as I wish to be) forbye. I needn't add that all I've written tonight is for your private ear alone, & that not for worlds would I talk as freely as I have to anyone but R.L.S.

I shall hope to see your 'Pilgrim's Progress' soon And to have an answer (in the affirmative) to the San Francisco proposal,[19] which you may consider as formal. Will you ask Symonds please, with reference to our 'Byways & Alleys of Book Illustration' series, if he could work off a little prelection about the Anatomy of Vesalius?[20] He knows the one I mean; the one that was said to have been illustrated by Titian. This is not formal; but I should like to hear his views ere I proceed further in the matter, & enquire into the questions of propriety, facsimiles, & so forth. I have thought of him in connection with several other books; but of these I won't say anything at present. Tell him, please, that Dobson is to do Bowdler's *Shakespeare*[21] for the series, & that I am bent on working off the Delacroix *Faust*.[22] I am going to tempt Lang into the Byway (or Alley) which is blocked with Major's edition of I. Walton's

---

[17] RLS's collection of Arabian tales and short stories *New Arabian Nights*, 2 vols (1882) first published as 'Latter-day Arabian Nights', *London*, 8 June 1878 to 26 October 1878.
[18] Ellen (Nellie) Epps (1850-1929) had married Gosse in 1875. She wrote children's stories, contributed to various journals, and also exhibited paintings at the Grosvenor Gallery, 1879-88.
[19] WEH had asked RLS for an article on San Francisco. It was published as 'A Modern Cosmopolis' in the May issue of the *Magazine of Art* 1883.
[20] No article was published. Andreas Vesalius (1514-64), a Flemish physician, born Andries Van Wesel, who wrote *De Humani Corporis Fabrica Septem* [*The Seven Books on the Structure of the Human Body*], published in 1543. It is more commonly known as the *Fabrica*.
[21] This did not materialise. Thomas Bowdler (1754-1825) published an expurgated edition of Shakespeare, suitable, as he felt, for family reading, in 1818.
[22] Delacroix had produced seventeen lithographs for a French edition of Goethe's *Faust* in 1828. The article was not written.

Complete Angler.[23] Tell Symonds, please, that for any hints or suggestions from him I shall be truly grateful, & that I have in mind, & at my tongue's end, to ask him for some note on certain of the castles of Lombardy:[24] the names of them to be sent on presently.

How about a Skelt?[25] Could you write one? We want some 'Art for Children'; badly. Let me know. I will sound, & discover meanwhile. Don't write a line, or think a thought, till you hear further, as Petter[26] is a tremendous Noncon, & holds the theatre an antechamber of hell.

How did you like my Thackeray?[27] There have been onslaughts more than one upon it. One in the *World*,[28] I hear; another in a sixpenny sheet, called *Life*,[29] which is owned & edited by a Hungarian Jew, & is (very naturally) inclined to dogmatise on the question of style. This one I had the pleasure of reading for myself. Oddly enough, I had never read a line of the journal before. I picked it up by accident, took my punishment meekly, & with some amazement, & went through the journal religiously. In no great while I found myself struggling with a prose-poem upon Robert Buchanan's new novel.[30] The I began to understand the why & wherefore of my whipping. I am not sure, by the way, that Sutton[31] is not in some way or other, concerned in *Life*. It would be complete, if he were. Wouldn't it?

Herewith I send you my Dickens note.[32] Macollie[33] (the beast!) has cut it down considerably, but it's a courageous, & not ineffective, little *palidoyer* for all that, I think. I had developed the 'Dickens a great artist' thesis at greater length than it stands; & I had gone so far as to institute a comparison between him & Hugo on this head, & to prove that, as an Artist, he is infinitely the Frenchman's superior. This I take to be self-evident. It's easily demonstrable, at any rate; & I had proved it so. MacColl was, I take it, afraid of Swinburne, so that my proof had to come out. When you read, you'll see that he has been daring in no mean degree, inasmuch as, though he has shrunk from publishing

[23] John Major wrote an introduction to the 1823 edition of Izaak Walton's *Complete Angler*. Lang's article was not written.

[24] Not written.

[25] RLS's 'A Penny Plain and Twopence Coloured', *Magazine of Art*, May 1884. This was an article on Skelt's Juvenile Drama or toy theatre.

[26] George William Petter (1823-88), a partner and editorial manager at Cassell's.

[27] WEH's review of *Extracts from the Works of W. M. Thackeray*, *Athenaeum* 12 November 1881.

[28] 'What the World says', *World*, 16 November 1881.

[29] 'In and Out of Society', *Life*, 17 November 1881. WEH is attacked for his lack of clarity in style when writing of Thackeray's style.

[30] A review of Buchanan's *God and Man*.

[31] This may have been Alfred Sutton, the publisher of *London* from 15 December 1877 to 5 April 1879.

[32] WEH's unsigned review of volume three of *The Letters of Charles Dickens*, in the *Athenaeum*, 19 November 1881.

[33] Norman MacColl.

the demonstration; & rather belittled my adjectivity all over the article, he has not refrained from the comparison of Dickens with the Frenchman generally, but he has even let me do more than hint at Gautier & Hugo particularly. I am afraid that if he'd published me as I stood, there would have been war in Israel with a vengeance. I was as respectful as I could be; but I couldn't help noting that Hugo is still the Hugo of *Hernani* & the *Orientales*;[34] that in 50 years he has not learned anything, nor forgotten anything; & that at eighty years old he is as capable of attitude, of insincerity, of mendacity, of ineptitude, as he was when he put forth *Cromwell*[35] as a serious contribution to the literature of drama, & Didier, the gent in *Marion Lorme*,[36] as an essay in the manner of Shakespeare. I added that extraordinary popularity had demoralised him, & that he had got to be conscious of his own Godhead as to have contemptuous of merely human means. And I contrasted all these facts with the facts that make up the artistic life of Dickens. I think I was justified in my conclusions if I was a little premature in my argument. Don't you? Now confess you do. Confess, Ye bitch, that you wouldn't write that 'Victor Hugo Romances'[37] of yours like that nowadays. You know you wouldn't. You wouldn't be R.L.S. if you could write it. If you say me nay to all this, I renounce you. I'll have no more to do with you. And I'll jump on your next book in these journals.

Of course this is only my little jest. I know that you are with me in heart & soul in this matter, & that, whoever may cant of France & the French, you hold the even tenor of your way, & listen to nobody. To me Hugo is, like Shelley, an incarnation of the Evil Principle of Æsthetics. They may call him an Artist who will. He is really the most gigantic Amateur in history. Meredith & Swinburne monstrositical of the same type. Their idea of art is the Amateur's merely; — to be mannered, as personal, as egoistic, as eccentric, as abnormal, as one can possibly be; never to set down a sentence that, by the operation of inscription, does not become consecrate to immortality; never to deny oneself a single freak in the matter of epigram, or a single frenzy in the matter of antithesis, or a single orgasm in the matter of rhetoric; to have no law but one's appetite, no canons of compositions but one's own desires — this is to be an Artist. You can't deny it, my dear boy. It's the old dispute — the Personal V. the Absolute — embodied in a fact; & if some of our swell critics would only condescend to talk about art a little less, & think about art a little more, they wouldn't be the blind guides they are. As for me, I think, by my soul I do! old Dumas[38] [is] worth sixteen Hugos & eight & forty Gautiers as an artist, & I think Dickens even better than Dumas. And so, I believe, do you.

[34] Hugo's play *Hernani* was published in 1830 and his collection of verses in 1829.
[35] The play was published in 1827.
[36] Hugo's play *Marion de Lorme* (1829).
[37] RLS's first contribution to the *Cornhill Magazine*, August 1874.
[38] Alexandre Dumas *père*.

Truly, it's odd to find how fearfully a clever man can blunder. Symonds, for instance, gravely applies to Italian tragedy old Goethe's test of drama, & opines that as it is lacking 'in essentials of tragedy; action, that is, & the *motiviren* of each incident',[39] it is therefore a failure. Not a word about emotion, you see; not a hint of the only true essential in drama; not a suspicion that Goethe's description applies far better & far more closely to *Une Cause Célèbre*[40] than to *Othello*. 'Tis the same with Colvin & the dramatist in Landor.[41] He cannot be brought to see clearly that Landor is always Landor, & was absolutely incapable of true drama; he goes about spotting bits, & tips, & passing fancies, which mean nothing at all where they are, & would mean little even were they properly placed; & he addles his big head with the theory that Landor knew all about it, & that this sort of thing, though it isn't absolute drama, is as who should say a beginning of it, & that these scattered notions prove their author to have had in him dramatic embryonisms — dramatic ovaries, even! — not much inferior to Shakespeare. Swinburne — God bless him! — goes miles farther than Colvin, &, gravely maniacal, writes down Landor as 'a second Shakespeare' right away. Blest if I don't think honest, cautious, old Stephen — the walking negation that he is — a thousand miles nearer the truth than the nearest of 'em.

I talked with Colvin tother day, & was moved to own that Whitman, in very many ways, far stronger as a man, & far more vivifying & ennobling as an influence, than W.S.L. But he regarded me with an astonished coldness that made me feel afraid; & I made haste to change the subject.

Meanwhile, read my Dickens, & report on it, & on the Thackeray, at your leisure. I must tell you that the Dickens proof was lost in the post, so, that the article — which must have been originally some six or seven columns long, & was written & transcribed in two evenings — went to press unrevised. I wish it hadn't, for I wanted much to look it over, having been too tired to go through the *MS.* ere I sent it off. I felt sure, too, that my editor would chip, & prune, & frigg about the thing; & I meant to restore after him as much as I could. I don't say this apologetically, for I really think the thing runs smoothly in its way, & will serve its purpose as well as most Athenaeumisms; but lest you should think me more slovenly than usual, & reproach me with crimes of which I ain't guilty.

Now for a little news, & then to bed. We are all well, & we are all anxious to have good news of you. Teddy has been staying for a day or two with C.B. He has likewise been playing old Eccles (Henry's part in *Caste*, one of the most

---

[39] 'The two essentials of dramatic art, action evolved before the spectators, and what Goethe called the *motiviren* of each incident, are conspicuous by their absence.' J. A. Symonds, *Italian Literature*, vol. 5 of his *Renaissance in Italy* (1875-86), 128.

[40] A play in six acts by A. D'Ennery and P.-E. Cormon (Paris 1877).

[41] WEH is referring to Colvin's *Landor* (1881) in the English Men of Letters series.

trying games in the Robertsonian repertory)[42] &, apparently doing the thing quite cleverly & well. I think, dear lad, that he'll do, & that we shall take our whack of H. Irving Esq. in several ways. Anthony has made a great stride forward of late, & is actually painting pictures. I am more pleased than I can say with him. I really do think cheerfully of him at last. Nigel has framed the two Canalettos for your father, & very well he did 'em. I wished he had worked off your Piranesis at the same time. Your father seems very much pleased with the Canalettos, I am glad to say; & I feel very happy that I thought of asking him to accept them. Bob I haven't seen for an age; I must write to him next week. If I hadn't been so busy all this while, of course I'd have written before. Of Ferrier I heard this morning. I hadn't seen him since the beginning of my official life; & wrote off to him my first chance. He replies that he has had a haemorrhage, & is very dicky. Poor old boy! I am fond of him, & that's the truth. I hope & trust he'll mend; & I am inclined to think he will. Of Runciman I haven't heard for an age. The latest news from Rothesay Place[43] is amusing. I sent on there, to complete the drawn room decoration, Michelanglo's *Night & Twilight* — the two tremendous nudities — tremendously nude they are, *too*! From the tomb of Guiliano di Medici.[44] Mrs. B. refused to hang them in the salon; Charles insisted; it was haul devil, pull baker for many days. Charles says it was almost causing a petition for divorce. He has taken the nudities down into the smoking room, & there Mrs. B. vows & declares she nevermore will sit. He says that, if she don't, she shall sit nowhere, & if the figures were good enough for Miche, they're good enough for Charles Baxter, & his wife also. There the matter stands. The figures are colossally naked to be sure; but indecent they're not. I fear that Mrs. Baxter's sense of decency is exaggerated. I have written to make peace, & of course I have declared her absolutely justified in excluding the things from her drawing room.

How are you? How is it, my dear Mrs. Louis, that you don't secretary it a little oftener? I am ashamed of you. So is my wife. Our love to you all the same. And our love to Louis, too. How is he? Do please tell us. Not that I think you will; you'll never get so far as this; you'll stop at page 12 or so. never mind. You asked for a letter, & here one is. If you're not very good, you shall have another the very first opportunity. Meanwhile, God bless you both. We would give much to be near you.

W.E.H.

---

[42] T. W. Robertson's *Caste*, at the Theatre Royal, Edinburgh, from 24 October to 29 October 1881. Thomas William Robertson (1829-71), actor and playwright.
[43] WEH was sending various pictures to Baxter and he also seems to have been involved in advising on the decoration of at least one of Baxter's rooms (WEH to Baxter, Thursday [Autumn 1881], Yale).
[44] Michelangelo's four reclining marble figures representing the times of the day in the Medici Chapel, Florence.

To Robert Louis Stevenson, Saturday Night, 17 December 1881
ALS: Yale

51 Richmond Gardens, Shepherds Bush, W.

My dear Lewis,

I blush for my ingratitude. Of my silence I am fearfully ashamed. But I do get so damned bored with editing & jawing that when I am at last *chez moi*, which seldom comes off before four or five o'clock, I feel more bust than I can say. This is why I haven't been writing so free as I ought. I've been hoping, too, to have had news to send when I did write; & so I find myself axing [*sic*] pardon, & imploring you not to believe me forgetful & unkind.

I saw Chatto[1] on Friday, & concluded the purchase. The coins will be paid, by a bill at 3 months, the day of publication. The said bill is instantly negotiable; & if the thing is necessary, a banker will be provided who will cash on the spot.

The day of publication wholly depends on yourself. Chatto is anxious to get the book out as early next year as possible; & we only wait for the typification of the 'Pepys', & for the *MS*. of the 'Preface'. You had better write to Chatto I think,[2] & say something nice to him, as it's plain he means to be as nice as a publisher can be to you. Likewise, please, give him your new title. I have forgot it; but I told him, as an approximation, that it would be something like *Studies in Men & Books*. That was as near as I could get it. He approved of it highly.

I have Chatto in communication with C.B., as your agent; & I have asked your father to transfer his account with Clark[3] to the new publisher. So that the thing is as good as settled. I am happy to say that, so far as I know, it shouldn't cost your father a single pound.

I have more to tell. Colvin & I discussed the advisability of getting Chatto to take over your copyrights from the Keg. I broached the matter to Chatto, & found him very willing indeed to consider it. I rather fancy that, if you're that way inclined, the business may be done. What do you say?[4] Write at once, to Colvin or to me, & let us know your views. Just now Colvin is a gay Londoner, & if you thought well of the tip, it might be worked out ere he returns to Cambridge & becomes once more a Don. I shall add that he goes for the idea like fun.

If the thing were done at all, it would have to be done through your father, I

---

[1] RLS's *Familiar Studies of Men and Books* was published by Chatto and Windus in February 1882 and reviewed by WEH in the *Academy*, 1 April 1882.
[2] RLS wrote to Chatto on or about 22 December 1881 enclosing the letter with his to WEH of the same date asking him to forward it to Chatto and Windus.
[3] The Edinburgh printers R. and R. Clark.
[4] RLS agreed and Chatto and Windus finally acquired the copyright from Kegan Paul in January 1884.

think, who would take over & transfer. All depends on the price the Paul & Partner Joe put on their victims spoils. The robber-in-chief declares, I know, that the property is not worth sixpence to him; but I imagine that if we put him to the proof, it would turn out a horse of another colour. We shall see, no doubt, strange things, in fact, if we come at him practically.

That's all my business talk for the present. Except that I think it will be well for you to take to thinking out the Theatre on Style as seriously & steadily as you can; & that you won't do any harm by letting me have full proofs of *Treasure Island*,[5] when such is the will of your good editor.[6]

The 'Pilgrim's Progress'[7] is not in your best vein, I admit. Still it's a green island in my sea of misery: a place of palms, & fountains, & the song of birds in the midst of that waste & idle desert which men call the *Mag. of Art*. Colvin overlooked the slips, & suggested some changes, several of which I made bold to adopt. I am just now waiting for electros of some twenty of the cuts, & hope to have it out in my February issue. That's as much as to say that I shall be pasting it up on Monday or Tuesday next. As yet I've found out nothing about Mr. T. Conder,[8] about whom I've written to Garnett[9] at the B.M., & to Cundall likewise: both swells, & up to all sorts of tips. As it happens, the edition is no longer Bagster's. It is reissuing by a brute named Benjamin West,[10] at 2/6 (in French & English; dedicated to W. Ewart G.), at 1/0, 5d., & 1d — and, in pamphlet form, in French likewise, so an article will help it off a good deal. West has suppressed the plan of the route, & put in its place a staring *frontis* representing the Bunyan statue. He has also inserted a dithyrambic inscription in praise of W.E.G. In other respects, his issue is the same with Bagster's.

I hope to put you on the free list, & so let you see how I am working month

[5] RLS's *Treasure Island* was serialised in the children's magazine *Young Folks*, 1 October 1881-28 January 1882, in seventeen weekly instalments. WEH was instrumental in getting Cassells to publish *Treasure Island* as he acted as RLS's 'unpaid agent: an admirable arrangement for me, and one that has rather more than doubled my income on the spot' (RLS to Edmund Gosse, *Stevenson Letters*, 4, 125). WEH was also the model for Long John Silver in *Treasure Island*. 'It was the sight of your maimed strength and masterfulness that begot John Silver in *Treasure Island*. Of course, he is not in any other quality of feature the least like you; but the idea of the maimed man, ruling and dreaded by sound, was entirely taken from you' (RLS to WEH, *Stevenson Letters*, 4, 129).
[6] James Henderson (1822/23-1906), founder of *Young Folks*.
[7] 'Byways of Book Illustration: Bagster's *Pilgrim's Progress*', *Magazine of Art*, February 1882.
[8] T. Condor had drawn the pictorial 'Plan of the Road' which formed the frontispiece and RLS thought he might have done all the illustrations. In fact they were by the late Eunice Bagster, daughter of the publisher Samuel Bagster. The Art Notes for the January edition of the *Magazine of Art* confirm this.
[9] WEH wrote on 16 December 1881 (Texas). Richard Garnett (1835-1906), Superintendent of the Reading Room at the British Museum, 1875-1890, then Keeper of Printed Books, 1890-99. He was editor of the first catalogue of the library at the British Museum.
[10] *The Illustrated Polyglot Pilgrim's Progress* published by Benjamin West in 1876.

by month. I shall have a good number in March; — Lang, Colvin, Creighton, B. Champneys, & Monkhouse to the front.[11] *Qu'en penses-tu*? That is, if all comes off, as I have arranged. Which, in all probability, it won't. To these, you may add, if so disposed, Percy Fitzgerald & Mrs. Sitwell[12] — the one on 'Coalscuttles', & the other on 'Art Needlework' — & yours truly on things in general. Altogether *ça a l'air pas mal*. If I hadn't so much vile matter to work off, so much dead horse to flog into space, I would show such a clean pair of heels to Messrs. *Portfolio*, *Art-Journal*, & Co. as never were seen before.

Gosse's poem, 'The Cruise of the Rover' is really devilish good. I am much pleased, & a little surprised. Gosse & I are now, I may add, sworn friends. Dobson tells me that he's very anxious to be nice to me & — . As a matter of fact I have been as pleasant & as amiable over his poem — practically so, I mean — as I know how; & I think, dear lad, you'll confess that when I do go in for that sort of thing, I am rather a swell at it. I hear from Colvin that Gosse met Gell at dinner, & spent a long time talking of me very magnificly indeed to him. I was a little hurt by this, for some days after the conversation I had amused myself by describing Gosse to Gell, & had been anxious that I was rather on the spot in my description. I felt easier in my conscience when Gosse, in his neatest & best style, — . Still I thought it best to dish matters up a little to Gell; so I said to him, with the air of mingled candour & remorse you would have liked to see, 'By the way, Gosse is fearfully kind to me that I must ask you to forget what I said tother day of him. I don't retract a word of it (I went on) but you must forget it as soon as ever you can.' Gell, who is an intelligent creature, & very full of tact & amiability, enjoyed the jest as much, I think, as I did.

Gosse has discovered Benjamin for me. Benjamin is by no means the Hannibal Chollup[13] we had supposed. He is a mild, short, bald elderly gent who is always borrowing money, & who wouldn't (& couldn't) hurt a worm. He has filled with credit to himself, the honourable office of art-critic to the *Denver* (or *Danbury*, or *Durgan*) *Banner & Courant*,[14] I don't know the name of the place, but it's somewhere in Massachusetts. It was considered by his friends that the *Magazine of Art* was sent from heaven to relieve his wants & save their purses. *Voilà*. I am afraid the poor old boy has not much to hope for now. I feel sorry for him. Don't you? I do indeed. But he really ought to have taken the pains to learn to write something like English. It was damn artful of him, too, refusing to put pen to paper under 50 dolls., wasn't it? and giving himself out for a

---

[11] Sidney Colvin, 'A New Raphael'; M. Creighton, 'Alnwick Castle'; Basil Champneys, 'The Towers of Sir Christopher Wren'; Cosmo Monkhouse, 'The Watts Exhibition'. All these appeared in the *Magazine of Art* for March 1882.

[12] Percy Fitzgerald, 'The Coal-Scuttle from an Artistic Point of View'; [Mrs. Frances Sitwell], 'The Royal School of Art-Needlework'. WEH would have written the monthly 'Art Notes'.

[13] An American frontiersman in *Martin Chuzzlewit*. He 'was a man of roving disposition; and, in any less advanced community, might have been taken for a violent vagabond'.

[14] The *Danvers Courier*, Danvers, a weekly newspaper, 15 March 1845-1902.

regular tiger, to boot! — upon my word, if only he were a little better I wouldn't have the heart to send him packing. Editor as I am (& editing hardens the heart most fearfully), I would cherish & make much of him, & show him for the Tiger of the Tribe of Benjamin he isn't.[15]

I heard yesterday, from Payn, that you'd been writing nuts to him. 'Tis the vainest, cheeriest, kindest creature living! He seemed immensely pleased, & roared with laughter when I quoted your last letter to him. Bob I saw last night; & to day we went & heard a Razimoffsky quartet together.[16] Reis, Zerbini, & Piatti were on the spot; & I had hard work not to fall asleep. Bob & yourself have had a like experience over another Razimoffsky, I believe. The fact is Razimoffsky is my eye. Santley[17] came on next, & electrified us with a *mauvaise* romance d'Arthur Sullivan. What a gorgeous thing it is to deal with a real, right-down, tip-top Artist, isn't it? Santley also sang a *chanson Arabe* of Gounod's[18] — a very jolly, sexual business, it is — & sang it magnificently. We were enchanted. The Æsthetes, I should note, prefer Henschel[19] to Santley almost to a man; & Henschel, who's a clever fellow & a good musician, is worthy to be let cough in the same field with him. Tis another proof that to be an Aesthete is to have not a single glimmering of the meaning of Art. I needn't remind you that most of the Aesthetes batten on Chopin, & think Wagner a far greater swell, not only than Berlioz & Handel & Gluck & Bach, but than J. Beethoven himself. I met one tother day — he's not so much an Aesthete as a gent gone maniacal with translating Wagner's operas & Hugo's dramas, by the way — & he confessed that he thought it absurd to prefer Wagner to Beethoven. He said he thought them about equal. Also the Wag. might very fairly be described as Shakespeare's brother, & his work the complement of the Æschylean & Shakespearean drammy. Such, dear lad, is the Art-talk of to-day.

The truth is, the artistic intelligence & sentiment are dousid rare & the culture-mongers, holding that culture would do everything, have only succeeded thus far in bashing the cause they uphold, by according to everybody a kind of certificate of permission to believe in himself as an artistic somebody. We all have learned to jaw & to be aesthetic; and as the world is a dull & dense & idiotic world, the first ass who chooses to lift his face & bray to the four winds has as much chance of attention & respect as Colvin himself. This I can't help telling Colvin now & then. Last Sunday I swore to him that he reminded me of the prentice wizard in Goethe's ballad,[20] who knew enough of the charm to raise the devil, but not enough to lay him, & so perished

[15] A reference to the Tribe of Benjamin in the *Old Testament*.

[16] Beethoven's String Quartet in C, opus 59, known as the *Rasumovsky* No. 3, performed at St James's Hall, London, on 17 December 1881.

[17] The great baritone, Charles Santley (1834-1922), sang Sullivan's 'Thou'rt passing hence'. Santley was knighted in 1907.

[18] Gounod's 'Medje'.

[19] The baritone George Henschel (1850-1934).

[20] 'Der Zauberlehrling' in *Die Musenalmanach für 1798*.

miserably. Oddly enough, he didn't seem to see the humour of the comparison. Strange, wasn't it? Bob, too, appears to have given him some shrewd knocks at Cambridge.[21] I fear that, between the two of us, he is not always happy.

He is lecturing at the Working Men's College to-night;[22] on Walter S. Landor, no less. I hoped to have gone to hear him; but I was dead tired when I got home, & hadn't coins for cabs. So I'm writing to you instead. I feel such a tenderness towards him, & such an admiration for his very weaknesses, that I've scarce heart enough to laugh at him. God bless him, I say, for a good & true man. You were a happy gent in your first friend, dear lad; & you deserved the happiness for your willingness to share him with the likes of me.

Àpropos de Bob. He is grinding at — what? What do you think? A Book On Art!!![23] When I said I'd make him write, I didn't know how near to consummation I was. He told me of it last night. If he gets through, it will be one of the most suggestive works in literature. His difficulty is, that he can't write. But that is a difficulty that we've all had to fight, & that we've all contrived, to a greater or less extent, to overcome. Be sure that if he fails, it won't be fault of mine. Be sure, too, that he has promised communication, & that I'll have him in print ere he knows where he is. He shall lose his virginity before he's aware of it. The day I send you the proofs thereof — the bloody sheet, so to speak; the — number of the *Magazine of Art* — I shall be a proud & happy gent.[24] Do you, when you write, encourage him by taking the fact, of authorship on his part, for granted, & express all the interest you have as imperiously & matter-of-factishly as you know how. Colvin & I'll answer for the rest.

Did I tell you that the Simp is grinding hard at his novel?[25] Baxter tells me that he has read the same, & that Lady S. & her talk are simply photographically perfect. I hope to take the book to Chatto. Charles himself has started literary composition. In the intervals of aestheticism & the study of M. Angelo, he wrestles with a Digest or a Codex — I don't know which — of certain points in Scots law. Simpson says he's 'reconciling the four Gospels'; but that's a Simpsonism. Probably I shall see the pair of 'em in a month or so; as, if I possibly can, I must go north & see *Griselda*. The Jenk is hard at work

[21] Bob taught an undergraduate painting class in connection with Colvin's work as Slade Professor.

[22] The college had been founded in 1854 by the Christian socialist Frederick Denison Maurice (1805-72) and others at Red Lion Square, London, to broaden the education of working men. From there it moved to Great Ormond Street and in 1905 to Crowndale Road, Camden. Maurice was its first Principal, 1854-78.

[23] WEH seems to suggest an original work by Bob but his first published book was a translation; see WEH to RLS, 13 April 1885. His major work was *The Art of Velasquez* (1895). WEH took the lead in encouraging Bob to write rather than paint.

[24] Bob's first contribution to the *Magazine of Art* was his 'Art in France' for September 1884.

[25] Simpson did not publish a novel.

on it; &, if he had but a Marquis, would be perfectly happy. But Burnett's[26] health has given way, & he hasn't. What he'll do I can't imagine.

Katherine I know not of. She has left De Mattos & that's all I can say. Rosy Simpson,[27] who has a wonderful capacity for finding people's destiny for them, is said to have written to say how very glad she was to hear that De Mattos is now a postman in Australia: that being a kind of lay for which, by nature & passion, he is pre-eminently suited. I ought to say that I got this story from Bob, & won't vouch for the truth of it.

I have heaps to write about yet. But I must draw in; for I'm getting dead beat. We are all very anxious about you, & sorely afraid that you may be unwise enough to leave Davos. What on earth is the matter with Mrs. Louis?[28] How much we regret your & her ill plight I cannot tell you. We do hope that, ere this, you have good news of her, & that you won't hesitate to communicate it. With all you can about yourself as well. Our love to both of you, meanwhile.

The Châtelaine is a trifle wretched to-day; for the Smike[29] took himself off last night, & — contrary to his usual habits; which are exemplary — has not yet returned. We suppose him to have gone seeking some charming fair; but we are a little upset about him, as he's a model of punctuality & domesticity, & has never been away so long before. As for the doggie, he is really more intelligent & uproarious than words can express. Tell Mrs. Louis that he reflects the highest honour on her judgement. I fully expect him to prove capable of acting as my secretary & amanuensis. If he were not so hungry, & so passionately interested in grub, I believe he would ere this have taken to reading the paper to me at breakfast. His intellect alarms & astonishes me. Talking of him, I fall to thinking of the Woggs, & hoping, with all my heart, that he is healed of his hurt, & able to companion you in your loneliness.

Anthony is painting very well indeed, but is not selling. His love to you. Nigel has knocked the Jenk with a frame, & is to have photos galore from him. Joe,[30] whom I think you've seen, marries two hundred a year & a nice girl, next Tuesday. I've so much to do, & am so far behind with it, that I fear I won't be able to be at the wedding. Such is the practical translation of '10 till 1½ daily'! Ted returns to-morrow, & is away three days after, with a new engagement. Mrs. Sitwell has been very poorly indeed, but she's now better.

Warner I've not seen for an age; nor Clayton; nor Shiel Barry.[31] I never seem to have a moment's time. More than ever do I see that I was wise to decline

[26] An amateur actor Mr A. Burnett.

[27] Lady Simpson?

[28] Fanny's ill-health had puzzled the doctors and worried RLS. She was sent to Berne in December 1881.

[29] The Henley's cat named after a character in *Nicholas Nickleby* (1839).

[30] WEH's brother Joseph Warton Henley (1857-1928) married Lillie Keane at St Peter's Church, Hammersmith, London, on 20 December 1881.

[31] The actor Shiel Barry (1841-97) was born in Ireland and played in Australia before coming to England. He also toured in Canada and the United States.

absorption, & to stand for my own hand. The drama — my one passion — is miles away as it is. Where it would have lain had I sworn myself a Cassellite, I don't think. Meanwhile, the work is doing me good. I am in right health, & writing fairly well at least. The worst is, that I've no time to read & none to think for myself. I suppose I'm safe for a year. After that, we'll see. By that time I shall know what I'm worth, and, as books are coming in fast (thanks entirely to me, I am bound to say) be the owner of a very fair art library. I shall likewise have paid off a little debt. The engagement, however, is plainly not so good as I had hoped & believed; and, between ourselves, I shouldn't be excessively sorry, if I knew that with '82 it would surely come to an end.

Don't resent these confidences. I write *à coeur ouvert* & can't help saying what I feel. And don't be afraid that I shall neglect my duties. I believe in doing things well, & I shall do as well as I know how. Indeed I am not sparing myself. I am a little vexed to think that much of my labour is in vain, & that I might have been spared the most of it had my predecessors been worth their salt. I have to repair their blunders; & I don't care for the job. They seem to have edited the *Magazine* much as the most of their contributors write English; & I am putting their work into shape as I'm putting their contribution into grammar. For the dear honour's sake, you may be sure that I am not going to fail.

I had almost forgot. Of Ferrier I haven't heard these some weeks past. I fear he is ill indeed.[32] I'll write to morrow. Runciman I never see, & seldom hear from. He is, I fancy, mad with vanity, & will end wildly. Ruskin (who is quite insane at times) & he exchange long & passionate letters. He is seldom himself just now; & will presently come forth with the air of a saint released (you can see him from here!) and the *MSS.* of his novel.[33] Which, of course, is a masterpiece. He is so bent on producing his wretched individuality, that (he writes) he is 'shutting himself from the consideration of all forms of art'. Can you imagine him? He has found out his Books, he says, & when the time comes is prepared to throw the wretch over. Did I tell you that he has been writing for Morley? He has; & he says his stuff 'looks well'. I'm afraid that I'm sick of him, & that, when I think of things, I let myself be d—d angry with, & contemptuous of, his new editor. That was my great chance; & that thick-headed, clever, brilliant doctrinaire declined to let him take it. [?My] life, but for that, had been just now a good & honest game. By God, I'll not forget, nor forgive, him, while that life lasts.

How I chatter, to be sure! Here I am at the end of my fourteenth page, & heaps on heaps to say yet. I am glad to be done for the moment, as I feel myself getting melancholy & I want to cheer & hearten you as much as I can.

[32] Ferrier was an alcoholic and died of 'chronic Bright's disease' in 1883.
[33] Runciman's *Romance of the Coast* (1883).

Since I wrote of Smike, he has turned up once more, & the Châtelaine is a happy young woman again. He is safe & sound but he has the air of one who has spent a number of hours in some such seclusion as that which is afforded by a coal-hole.

Affectionately Yours,
W.E.H.

To Henry James, 12 March 1882
ALS: Harvard

51 Richmond Gardens, Shepherds Bush, W.
My dear James,
Your letter is more like passion than anything I have seen from your pen.
Of course I won't take your no for an answer. As for the Concord fachement is concerned, I will.[1] I will because I must. But I cherish the hope that you will one day contribute to the *M. of A.*[2] Why shouldn't you? I am sure that you have in your head lots of aesthetic novelettes — such, for instance, as that one which is included in the 'Madame de Mauves'[3] volumes; stories about art & artists; improvements on the *Chef d'Oeuvre Inconnu* & the *Debut dans la Vie* of the Master;[4] games that leave *Manette Salomon*[5] & things of that sort nowhere! Confess that you have; & promise me the first offer of one of them — not the longest — & I shall be happy. If you don't I shall think you not half the cosmopolitan you would have us believe.

I imagine that what you say about the incompatibility of the two nations is pretty right. But I'm not my own master. I've a sale of over 20,000[6] (another reason why you should write for me); & a great part of it is American. Consequently I am in demand to cater for Columbia, happy land, & to do as much for the home of the brave & land of the free as I possibly can.[7] I believe that the command is a mistake; & that if your people buy me at all, they buy me because I tell them not about themselves, but about the art of England — such as it is. But my orders are imperative; & I must obey them. If, therefore, you know of any American who can write well & graphically about his own

---

[1] This has not been identified.
[2] James did not contribute to the *M. of A.*
[3] 'Madame De Mauves' is one of the stories in Henry James's *A Passionate Pilgrim and Other Tales* (Boston, 1875).
[4] Balzac's *Le Chef D'Oeuvre Inconnu* (Paris, 1845) and *Un Debut dans la Vie* (Paris, 1842).
[5] Edmund and Jules de Goncourt's *Manette Salomon* (Paris, 1867).
[6] WEH's circulation figure is not clear. Is it 2,000 or 20,000? Unfortunately there are no circulation figures available for the journal.
[7] WEH is quoting sarcastically from two American patriotic songs; 'Hail Columbia' (1798) and 'The Battle Hymn of the Republic' (1862).

country, I shall be grateful for his name & address.

I have read *Numa Roumestan*:[8] not without tears. It is an admirable book. The new Zolaisms — biographical, critical, & so forth — I have not seen, nor shall I be at the pains of seeing. I hate the whole movement. It's aesthetic syphilis. And as for the heavy handed & stupid insolence of the great man himself I have a very genuine disgust. Life is really too short to waste on such experiences. I think I'll never read a line of his again.

I don't know why I'm prattling to you in this vein. I suppose that Zolaism, Wagnerism, Whistlerism — aesthetic cockneyisms generally — put me into a passion, & make me roar. I am sure that as I grow older, I grow choicer; & that the less time I have to spend, the more I want to know what's best to spend it on. Hence these oaths. If I could I would purchase the works of Dumas, & forget that naturalism ever existed. I can't get rid of the thing any more than I can get rid of the 'Genius' of Wagner, & the 'Shakespearean quality' of Hugo's plays, & the 'generous & noble humanity' of Thackeray's novels. I think I must look about for a maniac with money, & make him found a journal, in which I may gild at everything. If I don't, I may end up in Colney Hatch: a Quixote who died of suppressed adventure.

I shall be glad indeed to call on you when you return. I hope that you are well in health & active in mind, & deep in a new Mrs. Prettyman.[9]

Truly Yours Always,
W. E. Henley

'Madame Delphine'[10] seems to me a very good work indeed. A little this side of white, if anything; but excellent in no mean degree. I am not sorry to say that I found it for myself.

I shall send you our March number to-morrow. It is, I think, the best that has yet appeared; & I hope to make the new ones better still. Of course the public is a pig; & I shall probably earn a rending. But I can't help it.

---

[8] A novel by the French journalist and writer Alphonse Daudet (1840-97) published in 1881.
[9] Mrs Penniman in James's *Washington Square*.
[10] G. W. Cable, 'Madame Delphine, *Scribner's Monthly*, May-July 1882. The American writer George Washington Cable (1844-1925).

To Charles Baxter, 15 April 1882
ALS: Yale

51 Richmond Gardens, Shepherds Bush, W.

My dear Charles,

I rejoice to hear of the new baby.[1] Anna sends her love to the mother, & hopes she will be able to the see the son next week or the week after, when she purposes to be in Edinburgh. We trust that things are as well as may be. From the fact that your letter seems to have been written under the influence of strong waters, we suppose that all was right & tight. Mind you let us know if rightness & tightness are still the words. As soon as ever you like.

Yes. Louis avows that Purcel[2] is meant for Becky. If there's any greater failure in literature, I'll eat my hat. Colvin is not there. Louis says he couldn't get him right, & had to cut him out, at a cost of £1..1. I am savage when I think of this; as I am when I think of the absence of J.W.F. — who would have made a noble picture — & the presence of Becky, who has led the poor dear young man astray.

I enclose a page of the *St. Jingo's*.[3] It has some good reading in it. You will, I know admire & batten upon the third & fourth 'Notes'. Of course I come out with my primroses on the 19th, & so, of course, do you. So, I hope, will your honoured father & ditto ditto of R.L.S. The *Emigrant* himself is much bitched with Iron Dookery[4] to do anything so sane.

I am glad to know that my sentiments & yours are one concerning the Gluckisms. I'll let you know of more (not in that vein) anon. For the moment, these should be enough. You must play them many times, or you won't get them. The Morbidezza,[5] in especial, must be nicked — as to a Hair's breadth.

Write soon. I can't say more now, being in a hurry to catch the post.

---

[1] The Baxters' son, Charles Stewart Baxter, was born on 13 April 1882 and died in 1930.

[2] RLS had published his 'Talker and Talkers ' in the *Cornhill Magazine*, April 1882. This essay was a portrait of friends of RLS. Those depicted were: WEH ('Burly'), Bob Stevenson ('Spring-Heel'd Jack'), Walter Simpson ('Athelred'), Symonds ('Opalstein') Gosse ('Purcel'), and Fleeming Jenkin ('Cockshot').

[3] 'Notes', *St James's Gazette*, 15 April 1882. The third note reported that a Post Office pamphlet *Aids to Thrift* had been distributed to all factories and workplaces in the UK. A few objections were raised, the fear being that the saving of postage stamps would encourage some people to turn to crime to acquire stamps. The fourth note read: 'It is understood that the passage in Mr. Gladstone's letter to Mr. Broadhurst in which the right honourable gentleman speaks of the "great and beneficial changes in our laws which have made this country illustrious", refers more particularly to the Irish legislation of 1881.'

[4] A projected biography of the Duke of Wellington by RLS.

[5] The life-like quality of flesh in painting.

Yesterday, I got home too late to do more than read your letter, & wish you both all good luck going.

Affectionately yours,
W.E.H.

Opalstein is Symonds. I hear that Becky has been telling people it's Lang. I wonder why? She must have a motive.

Ce secret. I've sold the *Arabian Nights* for £50. As much, that is, as Louis got for the *Donkey* & the *Voyage* put together.

To Robert Louis Stevenson, 30 May 1882
ALS: Yale

51 Richmond Gardens, Shepherds Bush W.

My dear Louis,

I am horrid vexed to hear of your pickle. What in God's name has put you into it? When I last saw Mennell, he said that Mrs. Louis, as she appeared at the Great Northern,[1] was very much better; & lo! the next I hear of you is, that you are all in the Downs to an extent that cannot be expressed in words. What is the reason?

I don't hate you at all. Why accuse me of wanting so to do? O Louis, Louis! Child that you are! Am I not W.E.H., & do I not owe myself to you? Of course I oughtn't to take you so seriously, I know. For what are you if not lyrical? Egad, dear boy — you are as personal as Byron; every whit! And I'm a jackass of the right Hyrcanian breed[2] — distinguished over all for length of ear & grossness of temperament — to take any notice of you.

I got your *very* formal note this morning.[3] It came to me intact, for you had carefully addressed it to me personally. However, there's no harm done; so don't go & tear at your little wool, & think yourself the hero of a complication *à la* Merry Andrew. 'Cos you ain't. As a fact, the photos ain't good; & as another, we'll need some more. But of this anon.

As regards the Japanee,[4] I insist on you taking your own time, & I promise you solemnly that if you go on forcing yourself to work, & sending me in an article not in your good vein, I'll refuse it. I'll decline it with thanks, by God. Beware, Sir, how you palter with a desperate Editor. When you are right, well

[1] Mennell would have seen the Stevensons at the Great Northern Hotel, London, on their return from Davos en route to Scotland.
[2] Hyrcania (Wolf's Land), part of Persia.
[3] This has not survived.
[4] RLS's 'Two Japanese Romances', versions of a Japanese legend published in the *Magazine of Art*, November 1882.

& good, *je ne dis pas non*. But meanwhile, no. You've heaps of other things to do. You've your Arabians,[5] for instance, to put straight. What's more, I'm in no immediate need of the article. If I asked you for't, twas that I believed you at leisure & fit. *Voilà*. Of course I accept the 'Agricola'[6] *d'avance*; & on the same terms.

My wife is still in the West. But to-morrow she'll be in Edinburgh, & she'll call on you at once. Had she been within visiting distance, she'd have seen you before. I think she has made up her mind to see Balfour.[7] I am very anxious that she should. So if you can be at all useful in that direction, I shall be grateful. As, dear lad, for any other kindness you may be able to show her during her stay, which — unless there happen something of untoward — will last a fortnight yet.

Now I must stop: having much to do, & not feeling very fit nor very willing. I am sorefooted; & I'm languid with weather & loneliness; & I've fractured a tooth; & I've a folio to read & review in two days. Altogether I'm a gent to be pitied. I'll write again soon; & in all probability I'll be beating up your quarters in person within two months at latest. Meanwhile, — !

Yours affectionately Always,
W.E.H.

[*Added by WEH at the top of the letter*] Have you seen my current number? If not, do — please! There is good fun to be had, I assure you.

[5] *New Arabian Nights*.
[6] RLS had been commissioned to write on the woodcuts of the German metallurgist Georgius Agricola (1495-1555). It was not written.
[7] Dr George William Balfour, L.R.C.S. (1823-1903), RLS's uncle.

To Robert Louis Stevenson, 19 September 1882
ALS: Yale

4 Clifton Gardens, Margate[1]

My dear Louis,

Frankly, I'm not pleased with you. I think it's unkind of you to be spreeing about in Paris, with Bob,[2] & me at Margate — in the rain, & *tiraillé* by the *Magazine of Art*.

Then, I consider it scandalous of you not to have taken Margate on your way to Dover,[3] or — failing that — to have bidden me up to town for the night.

[1] The Henleys were on holiday.
[2] Bob accompanied RLS to the south of France to find a suitable spot for Fanny and RLS.
[3] RLS was not well and Fanny had been left ill in Edinburgh. RLS was just passing through

This, as you're away for the winter, & we shall meet no more on this side of '83. Which I think beastly. Especially when there was so much to be talked about; & as you are, on business matters, about the worst correspondent that ever draw the breath of life. I know now the scent of Baxter's agonies & sweats — confound you!

Let me add, that in my opinion, you shine even less as a corrector of proofs than as a writer of business letters.

However, you always were a dam heggoist; & a dam heggoist you always will be. *Violà*!

I notice now that whenever you send me bad reports of your health, somebody instantly contradicts them. Thus Hake[4] pursued you to the club & learned from Middlemore[5] that you are looking famous. And I get the gayest accounts of you from the archangel besides.

Is Bob your travelling companion to the Riveria or Majorca? Let me know; as I may be able to arrange a little work in collaboration for you. You neither of you deserve it, you dogs; but d—n you, I love you with all my heart, & I should like very much to yoke you together to my chariot. If Majorca is the place, I shall think very seriously of the matter. What fun for you to be in Majorca! Why ain't you Chopin? and why haven't you a George Sand?[6] The ides of letting two such Uxorious Billies[7] loose in the tracks of G.S. is as about as comic as they make 'em.

How I wish I were with you! I wanted above all things to see the Louvre & Luxembourg with Bob, this year; & lo & behold! he has seen them, & I have not. Tell him, I shall expect much information when he returns; & that if he hasn't got me up a good Rousseau I'll kill him. A good Rousseau at least. And Ehe a Courbet, and a Delacroix. [*rest of letter missing*].

[*Added by WEH at the top of the letter*] Did you see yourself placarded in the *World*?[8]

London. In a reply to this letter RLS said that 'whatever appearances may have been' he 'was far from well' and that he had 'carried the art of spitting blood to a pitch not previously dreamed of in my philosophy' (*Stevenson Letters*, 4, 12).
[4] The journalist and writer Alfred Egmont Hake was a member of the Savile Club.
[5] Samuel George Chetwynd Middlemore (1848-90), journalist and member of the Savile Club. He was the translator of Jacob Burckhardt's *Die Kultur de Renaissance in Italien*.
[6] The French novelist George Sand (Baronne Dudevant) (1804-76) who formed a liaison with the composer Chopin and lived with him in Majorca.
[7] RLS had called himself 'Uxorious Billy' in a comic poem to Fanny the previous month.
[8] A comment in the *World*, 6 September 1882. The writer notes that similarities abound between works and cites RLS's 'Suicide Club' (*New Arabian Nights*) and a story by Charles Collins for a Dickens Christmas number.

To Austin Dobson, 18 October 1882
ALS: London

Magazine Of Art, London

My dear Dobson,

There is no objection to Miss Greenaway's terms.[1] We shall be glad to give her £10 for the page design, & to return the original. Of course, the thing must be appropriate & good; or we shall have to return it.

Will you tell Miss Greenaway all this, & encourage & counsel a little in her work? As the author of the verse she has to illustrate, you can approach her much more nearly & directly than we; & I feel sure that she will — you aiding — succeed quite brilliantly.

What we want, as you know, is some 'Mother Goose' in monochrome & more or less in outline. If we get that, we shall be content.

Very Faithfully Yours,
The Editor.

Austin Dobson Esq.

[1] Kate Greenaway illustrated Dobson's poem 'Home Beauty', *Magazine of Art*, May 1883.

To Robert Louis Stevenson, Friday [22 December 1882]
ALS: NLS

[12 Salem Street], Bradford[1]

Dear Lad,

As I expected, the proof cannot be received as final. As I did not expect, a great many good qualities revealed themselves. Crichton[2] declines to pronounce an opinion until after Saturday night, when — with an understudy of the Deacon — the piece will be tested on an audience three thousand strong.[3] I shall hear of this anon. Meanwhile, I will give you my own impressions.

We had everything against us. Crichton had been unlucky in his attempts at casting us appropriately & well. Nobody had come, & substitutes had to be

[1] WEH had lodgings here while attending the rehearsals of *Deacon Brodie* at Pullan's Theatre of Varieties.
[2] The actor-manager Haldane Crichton (1852-1938), who also played Smith. Crichton had offered to produce *Deacon Brodie* and then to tour with it. RLS and WEH gave him sole provincial rights for a year.
[3] This seems an unusually large number but WEH mentions it in a letter to Baxter (Thursday Night [21 December 1882], Pierpont Morgan). The play was produced on 21-23 December 1882.

found at the last moment. None of them knew his part, none of them looked his part; some — Bretton,[4] for instance were rehearsing pantomimes elsewhere. The stage at Pullan's is lightless, & was so dark that at times I could not follow my book; for the weather is bad & gloomy, & we could only get the people together in the afternoon. Then there were no properties & no scenery; no chair could be found for Old Brodie; no windows at the back could be put up for Leslie's & the Deacon's; the limelight wouldn't work; Leslie's door shut to in the midst of one of his most important speeches; & twice did the curtain fall a half-minute too soon — at the end of the third & fourth acts; the Procurator bungled his scene with the Deacon; Mary left a candle burning on the Deacon's table, & it was discovered within the empty room, waiting the broken door; Moore had to leave the stage during the scene at Clarke's, & Smith & Ainslie had to share his words for some few speeches; Smith did low comedy business in & out of season, sat down during Moore's defiance, made the audience laugh at the Deacon's downfall, & introduced several impertinent gags, and failed to score off our own with a quite depressing regularity; Mary & Jean were all but inaudible for the carpenters behind; & so forth. Then , the night was the worst of all the three hundred & sixty-five — the night on which the theatrical flood is at lowest ebb; the night between the season & the pantomimes. The audience was wretchedly cold & miserably thin. And for three minutes my heart stood still, & flight seemed beautiful & full of honour. Then, however, I lit a cigarette, & saw the curtain rise. And the play began.

I felt at once that I was well astride the thing & could look on pretty calmly. This feeling I never lost. Even the voice of Smith — which was like unto that of a cheap-jack — though it made me long for dynamite, did not succeed in making me a partizan. I watched the thing from end to end; & I believe that my behaviour under fire was good. I can assure you that I felt as cool as if I had been sitting in judgement upon a Byronism or an Adelphi melo. I incline from this to auger well of my future failure. I was born to be d—d; the Almighty who is responsible for my virtues & for me, could hardly have fitted me so well for endurance if he had not intended me to endure.

This, however, is by the way. The play's the thing just now. It was most ineptly done. Bretton took the Deacon at top speed, as if, 'hurry hurry' were indeed the road to safety, & played in a boisterous rough & ready way, with a certain rough & tumble energy & swagger, that were on the whole effective. He carried our fortunes on his shoulder; & though he bore himself too spasmodically & noisily, he pulled us fairly through. His absence was a loss & his presence a gain — no end! Mary was vulgar & inefficient; Leslie worked hard, but couldn't get up to the passion pitch; the Procurator, a lad of talent, approved himself a kind of actor; Smith, as I've said, did cheap-jack all the which — much to his satisfaction; Moore looked thin, & spoke sluggishly & with effort; Ainslie was English & inoffensive; Jean was inoffensive &

---

[4] E. W. Bretton played Deacon Brodie.

English; Hunt, an actor of the Hawtree[5] type, was more unlike a Bow St. Runner than one can be expressed in words; Old Brodie tried his best, & didn't come off. *Voilà.* There was never such a hodgepodge of blundering since time began.

But the play, dear lad, is a veritable play. It stood the strain superbly. The action moved on from point to point with a vigour & an assurance that surprised me. From situation to situation; from climax to climax; over bungle after bungle the interest advanced & grew. There was not a speech too much; but there were places where the speeches seemed too few. And at last, when the curtain had fallen on the Deacon dead, I was able to tell myself that my point was proved, & that we had really made a brilliant & practical play.

This was made clear to me by several circumstances. This among the number. At Pullan's we are an audience a-part. We are mostly mill hands, & we have a habit, no matter who, is on the stage, of dispersing at ten o'clock. Not even George Leybourne (it is said) can give us pause; for we have to be up at four & five in the morning, & we must early to bed. We smoke, too, steadily; & we have a habit, when we are displeased, of calling down the curtain. Now the Deacon did not begin this life before eight o'clock, & did not retire to the privacy of his dressing room until a quarter to eleven. When he did, not a soul had stirred. They didn't stay to applaud him; but till the curtain fell he fixed & held 'em. This (my landlady tells me) is *ironic*; only *The Green Lanes of England* has the same virtue.[6] Again, during the last tableau, *no pipes were lit*; the smokers were spectators &, their heads thrust forward, they followed their Deacon keenly till the end. At certain moments you might have heard a pin drop; Pullan,[7] the great Pullan, was seen looking on for the first & only time in history; none went out during the acts but returned as soon as the *entracte* music ceased from sounding. These facts, noted with wonder by old habitues of Pullan, were not communicated to me until I had formed my opinion of our merits. They rather confirmed me in it than otherwise.

The second act was loudly applauded, & the players had a recall; the third act was bungled, as I've said, but a recall was attempted; the fourth was listened to in desperate silence. The first was merely applauded; not very warmly. I felt that the Mary-Deacon scene in Act II was abominably short, & that in breaking off at 'what have you done' (Oh! so vilely said) you had been badly inspired. I also felt that a Leslie-Mary scene, before the Deacon's last entrance, would be an improvement, & a great one. The repulsiveness of the last tableau was not felt; Bretton, very judiciously, threw a touch of mania into his hysterics, I am convinced that the part thus read, would, if properly played,

[5] Charles Henry Hawtrey (1858-1923), actor, theatre manager, playwright and director. His most successful play was *The Private Secretary* (1884) which ran for two years. He was knighted in 1922.
[6] A play by George Conquest (1837-1901) and Henry Pettit (1848-93).
[7] The theatre manager Henry Pullan (?1816-1903).

produce a really tremendous effect. My landlady & her daughter owned to a touch of creepiness, but swore they would be delighted to go again & again. They also remarked that everybody in their party had been interested to know the end, & that nobody had been able to give a guess which was anything near the truth. They added that they'd never seen anything like it before. On the whole, they were fearfully fetched by it. I noted too that the *Observer* critic — a pompous young facetist & writer of — pantomimes — forgot to be captious during this last tableau; & when I remarked to him that the play was, after all, alive was uncommon ready to agree with me.

I saw Bretton after all was done, & smoked a pipe with him. He believes there's a future in the play, but as Crichton has got it, & as Mrs. Crichton & Mrs. Bretton do not agree, he plays it to-night — in all probability — for the last time. Crichton, himself, as I've said, refuses to pronounce an opinion until Sunday morning. For myself, I am devilish glad that the ice is broken, & that I've seen for myself that the play not only stands square on its feet, but moves at a d—d sight better pace — a pace unconceivably swifter & surer than that of any melodrama I know.

I hoped to go again to-night, when there will probably be a better house & a better performance. But I find that I've made a mistake in my trains, & that I must leave at 9.20 — an hour hence — instead of 11.15. So that, as far as I'm concerned, you'll hear no more.

To this I'll add no more than that I talked long with Crichton this morning, & that it is his intention, if Saturday is satisfactory, to produce the play, with a special company, & as many perfect rehearsals as he can give me, in Aberdeen; about April, '83.[8]

I wish my news were better. As I have felt it, however, it is good enough. We had every thing against us — season, theatre, company, scenery, audience; & we have rather won than lost, and at the worst we have fought a drawn battle.

Affectionately Yours,
W.E.H.

Crichton's theory of drama is this: 'No play is worth tuppence unless it has an abundant low comedy.'
[*Written by WEH vertically through paragraphs four and five*] The modern world is subject to many delusions.

---

[8] *Deacon Brodie* was produced at Her Majesty's Theatre, Aberdeen, from 16 April to 21 April 1883 and at the Royal Princess's Theatre, Glasgow, on 25 June 1883. It was produced some forty times in Scotland and the North of England during the summer of 1883.

To Robert Louis Stevenson, 1 March 1883
ALS: Yale

                                        51 Richmond Gardens, Shepherds Bush, W.
My dear Louis,
   Just a few lines. Not a letter. That's always impossible. Try & give me a
right answer, for it's mostly business.
   (1) Describe 'Labor'.[1] I don't seem to know it. If I like it, I will engrave it
for the *M. of A.*
   (2) Try & draw me your idea of 'The Wind'.[2] I've a mind to ask the
Greenaway, or the Caldecott, to work it off for me; & I should like to send him,
or her, your own idea. (3) Let me hear from you on the subject of Johannes
Agrippa,[3] or whatever is his name. I want a 'By-Way' badly. Dost hear? *Badly.*
   (4) They are bent on making me publish (a) A Volume of Verse; (b) a
selection from the *London* 'Novelists'.[4] The latter will be called *The
Posthumous Works of John Libbel,*[5] or something of that sort; *Edited with notes
by A. Egmont Hake, & with a Biographio-Critical Preface, by R. L. Stevenson.*
It will be published by a new publisher of whom more anon (& on whose
account I may possibly demand of you an introduction to Geo. Meredith); &
what I want to know is,' Will you look over the slips, & correct me as to
propriety & impropriety? and will you, if publication seems advisable,
undertake the memoir?' As you see from here, it will be a famous *blague*; and I
think we should have sport out of it.
   Did I tell you that 'Millet As An Art Critic' was translated *en feuilleton* for
the *Courier du Soir*?[6] and that the Editor asks for more? Did I tell you (no I
didn't that I am asked to make one — with Benedict, Sullivan, Stainer, Cusins,
Hallé,[7] & others — of the Berlioz Statue Committee? Such is life!

[1] Millet's *L'Homme à la Houe*. In a letter to WEH RLS had remarked that he had 'suddenly
beheld an etching of "Labor", and I fell off my horse and am being treated for scales' (late
January 1883, *Stevenson Letters*, 4, 62).
[2] WEH published RLS's three poems 'The Land of Counterpane', 'The Wind' and 'The Cow'
under the heading 'A Child's Fancies' in the *Magazine of Art*, July 1884. It was not illustrated.
The three poems were published in *A Child's Garden of Verses*.
[3] Georgius Agricola.
[4] WEH ran a series of forty-two 'Living Novelists' in *London* from 28 July 1877 to 11 May
1878, with concluding articles in the next two issues. The proposed book was not forthcoming.
[5] John Libbel was a joke name invented by Bob Stevenson. He and RLS developed the concept
of 'Libbelism'. RLS used the name as a signature in some letters to WEH.
[6] WEH's 'Millet as an art-critic,' *Magazine of Art*, January 1883. Neither I nor the Bibliothèque
National de France have been able to find the French version.
[7] A committee had been formed in France to subscribe for a monument on Berlioz's tomb. A
subcommittee was formed in England. Among its members were: Julius Benedict (1804-1885),
German composer; Sir John Stainer (1840-1901), composer and organist at St Paul's Cathedral,
London, 1872-88; Sir William George Cusins (1833-93), pianist, organist, violinist and
conductor; and Sir Charles Hallé (1819-95), German-born pianist and conductor, founder of the
Hallé Orchestra in 1858.

Somehow, or other, we must meet, & work off a new play. When? how? where? at whose expense? *Voyons, voyons*! It must be done. Must's the thundering word! But where? when, how? at whose cost — ? Ah, there you floor me! What's to be done with a collaborator whose bright home is the rising sun? *Ein Fichtenbaum steht einsam* is the situation exactly.[8] Meanwhile, I can see that letter writing is no good. I can also see that, we must finish *Old Glory*. That I must renounce journalism, in a word, & play King Log[9] at Belle Sauvage Yard, and leave King Stork to perish. But how? where? when? at whose expense? Ah, *voyons*! [*rest of letter missing*].

[8] Heine's two stanza poem number XXXIII in his *Buch der Lieder* (Hamburg, 1827).
[9] A spiritless king in one of Aesop's fables.

To Charles Baxter, 7 May 1883
ALS: Yale

Magazine Of Art, London

My dear Charles,
    Send me Louis's agreement with Henderson, in re *Treasure Island*.[1] Or a copy of it. I hope in a few days to place to his credit with you £100: for the said *T.I.* But of this anon.
    Mum, meanwhile.

Yours ever,
W.E.H.

How go the grouse? And the H.C's?[2] Princes Street (to judge by my feelings) must be perfectly honey-crushed with 'em.

[1] The agreement for the publication of *Treasure Island* in *Young Folks*. The book was published on 14 November 1883 by Cassell's and RLS received £100 (£50 for signing and £50 when the book was passed for press) in advance of royalties.
[2] Horse chestnut trees in Princes Street, Edinburgh.

To Robert Louis Stevenson, 14 July 1883
ALS: Yale

51 Richmond Gardens, Shepherds Bush, W.

Dear Lad,

Your 'Fontainebleau' is delicious.[1] You are the boy that can write! To read you gives me all the pleasure in life; & all the pain. I felt this time as though I'd never write again. I did, indeed.

I should. like to use you up at once; but it will take some time to get off the pictures. Anthony can hardly go before the early autumn.[2] So you can trot on with the 'Skelt' & 'Hokusai' as soon's you like.[3]

Is your *Otto* fit for a decent, sponsible, God-fearing picter-book?[4] If it is, there's a chance — if you don't mind — of my editing it; as a supplement to the *Magazine of Art*; in monthly issues.

I've ceased from making money; that, to say, I've had nothing in the *S.R.* for a fortnight; & I'm disgusted with life

Baxter has begun upon the Keg. I shall oblige him to render us an account. You see if I shan't. My object is, to get the three books out of his hands,[5] & republish them *chez* Chatto. I shall propose to buy them of the original Villain as remainders, & come on you, or your stern Parent, for a cheque for the amount. Then I shall sell the stock to Chatto, for its market value *plus* something handsome for the rights of publication. How does that suit your figure? Of course, the negotiation with Paul will be carried on in your name by Messers Mitchell & Baxter.

Ere this, I hope, you'll have received your copy of the *Paradox*,[6] for which, dear Lad, you must do what you can with the *Century*. Of course the dedication — as Hake himself was first to say — should have been mine. But that's nothing. The thing is to make it a success. The Wollock, & I, I should add, are not so thick as we were awhile ago. To get him to treat his knee in any otherwise than maniacally, I had to be as brutal & trenchant as I could. It hurt him very much & frightened him still more; & I think (but don't know) that he resents it. 'Tis a nice fellow, a good fellow, a clever fellow; but a reed — a reed, boy! I almost despair of him. In Hake & myself he has two such men at

---

[1] RLS's 'Fontainebleau: Village Communities of Painters' which was published in the *Magazine of Art*, May 1884 and June 1884.

[2] Anthony Henley went to France to produce illustrations for RLS's article.

[3] The essay on the Japanese artist Katsushika Hokusai (1760-1849) was not written.

[4] RLS replied: 'As thus, it is *very* moral, very, quite in my highest vein; of a nice morality, stap my vitals' (17 or 18 June 1883, *Stevenson Letters*, 4, 143). WEH did not publish RLS's *Prince Otto* but instead sent the manuscript in August 1884 to Andrew Chatto who published it the following year.

[5] The three books were *Travels with a Donkey*, *An Inland Voyage* and *Virginibus Puerisque*.

[6] Diderot's *Le Paradoxe sur le Comédien*, translated as *The Paradox of Acting* (1883) by Walter Herries Pollock.

his back as never in his life have been interested in him before. But I doubt he's incurable. However, we must hope for the best.

I saw him on Sunday *en famille*. Everything was explained. I breathed an atmosphere of childish vanity. Lady Pollock, Sir Frederick, the noble Maurice, Walter himself — oh, it was pitiful![7] As I drove home, I abandoned hope. I concluded that a vanity found in such a temperature & manured in such a mixen would prove too strong for me. Since then, I've a little got back my spirits. But, as I've said, the confidence I had is pined & peaky. Still, I mean to do my best.

Here would be a place for a comparison of opportunities; for a contrast between my own & other cases; for a trotting out of all sorts of might-have-beens, an enquiry into all sorts of destinies. Don't, on my account, treat with Gilder[8] at second-hand, but directly — from man to man. In spite of his bounce, the Becky[9] knows, or knew, nothing of the price you were to receive for the *Squatters*.[10] *The very first time he found himself alone with me, he asked me what you were going to get.* Remember this; & remember that you may have as much as you like. American prices are very different things from ours. Howells[11] or James or Cable could get £16 per page from Gilder for a *Squatters*. Your name is rising daily — will soon be on a level with theirs. Do you know that Howells asked, & got, a hundred pounds of Longman for that trumpery 'Lexington' thing of his in the first number of the *Magazine*?[12] If you don't feel equal to sticking up for yourself, turn the whole thing over to me; & I'll see that you make some money.

When I think of Paul, I am a little inclined to go & be a hermit at once. Fortunately or unfortunately, I can't afford to work off the drama. That leaves me no alternative but fighting. When I read his reply to Baxter's first letter, I vowed vengeance; & by God I'll have it.

I have been little at the club of late. I paid off a lot of debt this month, & left myself almost penniless. I think it was a mistake. I ought to be able to clubbize at least once a week. In the autumn I shall be more regular. I propose, as I think I told you, to spend the first few days of my holiday in bed — to get rid of that prolapsus (Mennell aiding), & become a new man. After that, I'll go seawards, & refresh me. After that, I'll emerge, & contrive a campaign to some purpose.

---

[7] Lady Juliet Pollock (1819/20-99), *née* Creed, wife of the author and lawyer Sir (William) Frederick Pollock, Bt (1815-88). Maurice Emillius Pollock (1857-1932), a brother of Walter.

[8] Richard Watson Gilder (1844-1909), American poet, and editor of the *Century* from 1881 until his death.

[9] Gosse was the English representative of the *Century*.

[10] RLS's 'The Silverado Squatters: Sketches from a Californian Mountain,' *Century Illustrated Monthly Magazine*, November 1883 and December 1883. RLS was paid £40 by Gilder.

[11] William Dean Howells (1837-1920), American novelist and journalist was editor of the *Atlantic Monthly*, 1871-81. He wrote the monthly 'Editor's Chair' in *Harper's Magazine*.

[12] Howells's 'Lexington', *Longman's Magazine*, November 1882.

Next year, if you're better — as God send you may be — we'll have at the drama once more.

Not, though, at the *Deacon*. That I refuse to touch. It is what it is; & it shall remain so for me. There is in it the germ of a new formula which — in the teeth of Cockshot & all his kind — I purpose to consider later on. It is vain to *escamoter* the Ugly. It's an essential in modern art; it is to us, perhaps, what the Beautiful was to the Greeks. Balzac has spoken, & Goethe, & Dickens. The Shakespeare of to morrow will take for his hero, not Othello, but Iago. The heroics of iniquity, the epic of immorality, the drama of vice — *voilà la vraie affaire*. In fifty years the *Deacon*, if we had but done it, might be a great work. We are syphilised to the core, & we don't know it. Zola is our popular eruption, as Balzac was our primary source. Presently, we shall get to our tertiaries; & the Ugly will be as the Beautiful, & *Esther Noble* will tragic & acceptable.

Meanwhile, I've an idea of another sort. I am on the track of a series for Cassell: — a series of Masterpieces of English,[13] to be edited by myself, & to be selected & prefaced & prepared by the men of my own generation. God knows if the idea will ever come to anything. If it does, I will show John Morley, & the bloody Radicals generally, that we are quite as good as they are. Swift I think in connection with Sainsbury;[14] Bacon, with Fred Pollock; Congreve, with the editor; Hazlitt, with R.L.S.; Gray, with Becky; Dryden, with David Hannay — a man you'll like to know; Borrow, with Hake; Richardson, with R.L.S.; Keats, with S.C. — the patriarch of the race. What do you think of it my son? Don't it smile on you? Some twenty or thirty volumes; comely to look at, agreeable to handle & read; each one the apotheosis of a masterpiece of English!! Let me hear your views when you write; & wish me all the fortune I deserve meanwhile.

Colvin's appointment[15] is a great joy to us. The poop, Wedmore & the mule, Stephens,[16] have shed tears over the retiring Reid; but that's nothing. The Print-Room is merely chaos. With the Archangel[17] at work, & *Fiat Lux* going forth

---

[13] A projected series of selections from major authors prefaced by modern writers. It did not materialise.

[14] The series was to have included Saintsbury on the poet and satirical writer Jonathan Swift; Sir Frederick Pollock on the philosopher Francis Bacon; WEH on William Congreve; RLS on the essayist and critic William Hazlitt and on the novelist Samuel Richardson; Gosse on the poet Thomas Gray; the journalist and naval historian David Hannay (1853-1934) on John Dryden; Alfred Egmont Hake on the traveller and writer George Henry Borrow (1803-81); and Colvin on John Keats.

[15] Colvin had been appointed Keeper of Prints and Drawings at the British Museum in July 1883 on the retirement of George William Reid (1819-1887).

[16] Frederick Wedmore (1844-1921), short-story writer and art critic. Knighted 1912. Frederic George Stephens (1828-1907), art critic for the *Athenaeum*, 1861-1901. He was a contributor to the *Magazine of Art*.

[17] Colvin.

continually from his lips, it'll presently be the institution it ought. Which is saying much.

Too dark to write any more, & a man waiting besides.

15 July 1883

This morning the Archangel breakfasted here. He looks well & happy as he deserves. He is booked for articles in my September & November issues.[18] I gave him your 'Fontainebleau', which he proceeded to revise & correct with great spirit & determination. He will send you on the set of slips; to digest at your leisure.

I've been hacking & hewing at Hake's *Story of Chinese Gordon*.[19] I can't yet say if it will do, or not. It has cost him a great deal of trouble; but it has been written against time. I don't think he should have attempted it under two years. But we shall see.

At the last Rabelais dinner but one I met Dew Smith.[20] He sought me out, & I feel disposed to like him. 'Tis a humorous bird, &, I should think, a good fellow.

I read nothing now. I am living on my capital & far from satisfied with the life. I seem always to have something to do & never to have done anything. In the next world we shall make plays, & have Shakespeare & Molière to sit at our first nights. At least I like to think so. Don't you? The prospect's a pleasing one; but you mustn't let it hurry you out of this world ere your time. On the contrary, you must take the very greatest care of yourself, & rush as little upon disaster as is consistent with the principles of a romantic life.

Farewell. Write soon. I had heaps more to say; but I've forgot 'em all. In my next, news (I hope) of Skelt.

Yours ever, dear lad,
W.E.H.

[*Added by WEH at the top of the letter*] Read Maxime du Camp, *Souvenirs Littéraires*,[21] if only for the pages on old Dumas. They will warm your heart. They have mine, I know.

---

[18] Colvin's 'Pictures in the Fitzwilliam Museum. II. Adam Elsheimer', *Magazine of Art*, September 1883 and 'Pictures at Palace Green', December 1883.

[19] Hake's *The Story of Chinese Gordon* (1883). Gordon was a cousin of Hake's. General Charles George Gordon (1833-85) was known as 'Chinese Gordon' after his exploits in China.

[20] Albert George Dew-Smith (1848-1903), skilled amateur photographer, and fellow member of the Savile Club.

[21] Maxime du Camp (1822-94), French journalist and novelist, and friend of Flaubert. His *Souvenirs Littéraires* was published 1882-83.

To Charles Baxter, 18 August 1883
ALS: Yale

[51 Richmond Gardens, Shepherds Bush, W.]

My dear Charles,

I hope to get away about September 6*th*. Next week I propose to get to bed & deliver up my fundament to the knife of Mennell.[1] After that I finish off my number; & then hay for the month.

Whether I'll can come or not & stay remains to be seen. Are you aware, Sir, that I am a married man? that your invitation seems addressed to me only? that you appear to ignore the existence of Madame? O imbecile! O block head!! O Ass!!! If you really want me to come & stay with you, is *that* the way to have your wish?

Ever yours,
W.E.H.

[*Added by WEH at the top of the letter*]
I'm 34 next Thursday!!
Ted was 22 yesterday!!![2]
Why was I not an actor!!!!

[1] The exact nature of the operation is not known though it may well have been for piles. WEH remarked later to Baxter that his prostate was bruised in the operation (19 October 1883, Yale).
[2] E. J. Henley was born on 17 August 1860.

To Andrew Chatto, [9] October 1883
Telegram: Yale

Edinburgh 11.38   Piccadilly 12.17 Oct 83
W. E. Henley, 7 Rothesay Place, Edinburgh
Andrew Chatto, 214 Piccadilly, London

Am arranging English copyright of Stevensons book[1] what date of publication in England will be best for you.
[*Reply in Chatto's hand*] Telegraphed reply same date. Almost any date will suit us for Stevensons book provided copyright is secured by first publication in England.

[1] English copyright was secured by issuing on 17 October 1883 (in an edition of ten copies) the November instalment from the *Century Magazine* in pamphlet form in advance of the publication of the magazine. *The Silverado Squatters* was published by Chatto and Windus on 8 January 1884.

To Charles Baxter, 4 December 1883
ALS: Yale

[51 Richmond Gardens, Shepherds Bush, W.]
My dear Charles,

It wasn't drink. It was haste & a bad pen.

And now to answer your letter categorically.[1]

(1) Hard up is all jimmy. *I* am hard up. You! — oh!!!

(2) Right you are. So am I. And Lewis will die if we fail.

(3) Let your creditors wait. Who are they that they shouldn't?

(4) D—n it. So you shall. An so will I.

(5) No! Oh no! That you will Not. Or if you do, you will alone. The 26*th* of this month is my eye. I can't do it. Say January 5*th*, & I'm on it bigger than an Injun. You see, the *M. of A.* has to appear; & by the 5*th* it will be all right. By the 26*th* it cannot.

(6) Yes — Good. But 5*th* Jan. in lieu of 26*th* December; and Henley will meet you for Paris morning mail.

(7*th*) 'We reach Paris that morning, & start same night for Marseilles.' Do we? yes! Well?

(8*th*) 'We reach Hyères' — True, true. As you were going to say.

(9*th*) 'We will stay four or five days & then return as before.' O D—n your sentiments.

(10*th*) I shall write to Mitchell,[2] & make it all right with him? of course I shall. What do you take me for.

So there you are. I agree to everything but the 26*th* December. That, as you see, is jimmy. If I'd a good side it might be so. But I've nobody but myself; & the exhibitions are heavy; & I must get off as much of the Magazine as I can ere I may depart & be free. So there you are.

I've given way to you in all besides. You must give way to me in this. Write & say you do.

In Paris, I've to see Coquelin, Rodin, Régamey, & W. C. Brownell.[3] *And to compare the Boulevard Sebastopol & the Bois de Boulogne with the sunny side* of Princes St. on a morning after a *nicht wi' Brown*. So you must give me at least a day, either coming or going.

---

[1] Baxter and WEH were planning to visit the Stevensons at their home, the Chalet La Solitude, Hyères, in southern France. They were at Hyères by 8 December 1883 and returned home before 20 January 1884.

[2] William Mitchell, Baxter's partner in the Edinburgh law firm.

[3] The well-known French actor Benôit Constant Coquelin (1841-1909). Probably the French artist Felix Régamey (1844-1907). William Carey Brownell (1851-1928), American writer and journalist who contributed to the *Magazine of Art*, and was editor of *Scribner's Magazine*, 1888-1928.

See *Athenaeum & Academy* of Sat. last for more puffs of *T.I.*[4] I expect a big one from the *P.M.G.* this week; & another from the *S.R.*[5] I hear, too, that the *Guardian* doats on the book; & that he'll give us a flamer.[6] Do not, I pray, neglect to bring all these beneath the eyes of Tom Stevenson, Gent, & to remark to him how little he knows about literature.

Ever yours, my dear Charles,
W.E.H.

Brown turned up on Saturday night. He abused Kirkhope's whisky; said it was wasted for the London market — I think to excuse himself beforehand for taking a lot of it. But I was obliged to dismiss him; for I [?wick] to the throat. I heard some pleasantries of you.

[4] An unsigned review by the Italian scholar Arthur John Butler (1844-1910) in the *Athenaeum*, 1 December 1883. The *Academy* reviewer of 1 December 1883 has not been identified.
[5] WEH's unsigned review of Stevenson's *Treasure Island* for the *Saturday Review* was that of 8 December 1883. In a letter to RLS he writes: 'Next week I hope to trot you over some notices of *Treasure Island*. Lang is after it for the *P.M.G.*; I, for *the S.R.*; a friend for the *Academy*; Runciman for the *Standard*. I think it will be a hit.' (25 November 1883, Yale). Lang reviewed it in the *Pall Mall Gazette* on 15 December 1883.
[6] The book was reviewed in the *Manchester Guardian* on 15 December 1883.

To Charles Baxter, 29 January 1884
ALS: Yale. Part published in *Stevenson Letters*, 4, 235-6.

[51 Richmond Gardens, Shepherds Bush, W.]
My dear Charles,
   Much thanks for your enclosure.[1] I return them all herewith.
   Simp, I fear is lost. But that, no fault of ours. Let us wipe it up & say no more about it.
   Colvin & I & Anna rejoice greatly to know the worst is over. Your telegram frightened me damnably. I thought it was for to receive his last wishes that Bob was called. To find that it's to help move him to Hyères is an immense relief.
   I got your telegram at eleven. I at once went round to Ionides,[2] & borrowed

[1] RLS had been taken ill at Nice as soon as Baxter and WEH had left. RLS was suffering from 'congestion of the lungs and kidneys' (Fanny Stevenson to Charles Baxter, *Baxter Letters*, 132). Presumably one of the enclosures would have been Fanny's letter to Baxter, received on 27 January 1884, complaining that she had not heard from Walter Simpson and that she was writing to Baxter as she did not know where WEH was.
[2] Constantine Alexander Ionides (1833-1900), art collector and friend of WEH. He made his fortune on the Stock Exchange and left his valuable art collection to the Victoria and Albert Museum. He was living at 8 Holland Villas Road, Kensington, at this time. WEH was borrowing money to pay for Bob to go to Nice and help Fanny.

the money. His house I left at midnight, & posted to St. John's Wood. There I lost my head & forgot the number of the house. At number seven I knocked up a yellow-haired person in the exercise of her calling, & brought her shivering to the door, to tell me I had made a mistake. I was naturally angry; so (which seems inexplicable) was she. This mistake settled me; & I had to post back again, hunt up a catalogue, find the address (which was next door to my yellow-headed one's), & post back again. The clock struck two as I started upon Bob's bell. Ten minutes after he was quaking before me. I handed out the notes, told him to leave at ten that morning, & returned to my own house. It was three ere I laid me down; the tiredest sorrowfullest gent in all London.

Colvin remarks that these attacks are periodical, & notes that last year, about this time, the lad fell ill, in much the same fashion, at St. Marcel.[3] I am to write to Drummond,[4] & ask what's really been the matter, whether Hyères is right for him, whether he should to sea, & so forth.

We passed a very pleasant evening together. I think that little brush you wot of has done good — has cleared the air.

Ever Yours, my dear Charles,
W.E.H.

What Fanny wants is reviews; of the *Squatters*.

[3] St Marcel, Marseilles, where the Stevensons lived before moving to Hyères.
[4] Dr James Drummond, Promenade des Anglais, Nice. The letter has not survived.

To Robert Louis Stevenson, [early May 1884][1]
ALS: Yale

[51 Richmond Gardens, Shepherds Bush, W.]
Dear Boy,

Have writ to T. junior,[2] accepting his offer; promising proof sheets of second edition: opining that £20 would be welcomer than £15, but placing ourselves entirely in his hands; & promising advance sheets of *Otto* & the *Sealskin*,[3] both of which, however, *must* ere they appear as books, come out as parts of

[1] Written on a letter to WEH from Tauchnitz junior of 30 April 1884 seeking publication of *Treasure Island* in his Continental Series. (Christian Carl) Bernhard von Tauchnitz, 2nd Baron (1842-1912), publisher. The Tauchnitz publishing firm was founded at Leipzig in 1841 by the first Baron Tauchnitz. It produced a large collection of English and American authors for circulation on the Continent.
[2] WEH secured £20 from Tauchnitz for *Treasure Island*.
[3] *The Man in the Sealskin Coat* was the title suggested by Andrew Lang for the stories which RLS and Fanny later published as *More New Arabian Nights: The Dynamiter* (1885). Tauchnitz published neither *Prince Otto* nor *The Dynamiter*.

magazines.

I have also provided T. junior with the *Voyage*, the *Travels* & the *Virginibus Puerisque*. To the end that he may make us some offers.[4]

Half-dead, but hopeful. Weather Aprilish in the extreme. No east wind, however. So begin to prepare to make up your mind for England home & beauty!

Your Affectionate Pal,
W.E.H.

[4] None of these was published by Tauchnitz.

To Robert Louis Stevenson, 3 May 1884
ALS: Yale

51 Richmond Gardens, Shepherds Bush, W.

Dear Boy,

Your telegram didn't come in till after eleven o'clock this morning.[1] Hence what must have seemed a dreadful & unpardonable delay. I hope that ere this the right result will have been secured, & that the prescription will finish what the injections have begun. Mennell says that it will stop any bleeding in no time. So that I feel pretty confident about it.

We are very miserable about you. Now, things seem darker than ever; for I can't but think that this last accident will delay your journey, from which I looked for much good. I hope it won't; & above all that it won't so far worsen your state as to make the Ionides place impossible.[2] If you come, I shall do with you exactly as though your life were in my hands, as, God save us, I suppose it will be. What I mean is, that Zeb will be appointed dictator, & instructed to rule with a rod of iron. Of course, it's a risky business; but I've thought things out, & am prepared to accept the responsibility, great as it is.

I've nothing much to say. Except that I'm damn tired. The picture shows have had hold of me all week, & I've written a long article about them, which is very incomplete & tedious & inefficient.[3] And today — Saturday — I am simply a wreck.

Your last letter[4] — with the Simoom's enclosure— to which my second paragraph is an answer — came in soon after the telegram. I am glad you think

[1] A telegram was received by WEH from Fanny stating that RLS had ruptured an artery in his lung and asking for help from Dr Mennell. After consulting Mennell WEH sent a telegram to Fanny with Mennell's advice.
[2] Constantine Ionides had offered to let RLS stay at his house *carte blanche* (WEH to RLS, 22 April 1884, Yale).
[3] 'Current Art. I', *Magazine of Art*, June 1884.
[4] Sent on 1 May 1884.

so well of the Fonties. For myself, I prefer the 'Wilderness' to the 'Bridge' by a good deal.[5] As you say, the 'Gluck' is first chop.[6] As you say, too, I am really no slouch of an editor.[7] By the rummest chance I learn that I've actually succeeded in editing Cassell & Co. themselves to the point of thinking the Houdons quite admirable & the stars of the number. I wish I could believe they thought any better of me for my work. But I reckon they don't, & that I'm only there as a visitor. Which sometimes makes me gloomy enough.

Did you see that they've repris *Antony* at the Odeon?[8] I'd like to have been at the *première*. 'Tis odd, is it not, that we've never seen Alexander Maximus in action? By the way, I've writ another note on him — In connection with the speeches delivered at the ceremony, tother day, of the unveiling of Dore's Monument, which seems, by the way, a poor affair — which I think you'll like.[9] Also I've purchased the complete edition — Fifteen Wollums — of his plays. Out of which something may come. I don't think I shall start on them till you're in a fit & proper state to discuss them verbally.

I heard the other day a very ugly story of Becky. But I am beginning to learn patience, I think; Alceste will soon become a highly respectable Philinte.[10] Such is life! Becky, the wretch, looks sleeker, fatter, more twinklingly prosperous than ever. W.H.P.[11] on the other hand, is vaguer, ruder, less personal, less dependable than ever. I really believe that he now regards himself as a representative of the British Aristocracy. That he'll long continue to misedit the *S.R.* is not, I fear me, certain.

Colvin has disappeared into space; at least I've not heard of him for weeks. I suppose he's arranging his new Museum at Cambridge, for the ceremony of inauguration.[12] My chief comforts are Hake & Eustace Balfour (sometimes),[13] & Hannay & Bob, & this last week Hennessy.[14]

As coins are a consideration, shall I offer Carr[15] the 'Bed Trilogy' from the

[5] Anthony Henley's illustrations for 'Fontainbleau'.
[6] *Gluck*, by the French sculptor Jean-Antoine Houdon (1741-1828), was one of the illustrations to A. E. Hake's 'Sculpture at the Comédie Française: Houdon,' *Magazine of Art*, May 1884.
[7] RLS had written to WEH: 'Man, you're a great editor' (*Stevenson Letters, 4*, 286).
[8] Dumas *père*'s play *Antony* at the Odéon theatre, Paris.
[9] 'The Dumas Memorial,' *Saturday Review*, 24 May 1884. (Louis Auguste) Gustave Doré (1832-83), French illustrator and engraver.
[10] Alceste, the caustic character of Molière's *Le Misanthrope* who is disgusted with the hypocrisy of society.
[11] Pollock.
[12] A new gallery of casts from antique sculpture was opened at the Fitzwilliam Museum in April 1884.
[13] Colonel Eustace James Anthony Balfour (1854-1911), writer on architectural and military matters. He was the brother of Arthur James Balfour (1848-1930), statesman and writer, Prime Minister 1902-05.
[14] William John Hennessy (1840-1917), artist. His *Twixt Day and Night* is discussed by WEH in 'Current Art. II', *Magazine of Art*, July 1884.
[15] Joseph W. Comyns Carr (1849-1916), critic and journalist, founding editor of the monthly *English Illustrated Magazine* (1883-1913).

Garden?

I'd a talk with Besant about the proper form of publication of the *Sealskin Coat*. He says that 'tis to the magazine that you must look for real coins. And he gave me the figures of his *Revolt of Woman*,[16] published, at half profits, by Blackwood. It is a small book; & was sold at two prices, at 6/ & 3/6, to the amount of 11,000 copies, on which the author received about a hundred and sixty pounds. It was anonymous, as you know; so that a book of yours would have a better chance. But it had a very great success, & that a book of yours, however good, might possibly not achieve.

Talking of that reminds me that yesterday I went to see Payn to thank him for the Tauchnitz introduction. I spoke of the *Sealskin Coat*, but firmly & judiciously. I told him there was a prospect of it's going on to Carr, but added that of course I'd thought of him as well. He asked how much it made; I told him & added that I wanted at least £250 for the magazine right. He was startled; but I told him that Longmans had just given you as much for another story about the same size,[17] which he (Longmans) considered inferior to *T.I.* After which he calmed down, & said he'd be glad to have the refusal.

From him I learnt, too, that a three-vol novel (even) is not nearly so profitable as it used to be. Wm. Black, for instance, is not worth more than £500 in three volume form, & of old he was as good as Croesus. The reason is that the librarians have taken to buying up the magazines, & issuing the stories in this form, instead of in their proper three volume clo'. The only way — a difficult one with a short story — is to get the start of them, & publish two or even three months in advance.

I can't understand why it is that I've not had proofs of the *Garden*. That I hope to do next week at latest. Meanwhile, the delay is quite inconceivable.

I am glad that 'Tauchnitz' has responded. Aren't you? I think I'll have my copy magnificently bound. There should be no difficulty with Cassell & Co. They have absolutely nothing to do with it. The book, having been published originally in a periodical, with no rights reserved, is not copyright in Germany; so that Tauchnitz his fee is pure benevolence & good feeling.

Mennell seemed to think nothing of the rupture, nor to anticipate that it would throw any obstacle in the way of the proposed journey. So that, as you see, I am right to hope.

Did I tell you that Ted is married?[18] Yes, I remember. The bride is a nice little girl; a *chanteuse*, with a remarkable voice; very ladylike & pretty, & absolutely unprofessional; Grace the name of her. She should, I think, be the making of him; but they are very young — I call them Mr. & Mrs. Harry

---

[16] WEH is incorrect in the title. The book was *The Revolt of Man* (Edinburgh, 1882).

[17] *Prince Otto*. RLS received £250 for the serial rights in *Longman's Magazine*.

[18] Ted Henley had married Kate Grace Padley (b. 1863) at St George's Church, Bloomsbury, on 24 April 1884.

Walmers Junior,[19] after the young couple of whom Charles Dickens heard, at the Hollytree Inn (a story which, being a conceited & impure minded ass You professed to scorn). I'm glad to say, too, that his Duc de Blingy[20] is vastly improved since he wrote of it. So much was to be expected, the boy being really an actor.

I ought to tell you that Sir Henry Gordon[21] doesn't believe his brother in any danger, doesn't believe he's ever asked for money or troops, doesn't believe that he wants more than a definite policy on the part of our noble & most damnable government, & does believe that his isolation at Khartoum — I isolation from Gladstone's morality, & Granville's[22] impudence & all the rest of it — is a blessing.

I send the four journals as usual. The *S.R.* leader I commend to you;[23] also Lang in the *P.M.B.* on Besant's lecture on the Art of Fiction.[24] As is usual when Lang has a chance of mentioning R.L.S., he mentions him. The rest is silence, though here & there you may pick out a word that may interest you.

All the picters this year are damn bad; or if not damn bad, damn small. B.J.[25] on the spot, they say; but I don't see it. As for the rest — jimmy! The only real bit of heroic work in the sculpture is Rodin's *Age d'Airain.*[26] Young Browning's *Dryope*[27] (refused by the Academy) is *nu nu nu*, as vulgar & ungraceful as bronze can be. Bob is on view — but aloft, aloft![28] I'd like to boil

[19] Harry Walmers in Dickens's 'The Holly-Tree Inn,' in *Household Words*, Christmas Number, 1855. He was an eight-year-old boy who eloped to Yorkshire with a girl of seven.

[20] The Duc d'Blingy in the play *Ironmaster* by the French playwright Georges Ohnet (1848-1918).

[21] Sir Henry William Gordon (1818-87). His brother was besieged at Khartoum, in the Sudan, from 12 March 1884, by a religious leader called the Mahdi, who was leading a Sudanese revolt against Egyptian rule. The British Government was finally forced to send troops but Khartoum fell with Gordon's death on 26 January 1885.

[22] Granville George Leverson-Gower, 2nd Earl Granville (1815-91), statesman. At this time he was Secretary of State for Foreign Affairs.

[23] Probably 'Egypt,' *Saturday Review*, 3 May 1884.

[24] Lang's 'The Art of Fiction,' *Pall Mall Budget*, 2 May 1884. This was a review of Besant lecture at the Royal Institution on 25 April 1884.

[25] Edward Coley Burne-Jones (1833-98), one of the major Victorian artists and uncle by marriage to Rudyard Kipling. Baronet 1894.

[26] Rodin's *Age of Bronze* exhibited at the Royal Academy.

[27] Robert Wiedemann Barrett Browning (1849-1913), known almost universally as 'Pen', painter and sculptor, son of Robert and Elizabeth Browning.

[28] Bob Stevenson's *Afterglow*.

Carr, Hallé, Lindsay,[29] Wedmore & most of the Forty Academies in their own piss. I would, by God!

Affectionately Yours, dear Louis,
W.E.H.

[29] Charles E. Hallé (1846-1919), portrait painter, born in Paris but lived in London. He co-founded the Grosvenor Gallery with Lindsay. He later founded the New Gallery. Sir Coutts Trotter Lindsay, Bt (1824-1913), painter and playwright.

Formal document, 4 May 1884
ALS: Huntington

51 Richmond Gardens, Shepherds Bush, W.
Yesterday morning, I — W. E. Henley — received a telegram from Hyères. Louis, it said, had broken a blood vessel; & it instructed me to telegraph Mennell's advice. This I did; & in the course of the day I found that Charles Baxter had been advised of the event through Dr. George Balfour, & that Mennell, on being consulted, thought the circumstances exceedingly alarming.

To-day, Sunday, we the undersigned — W. E. Henley, Charles Baxter, & R. A. M. Stevenson — have debated the question thoroughly; have determined to request Mennell to proceed, as our agent & on our commission, to Hyères, & there take charge of Louis's case; & have resolved, at our own risk, to guarantee him the payment of his fee & all his incidental expenses, & to accept in full the responsibility of his actions.[1]

Our reasons are: that we believe the break in Louis's health to have been preventable; that we do not believe his present medical adviser to understand or care for his case;[2] & that we think it our duty, as his friends & agents, to place him in the hands of a man in whom we have complete confidence.

W. E. Henley,
51 Richmond Gardens,
Shepherds Bush.

R. A. M. Stevenson,
7 King's Road,
Chelsea S.W.

[1] Mennell duly went to Hyères on 6 May armed with a letter of authority.
[2] Dr L.-Emp. Vidal, the local doctor.

Charles Baxter,
11 South Charlotte St., Edin.
National Club. Whitehall.

Postscriptum. It was further resolved that we would take this action on our own account, & without inflicting unnecessary alarm upon Louis's parents. This we did on Mennell's advice, based on such facts of the case as we had been able to bring to his notice, which facts, led him to hope a favourable issue.

W. E. Henley
A. M. Stevenson
C. Baxter

To Charles Baxter, 6 May 1884
ALS: Yale

51 Richmond Gardens, Shepherds Bush, W.

Dear Boy,

Another letter from Hyères this morning, written some time (I conceive) on Saturday.[1] Haemorrhage still going on. My telegram received, but — apparently — no attempt to apply treatment received. Vidal anxious to cup: why God only knows. This is all. The more I think, the ever I am that we have done the right thing. If the worst must come, it must. But we know this that unless Mennell arrives too late (he left this morning), there will be a fight for it.

I telegraphed his departure this morning. 'Tis encouraging that we have had no more telegrams. Yesterday Fanny must have received my letter, & with it the prescription which, if she only used it, must certainly have stayed the haemorrhage, even though it did no more. Mennell will telegraph as soon as he arrives; so that we shall know very soon what to expect.

Order *Monsieur Nicholas* (Paris: Isadore Liseux) by Retif de la Bretonne in 14 vols. at 5 fr. the vol. Williams & Norgate.[2] 'Tis a larger & richer & ranker Casanova.

In haste to catch post.

Ever yours Affectionately,
W.E.H.

---

[1] Fanny Stevenson to WEH, 3 May 1884, Yale. In this letter Fanny acknowledges WEH's telegram of 3 May 1884 (not found).
[2] Restif de la Bretonne, *Monsieur Nicolas*, 14 vols (Paris, 1883). Nicholas Restif (or Rétif) de la Bretonne (1734-1806), French novelist. Williams and Norgate, 20 Frederick Street, Edinburgh.

I am very angry with you still. However, I punished you somewhat last night, at the Royal;[3] & I shall presently no doubt be able to punish you again. So that I'm not so angry as I was. I suppose you got your train? I looked for you outside, in Piccadilly, after the concert; but you were nowhere to be seen, whence I concluded — rather optimistically, I own — that you must certainly have evacuated Flanders. How much of this success in what I looked like a forlorn hope was due to native virtue, & how much to terror of the goblet I shall not stay — now — now to enquire.

[3] WEH had probably been to the Richter concert at St James's Hall on 5 May 1884.

To Robert Louis and Fanny Stevenson, 8 May 1884
ALS: Yale. Part published in *Stevenson Letters*, 4, 295, note 1.

51 Richmond Gardens, Shepherds Bush, W.

My dears,

As you know, I've doubted & detested Vidal from the first. My great hope is that Mennell will make good use of his opportunity, turn Pirate once more, & put henbane in Vidal's porridge. My great regret is not that till now have I given him his chance.

For the telegram last night we were grateful indeed.[1] It was better news than we dared to hope. I have telegraphed it on to Edinburgh & Cambridge this morning. I hope to have more & better in your next.

Why you write me for *Martin Chuzzlewit*, be dam if I know. Why you didn't write to the shop at Nice for a Tauchnitz edition, be dam if I know either. However, I sent it; by this same post. Tell Louis that once, years & years ago, when I had just been entered as a patient at Barklemy's, Bartlemy's, or Bardlemy's, I had just been told (at nineteen, mind!) that caries of the spine was what was the matter with me, I took up *Martin* (borrowed him from a nurse), & straightaway laughed & forgot & swore to live in spite of everything. And here I am! And there you are! And the omen is, I think, a good one.

Or can it be that the Pirate himself has conceived a passion for polite letters? has felt a longing for the ingenuous arts, & is passing *via* Dickens, to Burne Jones? I refuse to believe it. That bold bad medical man is incapable of such weakness.

Baxter left on Monday night. He didn't tell your mother, because he couldn't resolve, as George Balfour telegraphed, to keep the matter secret from your father.[2] Ere this, you'll no doubt have heard from him. Some day I shall tell you the story of that famous empowerment which Mennell carries in his

[1] Mennell's telegram of 7 May saying that there was hope for RLS.
[2] Baxter had been staying in London. George Balfour sent a telegram asking him not to tell RLS's parents as Thomas Stevenson's poor health would have been at risk.

pocket. *Ca vous fera rire*. It made me swear most horrible at the time. But since I've laughed; & so, when you hear it, will you.

By an odd chance an old passion of yours turned up promiscuous & free the other night at the third Richter. Do you remember the lyric in *Iphigenie auf Tauris* —

> *Sie aber, sie bleiben*
> *Im ewigen Feste*
> *Am goldenen Tischen*

and all the rest of it?[3] And how, from your belly's deepmost penetralia, from regions umbilical & cavernous, you used to declaim it to me? Lord, Lord! I read it, & I remembered me of much. 'Twas set to Brahms's music,[4] & as I hoped, for auld lang syne, it would turn up trumps. But it didn't. Brahms's had set it for an orchestra & a six part quire, in the Wagnerian mode, every word his note, & the devil take all form & melody; & the result, a kind of Germano-Irish Stew of vocal & instrumental discontent, was trying in the extreme. And these bitches pretend to teach us the secrets of a new art! when all they've done is to bedevil the old ones! — I thought of you, & your umbilical declamation, & was exceedingly wroth.

We are longing for another letter. Tonight we dine — Bob, Hannay & I — with the merry Greek, superb Ionides. So if your ear shall burn, you'll know the reason why.

You are not to worrit about coins. Mennell is our servant, not yours. We have guaranteed him his fee.[5] You are as a corpus vile in his hands. All you have to do is obey his orders, & get well. Your John O'Tripes has left us untouched.[6] We can, & will, see that Zebulon is paid. So fret no more; but think of art, & life, & friendship; & get well. Think of the Bust; & get well. Think of Becky's memoir;[7] & get well. Under penalty of the extreme Taboo!

I've been jibing & japing the Academy;[8] & my employers are sore angered wi' me. I've had to tone down my japes & unvenom my gibes. The world is too much with us — evidently.

---

[3] Goethe's play *Iphigenie auf Tauris*. It was quoted earlier by RLS in a letter to Frances Sitwell (*Stevenson Letters*, 2, 72).

[4] Brahms's *Gesang der Parzen* [*Song of the Fates*] for six voices and orchestra, opus 89. Trans Mrs N. Macfarren (Berlin, 1883).

[5] It was paid by RLS's father.

[6] RLS had written that 'John O'Tripes has ruined me, I cannot pay' and this had been relayed by Fanny to WEH in her letter of 6 May.

[7] This is probably a joke. Should RLS die Gosse would write a memoir!

[8] 'Current Art. 1', *Magazine of Art*, June 1884, 347. WEH criticises the lack of originality in English art and notes that even 'what is being borrowed from the French is only interesting by reason of the manner in which the obligation is discovered and acknowledged'.

Our dearest love, our heartiest wishes. O if Mennell were but a Rosicrucian,[9] & took in his pocket the *E*lixir! But, change & hope. *Dieu.*

Your friend,
W.E.H.

[9] A member of an order supposedly founded in 1484. Its members claimed secret powers to prolong life.

To Charles Baxter, 13 May 1884
ALS: Huntington

51 Richmond Gardens, Shepherds Bush, W.

My dear Charles,

The two enclosures came in last night.[1] Too late for dispatch until today. I thought best to wire you as I did; for it's no use, now we've gone so far, to refuse to go farther. Mennell must see his work out. Even if we're all of us bankrupt for years.

What you've now to do is to declare the whole position. You may consult George Balfour or not as you please. But at this pass the parents must be told; that Louis has been desperately ill, & that we took such steps as you know; all, in fact, that was agreed upon. You must do the work, & nobody else. In the first place, you are on the spot; in the next, Fanny, as you see, has completely broken down, & would tell it in such a way as to send the parents daft, & even at this date produce the identical effect we wished so much to avoid.

These two reasons are good enough; but there's a third, still better. I mean there's the question of supplies. The book Louis has in hand is worth at least £200;[2] but that has nothing to do with it, & of that — as it's unavailable & uncertain — we must not permit ourselves to think. Louis must be removed to Royat,[3] & that, as Mennell says, as soon as may be. While there, he must live well, have plenty, & be absolutely free from care of any sort. This can't be done without money; & plenty of it. And to ask for that, & get it, & — if necessary — take charge of its distribution, is your work, my boy, & nobody else's.

I shall therefore write today to Fanny, & tell her that matters are in our hands, & that she is to take no thought of anything save Louis. That we engage to deal with the parents, & to take on ourselves the whole responsibility of explaining & justifying our past action, & of finding the money for Royat. In fact, that she is to leave herself in our hands, & trust to us to pull things

[1] Fanny's letter of 10 May and Mennell's report on RLS.
[2] Presumably *Prince Otto.*
[3] A town in central France.

through, not only successfully, but quietly & decently as well. If you, on receipt of this, will write to her to the same effect, it will help matters much.

You will note the contradiction between the two letters. That Fanny's is almost desperate,[4] & that Mennell's is quite cheerful & satisfied. At the exact truth of things we cannot conceive until Mennell's return. Meanwhile, it will be best, I conceive, to accept no other report than his. So far he has succeeded brilliantly enough. Still, as Fanny says, this may be the beginning of the end. All the same, I don't purpose to believe it, unless he tells it me himself. I merely purpose to accept the fact that Louis is, for the moment safe, & to insist upon it that his parents must, if they wish his safety to have a chance of permanency, be prepared to make a certain sacrifice — any sacrifice, indeed, which may be necessary.

You will note, too, that Fanny is desperately anxious that the parents should know, & desperately afraid to tell them. The first emotion is right enough; the second is pure jimmy. Told they must be, & told right out. The worst is over, & the event has justified our action. To keep that knowledge back any longer than we can help would now be both impolite & unjust. I should like you therefore to wire Fanny at once that she must consider herself in our hands, & — as I've said — take no thought of anything or anybody but Louis.

If I can be of use, wire me, & I'll come on at once.

Ever Affectionately Yours,
W.E.H.

If necessary, you must be prepared to advance for Royat as for Mennell.

[*Added by WEH at the top of the letter*] Mennell's letter, dated the 9*th*, can only have been posted on Saturday, the 10*th*, & not early than.

[4] In her letter of 10 May Fanny wrote that: 'It is the beginning of the end.'

To Robert Louis Stevenson, [24 June 1884]
ALS: Yale

[51 Richmond Gardens, Shepherds Bush, W.]

Dear Boy,
    As you can see, the hatchet is buried, & I did our little friend an injustice.[1]

[1] The letter is written on a letter from Gosse to WEH dated 22 June 1884. WEH had been drumming up support for the production of *Deacon Brodie* on 2 July at the Prince's Theatre, London. WEH had written to RLS (23 June 1884, Yale) complaining that Gosse had not replied. In his letter to WEH Gosse explains that he has been ill and therefore unable to promote *Deacon Brodie*.

Enclosed are two cuttings one from yesterday's *P.M.G.*,[2] the other from yesterday's *Daily News*.[3] The first I wrote; for that ass Gell to send to *Truth*; why he sent it to the *P.M.G.* — where Gosse, Archer,[4] & Colvin were all burning to paragraph us — I know not. The other is Moy Thomas's. A third (a plain announcement) appeared in yesterday's *Morning Post*.[5]

I've booked Patchett Martin for the *Pictorial World* & Australia generally.[6] I expect a preliminary flourish in the *Times*;[7] & I'm in full cry after the *St. James's*, the *Observer*, & the *Scotsman*.[8]

E.J. assured me that he'll have to work all he knows to keep his head up before Cartwright[9] in the great scene — the scene of the play.

I can't write any more. The *M. of A.* (I begin to think) won't appear this month. I'm fairly busted, & can get nothing done but busting.

W.E.H.

[2] 'WEH's unsigned 'Theatrical Notes', *Pall Mall Gazette*, 23 June 1884.
[3] Moy Thomas's unsigned 'The Theatres', *Daily News*, 23 June 1884. William Moy Thomas (1828-1910), journalist and novelist. He was drama critic of the *Daily News*, 1868-?1901.
[4] William Archer (1856-1924), dramatic critic and translator of Ibsen. He contributed to the *Magazine of Art* under WEH and became a firm friend despite differing political views. He was drama critic of the *World* from March 1884 to January 1905.
[5] 'Theatrical and Musical Intelligence,' *Morning Post*, 23 June 1884.
[6] Arthur Patchett Martin (1851-1902), English born journalist and writer who lived in Australia from an early age until 1882 when he returned to England. Editor of the *Melbourne Review*, 1876-82. His notice 'Music and the Drama' appeared in the *Pictorial World*, 10 July 1884.
[7] *Deacon Brodie* was advertised in *The Times*, 30 June 1884.
[8] An advertisement for *Deacon Brodie* appeared in the *St James's Gazette* of 26 June, 27 June, 28 June and 30 June 1884. 'At the Play', *Observer*, 22 June 1884. Nothing has been found in the *Scotsman*.
[9] Ted Henley played Deacon Brodie and Charles Cartwright (1855-1916) played Walter Leslie.

To Robert Louis Stevenson, Saturday 28 June 1884
ALS: Yale

51 Richmond Gardens, Shepherds Bush, W.

Dear Boy,

Comfort and Joy! Your people are in town (they were with us last night), & they are delighted to know of your visit.[1] They will be near you, I guess, while you're here. So there you are!

Your father, who looks wonderfully well, spoke of the possibility of your going to Edinburgh. But I vetoed it in my best John Silver manner; so I guess you'll hear no more about it.

They are coming to see the *Deacon*. They pretend to be above it; but I think

[1] RLS and Fanny had arrived in London from France on 1 July.

(& so does the Châtelaine) that they're pleased no end with our pluck.

Speed me on the Bedlamitish Woman. A place is reserved for her; & she owes me my revenge. If it's humanly possible, quoit her along to the Princes Theatre by 2.30, on Wednesday afternoon;[2] & she shall see an original play.

Things are shaping well at rehearsal. We shall either make a big spoon, or spoil a mighty curious horn. 'Twill be a goodish all-rounder. I want some twenty rehearsals yet to make it what it should be; but it'll be no that bad as it is. Of course, we shall be out of pocket by it, for the moment. But that's no matter. The thing is, we shall have put our Bad Child on his legs, & seen him walk.

How well we knew our business, lad! & how ill! We seem to have done every thing right but one thing. What wouldn't I give — & E.J.! — to have you see it in action! what a lesson it would be! how right, & how wrong, you'd find your contempt to be! The dam thing has pulled the actors into enthusiasm; the very supers & sceneshifters are interested, & watch us from the front. And yet! and yet! Will it hit? I don't know. I think it over, & I think it can't. I see it moving, & I feel it must. *Voilà. I do not know nothing*! I retire hup. I decline to pass an opinion, & retire hup, as high as I can get. Is it to be five then? or bankruptcy? '*Je n'en sais rien. Priez Dieu.*'

As yet, the blunder that has hit me hardest is not the last tableau (which plays like fire, dam ugly as it is), but the paralysis in mid career of the scene between May & Brodie, in Act II. That, ye bitch, was *your* doing, not mine; & I blush when I recall the cowardice that made me consent to it. It brings me up with a round turn every time. If the 'three men' scene didn't come upon it instantly, I wouldn't sit things out. Fortunately it does — like a clap of thunder; so that nobody has time to mark the mistake. It's a very striking moment, dear boy; & to see how our Badger[3] takes the cake in it would warm your heart. I don't think he'll go wanting an engagement long! By the way, I cut the 'Portrait of George as a Guardian Hangel'; it bitched the whole concern. The Dook[4] wept tears of blood; but I was adamant.

I've cut those bloody kids, too; hewn them in pieces before the Lord. My Jean (a fine, canty, Bonnie Fishwife buddy) embraced me for the deed.[5] The text, a 'much' or two apart, & apart from these two acts stands as we wrote it. The Badger's 'bloody' & Ainslie's[6] 'bad disease' have been out from the first.

Our Procurator will thrive well enough.[7] His, boy, is the best written part in the play. After his, I'm undecided between Moore's & Hunt's. The latter seems to me real literature of its kind; but the former is one of the most effective bits

---

[2] Fanny and RLS's parents attended but RLS was too ill.
[3] Edmund Grace played Humphrey Moore.
[4] George Smith, played by the playwright Julian Cross (1851-1925).
[5] Minne Bell (fl.1881-92) played Jean Watt.
[6] Frederick Desmond.
[7] John Maclean (?1835-90).

of stage work I've seen. Our Hunt,[8] I should tell you is ideal. His lingo seems to have sucked in with his mother's milk! It oozes out of him like a natural perspiration. I expect his scene with Ainslie (who's Scotch is lovely, & who slinks quite beautiful) to be one of the good things of the performance.

The Smith is hard & dry; but not offensive. Him I should eliminate had I to recast the piece. With the others, not excepting May[9] even (who, by the way, is a capital part) I am mighty pleased. Ah, boy! for twenty more rehearsals! Or even ten! or as few as five! As it is, I'm content. A matinee's only a matinee after all; & for a matinee our show will be unrivalled.

I a little doubt the Brodie. 'Tis such a tremendous part; so full of motive, so charged with significance, so *crible* with opportunities. However, he'll make a better fight for it than any living Englishman; & that's something ain't it? If we mash 'em, & it *is* put on for the autumn (as it will be, if we do) I stipulate for thirty rehearsals; & then we'll see.

E.J. has a tip-top voice; so has Cartwright. There'll be wigs on the green when these two Greeks are met. Of that you may be certain, if of nothing else.

You'll hear no more from me till after the event, of which, I take it, you'll hear from my own lips. I've to distribute the press tickets, to revise the book, to try & organize a few more preliminary puffs, to call in a few more laggards to the stalls, to superintend two full rehearsals, to hot Leslie through his big scene, & Brodie through his two first soliloquies, & to rehearse the thrice tableau till it's passable; & to keep myself sane withal for Wednesday afternoon. That's wot's the matter with *me*; & if you find me a corpse, do not affect astonishment.

Take care of your precious carcase, I beg. If you must & will collaborate with J. Silver Esq., you must go into training for the act. Tell the Simoom that I expect her on Wednesday afternoon, & that one of us has to apologize to the other for his (or her) view of *Deacon Brodie, or The Double Life.* Which I know not, I; all being still in the laps of the Gods.

Affectionately Yours ever,
Ben Jonson Dubious Burly Bewildered Silver
(Pirate, Earwigger, & Retired Huppist)

Shall we? Shan't we? *Je n'en sais rien.*
Priez Dew!

[*Added by WEH at the top of the letter*] A seat for the Cog.[10] if she's to hand.

---

[8] Hubert Akhurst (?1850-88).
[9] Lizzie Williams played Mary Brodie.
[10] Walter Ferrier's sister Elizabeth Anne Ferrier (1844-1917) always known as 'Coggie'. She had helped nurse RLS at Hyères and had become a close friend.

To Robert Louis Stevenson, 12 November 1884
ALS: Yale

51 Richmond Gardens, Shepherds Bush, W.

Dear Lad,

To morrow being your birthday, You will receive, in memory thereof, a new & beautiful edition of the works of Poquelin.[1] That you may be found reading it for thirty year to come is our heartfelt wish. I have obliged the Châtelaine to put her initials on the title page of Vol. I beside my own; because it was she who remembered what was coming, & thereby became the prime mover in the transaction.

Next February, or January, we shall have been friends for ten years. Think of that, Master Brook![2] Ten years, dear boy, & all that in them is! — In ten years from now, I hope we shall have done a few good plays, & you'll be seeing your way to that new & true life of John Silver which of course it will be yours & nobody else's to write. You are a high-nosed classic, sipping your wine (good wine!) & talking Moliere to me, a disemboweled romantic; it may be in that very house which we are going to build on the site of the old semaphore station you wot of with the Mediterranean at our feet, & the Estourelles a bow shot off. What think you of that? for 1894! I see it very plainly; & I believe.

Our next play must be a common melo. I'm reading Yates his recollections,[3] which you shall have anon. Old Buckstone[4] got £70 per play, & sold his American right for a tenner. A cove of today (which his name appears to be Sims)[5] tells Yates that he has made £10,000 by one piece, & is clearing a hundred a week of it still. Decidedly, we must make a common melo. If it's only to get ourselves in funds, & earn the wherewithal to begin reorganization in earnest.

From the same book, I learn that in private life, O. Smith[6] was mild, formal, & old fashioned, & *painted agreeably in water colours*. Such is life!

I beseech you not to overwork yourself, but to think a little of your friends as well as of your principles, & something not only of duty, but of love.

If you care to send me such of the Arabs as is ready, I'll take it to Carr, & begin my bargain. Anyhow, I shall be glad indeed to know they're off your

---

[1] RLS expressed his thanks for the edition of Moliere in a warm letter of 14 November (*Stevenson Letters*, 5, 31). In this letter he also thanked WEH for 'John Silver's pistol', a gift from Joseph Henley.

[2] *The Merry Wives of Windsor*, III. v. 113. 'Master Brook' is the character Frank Ford.

[3] Edmund Hodgson Yates (1831-94), novelist and journalist. Editor of the *World*, July 1874-May 1894. *Edmund Yates: his Recollections and Experiences* (1884).

[4] John Baldwin Buckstone (1802-79), playwright.

[5] George Robert Sims (1847-1922), prolific playwright, writer and journalist. He is now remembered for his ballad 'In the workhouse: Christmas Day'.

[6] Richard John Smith (1786-1855), actor, famous for playing villains and sinister characters. He was known as O. Smith for his performance as Obi in the play *Three-Fingered Jack*. His quiet private life was in stark contrast to the dramatic performances on stage.

hands, & that you can rest. Rest you must, & rest you shall; work you must not, & work you shan't. Or I'll cut my calls, & leave you to negotiate yourself.

I would write more; but that infernal Purseyfull calls me,[7] & I must away.

Ever Affectionately Yours,
W.E.H.

[7] WEH may be referring to an unidentified review that he was writing of the performance of Parsifal at the Royal Albert Hall on 10 November 1884.

To Robert Louis Stevenson, 2 January 1885
ALS: Yale

[18 Camden Gardens, Shepherds Bush, W.][1]

Dear Boy,

On receipt of yours,[2] I telegraphed to the Barebottomed Tree,[3] to call here today. In reply, the enclosed. I will send on his letter when it comes. Meanwhile, suspend your travailing, & don't get enamoured of your own conceit. If we do this thing at all, we must do it not hastily & not unreflecting but seriously & after hard & hugious confabulation. I don't know now that we shall have the chance; but we may, & if we do, I'm with you to the hilt.

Some of your situations — e.g. the two fathers — I like very much.[4] But of these anon. I also have a notion, — an *idée mère* — & I'm not sure that it's not better than yours; if it be, we can work in the chest & the two fathers quite beautiful.

As regards the personalities of Robert & Bertrand I think we might retain them as they stand:[5] Robert, the intellectual believer in rascality; Bertrand the poor timid infidel — conforming, but conforming against his will. Of course, this is not the original Bertrand after all; but he'll serve nobly. And we can make such an effect of contrast (I see my way to a Robert of the rarest type!) as he'll take their breath away.

I'm glad you didn't send the letter to Tree. Had he called, I should have taken it on myself to suppress it, & put the question verbally, & as a matter of no consequence. For why, you says? Because, he wants the murder — they all

[1] The Henleys were here by 25 November 1884 (WEH to Constantine Ionides, 25 November 1884, Fitzwilliam Museum, Cambridge).
[2] RLS's letter of 1 January (*Stevenson Letters*, 5, 56-60).
[3] The actor and manager Herbert Beerbohm Tree (1853-1917) had suggested to RLS and WEH that they adapt Charles Selby's play *Robert Macaire* (1835). This they did resulting in *Macaire: A Melodramatic Farce in Three Acts* which was privately printed in 1885 and first published in Chicago in 1895.
[4] In *Macaire*.
[5] The two main characters in *Macaire*.

want the murder — they refuse to do without the murder — Macaire is the murder — the murder plays blague. What did I say in my first letter? There must (I said) be laughter & there must be terror. Macaire is Lacenaire[6] — Voilà It's this double capacity — of fantastic irony with the most revolting practical brutality — that makes the figure what it is — the temptation every actor has found it since Frédérick the Great.[7] In your cogitations, therefore, keep the bloody hand in view. Remember what in the vicious pride of your youth you seem to forget, that, as I said, Macaire has only existed hitherto as a colossal gag invented & perfected by an actor of genius. If we write it, we must write Frédérick. To turn the idea of Lemaître into black & white — that's the point. In other words, to produce, what you've long been hankering after, a comic melodrama.

Shall we? Shan't we? *Je n'en sais rien. Priez Dieu.* If we do, by God we'll give 'em something they won't forget in a hurry,

I yelled with laughter at your criticism of *Robert Macaire*.[8] As you say, 'I have read it, & may God the lord'....! You are a great critic; as I've always sworn.

I will make no plans till I hear from Tree: Then we'll concert measures.

I am all right — but feeble. If this business could be got off, I could leave town with a clear conscience.

All I say is, why didn't you settle Bogue while you were about it?

Ever Affectionately Yours,
W.E.H.

PS. The Archangel now sweats & pimps & worries & piddles at his copy as you were wont to do in the brave days ere you could write.

What these blasted 'East Suffolk memories' will be when they're done,[9] the Lord alone knows as he only can guess the amount of doing they've already taken. Meanwhile, the printers wait & sit & girn & swear.

PPS. Bogue is Macaire or rather a well bred & mannerly Pew.

---

[6] Pierre François Lacenaire (1800-36), French adventurer and criminal.
[7] This is a reference to the French actor Frédérick Lemaître (1800-76), who had created the part of Robert Macaire.
[8] RLS's long letter of 1 January.
[9] Sidney Colvin, 'East Suffolk Memories', *Magazine of Art*, April 1885 and May 1885.

To Robert Louis Stevenson, [28 March 1885] Saturday
ALS: Yale

[18 Camden Gardens, Shepherds Bush, W.]

Dear Boy,

It's terrible, I know but what else can you expect? You fall deadly ill with overwork; you live the life of an intellectual athlete; & hardly are you recovered, ere you fall to working again. It is natural — only natural & inevitable. The sword wears out the sheath, & gets blunted & dulled in the process. How should it be otherwise? And what are we to look for of a man who cannot be idle? Who plays blindfold chess by way of easing his mind? What but breakdowns every now & again, & presently a breakdown that shall leave us all mourning long ere our time.

Think of the work you've done since you came to England last year. Three plays written, & more made; the 'Humble Remonstrance'; the 'Style'; the 'Mortality';[1] the *Child's Garden* finished & published; the *Dynamiter*, ditto ditto; the *Otto* ditto ditto; the 'North Road'[2] invented, *Kidnapped*[3] invented & begun; the *Wellington*[4] mapped out & read for, & the bigger book projected & arranged.[5]

Allons, voyons! Aren't you a damnable glutton to be still unsatisfied? Aren't you a pernicious ass to look, with such a carcass as yours, for the capacity for more?

I know all about it: you'll say 'And how am I to live?' — As you've lived before; as you told me lang syne you'd made your mind up to live till you could do better. On your father. 'Tis a most honourable ambition to want other, & 'tis most honourable & beautiful to attempt the achievement of such an ambition. But see the results! Not only have you to exert to extremities, but you break yourself to pieces, to boot: a consequence fraught with misery to us all, & to your father most beyond comparison.

If I'm rude, forgive me. I feel strongly, & I can't help my rudeness. For I do anticipate the worst. If you cannot & will not take a decent amount of rest, then I cannot but believe the wretchedest. Learn a language; play patience; read in chronological order the works of Dumas *père* & George Sand; do anything rather than cripple yourself like this. Do you want company? here are any of us at your service. Do you want collaboration? behold me! Shall I borrow you Ruskin? I can & will. Only refrain from being an ass — a noble, honourable,

[1] 'A Humble Remonstrance', *Longman's Magazine*, December 1884; 'On Style in Literature: its Technical Elements', *Contemporary Review*, April 1885; and 'Old Mortality', *Longman's Magazine*, May 1884.
[2] *The Great North Road* was RLS's unfinished novel and the uncompleted manuscript was published posthumously in the Christmas *Illustrated London News*, 1895.
[3] *Kidnapped; Being Memoirs of the Adventures of David Balfour in the Year 1751* (1886).
[4] RLS's projected *The Duke of Wellington* for the Longmans English Worthies series.
[5] This may be a reference to RLS's *Memories and Portraits* (1887).

glorious ass; & I am — we are — content. I send the journals. Compare Bob in the *S.R.*,[6] with Purcell in the *Athenaeum*,[7] & the ass Shedlock in the *Academy*,[8] & revere my genius as a midwife.

Grosvenor yesterday, so couldn't write. Infamous exhibition. A clipping good Sargent.[9] If he paints you like that, hooray! Bob & I dined with Ionides in the evening: a pleasant wine, & a hundred Rembrandt etchings. Wished you'd been there. Your mother called, & talked of the furniture some.

Ever Affectionately Yours,

W.E.H.

[6] 'The Bach Commemoration', *Saturday Review*, 28 March 1885. The concert was at the Albert Hall on Saturday 21 March.
[7] 'Music. The Week', *Athenaeum*, 28 March 1885. Edmund Sheridan Purcell (1823-99), journalist.
[8] 'Recent Concerts', *Academy*, 28 March 1885. John South Shedlock (1843-1919), music teacher and music critic of the *Academy* from 1879 and later the *Athenaeum*, 1901-16.
[9] Sargent's portrait of *Mrs Mason*. John Singer Sargent (1856-1925), American portrait painter born in Florence, who settled in England. He established himself as a painter of the rich and famous with a distinctive style.

To Robert Louis Stevenson, 13 April 1885
ALS: Yale

18 Camden Gardens, Shepherds Bush, W.

Dear Boy,

What must be must. I bow to the Gods; more especially as they elected to keep me poor. If by sudden oversight, they make me rich, down I come, meals or more, & do my best to pull off a plan of campaign & a scenario.

The position is this: (1) I no longer receive £300 a year certain for the *M.* of *A.*, but £240 certain, & permission to edit myself to the amount of the other £60, if I can or will.

(2) Having been compelled to resign the *S.R.* music,[1] my connection with that noble print may be considered as ended & done. When I tell you that my last quarter's cheque was for £30 you will appreciate the fact at its true significance.

Now comes the question: Having been flung out of journalism, shall I re-enter by another gate? Would it not be wiser to accept the position, live within my income, & apply myself to other pursuits? Would it not be more provident to give my time & energy all to the great subject, & block out dramas to be finished in the summer & autumn? Answer me that; & you'll confer a favour.

[1] It would appear that WEH had been asked to stop reviewing for the *S.R.* (WEH to RLS, 23 April 1885, Yale).

Or rather, think it over, & as soon as I've settled with Tree, expect me down, if it is but for a day, & a talk between breakfast & luncheon.

I was with Clayton some hours yesterday. He seems to have been at the *Beau*[2] again, & his conviction is that it ought to be played at the Français, where it would be a great success. Presently (if we've the coins) we are going to try it at a *matinée*. Meanwhile, Pew is a marvellous good part, the *Admiral* marvellous good reading, & the last act 'of an admirable ingenuity'. Of Tree's *Macaire* he's any thing but sure; but if it's worth anything, the play will succeed greatly. His fear is, that it's too clever for the Barebum's intellectuals, & too well & oddly written for his elocution.

I send you Bob's second *S.R.*;[3] 'twas cut (of course), but not much, & only in the really critical parts. The *Handel* has come in,[4] & will do finely well, & there's a *Fuseli* in hand:[5] likewise a treatise on engraving (translation) for C. & Co.[6] Next Saturday he tackles Berlioz's *Te Deum*,[7] & we shall see how he handles a big subject. I expect him to night with last Saturday's results.[8] On the whole, I think we have him.

I rejoice to hear from Colvin that the *Garden* is mashing 'em right & left, & that (according to Bain)[9] a second edition should be in preparation even now. I have flaunted these results before the eyes of C. & Co. with much glee. Of the *Dynamiter* in its shilling gown I confess myself afeard; indeed, I've no faith in it at all. You'll have to sell some 20,000 to take a penny more than you've got; & I doubt — I doubt! Still, I'm glad it's not for the *P.M.G.*, which is simply a Russian paper published in London.

I'm all right; but a poor poor creature. I hope & trust you're by this time ceased from Bloody-Jackey,[10] & are well through the horrors of flitting.[11] Our love to you both, anyhow.

W.E.H.

[2] Their play *Beau Austin: A Play in Four Acts* which was completed in the autumn of 1884 together with *Admiral Guinea: A Melodrama in Four Acts*. Both were privately printed in 1884.
[3] 'The Crystal Palace Concerts', *Saturday Review*, 11 April 1885.
[4] Bob Stevenson's 'Handel and his Portraits', *Magazine of Art*, June 1885.
[5] No article on the artist Henry Fuseli (Johann Heinrick Fuessli) (1741-1825) appeared in the *Magazine of Art*.
[6] Henri Delaborde's *La Gravure* translated by Bob Stevenson as *Engraving: its Origin, Process, and History* (1886). In fact, most of the work was done by Katharine de Mattos under Bob's supervision.
[7] 'Berlioz's Te Deum [at the Crystal Palace, 18 April 1885]', *Saturday Review*, 25 April 1885.
[8] 'The Crystal Palace Concerts', *Saturday Review*, 18 April 1885.
[9] James and Thomas Bain, Booksellers, 1 Haymarket, London.
[10] RLS had had a haemorrhage on 7 April.
[11] RLS's parents had bought a house (Skerryvore), in Bournemouth, for RLS and Fanny who moved in before 13 April.

To Robert Louis Stevenson, 16 October 1885
ALS: Yale

[18 Camden Gardens, Shepherds Bush, W.]
Dear Boy,
   Herewith *Athenaeum*, with an article of mine on the new volume of Thackeray;[1] & to-night's *St. James's* with the Merry Andrew on Alexander Dumas.[2] Of course I had conversed with him on the subject ere the letter was written; but that's no matter. The thing is, that he has come off nobly. I am sure he will please you; so I send him. I think (if I might advise an eminent literary man) I think you might write & congratulate him.
   How do you like *King Solomon's Mines*?[3] I think it's blamed good. Not art, of course; but a good deal of blazing imagination.
   Where is the Infant Samivel?[4] He cometh not: nor any news of his coming. Why tarrieth his hansom? Why tarry the wheels of his hansom?[5]
   I am wearying for a sight of you, & soon I shall try to compass one. Not this month, maybe; for I am *deravé*. But soon.
   The Meredith scheme goes on bravely.[6] G.M. has uttered a kind of *nolo episcopari*; but of course we don't take that for an answer. Harrison[7] goes down to Box Hill to-morrow; & next week there is (I believe) to be a general meeting at the monument.[8] Of all which things anon.
   I think I've succeeded in nailing Bob's ear to the *S.R.* He has resumed his function as a musical critic, & Pollock is anxious to get him on about pictures.
   Hake's success as a lecturer is startling. He had 4000 people at Birmingham,[9] & an ovation at the end: they stood up & shouted at him. As for Edinburgh, Charles was impressed by him to the point of persuading [him] to return in November,[10] & speak in the Music Hall on alternate nights with the Old Man Flatulent himself. He has (in fact) *temperament. C'est moi qui te le dis!*

[1] WEH's review of Thackeray's *Miscellaneous Essays, Sketches, and Reviews* in the *Athenaeum*, 17 October 1885.
[2] Lang's 'Letters to Eminent Authors. XII. To Alexander Dumas', *St James's Gazette*, 16 October 1885.
[3] Rider Haggard, *King Solomon's Mines* (1885). Henry Rider Haggard (1856-1925), traveller and novelist, well-known for his stories of South Africa. Knighted 1912. WEH, with Andrew Lang, was instrumental in getting Cassell to publish the book.
[4] Fanny's son Samuel Lloyd Osbourne (1868-1947), later called Lloyd.
[5] 'Why is his chariot so long in coming? Why tarry the wheels of his chariot?' *Judges* 5. 28.
[6] A suggested subscription portrait of Meredith. However, he declined and instead suggested a photograph of himself. See George Meredith to F. H. Evans, 29 December 1885, *The Letters of George Meredith*, ed. C. L. Cline (Oxford, 1970), *3*, 803.
[7] Frederic Harrison (1831-1923), barrister, positivist philosopher and writer on social reform.
[8] RLS's joke name for Colvin's house at the British Museum.
[9] A. E. Hake's lecture on General Gordon at the Town Hall, Birmingham, 9 October 1885.
[10] Hake gave his lecture in Edinburgh on 5 October 1885. No lecture was given in November.

When is one to have of your news? What are you doing? and how are you faring? Let it be soon.

Ever Affectionately Yours,
W.E.H.

Did I tell you I found C.B. *ferré* on the Subject of Greek plays, & preferring the *Oedipus Coloneus* (*de beaucoup*) to *Lear*?[11]

[11] Sophocles's *Oedipus at Colonus*.

To Brander Matthews,[1] 24 December 1885
ALS: Columbia

18 Camden Gardens, Shepherds Bush, W.

Dear Matthews,

All manner of thanks to you. If the offer comes I shall be gratified.[2] Whether I accept or reject it, to have had it made will be always a real pleasure.

I am going to send Louis the *Last Meeting*.[3] Whatever he says of it you shall hear. For myself, I've read it with interest & a certain pleasure. It is dreadfully like you talk; that's my chief objection to it. Not that I don't like your talk; you know very well that I do. But talk is talk & writing's writing, & both are best in their proper places.

What I complain of is a certain constancy of smartness — a cackle of cleverness that goes on all the time like the noise of an electrical spark. Everybody's so diabolically *éveillé*, so infernally neat & on the spot, that I get tired of you, & them, as I do of a high-spirited lunch table at the Savile. I long for a few brilliant flashes of stupidity; I am tired of being amused, & cry out to be interested & stirred; & I beg of you when next you write romance, to forget that you are yourself, & that melodrama needn't sparkle to be affecting, but affects the more, the solider it feels & the less glittering it looks.

All this is very brutal, no doubt; but you ask, & I answer. Forgive me if my response is a hit.

[1] (James) Brander Matthews (1852-1929), American teacher, critic and writer on the theatre. Professor of Literature at Columbia University, 1892-1900, and then Professor of Dramatic Literature, 1900-24. He edited, with Laurence Hutton, the *Actors and Actresses of Great Britain and the United States* (New York, 1886). In the early 1880s Matthews regularly spent the summer months in London where he saw much of WEH and contributed to the *Magazine of Art*.
[2] Matthews suggested WEH as a contributor to the New York *Critic*.
[3] Brander Matthews's *The Last Meeting* (New York, 1885) was sent to RLS and acknowledged in a letter of early January 1886 (*Stevenson Letters*, 5, 174). He called it 'a swindle of a story'.

Ever Yours,
W.E.H.

There are hopes that ere long my brother may appear as our Macaire. Say nought about it till it's sure. Meanwhile, what of *Dark Days*?[4] And did you see & like the tramp of our excellent Edmund Grace.

[*Added by WEH at the top of the letter*] Tis old fashioned, I know; but I can't help wishing you the good old-world wishes proper to the time of year.

[4] *Dark Days*, a play by Comyns Carr and Hugh Conway (1845-85), based on Conway's sensation novel, at the Theatre Royal from 26 September 1885 to 19 December 1885.

To William Archer, 25 January 1886
ALS: BL

[18 Camden Gardens, Shepherds Bush, W.]
My dear Archer,
I am glad indeed that you think so well of the *Beau*.[1] Tis a serious disappointment, of course, to project a joint & find you've only produced an *entrée*. But to disappointments in this particular line we are getting hardened. I will own to you, moreover, that we have yet a certain faith in the *B.A.*, & mean to keep him on hand some time still. Otherwise, I believe your plan of publication would suit us down to the ground.
I agree with what you say about the abruptness & slenderness of the thing. I fear it's an ineradicable defeat; for to go back on dead work is to me impossible & hateful. The other objection I don't take on. We are not sure that Dorothy[2] is damned in her single fault. Indeed, our position towards the Penshurst business[3] is not that of any but ourselves; & I doubt we shall never win followers, or be persuaded of the errors of our own ways. Which leaves things at a deadlock no Beefeater may do away withal.
By all means send the book to your brother. Only let me have it back some time or other. I should be delighted to ask you to keep it. But I've almost none in hand.
The *Macaire* cloud-castle has vanished into air — into thin air. In the autumn we hope to pull the production off; but — !! We have a promise, & we are preparing to work up to that promise. But in theatres there is no safety; & it may be that we are only laying up failures for the near future.

[1] Archer's letter of 24 January (BL) saying that although he regarded the play 'as one of the most delicious pieces of caviar I ever tasted, but I certainly don't think "the general" would appreciate it, and for my part I could scarcely blame them'.
[2] Dorothy Musgrave, the sister of Beau Austin.
[3] *Beau Austin*, I. iii.

By the way, if you are game to read the said *Macaire*, tis very heartily at your service.

I will not forget the poet Gosse; I shall have opportunity to talk about it on Wednesday. On Thursday I go down to Bournemouth for the rest of the week. I am sending on your letter later to-night.

Always Sincerely Yours,
W.E.H

To Robert Louis Stevenson, 8 February 1886
ALS: Yale

[18 Camden Gardens, Shepherds Bush, W.]
Dear Boy,

Please deal with the two enclosures from M. le Barong T.[1]

As soon as I could, I went off today to consult with the Colvangle. He had thought of it, too; & had it not been that, in his view & by his thirteen years' practise, the object of the chair is historical & archaeological, he would have pushed the Bobus before any one.[2] As it is, he is divided between Henry Middleton (who ought to get the chair) & Martin Conway,[3] & could only give Bob a testimonial. Others could be had, of course, from Pollock, from myself, from Legros, from you; but I doubt if they would have any weight with the electors, who are all of em cut of a spear. On the whole, there fore, I conclude that the less said about it the better: that Bob has not the ghost of a chance this time, & that though would do himself no harm by candidating, he would have a world of trouble for very little good.

I am amazed to hear of the non-arrival of the books. They were sent off the same day as the *Mousquetaires*;[4] not by post, but per P.D.C. You had better enquire about them; as there's no ready money to get more.

I hear that Arthur Balfour is mad about *Otto*; & other swells besides. I fear I shall have to discontinue your society; owing to incapacity to live up to such a nob.

---

[1] Tauchnitz.

[2] Colvin had resigned the Slade Professorship of Fine Art at Cambridge University. He was appointed in 1873 for a three year period and re-elected 1876, 1879, 1882 and 1885.

[3] John Henry Middleton (1846-96), archaeologist and architect, Keeper of the Prints and Drawings at the British Museum, 1884-1912. He was elected Slade Professor after Colvin until 1892. William Martin Conway (1856-1937), art critic, collector and mountaineer. Knighted in 1895, he was created Lord Conway in 1931.

[4] Alexandre Dumas *père*, *Les Trois Mousquetaires* (Paris, 1875). WEH and RLS were working on an uncompleted anthology to be called the *Masterpieces of Prose Literature* and WEH had sent RLS *Les Trois Mousquetaires* to this end.

Anderson has writ to Japan for the big Hiroshige;[5] it's just possible there may be one going. Meanwhile, to stay on cravings, he desires me to accept some loose sheets, which have just come in. I've not yet looked at them; but you shall share.

Let me know, if the books have turned up meanwhile, what you decide to do; for I hunger to send in an ultimatorium to Longman;[6] *au plus veto.*

I fear that to read Warner the *Rubies*[7] was a mistake. He hasn't yet replied to my demand for an appointment.

I asked the practical Jones[8] about electrical lights on Saturday night. He says to hell with 'em. They are worse than useless; & you'd need to have a workman constantly on the premises looking after them. He advises a new gas-burner which cost £2; save you gas; & give the light of ten or twelve jets. Of which — particularly suitable, it seems, for the lighthouse — more anon.

Ever Affectionately Yours,
W.E.H.

This should reach you first delivery on Tuesday.

[*Added by WEH at the top of the letter*] The book-parcel contained all G. W. M. Reynolds.[9] Hence my last night's allusion to *brandade*.

[5] William Anderson (1842-1900), writer and expert on Japanese painting. He formed the finest collection of Japanese art in Europe which is now in the British Museum. The Japanese artist Ando Hiroshige (1797-1858) was a master of the ukiyo-e or colour-print school of painting.
[6] Charles James Longman (1852-1934), editor of *Longman's Magazine*, 1882-1905.
[7] RLS and WEH had produced an outline of their projected play *The King's Rubies* on 21 December 1885. In a previous letter to RLS (20 January 1886, Yale) WEH had written: 'As for Warner, 'tis advisable, I think, that we should not resign his interest on a single rebuff.'
[8] Henry Arthur Jones (1851-1929), one of the most successful playwrights of the nineteenth century. His most popular play, *The Dancing Girl*, ran for three hundred and ten nights at the Haymarket Theatre, London, 1891.
[9] G(eorge) W(illiam) M(cArthur) Reynolds (1814-79), politician, journalist and sensation novelist. Founder of *Reynold's Weekly Newspaper* in 1850.

To Robert Louis Stevenson, [?18 March 1886]
ALS: Yale

[18 Camden Gardens, Shepherds Bush, W.]
Who the devil is Bernard Shaw?[1] I've been at him all morning: with astonishment & delight. He feels like a new force in fiction.

[1] In another letter WEH used a similar opening: 'Who the deuce is Bernard Shaw?' (WEH to William Archer, 18 March 1886, Pennsylvania State University), quoted by Williamson, 141. Archer had reviewed Shaw's *Cashel Byron's Profession* in the *P.M.G.* and RLS was also taken by it.

I thought of coming down this Saturday; but I fear I can't.

I fear that Sam has misled you. Assuredly he has if he says that it was only a Blow Out. I think you'd have enjoyed it.

Ever Yours,
W.E.H.

To Robert Louis Stevenson, 8 May 1886
ALS: Yale

[18 Camden Gardens, Shepherds Bush, W.]

Dear Boy,

Herewith *S.R.* (two articles of Bob's), *Athenaeum*, *Academy*, & *Critic*,[1] with a note on Sir Henry Taylor (in my London letter) & sundry references to R.L.S.

Have you seen *The State*? The review of Vernon Lee[2] (3 cols) is by nobody less than la De M.

A fine little scandal is toward. A certain article, on 'Author Critics' in the current *S.R.*,[3] appears to have galled the animal; also to be ascribed to yours truly. In *The Stage* of this week, is a very spiteful paragraph, accusing me of (1) being the dramatic critic of the *S.R.*; (2) being the ditto of *The State*; & (3) writing the article on my brother's performance in The *Pickpocket*.[4] All are untrue. Hence we demand an apology, with the alternative of proceedings. For the next step, see the first para. of the notice of *Clito* in the current *S.R.*[5]

I must see & discuss with Hawtrey ere I discuss the *Sleeper*.[6] It isn't suitable enough to do on spec.

---

[1] WEH's unsigned 'Notes', New York *Critic*, 3 April 1886. WEH writes that Sir Henry Taylor (1800-86), a friend of RLS, had died, aged eighty-six.

[2] A review of Vernon Lee's *Baldwin: A Book of Dialogues* in the *State*, 6 May 1886, by Katharine De Mattos. Violet Paget (1856-1935), the novelist and critic wrote under the name Vernon Lee. The *State* was a very short-lived weekly (10 April to 1 July 1886) edited by Alfred Egmont Hake.

[3] 'Author Critics', *Saturday Review*, 10 April 1886. This was a general attack on those dramatists who were also drama critics.

[4] 'Chit-Chat', *Stage*, 7 May 1886. 'And if critics may not be dramatists, because it would make them unfair, what is to be said of a critic [WEH] who this week writes of his own brother.' An apology was made both to WEH and E. J. Henley in the next issue; see 'Chit-Chat', *Stage*, 14 May 1886. The play *The Pickpocket* was reviewed in the *State*, 29 April 1886, 18-19. *The Pickpocket*, adapted from the German by George Procter Hawtrey, opened at the Globe Theatre on 24 April 1886 and closed on 15 January 1887. E. J. Henley played Frederick Hope and 'his success was beyond dispute' (*Era*, 1 May 1886).

[5] 'Clito', *Saturday Review*, 8 May 1886. An attack on the favourable bias of the review of the play *Clito* at the Princess's Theatre, the bias being that of an author-critic.

[6] WEH and RLS's uncompleted play *The Sleeper Awakened*.

Love to you all. Louisa[7] has been very ill, & is still abed. I am dead beat. Bob and Katharine are quite the successful journalists.

Ever Affectionately Yours,
W.E.H.

[7] Bob's wife, Harriet Louisa Purland Stevenson (1856-1909).

To Robert Louis Stevenson, 28 July 1886
ALS: Yale

[18 Camden Gardens, Shepherds Bush, W.]
Dear Boy,
    I've been other than myself these many weeks; so you must forgive me if my behaviour seem strange. I, too, am sorry; I, too, am disappointed. I thought that, for once, I was doing wisely, in electing not to come. Sam told me of the dinner at Morven;[1] I remembered your last break-down; I knew there would be much talk, as usual; & I decided to refrain. And now it appears my sacrifice has gone for nothing! That you may not be going after all! That we've mistrusted damnably! It's enough to make one selfish for the rest of one's days.
    Things are looking up a little. This note of Scribners is promising; & I am negotiating with the *Art Journal*,[2] so that I shan't be utterly penniless. These last days, too, I am better in health & mind. I have lost my old virtues, but not, I hope, irrevocably. Happy days are (may be) in store for the pore hartis still.
    There is but one opinion about *Kidnapped*. The severe Hannay himself is enchanted with it. I met him yesterday, & says he to me: 'Upon my soul (says he) Allan Breck is as good a Highlander as there is in Sir Walter.' Says I to him, in a whisper, 'Confess (says I) that that's not saying enough; Sir Walter's Highlanders are not good; & Allan Breck is worth the lot.' Says he to me, 'You're right; but we mustn't say so in public.' *Etcetra* — , *etcetra*. Henry James, Lang, Colvin — everyone to whom I've spoken or of whom I've heard — all are in a tell. And if David[3] doesn't double the cape of 20,000 I am a fool.
    Of course the *Longman* thing was written to draw Charles Baxter;[4] I want to

[1] The country home of the Fleeming Jenkins, West Highlands, Scotland. RLS had been planning to stay with them.
[2] WEH had disagreed with the partners of Cassell and resigned his editorship of the *Magazine of Art* in late summer or early autumn 1886, although the exact date is unknown. Prior to that he was looking for employment and was offered a consultative editorship on the *Art Journal* by its editor Marcus Bourne Huish (1843-1921) which he accepted.
[3] David Balfour, the hero of *Kidnapped*.
[4] WEH had contributed the first section (signed) of what was normally Lang's *causerie*, 'At the Sign of the Ship', *Longman's Magazine*, August 1886. WEH praises *Kidnapped* but asks that the dedicatee [Baxter] explain 'L.J.R.' mentioned in the dedication. Baxter did not contribute an explanation. The Liberty, Justice and Reverence club was a secret society whose members

make him answer the challenge in a letter to Lang. Lang would probably print his communication, & the advert would do no harm. Twig? He (C.B.) is pleased with the dedication; & with the terms in which I've dealt with it in the *Critic*,[5] & of which I hope your Highness also will deign to approve.

I met Miss Gilder[6] yestern, & had a long talk with her. A kindly intelligent woman, with a pleasant face & amiable manners. She has been scouring Europe with Miss Kellogg,[7] the *prima donna*, & returns to the States to-morrow (Thursday). Her great regret is not to have seen the noble R.L.S. Her brothers (she informs me) are Stevensonians of the acutest type. The letters, it appears, are a great success; & Richard, after reading the first, rushed round to Joe, in great excitement, & told him that he'd 'struck it rich in the matter of London correspondence'. Which is very gratifyin' to be sure.

I am giving Meredith a clinker in the next *Athenaeum*,[8] in respect of *Rhoda Fleming*. I hope he'll read it. If all goes well, I shall make him the subject of my next letter.[9]

I agree with Scribners that you should stick to your old title for your new edition; & suggest that you add your new title as a sub & see that the book is advertized as both.[10]

Are those letters of Katharine's any good?[11] This is the third time of asking.

A world of thanks for the cheque. I fear I shall have to return it. I've put things off too long, & must stay in town to pass the September part of the magazine. I leave for Paris (I hope) on Saturday week at least;[12] & between this & then, I've a heap to do, & little energy or inclination to do it. I'll keep the document for a day or two; for tis just possible that I might use a part of it in running down on Sunday. But I fear me much that I've baulked myself & you; & that there's nothing more to be said about it.

I'd almost forgot that yesterday I saw Balfour. He hadn't written because he hadn't exhausted his list of applications. The last chance was only done with a day or two ago. I told him you were coming to town, so that perhaps he will not write to you, as he expects to see you soon.

were Baxter, Bob Stevenson, Walter Ferrier and two others. They met at a pub in the Advocate's Close, Edinburgh. Among its objects was the abolition of the House of Lords.
[5] 'London Letter', *Critic*, 17 July 1886.
[6] Jeanette Leonard Gilder (1849-1916), and her brother Joseph Benson Gilder (1858-1936) were editors of the *Critic*, a New York journal.
[7] The American soprano Clara Louise Kellogg (1842-1916).
[8] WEH's unsigned review of *Rhoda Fleming*, *Athenaeum*, 31 July 1886.
[9] 'London Letter', *Critic*, 14 August 1886.
[10] *Kidnapped*.
[11] In a letter to RLS, WEH had written: ' Your praise of Katharine's letters gave me an idea. Don't you think the correspondence might be redacted into a sort of comic *nouvelle* in letters? To go in fifteen or twenty pages of the *Cornhill*, & be impressed on Jimmy Payn by one or other of us?' (2 July 1886, Yale). Nothing came of it, but WEH refers to it in his letter to Graham Balfour (20 June 1900).
[12] WEH was to sit for his bust by Rodin.

I've not seen old Galpin.[13] Why should I see him? I've been scurvily used: & there's an end of it.

Ever Affectionately Yours,

W.E.H.

Keep well & lusty. There must be a campaign this autumn.

[*Added by WEH at the top of the letter*] The Dilke business is a pity.[14] I hope Robertson won't use it. For your sake, most of all.

[13] Thomas Dixon Galpin (1828-1910) a partner in Cassell.
[14] RLS had written a letter criticising the behaviour of Sir Charles Dilke, Bt (1843-1911), in a divorce case and it was published in the *Court and Society Review*, 29 July 1886. Charles Gray Robertson was the editor.

To Robert T. Hamilton Bruce,[1] 24 August 1886
ALS: Yale

18 Camden Gardens, Shepherds Bush, W.

My dear Hamilton Bruce,
    I can't conceive what has become of you. What grief sits on your noble heart? What passion stops that weekly flood of magnanimity & Ruskinism that erst was wont to whelm us as we sat / At breakfast, dallying with the cheerful egg, / The sprightly ham, the crisp & sparkling toast? / Answer me quick, for I am fain to hear!
    I am from Paris late, the capital / *Of* girdy France, where I, my boy, have been / *A*-sitting for my bust; where I have looked / *U*pon the red wine & the white with Eyes / *Of* wisdom & discernment; where I have heard / *S*trange things, such things as I have joyed to hear / *Of* Monticelli,[2] which I will in time / *C*ommunicate to thee; where I have learned / *T*hat, lacking Rodin & his works, thy house / That house of art in which thou gettest drunk / With such complacency of heart & mind, / *A*nd such aesthetic feeling is not worth / *A* common damn! All which thou may'st perpend.
    I hope to be with you some time next month. Armed for the fray, eager & valiant / And worth a world of Bruces, drunk or not. / Be-Marised or bemused![3]

[1] Robert Tyndale Hamilton Bruce (1828-99), an Edinburgh collector of fine art and friend of Baxter. He and WEH were firm friends and WEH later dedicated his poem 'Invictus' to him. Later he became one of the founders of the *Scots Observer* of which WEH became editor.
[2] Adolphe Monticelli (1824-86), French painter.
[3] A reference to the Dutch artist brothers Jacobus Henricus Maris (1837-99), Matthijs Maris (1839-1919), and Willem Maris (1844-1910).

And so farewell.

Ever Yours,
W.E.H.

There is a chance, my Bruce, that I shall pass
From Cassell unto Virtue,[4] & assist
In editing the venerable *Art-Journal*.
Then may'st thou look for recognition swift
Of Matthew Maris, William, James, & all
The sainthings of thy calendar — the Mauves,
The Bosbooms & Artzes.[5] Every one
From Corot up to Cottier himself,[6]
Greatest, the chief of all!

If thou couldst sell
Some black-&-whites just now thou wouldst confer
A mighty favour, as the family
Is bust, stone-broke, & in a manner dead
And drained.

Tis thus I woo the Muse,
My Hamilton, be thine the witness, brief
But brave, of an endearment this fair morn
Of August, now the bloom is on the eye.

[4] Virtue and Co., publishers of the *Art Journal*.
[5] Anton Mauve (1838-88), Dutch painter. Johannes Bosboom (1817-91), Dutch painter. David Adolf Constant Artz (1837-90), Dutch painter.
[6] Daniel Cottier (1838-91), a well-known collector of paintings.

To Robert T. Hamilton Bruce, 6 October 1886
ALS: Yale

18 Camden Gardens, Shepherds Bush, W.

My dear Bruce,
    I am delighted to hear that the catalogue is launched;[1] &, though I think

[1] Bruce was instrumental in arranging an exhibition of French and Dutch paintings for the Edinburgh International Exhibition of Industry, Science and Art, from 6 May to 30 October 1886. WEH is referring to Bob Stevenson as the better man for the preface of the *Memorial Catalogue*. WEH contributed 'A Note on Romanticism' to the *Memorial Catalogue of the French and Dutch Loan Collection*. Edinburgh International Exhibition 1886 (Edinburgh, 1888). The 'Note' was reprinted in his *Views and Reviews: Essays in Appreciation*. II Art (1902).

Stevenson the better man, I shall be glad to contribute the preface.

But I want to know, first of all, what sort of thing you want? how much of it you want? & when you want it by? Also — for I am busy just now, & a good deal perplexed as to my movements — how long the show remains on view?

Write me all this; & I doubt not we shall hit things off exactly.

That the thing has been a failure I don't a bit believe; nor, if you are candid, do you either.

I've a vile influenza, & my wife's neuralgic. Such is life.

Ever Yours,
W.E.H.

To Auguste Rodin, 28 October 1886
ALS: Musée Rodin

18 Camden Gardens, Shepherds Bush, W.

Mon ami,

Stevenson va mieux; mais reste tojours malade. Je lui ai fait parvenir votre lettre.

Je suis de retour d'Edinbourg. Il y a là un de mes amis, qui voudrait avoir une épreuve du buste. Est-ce que cela se pourrait faire au prix de la fonte? Je vous prie de me le dire, et de me dire aussi le prix des épreuves en plâtre.

Nous avons le dessein de faire dans l'hiver de '87 une exposition des grands peintres français de l'école moderne — Delacroix, Millet, Corot, Rousseau, Diaz — et de leurs successeurs hollandais et français. Je ne sais pas si cela sera possible. Mais si cela se fait, il faut que vous en soyez, et que la collection comprenne un choix sérieux de vos oeuvres. C'est pourquoi je vous engage de ne rien faire pour percer à Londres sans me consulter.

Ce sera assez difficile; mais je ne désespère pas d'y parvenir. Je n'ai pas besoin de vous combien il me plairait de vous faire passer avec de tels hommes. Vous gagneriez beaucoup, et eux aussi.

Claude Phillips me paraît enthousiasmé de voses choses. Je n'ai pas encore vu Monkhouse, mais je vais le voir samedi soir, et j'attends de lui un enthousiasme pareil.

Nous ferons tout pour vous, mais à la condition seule que vous restiez tourjours le grand artiste que nous avons salé dès le commencement.

A vous,
W.E.H.

On trouve le buste très beau et très *Moi*, mais un peu trop maigre et trop rêveur et pas tout à fait si flamboyant ni si anglais que le pauvre modèle.

Translation

My friend,
      Stevenson is better; but still ill. I showed him your letter.
I am just back from Edinburgh. One of my friends there would like a copy of
the bust.[1] Could this be done for the cost of the casting? Please let me know,
and let me know as well the price of the plaster copies.
      We plan to organise in the winter of '87 an exhibition of the important
painters of the modern school[2] — Delacroix, Corot, Rousseau, Diaz — and of
their French and Dutch successors. I don't know whether it will be possible.
But if it does happen, you have to be a part of it, and the collection will have to
include a good selection of your works.[3] That is why I entreat you not to do
anything to get yourself known in London without consulting me.
      The thing will be quite difficult; but I am very hopeful that I'll manage it. I
need not tell you how delighted I would be to have you in the company of such
men. You would gain a lot, and so would they.
      Claude Phillips[4] seems very enthusiastic about your stuff. I have not yet
seen Monkhouse, but I will see him Saturday night, and I expect him to be
equally enthusiastic.
      We shall do everything we can for you, the only condition is that you should
always remain the great artist whom we recognized from the start.

Yours,
W.E.H.

Everyone finds the bust very handsome and very *Me*, if a little too skinny and
too dreamy, and not quite as flamboyant or English as the poor model.

---

[1] Most likely Hamilton Bruce. A copy of WEH's bust was not made.
[2] This was the exhibition for which WEH contributed historical and biographical notes in *A
Century of Artists: A Memorial of the Glasgow International Exhibition 1888*, (Glasgow,
1889). The Exhibition was opened on 8 May 1888 by the Prince and Princess of Wales and
closed on 10 November 1888.
[3] Three pieces by Rodin were in the exhibition: WEH lent his bust, Rodin sent his bust of
Victor Hugo and the German sculptor Gustave Natorp (1836-?), resident in England from 1884
to 1898, sent the *Recumbent Girl*.
[4] Claude Phillips (1846-1924), barrister, art critic for the *Daily Telegraph*, Keeper of the
Wallace Collection, 1897-1911. Knighted 1911.

To William Archer, 10 November 1886
ALS: BL

18 Camden Gardens, Shepherds Bush, W.

My dear Archer,

I want you, if *you* will, to write a couple of articles (3000 words each) for the *Art Journal*, on the collection of West's toy-theatre prints,[1] now in the Print Room. The *A.J.* page is 1250 words, & the pay is £2..2 per page.

If you consent (and I hope you will) I must ask you to keep the thing close; at all events until the *A.J.* is furnished. As I've engaged to do it for the *S R*.[2]

Colvin will tell you every thing you want to know; especially if you tell him that you are questing for me. If you are on, tell me, & we'll settle about pictures afterwards.

I think you'll find a couple of articles in the collection. There are the plays to begin with; & there are the character portraits after.

I should (I may tell you) have gone for this to R.L.S., had he been in working order. (Do you remember his Skelt article in the *M. of A.*?) As I've to choose between myself & you, I am glad to be unselfish, & come down upon you.

Always Yours,
W.E.H.

[1] William Archer's 'The Drama in Pasteboard', *Art Journal*, April 1887 and May 1887.
[2] This has not been found.

To Robert Louis Stevenson, Monday [?February 1887]
ALS: Yale

[18 Camden Gardens, Shepherds Bush, W.]

Dear Lad,

I got back on Friday morning; but had to start next day for Cambridge & the Dew.[1] Hence I returned last night. Dead beat; for I'd a wild time in Edinburgh, & in Cambridge, to say nothing of the violent delights of photography. I talked till three o' the clock on Sunday morning. To-day I feel refreshed; but not so much as you might believe.

The catalogue is so far a great success. They are going to double the screw, & will give me not £50, but £100. What do you think of that? And moreover, I think there's a 'Thomson of Duddingstone' in the wind as well.[2] And I feel

[1] Dew-Smith.
[2] WEH did not produce an essay on the Scottish landscape painter John Thomson (1778-1840) apart from 'Rev. John Thomson, Hon. R.S.A.' in *A Century of Artists*: It was reprinted in his *Views and Reviews: Essays in Appreciation*. II Art.

strongly inclined to think that a certain *Specimens of Prose Narrative* is worth
ready money also. What says't thou there to? I purpose to go back in June; for
the illuminations, & I think I could bring back the contract in my pocket.

Meanwhile please look over these few pages of proof;[3] & suggest any
changes you feel disposed to do. And let them come back soon — soon.

Donkin is anxiously expecting yes or no from you.[4] Which is it to be? Copy
by the 1*st* May. *R.S.V.P.*

I called at the Infirmary, & presented Mrs P.[5] with my portrait & Anna's.
She is still afoot, but greatly softened & a little enfeebled. I took Bruce to see
her, & the Châtelaine likewise. Also I proposed Edmund Baxter's health on the
occasion of his 75*th* birthday;[6] he looks wonderfully fresh, & his brain's as
active & as clear as ever. What a puny & a wretched generation is ours!

At Bruce's there was much talk of you & Rider Haggard. I didn't need to set
any of them in the right way: they were there already. They know the
difference between literature & London Journalism a good deal better than
Andrew Lang.

Much to tell you, when we meet. When's that to be? Write soon, & say.

Ever Affectionately Yours.
W.E.H.

Tell Fanny, with my love & the Châtla's, I've her umbrella in the hall, & owe
her six bob on it. Love to the Commercial Traveller.

[*Added by WEH at the top of the letter*] Still tired — tired. But the cloud has
lifted, & shows no sign of gathering again. God bless *that* time at Skerryvore.
How goeth the *Judge*?[7]

---

[3] Proofs of WEH verses for *Voluntaries for an East London Hospital* (1887), edited by the
physician Horatio Bryan Donkin (1845-1927). These were the revised and extended versions of
his *Cornhill* 'Hospital Outlines'. Donkin was at the East London Hospital for Children and a
writer on criminology. He was knighted in 1911.

[4] RLS contributed his poem 'Ad Matrem'.

[5] Mrs Porter, the subject of WEH's poem 'Staff-Nurse: Old Style' in 'Hospital Outlines:
Sketches and Portraits', *Cornhill Magazine*, July 1875. She is identified in Martin Goldman,
Lister Ward (Bristol and Boston, 1987), 46-8.

[6] Charles's father Edmund Baxter (1813-94), an Edinburgh lawyer.

[7] RLS and Fanny's, *The Hanging Judge: A Drama in Three Acts and Six Tableaux* (1887).

To J. W. Gleeson White,[1] 16 June 1887
ALS: Bodleian

18 Camden Gardens, Shepherds Bush, W.

Dear Sir,

It has just occurred to me that you may have overlooked the very pretty ballades published by Miss Robinson in her *Handful of Honeysuckles*. If you have, & you care to write to her (20 Earl's Terrace, Kensington) mentioning my name, I imagine you would get them at once.

What you say about my verses has given me great pleasure. At one time I should have been glad enough to take your advice, & publish a book of them. But that was years ago & since then, as Lang says of me, I have 'retired from business', & gone into prose. I imagined that what I printed would quietly rest in oblivion undisturbed; with all that I never succeeded in printing as well. I confess to a certain pleasure in the task of resurrection; but tis resurrection after all, & I doubt I shall not go back to it.

Oddly enough, I have just found place for a set of copies of verse written a dozen years ago, & rejected *sur place* by every editor in London. If you come upon a little volume of *Voluntaries* published in aid of the East London Hospital for children, you will find a W.E.H. who has much in common with the troubadour of *London*.

I have no doubt that the difficulty of selection is very great. If I can assist you in it, pray command me.

Very Sincerely Yours,
W.E.H.

I've not heard from Stevenson; but I hope to see him soon, as we've something to do in collaboration, which has got to be done at once.

[1] Joseph William Gleeson White (1851-98), journalist. A co-founder of the art magazine *The Studio* in 1893. At this time he was editing *Ballades and Rondeaus* (1887) in 'The Canterbury Poets' series to which WEH contributed thirty-one poems, most of which had appeared in *London*. The edition also contained poems by among others RLS, Austin Dobson, Lang, Swinburne, Gosse, Oscar Wilde, Robert Bridges (1844-1930), later Poet Laureate from 1913 and Arthur Symons (1865-1945), later editor of *The Savoy*, 1896.

To William Archer, 1 October 1887
ALS: BL

1 Fort Crescent, Margate[1]

My dear Archer,

I can't tell you much about Rodin by letter.[2] If I had you hip to lunch,

[1] WEH was on holiday and staying at a lodging house.
[2] In a letter to Archer WEH had asked: 'Have you read the little series it [*The Critic*] is

twould be other guess work.

As it is, I must refer you to an article — with a portrait you may have seen on Louis's bedroom mantel — in the *Court & Society*[3] some three months back (I believe) & to another in the *M. of A.* on 'Two Busts of Victor Hugo',[4] sometime in 1885.

If I were *chez moi*, I could show you both & more besides. Also Louis's letter to *The Times* in August-September '86,[5] defending R. from the ass Armytage's description of him as 'the Zola of sculpture',[6] & describing his visit to the studio, with Low & others, & the impression it left on their minds. If you look up this last take care to read 'forceful' for the 'fanciful' of the printers, in L's definition of Rodin's talent.

They met in Paris last year, on my introduction (I was sitting to R. for my bust which I remember now you haven't seen), & fell in love with each other. Louis presented R. with copies of *L'Ile au Trésor* & *Le Suicide Club* (he told me he felt dam mean in the presence of the sculptor's works) & Rodin presented L. with a plaster of his *Printemps qui Passe*, which is a group ⅓ life size, in the round.

Louis has promised me an article on Rodin for the *A.J.* next year, & as soon as I return I shall, as per contract, dispatch him the materials. Meanwhile, I may tell you that Rodin is about 45; is a pupil of Lecoq de Boisbaudran, Barye, & Carrier-Belleuse;[7] has (thank God!) be[en] only once medalled;[8] is the sculptor of a *St. Jean* & an *Age d'airain* (both in the Luxembourg); a wonderful *Eve*, a *Paolo & Francesca* which is — but there!), some extraordinary busts, Hugo, Jean-Paul Laurens, Henri Becque, W.E.H., Carrier-Belleuse[9] — & a multitude of *figurines* — incomparably passionate & expressive; & was last year rejected by the Royal Academy through (I suppose) Mr. W. Calder Marshall.[10] His game is the expression of passion. His technical accomplishment is very remarkable; his imagination, intensity are more remarkable still. His *Dante* door[11] (says Dalou, the sculptor, & no great friend of his) will be the great work of the present century. *Voilà*.

publishing of 'Authors at Home'? I don't know if you'd care to do it; but if you would, a 'Stevenson at Skerryvore' would just now be very acceptable indeed to them' (20 September 1887, BL). Archer's 'Robert Louis Stevenson at Skerryvore' was published in the *Critic*, 5 November 1887.
[3] The unsigned 'Auguste Rodin', *Court and Society Review*, 19 January 1887.
[4] WEH's 'Two Busts of Victor Hugo,' *Magazine of Art*, January 1884.
[5] *The Times*, 6 September 1886. Reprinted in *Stevenson Letters*, 5, 311-12.
[6] Letter, *The Times*, 30 August 1886. Edward Armitage, RA (1817-96), artist.
[7] Horace Lecoq de Boisbaudran (1802-97), French sculptor. Antoine-Louis Barye (1796-1875), French sculptor of animals. Albert-Ernest Carrier-Belleuse (1824-87), French sculptor.
[8] Rodin received third prize for his *St John the Baptist Preaching* at the Paris Salon of 1880.
[9] Jean-Paul Laurens (1838-1921), French painter. Henri Becque (1837-?1899), French actor.
[10] William Calder Marshall, R.A. (1813-94), Scottish sculptor who was elected a Royal Academician in 1852. He was of the established classical style and became very popular and produced the 'Agriculture' group on the Albert Memorial, London.
[11] Rodin's famous *Gates of Hell*, commissioned by the French Government in 1880, but never completed. They were based on Dante's *Inferno*. Jules Dalou (1838-1902), French sculptor.

About collaboration: yes, I've always understood that the order is alphabetical, your instance to the contrary. I've discussed it with Louis. When we wrote the *Deacon*, it was decided, on his suggestion, that his name, being better known than mine, should go first, and its precedence might help the play. When we wrote the *Beau*, *Macaire* & the *Admiral*, it was determined also on his suggestion, to revert to the established rule. That is all I can tell you.

Ever Yours,
W.E.H.

Low's etching is but a trifle: a sort of *petite femme*; you needn't say anything but that it's 'graceful'.

I find I've forgotten to refer you to a very temperate, intelligent, & well-considered account of Rodin by Cosmo Monkhouse in (I think) the January ('87) *Portfolio*;[12] & to mention one of the sculptor's master-works — the great group of the Calais Burghers — Eustache de Saint-Pierre & his pals[13] — just set in the square at Calais.

I see that Sharp is more of Gosse's way of thinking about *Underwoods* than yours.[14]

[12] 'Auguste Rodin', *Portfolio*, January 1887.
[13] Eustache de Saint-Pierre was a leading burgher of Calais when it was besieged by King Edward III in 1347. Rodin was commissioned to produce a work, the *Burghers of Calais*, to commemorate the six burghers who offered their lives to the King in return for the safety of the city.
[14] Sharp's review of RLS's *Underwoods* in the *Academy*, 1 October 1887. William Sharp ('Fiona Macleod') (1856-1905), Scottish poet, journalist and novelist. Gosse had reviewed *Underwoods* in a general article 'R. L. Stevenson as a Poet' in *Longman's Magazine*, October 1887. Archer's review was in the *Pall Mall Gazette*, 20 August 1887.

To Robert Louis Stevenson, 10 October 1887
ALS: Yale

18 Camden Gardens, Shepherds Bush, W.

Dear Lad,
I got back on Saturday, & found your good letter.[1] I meant to answer it as it deserves, but was too ill; so you must take what I can give, which ain't too much.

The *Antient Nightingale*,[2] I hear is delighted. He is turning up anew, & you may presently look for more music. You shd. publish all three in *Scribner's*. 'Twould please him, I think, who is a little forgotten & foregone, & now waits quickly for death, contented in his brave old heart, & with as much wits as most of us still working & busy in his brave old head.

[1] The letter of mid to late September 1887 from New York (*Stevenson Letters*, 6, 11).
[2] Dr Thomas Gordon Hake (1809-1895), physician and poet, father of A. E. Hake. RLS had sent some verses to WEH for Hake.

Lang was here yesterday. I showed him your letter. He was grateful. He said, 'they don't pay *me* as much as that in *Longman's*';[3] & suggested that, when you ain't quite up to it, you should turn in W.H.P. He hoped you wouldn't be huffed by his 'Dear Louis of the *A*wful Cheek',[4] & I took it on myself to promise & vow in your name that you couldn't. I added that I thought the patronage of Chadband *fils*[5] would be a damned sight more likely to put your back up than a world of Awful Cheek; & I believe that he agreed with me.

I think that the salary is good, & worth trying for. Anyhow, you can keep it for a year. After that, I feel doubtful. Just now, you are fuller of delicate matters than ever; you have mastered your trade; your interest in life, letters, morals, art, is quick, bright, undefatigable; you shd. find the task not difficult. And, if it were to give way, £600 is £600.

(Meanwhile, remember, please, that you are booked for a 'Rodin' for me. I will gather & send materials as soon as may be; & as soon as may be you can get it off your hands. You may write from 3000 to 3500 words.)

I am delighted you've fallen into the hands of St. Gaudens.[6] Save Auguste Imperator, he's about the best going. Or one of the best anyhow. Oddly enough, I've just been arranging that Clarence Cook[7] (Low[8] will tell you about him) is to write an article on St. Gaudens for the *A.J.*; so that the medallion will come in beautifully. Of course I took it for England. And of course I claim *épreuve* for home consumptions. In which I imagine I am more magnanimous than you, who have neglected your opportunities of acquiring a certain Bust in a manner not to be adequately condemned in words.

I got the Montreal *Gazette* this morning.[9] I am much pleased with our reception so far. It seems to have been all our fancy could have possibly painted. If we go on so, I shall marshall our legions in person in New York; there's no doubt of that. Annie Robe seems to be well worth her £40 a week;[10] Grace, Desmond, Lyons, Stewart, Coote[11]— all seem to have scored; the gifted Saker[12]

---

[3] RLS's had written: 'O, I am now a salaried person, £600 a year, to write twelve articles in *Scribner's Magazine*' (*Stevenson Letters*, 6, 11).

[4] Lang's poem to RLS in *Longman's Magazine*, October 1887 in response to RLS's poem beginning 'Dear Andrew, with the brindled hair' (*Underwoods*, Book I, xiv).

[5] Presumably Gosse. A hypocritical character in Dickens's *Bleak House* (1852-53).

[6] Augustus Saint-Gaudens (1848-1907), Irish born American sculptor, produced a medallion of RLS in 1887/8.

[7] Clarence Chatham Cook (1828-1900), American art critic, editor and writer. He was art critic of *The New York Tribune*, 1863-69, and editor of the *Studio*, 1884-92. The article was not written.

[8] Will Hicok Low (1853-1932), American artist and friend of RLS and Bob Stevenson.

[9] Ted Henley headed a theatrical company touring with *Deacon Brodie*. The first performance of *Deacon Brodie* at the Academy of Music, Montreal, was reviewed in *The Montreal Gazette*, 27 September 1887.

[10] Annie Robe (d. 1922) played Mary Brodie.

[11] Frederick Desmond played Andrew Ainslie; Edmund Lyons (1851-1906) played William Lawson; Graham Stewart played Walter Leslie; Caroline (Carrie) Eva Coote (1870-1907), married Sir William George Pearce, Bt, in 1905.

[12] Horatio Saker (?1848-1902) played George Smith.

alone does not appear to have come off. Of Ted's own share there was never any doubt in my mind. I only hope that *you* may be able to see him; I don't see why you shouldn't; you will have a soft place in your heart for your 'old schoolboy dream' while life lasts if you do. Meanwhile, dear lad, let us be thankful as we may that the boy is an Artist, & will give us, if we can give him the material, as complete a realization of our vision as can be got. That, to my mind, is the best of all. We need not be at the pains of writing one-part machines; we may write *plays*, if we can, with the certainty that right will be done them.

I've been really very ill. I know now what colic is, & what is flatulence. *Histoire de ne plus donner dans la spiritueux*! I came up on Saturday to see Mennell: I couldn't help myself; so that my holiday has been brief indeed. He has exhibited a solution from the pharmacopoeia, with his wonted audacity & success; & I'm now in the way of salvation. Which is all, I think, I need say about myself.

Gleeson White has been reviewed in the *P.M.G.*,[13] & the reviewer is good enough to give me second place after Dobson. 'Tis a vast deal more than I expected, & as much (to say the least) as I deserve. By the way, if you want to be revenged on Gosse for the *Longman* thing, you might turn to & peruse his *rondeaux*. One in particular delights me. I want to read it to Fanny, in whose bosom I know I shall find absolute sympathy. [*next two sentences deleted and illegible*]

Bob I haven't seen, or heard of, for weeks. He & Louisa are engaged in devouring my collection of Dumas: not, it is suspected, without designs upon the future of English literature. Katharine I saw yesterday: Maccoll has sent her the novel of the year — *Poor Nellie*,[14] it's called, & the writer is that mysterious creature who made such a hit, *ma pudeur* with *The Story of my Trivial Life & Misfortunes* — so that she prospers. She tells me that Dora,[15] who arrived on Friday, looks dreadfully ill. The Châtelaine is fairly well, but worried by bad news from Edinburgh. Hake may soon be within your gates: I saw him last night, & W.H.P. likewise; they didn't depart, indeed, till two this morning. I am now determined to cure the Wollock of alcohol, as I've cured myself; so you may send me the God speed I deserve. Colvin is custodizing, & studying the critics of his *Keats*:[16] with a mingling of agony & interest which to me, who don't give a tinker's dam for all the criticism ever produced, is a little *écœurant*. That's all I know.

Remember us to Low. We hope & pray that the agency may come off, & are sure that, if it don't, 'twill be no fault of yours. We hope too, that the

---

[13] Archer's unsigned review of *Ballades and Rondeaus* in the *Pall Mall Gazette*, 5 October 1887.

[14] *Poor Nellie*, 3 vols (Edinburgh, 1887) by the author of *My Trivial Life and Misfortunes*, 2 vols (Edinburgh, 1883).

[15] Bob's sister Dorothea ('Dora') Frances Alan Stevenson (1850-1931).

[16] Sidney Colvin's *Keats* in the English Men of Letters series (1887).

Hospitalisms[17] may smile upon Burlingame. You are often in our thoughts.
Our love to all of you.

Ever Affectionately Yours,
W.E.H.

[17] With a letter to Edward Burlingame RLS sent WEH's *In Hospital* poems with a view to
publication in *Scribner's Magazine* but he was unsuccessful (RLS to Burlingame, *Stevenson
Letters*, 6, 42). Edward Livermore Burlingame (1848-1922), American journalist. He joined
Scribner's in 1879 and was editor of *Scribner's Magazine*, 1887-1914.

To Auguste Rodin, 9 November 1887[1]
ALS: Musée Rodin

1 Merton Place, Chiswick, W.

Mon cher Rodin,
Vous avez bien lu: vous n'avez fait qu'une seule faut d'orthographie. Voici
l'addresse en plein: —
1 Merton Place,
High Road,
Chiswick,
London, W.
Si ce n'est pas lisible encore, dites-le moi, et je vais recommencer.
Je vais beaucoup mieux à présent. Je ne bois plus des spiritueux. Il m'a
coûté à en renoncer l'usage; mais les difficultés ne me déplaisent pas, j'ai
persisté, et voilà que je commence à m'en trouver bien.
Ç'a m'a rendu le travail excessivement dur. Je m'occupe d'achever, et de
passer par la presse, un espèce de *Catalogue*, avec des biographies des grand
artistes Romantiques — Corot, Millet, Rousseau, Delacroix. Je connais mon
Romantiques pas mal; et écrire une dizaine de pages là-dessus a été l'affaire
d'une dizaine de jours. Maintenant, les choses commencent à aller plus
facilement. J'en suis assez content, car c'ètait vraiment trop de peine.
Le *Catalogue* sera un superbe livre. Je crois aussi qu'il restera comme
document. Puis, je m'occupe d'un volume de *poéshie* j'ai publié quelques
imitations des antiques formes francaises — des ballades, des, des rondeaux,
des villanelles — dans une collection passablement hétérogène; et voici un
éditeur qui me demande un recueil fait par moi seul! C'est longtemps que je ne
rime plus; mais j'ai assez rimé dans le temps pour pouvoir lui donner ce qu'il
veut sans trop de peine.
Il y a aussi qu'on me demande un volume (à bon marché) sur le vieux
Dumas je le ferai de tout coeur. Puis mon frère a fait un grand succés en

[1] WEH appears to have written '9/11/81' and this has been previously accepted as correct but
the address and contents of the letter place the date as 1887. The Henleys had moved to Merton
Place on 21 October 1887 (WEH to Archer, 20 October 1887, BL).

Amérique avec le drame que j'ai fait en collaboration avec Stevenson. Je ne suis pas encore à faire de l'argent nulle part; mais je commence à entretenir des espérances un peu sérieuses.

La nouvelle maison est charmante. Elle date du commencement du siècle: c'est a dire, c'est bien bâtie, bien chaude, et bien confortable. Quand vous la verrez, vous nous en féliciterez, j'en suis sûr.

Stevenson va bien, à ce que je crois. Il va passer l'hiver à vingt-quatre heures de New York. Il sera content d'avoir des photographies de vois choses.

J'y pense, moi, bien souvent. Le buste vous rappelle toujours. Ça reste d'une éternelle beauté — la beauté du grand art. Vous n'avez pas manqué de déboires, mon ami — au contraire; je sais que vous avez beaucoup lutté, beaucoup souffert, beaucoup peiné. Et pourtant que vous devez être heureux! Vous travaillez pour les siècles de l'avenir; vous savez que ce que vous faites vous le faites bien. Oui, vous devez être bien heureux.

A vous de coeur,
W.E.H.

Translation

My dear Rodin,

You read properly: you made only one spelling mistake. Here is the full address: —

    1 Merton Place,
        High Road,
            Chiswick,
                London, W.

If it is still not legible, tell me and I'll start again.

I am much better now. I don't drink spirits anymore. Giving them up has been a great struggle; but I don't find difficulties unpleasant, I held on, and now I am beginning to feel all the better for it.

All that has made working excessively hard. I am busy finishing and putting through the press, a kind of *Catalogue*,[2] including the biographies of the great Romantic artists — Corot, Millet, Rousseau, Delacroix. I know my Romanticism quite well; and writing ten pages on that subject has only been the task of ten days or so. Now things are beginning to go more easily. I am quite pleased about that, for it really has been painful.

The *Catalogue* will be a superb book. I think it will remain as a document. I have also been busy with a book of poetry. I have published a few imitations of the old French forms — ballads, rondeaux and villanelles — in a collection which is quite heterogeneous; and now there is a publisher who is asking for a

---

[2] The Edinburgh *Memorial Catalogue*.

book containing only my own pieces![3] I have not written verse for ages; but I did enough of it a long time ago to be able to give him now what he wants without too much trouble.

Finally I have been asked to do a (cheap) volume on old Dumas, which I'll be delighted to do. Also my brother has met with great success in America with the tragedy I wrote with Stevenson. I have not yet got to the point where I am making money anywhere; but I am beginning to be fairly seriously hopeful.

The new house is charming. It was built at the beginning of the century: that is to say, it's well built, it's warm and very comfortable. When you see it, you will congratulate us for having got it, I am sure.

Stevenson is well, as far as I know. He is going to spend the winter twenty-four hours away from New York.[4] He will be pleased to have the photographs of your things.

As for me, I think about them a lot. The bust always reminds me of you. The beauty of it remains eternal — it is the beauty of great art. You have not been short of disappointments, my friend — quite the reverse; I know that you have had to fight hard, to suffer much, to labour. And yet how happy you must be! You are working for the centuries to come; you know that what you do, you do well. Indeed, you must be very happy.

With warmest good wishes,
W.E.H.

[3] Alfred Trubner Nutt (1856-1910), son of the founder of the publishing firm of David Nutt, and eventual publisher of WEH's verse. The firm started business as a bookshop at 158 Fleet Street, London, in 1837, finally moving to 57-59 Long Acre in 1890. Alfred Nutt published books on Celtic tradition, Gaelic and Icelandic texts. He founded the *Folk-Lore Journal* in 1883 and was a co-founder of the Folk-Lore Society in 1887. The business was finally sold to Simpkin, Marshall, Hamilton, Kent and Co. in 1916.

[4] RLS and Fanny spent the winter of 1887-88 in Saranac Lake in the Adirondacks, an area recommended for sufferers from tuberculosis.

To William Archer, 29 November 1887
ALS: BL

1 Melton Place, Chiswick, W

Dear Archer,

Your Skerryvore is capital.[1] I should think the Bedlamites are well pleased with it. Louis, when he wrote last week, was more or less maniacal: having given over the use of tobacco, & made himself thereby unfit for human food. By this time, no doubt he has regained his composure, though I fear that your remarks about his moustache[2] — which is the apple of his eye — may test his philosophy

[1] Archer's 'Robert Louis Stevenson at Skerryvore', *Critic*, 5 November 1887.
[2] Archer replied that the remark was WEH's and not his (30 November 1887, Pierpont

deeply.

What is the meaning of 'heroic mould'?[3] Is it an euphemism for a certain tendency to obesity? I believe it is, & I shall write & congratulate the lady on her Band![4]

Did I tell you that your unpublished wish has come off, & that a publisher has asked me for a volume of verse? Well, that's what's the matter with me; & a disappointed man you're like to be with the result.

The *Deacon* has scored terrifically in Chicago.[5] The notices are really astonishing. If I'd written them myself I couldn't have done better. More than that, the actor has scored as heavily as the play.

When are we to meet?

Ever Yours Sincerely,
W.E.H.

Morgan). WEH in his 'London Letter' in the *Critic* had remarked on J. W. Alexander's portrait of RLS that his 'moustache [was] of a few damp hairs'. Archer had referred to RLS's 'thin-lipped sensitive mouth'.
[3] Archer had described Fanny as 'a woman of small physical stature, but surely of a heroic mould' in his *Critic* article.
[4] Waist.
[5] *Deacon Brodie* was at M'Vicker's Theater, Chicago, from 31 October to 12 November 1887 where it had been retained for a second week. Elsewhere it was a failure.

To Austin Dobson, 30 December 1887
ALS: London

Merton Place, Chiswick, W.

My dear Dobbie,

Your Goldie arrived last night.[1] A thousand thanks for him. I read much of him ere I slept, & he struck me as being, so far, your best in prose. He gave me ideas: — thus, perhaps, you have but to go on, & do best what you like doing, to excel in this medium as in the other.

All good wishes from both of us for '88. As for the 'Sequence',[2] I should have called you in already; but a piece of hack-work fell in (from *The Graphic*),[3] & till that's done there's no rest for me. Next week I hope to see the *Smollett or hinder parts* of it;[4] & that month, with your help, to have the whole

[1] Dobson's *Life of Oliver Goldsmith* in the Great Writers series (1887).
[2] WEH is probably referring to the 'In Hospital' section of his *Book of Verses* (1888).
[3] WEH's *'The Graphic' Gallery of Shakespeare's Heroines. The Stories of the Several Plays from which the Pictures are taken are Written by W. E. Henley* (1888). Another issue of this book was limited to one hundred copies. This was a series of portraits of Shakespeare's heroines by leading artists.
[4] Possibly a review of David Hannay's *Life of T. G. Smollett* in the Great Writers series (1887). The second part of this sentence refers to WEH's selection for his *Book of Verses* and Dobson's help in that choice.

selection done & out of hand.

I wish I could have sent you the *Catalogue*.[5] But the impression is so small, & the rule so strict, that I've been able to smouch a copy for nobody outside the press. Is there none for whom you could write a high-handed & fiery review? Later on, perhaps, I may be able, in any case, to do my duty by you.

I am going to ask you to accept that illustrated *Rabelais*.[6] But it will mark the close of our campaign against the Muse.

Ever Yours,

W.E.H.

[5] *Memorial Catalogue of the French and Dutch Loan Collection.*
[6] Probably Rabelais's *Three Good Giants*, trans. John Dimitry (Boston, MA, 1888).

To Robert Louis Stevenson, 9 March 1888

ALS: NLS. Published in *Stevenson Letters*, 6, 129-30; *Baxter Letters*, 189-91.

Merton Place, Chiswick, W.

Private and Confidential

Dear Boy,

If you will wash dishes, & haunt back-kitchens, in the lovely climate of the Eastern States, you must put up with the consequences.[1] Very angry I was with you when I heard of it; & very glad I am to know that you'd got off so cheaply. That attack of *The Newcomes* is a distressing symptom,[2] it is true; but no doubt you'll get over it in time. But wash no more dishes, meanwhile. 'Tis gay, 'tis romantic, 'tis Bohemian, 'tis even useful and cleanly; but it's too desperate a delight to be often yours.

What a swell you are getting, to be sure! I shall address you in future as R.L.S. Esq., M.A.[3]; or as Dear M.A., or as 'Great, good, & just M.A.', or as 'Illustrious M.A.' — *Enfin*! You have it, & you deserve it. Pollock has it too; and doesn't deserve it. The difference is subtle, perhaps; but by an Intellectual M.A. it may, & doubtless will, be apprehended.

I am out of key to-day. The spring, sir, is not what it used to be. It amuses, & distresses, me to hear your view of life. 'Uncommonly like rot', is it? Have you only just begun to find that out; O Poet of the *Counterblast*?[4] These three years past I've been entertaining the idea, & it promises to master me. I've work in hand; I owe not more than a hundred pounds; I am beginning to make a reputation; my verse is printing & promises well enough; other joys are in

[1] For two days in February RLS and Lloyd Osbourne had to do the household chores as Fanny and the servant were ill. As a result RLS became ill.
[2] WEH is referring to Thackeray's sentimental novel *The Newcomes* (1855), where the characters are reduced to extreme poverty.
[3] RLS had been elected a member of the Athenaeum Club.
[4] RLS's *Underwoods*, Book II, viii.

store,[5] I believe; & I'd give the whole lot ten times over for — *enfin*! Life is uncommon like rot. *C'est convenu*. If it weren't that I am a sort of centre of strength for a number of feebler folk than myself, I think I'd be shut of it dam soon.

You will be bitterly disappointed in my *Dumas*.[6] I think I'll withdraw the dedication now. How am I to content you, wretch that you are? How, between two *Saturdays* & two *Art Journals*, produce a decent piece of work of that sort? I should have three months clear for it at least; & I shall get only a day or so now & then.

I read the 'Nixie' with considerable amazement.[7] It's Katharine's; surely it's Katharine's? The situation, the environment, the principal figure — *voyons*! There are even reminiscences of phrases & imagery, parallel incidents — *que sais-je*? It is all better focused, no doubt; but I think it has lost as much (at least) as it has gained; & why there wasn't a double signature is what I've not been able to understand.

Still no news of the *Deacon*! The young man is about the coolest hand ever dealt,[8] I think. There's one thing pleasant to reflect about, however; & that is that, as you say, if the play has failed in N.Y., there's an end of it. I wish I knew. Better aff as aye waggin', ye ken![9] And it has been waggin'ower lang.

Louis, dear lad, I am dam tired. The Châtelaine's away. The spring is spring no more. I am thirty-nine this year. I am dam, dam tired. What I want is the wings of a dove — a soiled dove even![10] — that I might flee away & be at rest. Don't show this to *anybody*, & when you write, don't do more than note it in a general way, if at all. By the time you *do* write you will have forgot all about it,

---

[5] Anna Henley was pregnant.

[6] WEH had intended writing a book on Dumas for the Great Writers series but nothing was done.

[7] Fanny's story had been published in *Scribner's Magazine*, March 1888. This letter, with its casual accusation of plagiarism by Fanny of Katharine's unpublished story, led to a bitter quarrel and estrangement between WEH and RLS. There may have been some truth in WEH's accusation. RLS saw it as another example of WEH stirring up trouble and speaking ill of him behind his back. RLS certainly felt deeply about the unwarranted attack (as he saw it) on his wife but neither would give way. Charles Baxter did his best to serve as mediator to both. WEH always believed himself to be right and RLS even though he could not forgive WEH showed concern for him in his letters to Baxter, even to the extent of making some form of indirect financial allowance to WEH. Although correspondence did continue occasionally after the initial argument their old, boyish friendship was to be no more. WEH did offer a reconciliation in his letter of 7 May 1888. Perhaps if RLS had been in England and not in America they may have resolved it? This was not the first major disagreement between the two for RLS remarks in a letter to Baxter (April 1888): 'And it is just a year since the reconciliation, when I forgave him all — God knows how gladly and wholly — and felt a boy again to be reconciled to my old friend' (*Stevenson Letters*, 6, 147). The final break came in 1890 after WEH failed to visit RLS's mother (*Stevenson Letters*, 7, 52-3).

[8] Ted Henley was playing the title role in the production in New York.

[9] 'Better a finger off, as aye wagging', Walter Scott's *Rob Roy*, ch. 18.

[10] Mendelsohn's 'O, for the wings of a dove'.

no doubt. But if you haven't, deal vaguely with my malady. I wish you were nearer. Why the devil do you go & bury yourself in that bloody country of dollars & spew? And you don't even get better! *C'est trop raide.* And you are 4000 miles from your friends! *C'est vraiment trop fort.* However, I suppose you must be forgiven, for you have loved me much. Let us go on so till the end. You & I & Charles — D'A., & Porthos, & *le nommé* Aramis![11] 'Twas a blessed hour for us all, that day 13 years syne, when old Stephen brought you into my back kitchen, wasn't it? *Enfin* — ! We have lived, we have loved, we have suffered; & the end is the best of all. Life is uncommon like rot; but it has been uncommon like something else, & that it will be so again — once again, dear! — is certain. Forgive this babble, & take care of yourself, & *burn this letter.*

Your friend,
W.E.H.

[11] In his poem 'Envoy: to Charles Baxter' written in the same month as this letter, WEH refers to 'the immortal *Musketeers*'. The remaining musketeer, Athos, was James Walter Ferrier.

To Charles Baxter, 7 April 1888
ALS: Yale. Published in *Stevenson Letters*, 6, 168.

1 Merton Place, Chiswick, W.

My dear Charles,
    You are a brick. But Lewis's letter has exasperated me;[1] I confess it's hard to endure.
    The immense superiority; the sham of 'facts'; the assumption that I am necessarily guilty, the complete ignoring of the circumstance that my acquaintance with the case is probably a good deal more intimate & peculiar than his own; the reference to Gosse; the directions as to conduct and action — all these things have set me wild.
    I prepared a reply (with Bob's assistance) in which, in a perfectly friendly way, I knocked his house of cards about his ears. At the last moment K., who is naturally indignant at the impudence of being arraigned as a criminal instead of deferred to as a sufferer, forbade me to interfere, & wrote herself. Of course I had no choice. I tore my letter up, & have written no other.

[1] RLS's letter of [22?] March (*Stevenson Letters*, 6, 131-2) in reply to WEH's letter of 9 March. In his reply RLS stated that he wrote 'with indescribable difficulty; and if not with perfect temper, you are to remember how very rarely a husband is expected to receive such accusations against his wife'. He asked WEH to refer to Katharine for the truth of the matter. He finished the letter with: 'You will pardon me if I can find no form of signature; I pray God such a blank will not be of long endurance. Robert Louis Stevenson.'

Of course another must be written. But in what sense I can't yet decide. Nothing shall go from me unless you approve of it: I promise you that. Meanwhile, I sit & gnaw my fists in silence.[2]

Anna tells me that Lewis (God help him!) has written you eighteen pages on the subject, & thinks we're all turning against him. How can he think that — *Enfin!* I've been writing three or four letters to his one; & always as always. Even the matter which has set him posing was mentioned in terms not accusatory but of astonishment. And he writes to me as you read. I am a person to be ordered about like a common footman, & K. is as it were arraigned & put on her defence! It's really incredible.

However, you shall hear all when you come up. Bob, whose temper is angelic, & whose sense of propriety is not inferior (to say the least) to Lewis's own, is indignant as any of us. He shall tell you the story; & you shall judge for yourself.

Lewis has known me longer than his spouse, & has never known me lie or truckle or do anything that is base. He can't have slept with Fanny all these years, & not have caught her in the act of lying.

However, least said soonest mended. Nothing shall go you have not seen & approved. *Voilà.*

Ever affectionately yours,
W.E.H.

[2] A rough draft of part of this letter is in *Stevenson Letters*, 6, 163-5.

To Robert Louis Stevenson, 11 April 1888

ALS: NLS. Published in *Stevenson Letters*, 6, 169-70 and *Baxter Letters*, 207-8.

Merton Place, Chiswick, W.

Since the above was written, your last has come in.[1] I know not whether to laugh or cry over it. Try the dates, however; & be resolved on one point — that the official letter was meant, not as an affront, but merely as a reminder. If I remember aright, it was written before there had dawned upon me any suspicion that my remarks upon the *Nixie-Watersprite* coincidences could possibly go near to turning our lives into separate tragedies. In any case, it was written, at my request, with a view to reminding you that you were down for the article, & that the sooner we had the copy the better we should be pleased, & with no other object whatever.

[1] RLS's letter at the end of March (*Stevenson Letters*, 6, 141) saying that he was sorry that WEH could no longer correspond with him. This was based on RLS receiving a letter not from him but from Marcus Huish, editor of the *Art Journal*, reminding him that his article on Rodin was needed.

Do you remember an official letter addressed to Bob, by the (then) editor of the *M. of A.*, & which, beginning 'My dear Stevenson', struck cold to the heart of the recipient. You were able to reassure him on the point. Try & be as sagacious & far-seeing in your own interest as you were in his. Won't you?

I want this to go to-night; so I will only say again, forgive me, & have faith in me yet. I am not ungrateful nor disloyal. Surely you should *know* that much of me by now? And the old affection, the old kinship, the old affinity (*enfin!*) is as living & dear as ever.

W.E.H.

I forget the names of the Rodins. The bust of Hugo, the bust of W.E.H., the bust of J. P. Laurens, the *Eve*: — I think these were of them. For the rest, I thought you'd write of what you saw in the round, & sent them merely as reminders of the general style.

To Charles Baxter, 25 April 1888
ALS: Yale. Published in *Stevenson Letters*, 6, 177-8.

Merton Place, Chiswick, W.

My dear Charles,

It is most distressing; & I know not what to say or do. If you think I should write, I will write; if you think not, I will not. I will be guided by you. I cannot endure to think of this lonely sufferer; & I cannot see a way to put him out of his misery.

The first letter is the wisest & sanest. He is right in saying that if his attitude had been better, no more would have been heard of it. I had said my say, & confessed my astonishment, as I had a right to do; & since then I've made no further references to the matter. Had his answer been made in the same spirit as my question was made, nothing could have come of it but good will. We believe that F. stole the story; I believe that K., out of liking for Louis, never made it plain to him that she resented F.'s interference; & having said what I had to say, I should have said no more. What to do now is more than I can tell. This babble about the 'rearrangement of facts' on our side is all too significant: it shows in a what a hopeless tangle of lies and half-truths which are worse than lies he has been involved. I am more than ever thankful that my answer was not sent: it would have killed him like a bullet from a gun.

If you write about the matter at all, you had best make clear to him (1) that, as he did me the honour to put me on my defence, I drew up a reply to his charge, which, on your advice, I suppressed; & (2) that the manner of his letter to me has made it impossible for me to address him in any other terms than those of the suppressed reply. You may add that I am absolutely unconscious of any offence to him of any kind since he quitted these shores: as (he will remember) I was of the estrangement to which he refers in one of these letters to you. I have been in great trouble more than once; & trouble makes one selfish. But there has been no more estrangement than that, & no more disloyalty either.

And this brings me to another question: — Is it not vain to attempt to satisfy him at all in this matter of friendship? I begin to suspect that from the first I have given him too much: so much, indeed, that he has been conscious, when I myself have not, of a momentary transfer of interest from him to myself & my own immediate griefs & troubles. Such a perception as his is too feminine to be baffled; such an affection is too feminine to be endured. If all my thirteen years of loyal service count for nothing now, how am I, at my present age & with my present interests, to surpass them? how to rise to such heights as, 'tis evident, he finds the only place where friendship can dwell?

Of one thing I am resolved: — that this burst was inevitable. I had as lief, since it was to come, that it came on this question. For months past, you tell me, he has complained of me; & now, in a cause that is not directly my own, I am openly accused of leze-friendship. I repeat, it as well. For my own part, I can truly say that, throughout our companionship, I have been absolutely loyal. I reserve to myself the right to be angry with my friends, to be rude to them, to criticize their work or their morals as I please; but I do not think that this is incompatible with friendship. On the contrary, I hold that the friendship which excludes it isn't friendship at all.

Of course, it's useless arguing, I know. We go round and round, & *que faire*? is still the only issue. Here you can help, and will. Tell me what to do; & I'll do it.

The reference to the will is touching indeed. But what a queer creature it is! and how terribly the life he leads has told upon his sense of reality & the practice of life! Is it possible that he can believe of me — of any of us — that Fanny & Sam are the same to us as himself? that in a difficulty I could go to them as to him? that I could accept of them as of him? that (to take in all the points I can suspect as existing) I could even go to Bob or Katharine as I might to him? Rede me this riddle; & , if it seems to good to you, ask him to rede it to you. Not as something coming from me but from yourself.

I want you, when you write, to tell him what I propose to do with the *Deacon*, & to ask if it has his approval.[1] Don't forget this, on any account. It is important; & it may help the business generally.

Say what you like about *Mexico*;[2] & be sure to add that from the final copy everything which suggests his hand & style will be carefully eliminated. I doubt not that he will order you to destroy the thing; & great as is my faith in you, I don't see how you can evade the order.

We are glad to have been able to make you comfortable, & grateful — most

---

[1] The play was privately printed in 1888 as a revised edition of the 1880 version.
[2] RLS was worried that what he termed 'unprofitable exercises' (pornographic or obscene) were still in WEH's possession and he wished them destroyed.

grateful — for your return. Do not lose sight of Twickenham & the river; but come soon again, & make us happy.

Ever Affectionately Yours,
W.E.H.

To Robert Louis Stevenson, 7 May 1885 [1888]
ALS: NLS.[1] Published in *Stevenson Letters, 6,* 188-89 and *Baxter Letters,* 216-17.

Merton Place, Chiswick, W.

My dear Lad,
 Your letter is heart-breaking; & I do not know how to reply to it, for it convicts me (I now see) of a piece of real unkindness, unworthy of myself & our old tried friendship. You may blame me in the bitterest terms you will for the cruel blunder I made in opening my mind to you; & I shall not complain, for I deserve them all. I should, I know now, have said nothing; & I shall never cease from regretting that I gave you this useless, this unnecessary pain.
 You must not believe, though, that I struck to hurt. I did not. I thought the matter one of little consequence. It seemed right that you should know how it looked to myself, & that there might well be the end of it. I was elbows deep in the business from the first, & I had (I thought) a right to make remarks. It was surely as well (I reasoned) that you should hear of certain coincidences from me as from another quarter. That I had any feeling of unfriendliness is what I want now explicitly to deny. It is your mistake, dear lad, to imagine that I've ever been any other than your true friend & servant. I have not; I could not. Twice before (I want you to remember) you have put this same charge upon me: each time, as you know, to my astonishment. In this case, as in the others, I can truly say the amazement is the same. How much greater the distress has been I leave you to judge.
 All this, & more, I should have said long since; but I could not answer your first letter. It put me (as it were) into the dock, & I preferred to keep silence till I could speak on the old footing & in the old terms. Now I can do that, I make haste to own that I spoke without a full sense of the regard that was due to you, & that I beg your forgiveness.
 The good Charles was with us not long since, & our talk ran much on you. I doubt not that he has written, & told you all he could, & that you know ere this why I have not spoken & how I — we — have felt. Let me add that neither he nor you can know how grievous the estrangement has been to all of us, nor what a relief it is to think that it may now be at an end.
 Forgive me if I write no more. I am far from well, & there are many things

[1] A draft of this letter with some changes is at Yale. The changes are noted in the *Stevenson Letters, 6,* 188.

for which I am perplexed. And do not doubt me again, if you can help it. Life is short enough & cruel enough, as it is; & you & I, dear Louis, should know better than to waste the good that is in it — the good that we have made for ourselves — like this.

Ever your friend,
W.E.H.

[RLS note at top of letter when sending it to Baxter]

His original position carefully saved throughout; (1) and yet I gave him my word as to certain matters of fact; (2) and yet the letter (in consequence of this) can never be shown to my wife; (3) and yet, even if he still thinks as he did, I think a kind spirit would have even lied.

To Charles Baxter, 26 May 1888
ALS: Yale

Merton Place, Chiswick, W.

My dear Baxter,
    You are the reverse of in disgrace. But I've been dreadful busy. This piece of tom fooling which I've been doing with Lang (*Vide* first par. in the *Literary Gossip* of the current Assineaum,[1] which also contains a note on Henry James) has given much trouble; & then I've been busy distributing the book. *Voilà.* You see the little busy B. is not the only conference of the shining hour.
    I am glad no end to hear of the proposed discussion.[2] Don't let them belted Earls look down on us too much, & believe that the demon proposal jumps with my humour exactly. I've sent your letter to W.H.P., & requested him to ponder & perpend. Let me know *when* to support you, & I will do the needful, & the Literary Lodge shall establish its fundamentals.
    The first review appeared this morning in our common Grandmother, the *Spectator*.[3] Get it, an you love me. I am (it appears) 'a true poet, though perhaps a minor one'. Also the hospital things are 'some of 'em not a little rough'. I wish I

---

[1] Lang and WEH had produced a light-hearted attack on the main London art galleries called *Pictures at Play or Dialogues of the Galleries By Two Art-Critics*. Illustrated by Harry Furniss (1888; rptd New York, 1970). Harry Furniss (1854-1925), artist. WEH's unsigned 'Literary Gossip [1st. para.]', *Athenaeum*, 26 May 1888.

[2] This is a reference to the *Scottish Art Review* and a possible takeover by Baxter and Hamilton Bruce. In a letter to the Glasgow bookseller William Craibe Angus (1829-99) WEH talks of the possibility of his editing the journal should it be bought by Hamilton Bruce (5 July 1888, Hornel Library, Kircudbright). The *Scottish Art Review* ran from June 1888 to December 1889, then as the *Art Review* until 1890.

[3] A review of WEH's first volume of poetry, *A Book of Verses*, in the *Spectator*, 26 May 1888. RLS had used the expression 'common Grandmother' in a poem of 1880 (*Stevenson Letters*, 3, 96, n.3).

could know what is meant by rough! But tis vain to try & understand these literary fellows. Being one of them I know that half their time they don't quite understand themselves.

Blaikie writes that my portrait is wanted for the *Evening Dispatch*,[4] & that a great eulogy is to be looked for in Monday's *Scotsman*.[5] I took measures to get us the *Scottish Leader*;[6] so my renown in the city of my adoption should be sudden & violent. Take my tip, meanwhile, & get yourself a copy of the cheap edition. Send to Nutt's for it; or you'll may be get fobbed off with the imperfect copy.[7] 'Tis (*sans blague*) a really *distinguished* little book, & I believe you'll prefer it to the more sumptuous form.

I've bought Anthony an etching-press, & am pretty confident that he'll make such use of it that he will be asked to co-operate in the production of the *Constable*.

I wrote to Tauchnitz, & asked him to remit the £20 to Messers. M. & B., who would send him a receipt in due course.

The Châtelaine is wonderous well, & I am vastly better.

Ever Affectionately Yours,

W.E.H.

[*Added by WEH at the top of the letter*] Nigel has the *Bismark* in hand. I think you'll grin over *Pictures at Play*. Furniss's pictures are said to be first chop.

[4] Walter Biggar Blaikie (1847-1928), railway engineer, historian, printer, partner and later chairman of T. and A. Constable. 'A New Poet. A Memorial of the "Old Infirmary",' *Edinburgh Evening Dispatch*, 26 May 1888, 3rd edition.

[5] *Scotsman*, 28 May 1888.

[6] *Scottish Leader*, 21 June 1888.

[7] The first edition consisted of 1050 ordinary copies, seventy-five hand-made copies, and twenty on Japanese vellum. The imperfect copy would have been the special issue, the imperfection being in the copy not the poetry.

To J. M. Barrie,[1] 28 May 1888
ALS: British Columbia

Merton Place, Chiswick, W.

Dear Sir,

I am very glad to have 'Auld Licht Idylls', which I read in the *St. James's Gazette*, with peculiar pleasure.[2] I am glad, too, that you find my own little book good reading. I sent it (I should tell you) at the suggestion of Mr. John Geddie,[3]

[1] Barrie and WEH established a friendship which lasted until WEH's death. This is the first of two known extant letters to Barrie from WEH.

[2] Barrie published his 'Auld Licht Idylls' in the *St James's Gazette* between 17 December 1884 and 12 March 1885. They were later published in book form in 1888.

[3] John Geddie (1848-1937), Scottish journalist.

who has been good enough to take notice of it in the *Evening Dispatch*, & who gave your name to a common friend (Mr. W. B. Blaikie, of the University Press) as that of an Edinburgh reviewer — as, in fact, one having authority in the *British Weekly*.[4]

I was not a student, I'm sorry to say. I was a patient in the Old Infirmary.[5] I had heard of Lister & Listerism, & went to Edinburgh, as a sort of forlorn hope, on the chance of saving my foot. The great surgeon received me — as he did, & does everybody — with the greatest kindness; & for twenty months I lay in one or other ward of the old place in Infirmary Rd. under his care. It was a desperate business, but he saved my foot, & here I am! The sonnets were written on the spot, & published with others I haven't reprinted (1875) in the *Cornhill* a month or two after I left the infirmary. The experiments in blank verse were the work of my first weeks of liberty. Both have been a good deal wrought & touched up for publication since; but I think there's nothing in them that isn't *true* & authentic.

It may interest you to know that Lister sat for 'The Chief';[6] that the original of the 'Staff-Nurse: Old Style'[7] is still alive & had a ward in the New Infirmary; that the original of the 'Lady Probationer', a Miss Matthews, died — on duty — before the sonnets were printed, I believe; that the original of the 'Visitor' was a Miss (Barbara) Abercrombie; & that Louis Stevenson sat for the 'Apparition', which has not been printed elsewhere than here. The 'House Surgeon' is in practice at Portobello;[8] the 'Scrubber' lives in Edinburgh;[9] & so with the rest, only the 'Staff-Nurse: New style' being (as it were) a composition.[10]

Forgive me all this egoism. I've been betrayed into it by the knowledge that you were an Edinburgh student, & the reflection that perhaps you knew the Infirmary when I knew it, though from another point of view.

Stevenson's address is c/o Messrs. Scribner's Sons, 743 Broadway, N.Y.C., N.Y., U.S.A. That will find him until his return to England.

Very Faithfully Yours,
W.E.H.

J. M. Barrie Esq.

---

[4] Barrie was a regular writer for the *British Weekly, a Journal of Social and Christian Progress*.
[5] The second to the fourth sentences of the second paragraph were quoted by Barrie in his Rectorial Address at St Andrews University, 3 May 1922 and subsequently published in his *Courage* [1922], 29-30.
[6] This and the following verse titles are in WEH's *A Book of Verses*.
[7] Mrs Porter.
[8] The 'Surgeon' was Dr Young who 'attended me at Portobello, 1875'; document (in private hands) listing, in WEH's hand, information about some of his poems. The physician Peter Alexander Young gained his M.B. at Edinburgh University in 1867 and his M.D. in 1870. He worked in Heidelberg during the Franco-Prussion war and then at the Edinburgh Infirmary.
[9] The 'Scrubber' was Mary MacDonnell.
[10] This poem was based on the following, among others, Miss Pringle, Miss Logan, Miss Mitchelson, Nurse Robinson and Nurse Watson 'with a great deal of the author'.

To Alice Meynell,[1] **6 June 1888**
ALS: Texas

Merton Place, Chiswick, W

My dear Mrs. Meynell,

I have just read your note in *Merry England.*[2] 'Tis the greatest pleasure of all, as you know, to be well read; & this you have given me. Thank you for it *from the heart*; &, believe me, there is more in the expression than it is wont to convey.

Some day I hope to talk with you of better & worse. Then you will tell me more of your dislikes, & I shall make bold to tell you something of my likes. For the moment, I will content myself with the confession that your selection has interested me, & that I don't at all agree with it. For instance, I do believe that my best is to be found among my lyrics; & I certainly prefer the last 'poem' in the book to the last but one;[3] & I am more or less in, among the ballades, with the 'Ballade of a Toyokuni Colour Print'; & — but I will not take myself too seriously! You must forgive me if I seem to do so. Everybody — the likeliest & all — has been so kind about these things that there are moments when I lose my head, & feel inclined to pose *en poète.*

I am grateful, above all, for the recognition that what I have aimed at is simplicity. I began with Rossetti;[4] I end (for I believe this is the end) with Heine & Burns, I think (there is certainly more *I* in this letter than may be pardoned to even a minor poet!) that a return to them is what we want; & I thank you for your applause of what throughout, was nearest my heart.

Let me correct a detail — historical — in your account of me. I am not a Scotsman but a wretched Saxon: Gloucester born & Gloucester bred, indeed, with not so much as a touch of the Scot about me. And Stevenson's first work[5] was *not* published in *London*, but *chez* Kegan Paul. He had written many of his essays & all his *Inland Voyage* before he wrote for me his *New Arabian Nights*, & therewith (they told me) murdered the journal. 'Twas in Edinburgh that I met him; you will find a kind of sketch of him in the number (In Hospital) called 'Apparition'. It was like him then, & I ran it in for old sake's sake. For, indeed, we have been much together.

---

[1] Alice Christina Gertrude Meynell, *née* Thompson (1847-1922), poet and essayist. A convert to Roman Catholicism, she published her first book of poems *Preludes* in 1875 and in 1877 she married the critic and writer Wilfrid Meynell (1852-1948). With her husband she co-edited the *Weekly Register* (1881-98) and *Merry England* (1883-95). Wilfrid was godfather to the Henley's only child Margaret Emma, born on 4 September 1888, whom Alice called 'the Golden Child'.
[2] Alice Meynell's review of *A Book of Verses* in *Merry England*, June 1888.
[3] The last poem is 'What is to come we know not', *A Book of Verses*. The penultimate poem is 'When you are old, and I am passed away'.
[4] Dante Gabriel Rossetti .
[5] *An Inland Voyage* (1878).

It may interest you to know that the original of the 'Staff Nurse — Old Style' is still afoot & still at work. She has a ward in the New Infirmary. I see her when I go north. She must be long past seventy, but she looks to me to have changed but little — to be only — little older & less active than she was in '73-'74, when I lived beneath her sway.

Always Sincerely Yours,
W.E.H.

PS. My wife — who looks to meet you one day — is Scotch as R.L.S. himself.

To Edmund Gosse, [19 November 1888]
ALS: Brotherton

Merton Place, Chiswick, W.
My dear Gosse,

I am very glad to know that you like the article.[1] I really mean all that it says, & to write it was a great pleasure. I intended to have discussed the cause — & effect — of that sudden drying up of the Congrevian fount, which is one of the most curious & perplexing points about a curious & perplexing personality; but I had — or thought I had — no room. I should have said all I want to say just now if I add that Maccoll demanded the thing at point of fix, & then left it on his table, in proof, for three weeks or a month before using it.

I've always liked Farquhar.[2] He's the most generous & humane spirit of the whole set. As far as I remember he is never brutal & offensive; & those high spirits of his go to the head like good champagne. But the *Dramatist* is Vanburgh.[3] Then if he could but have mastered something like a style — there was a great comic part. Why don't you take him up for this same series? He is worth it, I should think, as a man; & to have the chance of saying the right thing for the first time about such work as the *Provoked Wife* and the *Confederacy* should tempt you.

But (if I may presume to advise you on such a point) I would leave Molière out of my list of comparisons. Truly, there is no sort of parallel to be made between him & any of them. The aim, the convention, the morals, the style, the achievement — *everything* is different. I intended (to finish my lecture in a breath) to have objected to a certain 'Otway *or* Racine' in the *Congreve*;[4] but

[1] WEH's review of Gosse's *Life of William* Congreve in the *Athenaeum*, 17 November 1888. Gosse wrote the same day saying how pleased he was (Pierpont Morgan).
[2] George Farquhar (1678-1707), Irish playwright. His best-known plays are *The Recruiting Officer* (1706) and *The Beaux Stratagem* (1705).
[3] Sir John Vanbrugh (1664-1726), playwright and architect. Two of his main comedies are *The Provoked Wife* (1697) and *The Confederacy* (1705). He built Castle Howard, Yorkshire, and Blenheim Place, Oxfordshire.
[4] Thomas Otway (1652-85), playwright; Jean Racine (1639-99), French playwright.

somehow it dropped out of my scheme. I quote it now — to show you what I want to be at. It is misleading to the general — to talk of two absolutes of incompatibility in the same breath; & I could with that you hadn't given me this opening.

I fear that (as usual) I have said too much. But I think so well of the book that I hope to be forgiven this creepiness. *Quia multum amavi*.[5] I hope to handle your *Vanburgh* in the same spirit.

Our tumble was very great, & I think that it will be long ere life is quite the same. Thank you much for remembering that sympathy at these times is really a necessary of life.[6] Some little time ago I recalled the tunes of a certain letter which you once showed to me, & was moved to write to you. I have regretted ever since that I allowed myself to be moved in vain.

Always Sincerely Yours,
W.E.H.

[5] Wilde's poem 'Quia multum amavi' in his *Poems* (Boston 1881). Although WEH may be referring to Swinburne's 'Quia multum amavit' in his *Songs before Sunrise* (1871).
[6] WEH's mother had died on 25 October 1888.

To Oscar Wilde, 25 November 1888
ALS: Texas

Merton Place, Chiswick, W.

The 'prose of France', my Oscar, is all my fancy paints. Flaubert indeed is the prose of France, but not precisely French prose, the which (so far as I can recall myself to myself) I didn't accuse you of coming off in.[1]

That, however, is nothing to the point. The point is that, as I think, you've assimilated your Flaubert to an extent that seems to me quite wonderful.[2] His style to you is what rhyme is to *some* poets: it gives you ideas; you come up with it, & it whispers inventions! I am not sure that I altogether approve; but I do honestly *admire*. And that, as you know, is much.

I will read the *Prince* again, & mark the lapses. Then (*D.V.*), if you are not too violent, & will swear to me, upon your honour as a poet, to respect my grey hairs, I will go through the whole thing with you, & you shall perpend, & own that I am right.

What a strange monster is your critic! *You* praise me for sanity, cheerfulness, a practical optimism;[3] & here's an American (in the *New*

[1] If this was a review of Wilde's *The Happy Prince and Other Tales* (1888) it has not been found. However, it may have been in a previous letter to Wilde.
[2] Wilde replied to this letter: 'Yes! Flaubert is my master' (*The Letters of Oscar Wilde*, ed Rupert Hart-Davis, 1962, 233).
[3] Wilde's review of WEH's *A Book of Verses* in the *Woman's World*, December 1888.

Princeton)⁴ who hopes that next time I may be more human, lively, & [   ]! *You* reproach me with experiments in prose; & here is a Scotsman who — *enfin*! Your critic is a weird & curious being. And there's the *fin mot* of the whole business.

How I wish (now) that I had consented to attend that Congress at Liverpool!⁵ What sport, what discussions, what noble talk we would have had! However, you will meet Stevenson,⁶ &, if he's in the vein, there will be words enough between you, & ideas enough, to make all Liverpool mad for a month. Truly I'd like to be there.

Ever Yours,
W.E.H.

Let us meet soon.

---

⁴ An unsigned review of WEH's *A Book of Verses* in the *New Princeton Review*, November 1888. The reviewer remarked that: 'As poetry, these verses deserve almost unqualified praise. They have a vigour of thought, an unusualness of diction, often a melodiousness of rhyme, that excite admiration. There is much more than versification here. ... It may not be out of place to urge Mr. Henley to make the philosophy of his next verses more cheerful.'
⁵ The first Congress of the *Association for the Advancement of Art and its Application to Industry* was held in Liverpool from 3 to 8 December 1888.
⁶ Bob Stevenson.

Charles Whibley

Henley in later life

Photograph of J.M. Barrie given by him to
Anna Henley after Henley's death

Henley (from *Some Letters of William Ernest Henley*
by V. Payen-Payne, 1933)

3. The *Scots Observer* and the *New Review*: 1889-97

The *Scots Observer* was founded by Robert Hamilton Bruce, the printer William Blaikie and the lawyer Robert Fitzroy Bell, with its offices in Edinburgh. After the first issue on 24 November 1888, it was soon realised that a firm editorial hand was needed and Henley was asked to come north and take control. Thus started his most successful and influential period as an editor with his first edition on 19 January 1889. The gap left by Stevenson was partly filled by the young scholar and high Tory Charles Whibley and a firm and lasting friendship ensued though without the depth of that with Stevenson. Henley had Whibley writing for him but Whibley needed constantly reminding to have his copy in on time and this fault was also evident when Henley took on the general editorship of the *Tudor Translations* in the 1890s. Throughout his editorship Henley was fearless in his imperialism and Tory politics and he gathered round him a circle of young writers some of whom were to achieve fame, such as H. G. Wells, Kenneth Grahame, Kipling and W. B. Yeats.

This was the most productive period of his career as editor and writer. He wrote two guides or memorials to major art exhibitions in Glasgow and Edinburgh. His *Views and Reviews* on literature was followed by his very successful anthology for boys, *Lyra Heroica*, in 1891. He began the collaboration with John Farmer on *Slang* which kept him busy for the rest of his life. He published the first and only volume of his edition of the works of Byron, the project collapsing due to copyright problems. His important edition of Burns, in collaboration with T. F. Henderson, was published in 1896-97 and included his reassessment of Burns which was ill received in Scotland.

His recognition as a man of letters prompted his friends to put him forward for the Professorship of Rhetoric and English Literature at Edinburgh University in 1895 and then the Poet Laureateship on the death of Tennyson. Both ventures were unsuccessful. He published more poetry and collaborated with Charles Whibley on an anthology of English prose. An attempt in 1895 to produce a series of *English Classics* managed only five titles.

The *National Observer* was in serious financial difficulties at the end of 1893 and it was sold in March of the following year. Not only did Henley lose his position, but in February of 1894 his daughter Margaret died leaving him a broken man. Thanks to his friends he became editor of the *New Review* in 1895 but he resigned at the end of 1897 to concentrate on his literary work.

To Charles Whibley,[1] 21 January 1889
ALS: Morgan. Published in Connell, 150.

The Scots Observer, 9 Thistle Street, Edinburgh[2]

My dear Whibley,

I want you to try your hand at a column & a half on the Grosvenor Gallery.[3]
Avoid literary criticism, & remember that the merit of a picture begins — &
ends — in paint; so we shall do.

I am counting on you for Henry Bradley[4] & the other things.

Always yours,
W.E.H.

It would help me on if I got your *Grosvenor* copy on Wednesday.

[1] Charles Whibley (1860-1930), scholar, critic and journalist. After a first in classics at
Cambridge Whibley worked for three years in the editorial department at Cassells where he
met WEH. He became WEH's second-in-command on the *Scots Observer*, later the *National
Observer*, and later joined the *Pall Mall Gazette* as Paris correspondent. In 1896 he married
Ethel Philip, daughter of the sculptor John Birnie Philip (1824-75), and sister-in-law of
Whistler. On her death he married Philippa Raleigh, daughter of Sir Walter Raleigh, in 1927.
He and WEH shared a common belief in the Conservative Party and the strength of the British
Empire. Their relationship was more of nephew and uncle than mere friends.
[2] WEH had been staying with Hamilton Bruce at 32 George Square, Edinburgh, since the end
of November 1888 (Connell, 135). He had been asked by Baxter, Bruce, Blaikie and Fitzroy
Bell to edit *The Scots Observer*. Robert Fitzroy Bell (1859-1908), Edinburgh advocate and
secretary to the Scottish University Commission, 1889-1900.
[3] 'The Grosvenor Gallery', *Scots Observer*, 26 January 1889.
[4] WEH was confused and had written 'Bradley' instead of 'Bradshaw'. He was reminding
Whibley that he was to review G. W. Prothero's *A Memoir of Henry Bradshaw* (1889). Henry
Bradshaw (1831-86) had been the Librarian of Cambridge University, 1867-88. Whibley's
review duly appeared on 9 February 1889.

To William Archer, 28 January 1889
ALS: BL

The Scots Observer, Edinburgh

My dear Archer,

I have taken over the *S.O.*, & I mean to make a shaft or bolt of it.

I hope that (as a brother Scot) you'll help us all you can.

We have put you on the free list, & with this you will receive my second
number. I want you to note the 'R.L.S.'[1] 'Tis the first of a series to which I

[1] Andrew Lang's 'Modern Men: R. L. Stevenson', in the *Scots Observer*, 26 January 1889.
This was the first in a series of articles about major figures of the period and became a regular
feature of the paper. These portraits in print were collected in two publications, *Modern Men*

should like you to contribute.

Couldn't you do us a 'Henry Irving'?[2] An intellectual portrait of that distinguished creature would suit us down to the ground especially if it were down in the fearless old fashion you remember.

For any suggestions or proposals I shall be most grateful.

Ever Yours,

W.E.H.

from the Scots Observer (1890) and *Twenty Modern Men from the National Observer* (1891).
[2] A 'Henry Irving' appeared on 29 June 1889 probably written by Archer.

To Alice Meynell, 19 March 1889
ALS: Texas

The Scots Observer, Edinburgh

Dear Mrs. Meynell,

I want to thank you for 'The Rhythm of Life'[1] as for one of the best things it has so far been my privilege to print.

Soon, very soon, I shall have the pleasure of sending you a copy of the second edition of *A. B. of V.*

With kindest regards,

Sincerely Yours Always,

W.E.H.

[1] 'The Rhythm of Life', *Scots Observer*, 16 March 1889. This essay was subsequently reprinted in her book of essays of the same name in 1893.

To Charles Whibley, 19 April 1889
ALS: Morgan. Part published in Connell, 156-7.

The Scots Observer, Edinburgh

My dear Whibley,

I had to hold over the leader. I am not very sorry, for it is scarce up to *S.O.* form, & I want you in your next to be more careful of your phrases & to have a better interest in your style.

Will you try Claude Monet for me next week?[1] If you will, this is how — if you can — I should like you to look at him.

[1] Whibley wrote of him in 'French art in London' in the *Scots Observer* of 27 April 1889.

Impressionism, as I said in my Dowdeswell catalogue,[2] is only a move in the direction of fresh material. Monet, who is amazingly clever, is interested not in art but in new facts. He has observed a good many, & recorded them in terms of singular energy; but as yet he has not succeeded in making art of them. He has thrown over convention, & put nothing but facts & his own damn personality in its place, & he remains an experimentalist & no more. Whether the material in which he experimentalizes is appropriate to art remains to be seen. What is certain is that, as treated by him, it appears to be particularly *un*beautiful. Is this the fault of the material? Is it not rather the fault of the man, whose eye is so vicious, or so naïve, that it can, & does, rest with pleasure on the [   ] quality in nature, & satisfy his sense of colour with these hot pinks & atrocious purples? Colour is of the essence of art; Monet's colour is mostly offensive; therefore Monet is a bad colourist. In what then does Monet's merit consist? What is Monet's message? And where is the man who is to take it up, & express it in the terms of art?

Ever Yours,
W.E.H.

I am prickling a little at your preface.[3]

[2] *Catalogue of a Loan Collection of Pictures by the Great French and Dutch Romanticists of this Century with an Introduction and Biographical Notes of the Artists by William Ernest Henley.* (The Dowdeswell Galleries, 1889). The first impression was withdrawn because of the severe criticism.
[3] This probably refers to Whibley's preface of his *In Cap and Gown: Three Centuries of Cambridge Wit* (1889).

To Austin Dobson, 10 May 1889
ALS: London

The Scots Observer, Edinburgh

My dear Dobbie,
   I thought the review would please you.[1] I should like you to waste a copy on the reviewer, who is one of the most uncommon creatures I've ever met, & who writes a great deal more like me than I do myself.
   I think the distinction between poetry & society verses has never been so clearly drawn & so brilliantly illustrated as by him. *Qu-en dites-vous*?
   The gifted Nutt now writes that he has still some 80 copies of our First

[1] Whibley's unsigned review of Dobson's *Poems on Several Occasions*, *Scots Observer*, 4 May 1889.

Edition on hand. And this after hurrying a Second through the press at such a pace that I hadn't time to do justice to my proofs!! Such is publishing!

Cosmo's verses[2] have made him many friends.

Ever Yours,
W.E.H.

[2] Cosmo Monkhouse's 'Aex Triplex', *Scots Observer*, 20 April 1889; and 'The Secret,' 27 April 1889. Both poems were reprinted in Monkhouse's *Corn and Poppies* (1890).

To Alice Meynell, 14 June 1889
ALS: Texas

The Scots Observer, Edinburgh

My dear Mrs. Meynell,

I should like you, if you would, to undertake for us a pen-&-ink of His Holiness for Modern Men.[1]

I know several who might do me some thing of the kind, but none from whom I should like so much to hear as from the author of *The Rhythm of Life*. These studies demand something of *literature*; & that is why I come begging this one to you.

Will you let me know soon?

Always Sincerely Yours,
W.E.H.

[1] Alice Meynell's essay on Pope Leo XIII appeared in the *Scots Observer* of 10 August 1889. The Italian poet and priest, Gioacchino Pecci (1810-1903), was Pope from 1878 to 1903.

To Rider Haggard, 20 July 1889
Text: Haggard, 277.

11 Howard Place, Edinburgh[1]

My dear Haggard,

I got a week at Windermere and took *Cleopatra*[2] with me. I was alone, and found her very good company.

[1] The Henleys had moved here by 19 April 1889 (WEH to Austin Dobson, 19 April 1889, BL).
[2] Haggard's romantic novel had been published on 24 June 1889 and was reviewed in the *Scots Observer* of 27 July 1889 presumably by WEH who found the book 'the highest of the author's achievements' despite the fact that it 'lacked the open-air adventure — "the wild joy of living" on the veldt, which made Mr. Haggard's former stories such a bracing change from the conventional society novel'.

You were terribly handicapped by the inevitable comparison; but you came off better (to be frank) than I'd expected you would. The *invention* is admirable — is good enough, indeed, to carry off the archaeology and the archaical style, though they are both large orders.

And in Charmion you have given us, I think, your best creation; or if not that, a creation fit to rank with Umslopogas and the King in *Solomon's Mines*. And you know that I mean a good deal when I say that.

I am glad to have read the book, and glad to have it by me to read again. It has plenty of faults, but it has an abundance of promise and some excellent — some really excellent — achievement. There is never a sign of exhaustion, but on the contrary no end of proof that you have scarce got into your stride.

Yours always,
W.E.H.

To Alice Meynell, Friday [?16 August 1889]
ALS: Texas

Ivy Lodge, Levenhall, Musselburgh, N.B.[1]

Dear Mrs. Meynell,

I am not sure about Crispi.[2] But if your friend cares to adventure his article, I will give it every consideration.

There were some phrases in the *Leo XIII* which bothered us a good deal, & which I ventured to change — not being able to go with you in the use of them. Forgive me if I say that the article, while excellent in most ways, was not — is not — comparable with *The Rhythm of Life as a piece of writing*. Do you not agree with me? However, I am very glad to have it, & very glad to have asked you to write it.

There are but four new numbers in that ed. sec.;[3] but one of them is, I believe, my very best. I need not tell you which I mean.

Ever Sincerely Yours,
W.E.H.

---

[1] The Henleys spent August here.
[2] Francesco Crispi (1819-1901), Italian statesman. The author of the intended article has not been identified but it may well have been the poet Francis Thompson (1859-1907).
[3] According to David Nutt's advertisement for the second edition in the *Scots Observer*, 6 July 1889, 'Five New Pieces have been added'. However, the four additional poems were: (i) 'Friends, ... old friends', 111-12; (ii) 'If it should come to be', 113; (iii) 'Matri Dilectissimae I.M.,' 116-17; and (iv) 'Of June', 143-4.

To Robert Louis Stevenson, 22 November 1889
ALS: Yale

11 Howard Place, Edinburgh

Dear Lad,

We think these may interest you. The Naked Female was taken at nine months: the two others on her first birth-day.[1]

She is seldom off her feet now. Her energy is something paralysing. She has some taste for books & much for boys. *Enfin*, — —

Things go on, & go on, & go on. C.B. continues mad about free-masonry — a middle-aged man in want of religion; & we meet but seldom. The journal is up hill work; but we don't despair. Anyhow we've mortified & amazed the *S.R.* Letters come in from all manner of swells, & we are continually quoted; but — ! However, we don't as I said, despair; but enter this week on our third volume with a feeling of having done much.

I should have writ to thank you for your touching & affectionate verses; but I could not.[2]

I've sold the *Master* (which I do not like) to the Baron;[3] & I will post you a copy duly. I told him of the *Box*;[4] but he has not risen.

I am very tired: I've never worked so hard in my life as during the last ten months. I never see nor hear from Colvin now; but I hear that he looks parlous ill & 'painfully thin'.[5] The truth is, we are not so young as we were; [*rest of sentence deleted and illegible*].

W.E.H.

If you send me anything for the *S.O.*, please do.

---

[1] RLS replied to this letter in February 1890 (*Stevenson Letters*, 6, 363-65) addressing WEH as 'Dear lad' and closing 'Ever yours affectionately'. In this letter he offered WEH the poem 'A Voice from Home' for publication in the *Scots Observer*, which WEH duly published in the issue of 5 April 1890.
[2] RLS's poem 'In Memoriam E.H.', on the death of WEH's mother, in the *Scots Observer* of 11 May 1889.
[3] RLS's *The Master of Ballantrae*. Tauchnitz No. 2614 (Leipzig, 1889). The book had reviewed in the *Scots Observer* of 12 October 1889 by the journalist Walter Whyte and not by WEH as previously suggested (see Paul Maixner, *Robert Louis Stevenson: the Critical Heritage*, 349). In a letter to Hamilton Bruce WEH writes: 'When you get the new number read...Whyte on *The Master of Ballantrae*' (10 October 1889, Yale).
[4] RLS and Lloyd Osbourne's *The Wrong Box* had been published on 15 June 1889.
[5] Colvin had a breakdown in 1889 and received treatment in Paris.

To John Lane,[1] 31 January 1890
ALS: Berg

The Scots Observer, Edinburgh

My dear Lane,

It is hard to answer your question out of hand;[2] but I'll try.

The first article was in *London*;[3] but I can't give the date. I imagine it must have been very early in the *second* volume; one of the first three or four of a series of *Living Novelists*. I think, some time in '78.

After that, *Athenaeum* 1st Nov. 1879; 14th March, '85;[4] 31st July, '86; 11th June, '87.[5] *Pall Mall Gazette*, 3rd Nov, '79. *The Teacher*, [14 February 1880],[6] '79. *Saturday Review*, 11th June, '87.[7] *The Critic* — some time in '88.[8] *The Scots Observer*, Jan. 26, '89.[9]

To this last journal J. M. Barrie contributed *The Lost Works of Geo. Meredith*, 24th Nov., '88 — before my accession. I edited a George Meredith for the same print, 28*th* Sept, '89.[10] A note by Wm. Sharp appeared in the February issue (I think) of the *Scottish Art Review*, '89.[11]

I don't think it would be advisable to mention my name in connection with Meredith. For one thing, I am reprinting whatever seems worth salvation in a little book I am just now preparing for press: all of it selected from the *Athenaeum* Meredithisms;[12] & the others may go hang. *This is soonest*.

I have sent you the Meredith & the [?Woods]:[13] by registered post. The latter, *meo judicio*, is poor thin stuff poorly & thinly done. I ought to have known better than to expect anything good from a person procured by that

---

[1] John Lane (1854-1925), co-founder with Elkin Mathews, of the Bodley Head press, a major publishing house of the 1890s. Among its output was the *Yellow Book* (April 1894-April 1897).

[2] Lane had requested information on WEH's articles on Meredith for his bibliography in Richard Le Gallienne's *George Meredith: Some Characteristics*. Richard Le Gallienne (1866-1947), poet and critic.

[3] 'Living Novelists. V. George Meredith', *London*, 25 August 1877. This series ran from 28 July 1877 to 25 May 1878.

[4] *Diana of the Crossways*, *Athenaeum*, 14 March 1885; *Rhoda Fleming*, *Athenaeum*, 31 July 1886.

[5] Review of *Ballads and Poems of Tragic Life*, *Athenaeum*, 11 June 1887.

[6] WEH had left a space here, no doubt intending to insert the correct issue of the *Teacher*.

[7] Review of *Ballads and Poems of Tragic Life*, *Saturday Review*, 11 June 1887.

[8] 'London Letter', *Critic*, 14 August 1886.

[9] Review of *A Reading of Earth*, *Scots Observer*, 26 January 1889. WEH also contributed one other review of Meredith's *Works* in the *State*, 17 April 1886.

[10] It was written by the Scottish journalist and novelist James MacLaren Cobban (1849-1903).

[11] William Sharp, 'George Meredith's 'Reading of Earth', *Scottish Art Review*, February 1889.

[12] WEH's 'George Meredith' in his *Views and Reviews: Essays in Appreciation. Literature* (1890).

[13] Possibly an article by the novelist and poet Margaret Louisa Woods, *née* Bradley (1856-1945).

preposterous creature Frederick Harrison.[14]

Mrs. Henley duly received the cream, & enjoyed it thoroughly. She would have written her thanks — (which she now sends, through me) — at once, but I didn't know where to look for your address.

Very Sincerely Yours,
W.E.H.

I will try to send you the several articles — (all but the *London* extract) — very soon; but just now I am using them as copy for my book.

[14] WEH may be referring to the positivist Frederic Harrison rather than to Frederick Harrison (d. 1926) who later became joint manager of the Lyceum Theatre and the Haymarket.

To Robert T. Hamilton Bruce, 7 March 1890
ALS: Yale

11 Howard Place, Edinburgh

My dear Bruce,

I hope you are going on all right. Anyhow I hope you're well enough to take an interest in the new number. It is simply magnificent. We shall never beat it if we live a hundred years: as, by the way, there is every likelihood we may.

Whyte's 'A.C.S.' is first-chop;[1] & as for 'Cleared'[2] — the first leader — if it isn't genius, then I don't know genius when I see it. And the Barrack Room Ballad[3] is as good as you want. I must order you Kipling's books. I meant to do so, but forgot. No such gutsy person has appeared in English since Dickens. Write & let us know how you are.

Ever Yours,
W.E.H.

[1] Walter Whyte's 'Modern Men: Algernon Charles Swinburne', *Scots Observer*, 8 March 1890.
[2] Kipling's 'Cleared', *Scots Observer*, 8 March 1890. This was a political poem attacking the Special Commission for clearing Charles Parnell, M.P. and other Irish MPs of involvement in conspiracy and murder. The poem had been rejected by *The Times* and the *Fortnightly Review* before it was finally accepted by WEH who was anti-Gladstone and anything Liberal. Rudyard Kipling was born in India and came to England in 1871 returning as a journalist to India in 1882 for seven years.
[3] Kipling had sent his *Barrack Room Ballads* to WEH who immediately recognized their worth and published them. This was Kipling's third ballad 'Fuzzy-Wuzzy' in the issue of 8 March 1890.

I am going to talk material & style to the Art Students on the 19th April.[4] You must come & support me.

The Hindoo[5] is in mortal terror of being dragged to the bar of the House on account of 'Cleared'.

[4] I have failed to find where this took place in Edinburgh.
[5] Walter Blaikie.

To Charles Whibley, 14 July 1890
ALS: Morgan. Part published in Connell, 191.

Seaforth, Levenhall, Musselburgh, N.B.[1]

Dear Boy,

We shall be glad indeed of those reviews. Also in the middles on Jusserand & the N.S.[2]

The Nutt-Campbell review[3] is in hand & will go off this week.

Dobbie is the only one of the clique who has said a word in praise of *V. & R.*

What the devil does Furnivall[4] know about *me* personally?

Farmer (*this is private*) is in difficulties.[5] His printer has struck in

[1] The Henleys had now taken this cottage as a second home.
[2] Jean Adrien Antoine Jules Jusserand (1855-1932), French writer and diplomat. Whibley's 'middle', if it was written, was not used. 'The New Salon', *Scots Observer*, 19 July 1890.
[3] Whibley's unsigned review of *Waifs and Strays of Celtic Tradition*, edited and translated by D. MacInnes and with notes by him and Alfred Nutt, *Scots Observer*, 19 July 1890. His other review was of J. F. Campbell's *Popular Tales of the West Highlands, orally collected*, in the same issue.
[4] Frederick James Furnivall (1825-1910), scholar and educationalist. He proposed the idea of *The New English Dictionary* which later became the *Oxford English Dictionary*. He founded the Early English Texts Society in 1864, the Chaucer Society in 1868 and the New Shakespeare Society in 1873, among others. Whibley, under the guise of a 'Modern Man' on 18 January 1890, had attacked Furnivall, who as a 'prince of literary rag-pickers, is even as Leviathan among them that scramble and scratch in church-yards for the bones of the dead'. He went on to deprecate Furnivall's literary methods in the following issue of the *Scots Observer*. Furnivall's postcard reply was published: 'Have received your absurd caricature of me. What a furiously and mean-souled cad the writer must be! He attributes all his own low motives to me. Send him up to Barnum's as the champion skunk of Scotland.' WEH's published a rejoinder that: 'Our thanks are due to Mr. Furnivall for thus promptly and completely vindicating our position.'
[5] Since 1890 WEH had been helping John Stephen Farmer (1845-1915) with his *Dictionary of Slang*. WEH worked on it for the rest of his life, although his name did not appear as co-editor until volume two. See Farmer, John S. and W. E. Henley, eds *Slang and its Analogues Past and Present: a Dictionary, Historical and Comparative, of the Heterodox Speech of all Classes of Society for more than Three Hundred Years. With Synonyms in English, French, German, Italian, etc*, 7 vols (1890-1904).

consequence of having been asked to print *Cunt* in full & has destroyed the whole of his second volume. On the whole it is to the advantage of the book; for I doubt not we shall easily replace his printer, & we shall be able to revise his first pages more stringently & to fill up the blanks we left in a hurry. What say you? Do please let me know; & let me see your list of omissions. I shall get Millar[6] to take on the *Golf* slang. Indeed my interest, albeit Platonic, is very strong.

Have you seen my list of synonyms for 'Creamstick'? It is a marvellous performance.

I hope to heaven you've made up your mind to spend August at Strathpeffer. If you haven't you must, & at once. I imagine there's a woman in the case; but an Inamorata without rheumatism (I should say) is vastly preferable to an Inamorata with rheumatism. This is realism, perhaps; but it is sound sense, & should be put to the proof forthwith.

I am glad you liked the lyric. 'Piccadilly'[7] hangs fire: it is longer than most of my immortal works, & I can't get down to it for any length of time. But it will come, no doubt, in the end.

The Jap. copy is all right.

E.Y.A.,
W.E.H.

Is there a leader on the Cricket averages so far?

I haven't yet read Oscar his story.[8] I wish I had; for if he keeps us to our first utterance he has us in a tight place. Our second has *him*, I think; but he's a dexterous & slippery bitch.

As for your letter, write it & d—n the founders. You had better sign.

---

[6] John Hepburn Millar (1864-1929), advocate and writer, Professor of Constitutional Law and Constitutional History, Edinburgh University, 1909-25.

[7] This was the fourth section, but written first, of a four part poem entitled 'London Voluntaries'. The sequence was first published in WEH's *The Song of the Sword and Other Verses* (1892) and dedicated to Charles Whibley. A fifth section was added in WEH's *Poems* (1898).

[8] Oscar Wilde's *The Picture of Dorian Gray* had appeared in the July issue of *Lippincott's Monthly Magazine* and was attacked in an unsigned review (later identified as by Charles Whibley) in the *S.O.* of 5 July. The controversy as to the subject matter of *Dorian Gray*, moral corruption and the morality of art and the writer, continued in the *S.O.* for some weeks. Wilde defended himself in a letter to the *S.O.* of 12 July and WEH tried to find support for the paper's views.

To T. Fisher Unwin,[1] **28 July 1890**
ALS: Berg

Seaforth, Levenhall, Musselburgh, N.B.

Dear Mr. Unwin,

The best you can do with Pyle[2] is to make him the only pirate in the series, & pad him out with Johnson's life of Captain Roberts (by far the best of the crowd) & that of Captain Avery;[3] with Mary Read & Anne Bonny in an appendix.[4] That will give you a capital selection & the public an entertaining book.

For myself, I might possibly do a set of highwaymen or perhaps a selection of ruined characters from Johnson — highwaymen, burglars, street-walkers, & so forth. But I don't think either would serve your turn; for Pyle, as it seems to me, is gutting the volume (an excellent book in its way) month by month in the American magazine.[5]

Always Faithfully Yours,
W.E.H.

[1] Thomas Fisher Unwin (1848-1935), founder of the publishing firm. It is not known how he and WEH met but it would seem that WEH's apparent interest in, and knowledge of, pirates and such characters led him to help Unwin with suggestions for an adventure series.
[2] H. Pyle, ed., *Buccaneers and Marooners of America. Being an Account of the Famous Adventurers and Daring Deeds of Certain Notorious Freebooters of the Spanish Main.* The Adventure Series (1890). Howard Pyle (1853-1911), American illustrator and writer and later art editor of *McClure's Magazine.*
[3] Captain Charles Johnson (fl. 1724-36), *A General History of the Robberies and Murders of the Most Notorious Pyrates* (1724), arguably attributed to Daniel Defoe.
[4] An account of the pirates Mary Read and Anne Bonny was included in Johnson's book.
[5] Howard Pyle, 'Chapbook Heroes. 1.', *Harper's Monthly Magazine* [European edn], June 1890; and 'A Famous Chapbook Villain', July 1890.

To Alice Meynell, 21 August 1890
ALS: Texas

The Scots Observer, Edinburgh

Dear Mrs. Meynell,

Thank you for *Pocket Vocabularies*[1] a proof of which you shall shortly receive, *quam premum*.

I am sure that what you have to say about the Cardinal[2] will be worth

[1] Alice Meynell's 'Pocket Vocabularies', *Scots Observer*, 30 August 1890.
[2] Cardinal Newman had died on 11 August 1890. Alice Meynell did not write on him in the *S.O.*

hearing & noting; but I don't see how I can give you space for anything but a letter. Will that do? You see, you don't purpose to sign it; & I don't want to father it; & outside the correspondence section it is a rule with us that all signatures shall be genuine. Now you can sign a letter anything you please.

Yes, I laughed. It was a jest worth making. But how am I to please you? I insist upon woman's right to be woman & you laugh. And I point out that her duty is to avoid the making of bad verses; & you rage. Truly there is no pleasing you at all.

How do you like all this Art & Morality rubbish? I am rather pleased with it. Especially as it has — or ought to have — ruined O.W. whose letters really are, I think, the work of a common lunatic.

Ever Sincerely Yours,
W.E.H.

To James Payn, 26 November 1890
ALS: Fales

The National Observer, Edinburgh[1]

My dear Payn,

We propose to publish a series of literary supplements at intervals of six weeks to two months, consisting of (1) a story of some seven to eight thousand words long & (2) a series of selected reviews.[2]

Will you write us such a story?[3] And if you will, what are your terms, & when might I look for copy?

I hope to accompany you with Mrs. Oliphant,[4] Barrie, Rudyard Kipling, & R.L.S, & I am writing by this post to Anstey[5] to the same effect as to you.

Ever Yours,
W.E.H

---

[1] The following announcement appeared in the issue of 15 November 1890: 'On and after Saturday next, the 22nd curt., this Journal will appear under the style and title of *The National Observer*. As heretofore it will be published simultaneously in London and Edinburgh every Saturday morning.'

[2] The first supplement was the *Special Literary Supplement to The National Observer*, National Observer, 20 December 1890. It consisted of eight pages of book reviews with four pages of advertisements. In all there were five *Literary Supplements*: 20 December 1890, 9 May 1891, 14 November 1891, 12 December 1891, and 7 May 1892. At no time did they exceed eight pages of text.

[3] Payn did not have a story printed.

[4] Margaret Oliphant Oliphant (1827-97), prolific Scottish novelist and writer. She was a contributor to *Blackwood's Magazine* and most of her novels were serialised in the magazine.

[5] None of these had a story or article printed in the *Literary Supplements*. Thomas Anstey Guthrie (1856-1934), journalist and humorous writer, who wrote under the name of F. Anstey.

To Charles Whibley, 26 January 1891
ALS: Morgan

The National Observer, Edinburgh

Dear Boy,
   The Mahaffy has[1] gone to the printers. Please let me have your art-criticism in good time. And suggest your leader as early as you can.
   Gosse, I see, is again bust up.[2] I wonder when he will get really bust up beyond mending.
   You had better make your notes of Vols 2 & 3 of the *Century Dictionary*, & bring them down with you. You will find Vol 4 here & we must work off the lot at once.
   Don't forget your folk-lore either. I've Douglas Hyde,[3] & think you'd better take it on with the rest.
   I think I'd better send you no more till you've cleaned your slate.

Ever Affectionately Yours,
W.E.H.

[1] Whibley's review of J. P. Mahaffy's *Greek Pictures*, *National Observer*, 31 January 1891.
[2] Archer had attacked Gosse for his inaccurate and careless translation of Ibsen's *Hedda Gabler* (*Pall Mall Gazette*, 23 January 1891). They later collaborated on translations of Ibsen.
[3] Douglas Hyde (1860-1949), Irish poet and scholar. He was the first president of the National Literary Society, Dublin, in 1892 and he founded the Gaelic League the following year. He was interested in the revival of the Irish identity and folk-lore. He became the first President of Eire from 1938 to 1945. Hyde's *Beside the Fire* (1890) was reviewed in the *National Observer*, 28 February 1891 by W. B. Yeats.

To Robert T. Hamilton Bruce, 19 March 1891
ALS: Yale

Berkeley Hotel, [Piccadilly][1]

My dear Bruce,
   I've agreed to do a *Selected Burns* & a *Boys' Verses* for Nutt:[2] on my own

[1] WEH was in London for a short period.
[2] WEH did not do a Burns for Nutt. This is the only known reference to this project. The *Boys' Verses* was an anthology of poetry designed to show 'as only art can, the beauty and the joy of living, the beauty and the blessedness of death, the glory of battle and adventure, the nobility of devotion — to a cause, an ideal, a passion even — the dignity of resistance, the sacred quality of patriotism, that is my ambition' ('Preface', to his *Lyra Heroica*, 1892).

terms. Also I've settled the matter of the Tudor Translations.[3] All three books for the Hindoo!

I lunch with Graham R.[4] to-morrow (Friday), & I go to the play in the evening. But I shall be on view in the afternoon at 107.[5]

I don't know where you are; but Whistler's[6] to be here about nine to-night, so I think I'll send this round by hand on the chance of catching you, & bringing you on.

Ever Yours,

H.

[3] This is the first mention of a major series of reprints of sixteenth-century translations of classic works into English. The series known as the *Tudor Translations* was to consist of thirty-eight volumes published 1892-1904 under the general editorship of WEH with each title having an introduction by a suitable critic.

[4] Rosamund Marriott Watson (1860-1911), poetess and writer. As Rosamund Ball she had married George Francis Armytage, then the artist Arthur Graham Tomson (1858-1905) and finally she became the common law wife of the writer Henry Brereton Marriott Watson (1863-1921). Prior to living with Marriott Watson she had adopted the name Graham R. Tomson. She, together with Alice Meynell, Mrs Fanny Douglas and Katharine de Mattos, was one of the few women to contribute to the *Scots Observer* and the *National Observer*.

[5] The Savile Club.

[6] The American artist James Abbott McNeill Whistler had settled in London in 1859 where he soon established himself as the *enfant terrible* of the art world preferring 'art for art's sake' to the mere pictorial representational art of the establishment. His *Nocturnes*, particularly *Nocturne in Black and Gold* caused Ruskin to accuse him of 'flinging a pot of paint in the public's face'. Whistler sued and was awarded a farthing leaving him bankrupt. He produced a lithograph of WEH in 1896.

To Charles Whibley, 13 April 1891

ALS: Morgan. Part quoted in Connell, 210-11.

11 Howard Place, Edinburgh

Dear Boy,

I have just skipped a quinsy; at the cost of a tiny abscess in the throat. It was only a little one, but it made me delirious — (in which condition I wrote that Barnum doggerel)[1] — & it has left me very much the worse for wear.

The *Anthology* has grown & grown till, I fear, the Scots ballad will all have to come out of it. I am putting the scheme into type, & will send a proof this week. I now call it *On the Heights*, &, beginning with the *Henry V* chorus I end with Rudyard & *The Flag of England.*

I wish I'd seen Ravogli.[2] And why, A God's name, if you & Bob were both

[1] 'I.M. Phineas T. Barnum, 1810-1891,' *National Observer*, 11 April 1891. The American showman had died on 7 April worth five million dollars.

[2] The singers Giulia and Sofia Ravogli, members of the Royal Italian Opera, were appearing in

disgusted, why did not one or other descend upon the thing in the columns of
the *N. O.* If *this* is representing me in London, well, well! I say no more.

I am distressed about Cobban.[3] His work has been getting worse & worse, &
t'other day — but you saw, no doubt those parallel columns in the *Daily
Chronicle*? We've had no such kick in the breech since we began this life; & in
explaining the thing, he took it with a lightness & accounted for it in a way that
made me gasp. So I've writ to him urging him to take a holiday, to keep the
matter strictly private (that is, not to discuss it with Whyte & his wife), & to
advise him to take counsel of none but you. Whom I hereby warn; in case he
should follow my lead. It is possible — (for he's the vainest person) — that he
will tell me to go to hell. But it is also possible that he will take my advice. In
which you'll assure him that we like his work & him, & that *when* he has
rested, & got back a little of his interest in us, then he can come back. Till then,
as you know, we can do without him.

Tell me anything you hear & know about Whyte & the woman.

I got your telegram on Sunday morning. I've no doubt you'd good reasons
for being present. Only keep out the public Liar, & I am content. I hope you'd
a good time.

I expect a *pantomime* from you this week.[4] You don't need to be historical,
of course; but it might be well to say that Pierrot, a servant from the Commedia
del'Arte, had practically died out of art until Deburau[5] (one of the great
romantiques) renewed his life, & made him as popular & traditional a figure as
Macaire; that he suffered a certain eclipse, of course, in the hands of Paul
Legrand,[6] for whom Champfleury[7] wrote pantomimes; & that there is certainly

six performances of Gluck's *Orfeo* at Covent Garden between 6 April and 9 July. Both sisters
were also in the seven performances of Bizet's *Carmen* at Covent Garden from 9 April to 5
July. Giulia also appeared in Wagner's *Lohengrin* at Covent Garden from 11 April to 27 July.
The performances were reported in the major journals.

[3] Cobban had used some text from the *Daily Chronicle* of 20 March in his article of 28 March
in the *National Observer*. The *Daily Chronicle* commented on this on 6 April 1891 as follows:

> Has the *National Observer* secured the services of the Lord Mayor on its literary staff? We
> ask the question because there is a curious resemblance between certain portions of an
> article in its issue of March 28 and some remarks of our own which appeared on March 20,
> which seems to suggest a singular wave of thought-transference. … Evidently there is a
> great deal of thought-transference about. To borrow ideas from *The Daily Chronicle* is no
> doubt a good way to become popular, but the *National Observer* should acknowledge the
> source of its inspiration.

[4] Whibley's 'Drama without Words,' *National Observer*, 18 April 1891.
[5] Jean-Baptiste Gaspard Deburau (1796-1846), French actor famous for his role as the buffon
Pierrot.
[6] Paul Legrand (1816-98), French mimist and actor.
[7] *Nom de plume* of Jules François Félix Husson (1821-89), French novelist and critic.

a good deal of the tradition of Deburau in Paul Martinetti.[8] The Museum business can wait.

I am glad they quoted you in that way in the *St. James's*:[9] though I wish, for Barrie's sake, they'd quoted me instead. As regards this week's leader, the time seems ripe for a kick in the breech of Hubert Herkommer.[10] 'Tis plain he will not be drawn: indeed, 'tis plain that, if he were, it could only make bad worse for him. I see that the *P.M.G.* has turned agin him; but I don't think that will make much difference. If then, you think that we should wire in this week, then, my son, *à l'oeuvre*! Meanwhile, however, Hamerton is answering 'Theo Fox',[11] & there is just a chance that Emerson (the photographer man) will sign a communication he addressed us in which he falls on Joseph.[12] So that, if you think it would profit us more to keep our last until the next week — which is practically the opening of the R.A. — we will reserve our final volley till

---

[8] Paul Martinetti (d. 1924), French writer.

[9] A paragraph appeared in the 'Notes' section of the *St James's Gazette*, April 1891, praising Whibley's unsigned 'Literature and Democracy' published in the *National Observer*, 11 April 1891. The same edition of the *National Observer* contained WEH's prologue to Barrie and Marriott Watson's play *Richard Savage*.

[10] In an open letter to Professor Herkomer, R.A., published in the *National Observer* of 14 March, the illustrator and lithographer Joseph Pennell (1857-1926) attacked him for not stating clearly whether the illustrations produced for the limited edition of his book *An Idyll* were etchings produced by the artist himself, or photographic facsimiles of the etchings produced under his supervision. As no reply was forthcoming from Herkomer, Pennell published another open letter in the *National Observer* of 21 March asking for clarification which was not forthcoming. In a letter in the *National Observer* of 28 March, the artist Walter Sickert suggested that as Herkomer was still silent the Royal Society of Painter-Etchers should ask for his resignation. Whibley duly produced a leader 'Pennell *V.* Herkomer', in the edition of 18 April, repeating Sickert's suggestion. However, this fell upon deaf ears. Pennell had his final say in a letter in *The Times* of 27 April:

> After several weeks of waiting for a reply to the questions which I asked Professor Herkomer in the *National Observer*, he has admitted in your issue of to-day [*Times*, 24 April] that the purchasers of *An Idyll* have obtained prints from only 'seven plates produced entirely by his own hand' out of the 16 by Professor Herkomer himself promised in the prospectus of the book. This possibly explains the fact that Messers. Novello and Co. have offered to take back the copy I purchased and refund me the money I paid for it. And the admission of both artist and publisher satisfy me that I was fully warranted in putting my questions to Professor Herkomer.

Walter Richard Sickert (1860-1942), artist and member of the New English Art Club. Hubert von Herkomer (1849-1914), Bavarian born painter. In 1883 he founded the Herkomer School of Art from which he retired as Director in 1904. He was Slade Professor of Fine Art at Oxford, 1885-94. Knighted in 1907 .

[11] Hamerton's reply in the *National Observer*, 18 April, to a letter of Theo. Fox in the *National Observer* of 4 April concerning the terminology of producing etchings. Philip Gilbert Hamerton (1834-94), etcher and writer. Art critic for the *Saturday Review*, 1865-68. He was the founding editor of the *Portfolio* from 1870 until his death.

[12] This did not happen.

then.[13] Only let me know in good time.

I am wearying to back at my verses. We shall go down to the sea next week, I hope.

Nutt wants to publish *Admiral Guinea* at a fancy price.

E.Y.A.,
H.

Nothing from Murano![14]

---

[13] Whibley penned the final note on the controversy in the *National Observer* of 2 May 1891. In it he refers to Herkomer's letter in *The Times* as his only comment on the whole affair.
[14] Was WEH buying some Murano glassware?

To Alfred, Lord Tennyson, 25 April 1891
ALS: BL

The National Observer, Edinburgh

My Lord,

I am selecting an anthology for boys[1], designed — but the design is not avowed — to bring into particular relief the dignity of patriotism, the beauty of battle, the heroic quality of death. It begins with the chorus from *Henry V*;[2] includes excerpts from Drayton, Beaumont, Fletcher, Lovelace, Herrick, Montrose, Marvell, Dryden, Milton, Gray, Collins, Wordsworth, Byron, Sir Walter, Matthew Arnold, Whitman, Swinburne, Longfellow, & William Morris;[3] & ends with Mr. Kipling's 'East & West' & 'The English Flag',[4] to which last I did myself the honour to draw to your attention some two or three weeks ago.

I believe that the anthology will be a remarkable book; I believe, too, that its effect must certainly be good; & my purpose in writing to you is to ask permission to strengthen & dignify it by the addition of certain numbers of your own, who have spoken so well for England, & to whom we owe it that our antient civic feeling endures so vigorously yet. These are (1) 'The Charge of the Light Brigade', (2) 'Lucknow', & (3) 'The "Revenge"': your permission to reprint the which will be duly & gratefully acknowledged.[5]

---

[1] This was his *Lyra Heroica.*
[2] The Chorus before Act 1 in *Henry V.*
[3] Michael Drayton (1561-1631), poet; Francis Beaumont (1584-1616), playwright who collaborated with John Fletcher (1579-1625); Richard Lovelace (1616-57/8); James Graham Montrose (1612-50), 1st Earl of Montrose, who was executed during the English Civil War; William Collins (1721-59) was not included in *Lyra Heroica.*
[4] 'A Ballad of East and West' and 'The Flag of England'.
[5] Tennyson gave permission for 'A Ballad of the Fleet', commonly known as 'The Revenge', and 'The Heavy Brigade'.

In conclusion I will add that I propose to call my collection 'On the Heights' & *to use as its device the admirable quotation from Old Mortality.*[6] I have the honour to be, my Lord,

Your very obedient Servant,
W. E. Henley

Lord Tennyson.

I have pleasure in asking your attention to a little book of *Essays in Appreciation*[7] in which I have attempted to express something of my admiration for your work.

[6] 'Sound, sound the Clarion, fill the fife!
   To all the sensual world proclaim,
   One crowded hour of glorious life
   Is worth an age without a name.'

This quotation from Sir Walter Scott's *Old Mortality* (1816) appeared on the cover and the title page. Although attributed to Scott (he had used it as a motto in ch. 34) it is from 'Verses written during the War, 1756-1763' by Thomas Osbert Mordaunt (1730-1809) first published in the *Bee*, 12 October 1791.
[7] 'Tennyson,' *Views and Reviews: Literature.*

To William Blackwood,[1] 19 May 1891
MS: NLS

Seaforth, Levenhall, Musselburgh, N.B.

My dear Blackwood,
    The enclosed is too long for me, or I should certainly use it.[2] I send it to you (1) because I think it will suit you, & (2) because, if you like it, it may well be the starting-point of a conservation.
    The author, a lad of twenty-two, is still at Oxford.[3] To judge by the stuff he

[1] William Blackwood (1836-1912), publisher and editor of *Blackwood's Magazine*, November 1879-1912.
[2] 'Title of *MS. Love and Duty*' is noted in another hand at the top of the letter.
[3] George Warrington Steevens (1869-1900), writer and traveller. He died of illness as a war correspondent at the siege of Ladysmith during the Boer War. The Boers, or Dutch South Africans, rebelled against the British from October 1899 to May 1902. He married Mrs. Christina Adelaide Ethel Athanasia Rogerson (*née* Stewart) (1849-1911) on 25 August 1894.

is sending me — that excellent ghost-story, 'An Object Lesson', was his;[4] & so is 'A Smoking Compartment'[5] in the current number — he is going to be somebody.

Now, there's no earthly reason why he shouldn't be somebody for you & *Maga* (which he venerates); so I give him his chance.[6] I hope you'll think with me about him, & help.

Always Sincerely Yours,
W. E. Henley

I hope you are smitten with Barry Pain.[7]

[4] *National Observer*, 2 May 1891.
[5] *National Observer*, 16 May 1891.
[6] Steevens's first published *Blackwood's* article was 'A Naval Utopia', *Blackwood's Magazine*, June 1898.
[7] The journalist and comic writer Barry Eric Odell Pain (1864-1928). He published his first book *In a Canadian Canoe*, a collection of contributions to the Cambridge University undergraduate paper *Granta*, in 1891. He succeeded Jerome K. Jerome as editor of *To-Day* in 1897.

To Alice Meynell, 22 July 1891
ALS: Texas

The National Observer, Edinburgh.

My dear Mrs. Meynell,
    I've had an accident with the Patmore[1] which will make you more dissatisfied with it than ever.

Your revised proof was late; &, fearing lest it might not come, I myself prepared one for the press, & sent it up stairs. When yours came in, I sent it also up stairs: with clearly written instructions to cancel my own corrections & stick to yours. When I came this morning I found that both sets had been adopted, & that the result, with two thirds more, was already in page form, which made correcting impossible.

I am very sorry, but, as you see, it is not my fault but my misfortune, &, as you know, the monster is a strange wild animal. I will take care to have better fortune with your next: which I hope will come soon.

Yours Ever Sincerely,
W.E.H.

[1] Alice Meynell's 'Modern Men: Mr. Coventry Patmore', *Scots Observer*, 25 July 1891. Coventry Kersey Dighton Patmore (1823-96), poet. He was a convert to Roman Catholicism and a close friend of the Meynells.

To Edmund Gosse, 3 September 1891
ALS: Brotherton

11 Howard Place, Edinburgh

My dear Gosse,

The two numbers of the *N.O.*, with 'Cleared' & 'The B.B.', were posted to you to-day — to you at Dunster. The former, I believe, is not easy to get; so perhaps you may find it worth keeping.

'Tis the privilege of editors now & then to stumble upon a *writer*. And it is a very great pleasure to me to reflect that, with a single exception ('East & West'),[1] all R.K's best numbers have been passed out through me.

I must tell you about Old Masson & 'Danny Deever'.[2] 'Yes,' said he: 'I read it, & then I read it again; & I said to myself here is some thing new in English letters. A new taste: a new flavour; some thing — in short, it reminded me of *creosote*.'

It is kind & friendly of you to talk about my new book.[3] Next year, perhaps, you may see it a possibility. But the infernal bangle of this Struggle for Life, the immense & unending demands upon time & energy & invention which are implied in the production week by week of a journal like the *N.O.*, are very much against it. Especially as these later growths, with their complications of rhythm & their niceties of statement, are monstrous hard to turn into art. But I haven't yet lost heart, & I believe that the new book, when it comes, will be far better — & far less profitable — than the old. For the rest, the other stuff of which you speak disgusts me every time I try to get back to it; & I think that little if any of it will escape the fire.

I think highly of 'Cleared', which seems to me as vigorous & as inspired a piece of invention as late English holds. I should like to see the new & amended 'Blind Bug'.[4]

Yours Always Sincerely,
W.E.H.

I don't mind confessing that R.K. has given me a new interest in life.

---

[1] Kipling's 'The Ballad of East and West' was published in *Macmillan's Magazine*, November 1889.

[2] David Masson (1822-1907), editor of *Macmillan's Magazine*, 1858-67, and Professor of Rhetoric and English Literature, Edinburgh University, 1865-95. Kipling's 'Danny Deever' appeared in the *Scots Observer*, 22 February 1890.

[3] WEH was working on his book of poems *The Song of the Sword and Other Verses* which was published in 1892.

[4] Kipling's 'Blind Bug' had been published in the *National Observer* of 27 December 1890 and was revised as the dedication ('To Wolcott Balestier') in his *Barrack Room Ballads and Other Verses* (1892).

To Charles Whibley, 1 October 1891
ALS: Morgan

11 Howard Place, Edinburgh

My dear Boy,

Yours to hand. There is much in it. Something, too, that needs debating. But of that anon.

Try to get Sickert's 'Degas' or your own 'Tolstoi' in soon.[1]

I am sorry for poor Arnold-Forster.[2] Very soon, it may be, there will be no *N.O.* for him to enthuse about.[3] It will be a thousand pities; for we're £1000 better than last year. But one never knows. For myself, I feel pretty cheerful: especially as there is £1500 of promised money to the good; though as it is promised on condition that £2000 more will be forthcoming, this may mean nothing. But that advance — £1000 since last October — is encouraging, isn't it?

All this, of course, is the most deadly & desperate secrecy. So beware lest you blab so much as a syllable.

I had to cut your leader. It came so late that — *enfin!* I had to cut it.

The Châtelaine & the Emperor[4] have gone to Levenhall: the former is thoroughly done up. I remain in Edinburgh for some days at least. Bruce returns to-morrow, & is for town on Tuesday, Bell came back last night: looking & feeling uncommon fit — also cheerful.

E.Y.A.
W.E.H.

[1] Sickert's 'Modern Man' on the French artist Degas appeared in the *National Observer* of 31 October 1891 and Whibley's 'Modern Man' on Tolstoy was published on 14 November 1891.
[2] Hugh Oakeley Arnold-Forster (1855-1909), politician. Unionist MP for West Belfast, 1892-1906.
[3] The journal had been a financial risk from the start and despite the change of name from *Scots* to *National Observer* it was still losing money. In a letter to Whibley WEH wrote: 'I think the journal's safe. It is proposed — (between ourselves) — that F[rederick] G[reenwood] comes in as political editor, absorbs the *Anti-Jacobin* in us, & sinks £3,000 as well' (WEH to Charles Whibley, 16 July 1891, Pierpont Morgan). Nothing came of this.
[4] WEH's pet name for his daughter.

To Alice Meynell, 9 October 1891
ALS: Texas. Part published in Meynell, 73.

11 Howard Place, Edinburgh

My dear Mrs. Meynell,

I am very glad that you liked 'The Olympians'.[1] It is the work of a boy I've

[1] Grahame's 'The Olympians', *National Observer*, 19 September 1891. It was reprinted in his

never seen — one Kenneth Grahame: who is also responsible for a certain 'Justifiable Homicide' in the current number.[2]

I, too, am pleased with *Trees*,[3] but I think I can improve it. The pity is — for me at any rate — that I cannot get the time to do some more in the same strain. But the work of the *N.O.* grows heavier instead of lighter; & I begin to fear there may be no book next year after all.

Mr. Martin tells he thinks of asking you to write a certain study for a certain portrait in *Literary Opinion*.[4] I have told him in return that I think you would write well about a broomstick.

I shall be glad, as you know, to see those new articles.[5]

Yours Ever Sincerely,

W.E.H.

Pagan Papers (1893). Kenneth Grahame (1859-1932), writer and bank official. He is famous for his classic story *The Wind in the Willows* (1908). Grahame's first contribution for WEH was 'Of Smoking' in the *Scots Observer*, 18 October 1890. He contributed to the *National Observer* from 24 January 1891 to 25 August 1894; the contributions are listed in Peter Green's *Beyond the Wild Wood* (Exeter, 1982).

[2] 'Justifiable Homicide', *National Observer*, 10 October 1891, reprinted in his *Pagan Papers* (1894).

[3] WEH's 'Trees', *National Observer*, 29 August 1891. Connell incorrectly identifies this poem as 'Trees and the menace of the night'. 'Trees' was not included in WEH's *Works*.

[4] William Pethebridge Martin (1859-1933), editor of *Literary Opinion*, 1891-92. The 'certain study' was an article on WEH; see WEH to Whibley, 8 October 1891, Pierpont Morgan, quoted by Connell, 227. Alice Meynell declined and Whibley's unsigned 'W. E. Henley' appeared in *Literary Opinion*, November 1891.

[5] Alice Meynell's next signed article was 'Domus Angusta', *National Observer*, 28 November 1891. It was reprinted in her *Essays* (1914).

To Charles Baxter, 31 December 1891
ALS: Yale

11 Howard Place, Edinburgh

My dear Charles,

I hope & trust that 'my dear Baxter' duly received a communication in respect of one R.L.S. from his very sincerely W.E.H.[1]

All manner of thanks for the whisky. Which I am sampling day by day.

I had but ten days of St Andrews, but I managed to pull off a certain *Song of the Sword*,[2] which makes a record. Since I returned, I have lived the life of an

[1] WEH had written to Baxter (4 December 1891, Yale) sending a copy of his *Lyra Heroica* for RLS. RLS commented in a letter to Baxter of 1 February 1892 that 'I have received his *Lyra Heroica* and was knocked of a heap to find myself Lyring Heroically, which I thought beyond expectation. It was good of him to stretch a point for his old friend' (*Stevenson Letters*, 7, 233).

[2] WEH had been staying with Bruce at St Andrews. While there he completed *The Song of the Sword*, a patriotic poem of glory in Empire and destiny which was included in his *The Song of the Sword and Other Verses*.

overdriven hansom cab-horse: which is why you've neither seen nor heard of me.

When shall we meet, & where? Will you lunch with us to-morrow, New Year's Day? or a Saturday? or Sunday? When, please? You shall name your own time & place (so that you names the house or your own, that is). There is still a little champagne wine in these cellars, & there is, as ever, the greatest & the most cordial welcome for you & yours.

How sped you in London? Did you see the Book-Hawker? And did you meet the Automatic Drunkard & the Economist-Upside-Down? All these things I die to hear.

All good wishes, my dear Charles — the best possible — to you & yours, from us & ours, for '92.

Yours Ever Affectionately,
W.E.H.

I sent you a letter for Lemuel S. Bangs.[3]

[3] WEH had written to Lemuel W. Bangs (d. 1922), Scribner's agent in London, that Baxter wanted to discuss the American sale of RLS's *The Beach of Falesá* (14 December 1891, Yale).

To Charles Whibley, 28 January 1892
ALS: Morgan. Part published in Connell, 238.

11 Howard Place, Edinburgh

My dear Boy,

I am heartily glad to hear it. I hope & trust you'll beat the bugger off until the very end.

Bruce has all his servants down with it: they caught it in a church: which makes the grievance greater still!

The journal looks a little strange without you. But it ain't a bad number, take it all in all. Watson's piece of fancy[1] is uncommon gay, foppish & pleasant; & the leaders & reviews are on the spot. Also your letter should knock 'em.[2] Keep Sickert up to the mark, & we shall do. I am sick of that bloody Jew & all his works, & would fain bury him.

I confess to a serious liking for my own verses. I should like to hear if it's shared around. As for the Dawn,[3] two of your objections has been removed as they arrived. The third — the last — is more bloody: indeed, I'm not sure that ending isn't inevitable. But I'll see. Meanwhile, You & the Châtelaine are both pleased so far: so I don't regret the time & pains — though I could afford neither one nor the other at this juncture. The fourth version — if I do it — will be much

[1] H. B. Marriott Watson's story 'The Maze', *Scots Observer*, 30 January 1892.
[2] Whibley's letter, signed 'K', attacking the Royal Society of Painter-Etchers for electing Professor Herkomer a Fellow.
[3] WEH's 'Largo e mesto', the third part of his 'London Voluntaries' sequence.

shorter, I fancy; but we'll see. I am anxious now to get the book into type;[4] for the Americans, chiefly. And if the aforesaid fourth do not come readily — !

Tell Leonard[5] to read Lang's Burns Dinner speech in Thursday's *Times*;[6] he might do a good deal worse than ask the speaker to edit a reprint of the [   ] — though I reckon he'll be too late if he hasn't done so already.

Let me know if I may depend on you for Maetlinck[7] next week: by Saturday if possible. With anything else there is to come.

I had a letter from Parsons[8] (1 White Court Buildings) yesterday. You should look him up: he thinks he has a new hand; also he shows symptoms of returning to his dooty; also, I'd like him to see the *Sword*, as he has a peculiar affection for these rhythms.

It is important that we should get some swinging good names these next weeks. I wrote to Rud — (so far as I know 'Tomlinson' has been a dead frost)[9] — & offered him his own terms for a set of short stories; but the little bugger hasn't answered. If you see him, you might get a sort of answer. Barrie, too: I am on such terms with him, that I can't presume too far on his good nature. But you might sound him on the subject of short stories: at his own price of course. He will be stepping northward soon; so you can't be on view too readily.

Arthur Locker[10] wants me to write a fortnightly *causerie* for *The Graphic*. There's oof in it, of course; but how the devil can I take it own?

Spielmann[11] has written for my photograph, for publication in the *M. of A.*?

---

[4] WEH's *Song of the Sword*.

[5] Charles's brother Leonard Whibley (1863-1941), classical scholar and writer, Fellow of Pembroke College, Cambridge. 'He was for a time associated with the publishing firm of Methuen' (*DNB*). After that he embarked on an academic career at Cambridge being a University lecturer in Ancient History from 1899 to 1910. Apart from classical publications he co-edited, with P. J. Toynbee, the letters of the poet John Gray and edited other works.

[6] In proposing the toast of Robert Burns, Andrew Lang noted that there were 'thousands ... to damp his [Lang's] ecstasies in the newspapers. There was that singular, savoury Christian, the editor of the *National Observer*. This critic was convinced that his own opinion about Burns was verily the right opinion, and especially that it was infinitely superior to the view of tradition' ('Mr. Andrew Lang on Burns', *The Times*, 26 January 1892).

[7] Whibley's review of the play *Princess Maleine* by the Belgian poet and writer Maurice Maeterlinck (1862-1949) was in the *National Observer*, 6 February 1892.

[8] Harold George Parsons (1867-1905), lawyer and traveller, was the chief leader writer for the *National Observer*, 1891-92. After leaving Oxford he was called to the Bar in 1893 and later served in South Africa during the Boer War, as a Lieutenant in the 53rd East Kent Imperial Yeomanry, where he was wounded. He later worked in Africa and was a Fellow of the Royal Geographical Society.

[9] Kipling's poem published in the *National Observer*, 23 January 1892.

[10] Arthur Locker (1828-93), editor of the *Graphic*, 1870-91. Presumably he wanted WEH to write the fortnightly column 'The World of Letters' which was eventually written by the journalist Henry Duff Traill (1842-1900), later first editor of the weekly *Literature* in 1897.

[11] Marion Harry Alexander Spielmann (1858-1948), art critic, writer and editor of the *Magazine of Art* on WEH's resignation from 1887 to 1904 when the journal ceased publication. Spielmann wrote the 'The Press-Today and the Critics. - II. Glimpses of artist-life', *Magazine of Art*, May 1892, in which he commented on the major art critics of the press

Why, my God — *why?*

E.A.Y.
H.

The Emperor is getting truly wonderful. She lives a romance all day. Her mother scolded her for something or other, & says she —after a certain silence, in a very nearly breaking voice — 'Mother, you shouldn't: *my heart feels crying.*'

[*Added by WEH at the top of the letter*] I am much pleased with the *Mickado.*[12]

when viewing at the gallery. Photographs of some of these critics were published but not those of WEH or Charles Whibley, both of whom were but mentioned in passing.
[12] A 'Modern Man' of 30 January 1892 on the Emperor of Japan.

To Charles Whibley, 26 February 1892
ALS: Morgan. Part published in Connell, 242.

11 Howard Place, Edinburgh
Dear Boy,
    Farmer wants volunteers to read for words. Could you not turn on Bobby Ross?[1] I think he might go through Dryden (comedies) & Etherege[2] without hurting himself. Let me have your views, & I'll write to him.[3]
    What is your theory of *Greens*? Does it derive from *Grene* (Scots) = to long for? Or is it merely sprung by association from *Cauliflower* & *Garden* & sich? I believe it to be a modern coinage, & have never seen it in print. Have you?
    I must close without you, I fear.

Yours Ever,
H.

[1] Robert Baldwin Ross (1869-1918), writer, art critic and loyal friend of Oscar Wilde. Born of Canadian parents in France, he lived in England from 1872. He was director of the Carfax Gallery in London, 1901-09.
[2] Sir George Etherege (*c.*1634-91), playwright of the Restoration period. His best-known play was *The Man of Mode* (1676).
[3] WEH wrote on 18 March asking Ross to take on Dryden (18 March 1892; published in Ross, 23-4).

To Charles Baxter, 4 May 1892
ALS: Yale

11 Howard Place, Edinburgh

My dear Charles,

Then fire away, please, at *V. & R.*[1] *as soon as you can.* It is wanted *au plus vite*: indeed, it is supposed to be in the press e'en now.

I don't remember charging you with any message for Lewis. What was it? *Please* let me know. For I wouldn't for the world that anything of mine made further mischief.

The *Sword* appears to be doing fairly well: All the Japs & some sixty l. p. copies went last week. Do let me have your views about it: if only to the extent of which section you like best.

I go down again to-morrow night.[2]

Your Ever Affectionate,
H.

I think I told you that we — Blaikie & I & Nutt — are producing the initial number of a series of *Tudor Translations*. It may run to 30 volumes, or it may stop at 3. In any case, it will as beautiful a thing has [*sic*] British printing has achieved. The initial aforesaid is a reissue of Florio's *Montaigne*[3] in three volumes. The first is to be ready on the First June. We think of inscribing it thus:

To the R.L.S.
of
Virginibus Puerisque
Memories & Portraits
Across the Plains
This Reissue
Of the first Version of
His Renowned Acceptance.

Or words to that effect.[4] Would there be any objection, think you?

---

[1] WEH was preparing the second edition of his *Views and Reviews: Essays in Appreciation: Literature* which was published in June 1892.
[2] To Musselburgh.
[3] *The Essays of Montaigne. Translated by John Florio. 1603.* Introduction by George Saintsbury. *Tudor Translations*, 1-3 (1892).
[4] The final dedication was: To / Robert Louis Stevenson / This new fashioning of an / old and famous book is / Dedicated / by its contrivers.

To Charles Whibley, 28 May 1892
ALS: Morgan. Part published in Connell, 248.

Seaforth, Levenhall, Musselburgh, N. B.

My dear Boy,

Your news is appalling. How you contrived to get flooded on the first floor I don't exactly see. None the less do I regret.

Since writing, I've made up my mind about the rooms[1] — about one at all events. I'll simply reproduce the study. The woodwork a chestnut brown; the ceiling gold; cornice, a darkish red; gold the mantel; & the walls a light brown-paper hue, as near a bit of jute I shall send next week as possible. The bedroom & buttery I leave to you. Both should, I think, be warm alike in paper & woodwork.

I do hope the bog in the bath-room is a feature. Do your best to make it so, at any rate. I am so poor a bogster & I couldn't & wouldn't share with a double set of offices. Also, insist for me upon a *really decent bath*. If the whole thing —bath & bog — be to my mind, I am game to pay interest on the outlay.

The bath, by the way, should be fed with taps, as I want to lay on a cold water spray.

All this is trifling enough; but it makes the difference between comfort & discomfort: & that, to me, who spend my days in the house, means a very great deal indeed.

Besides, you volunteer to do your best; & I must e'en take you at your word.

I am woefully glad to have your letter: (1) because it says you've got rid of neuralgia; & (2) because it give a decent account of Bruce & Bell.

I've heard no more of George Moore.[2] If the copy don't turn up, I shall suspect with you, that Shorter[3] knows where it is. As the *Graphic* hasn't come, I suppose the R.A. is still too many for us. I note, from the *Fortnightly* announcement, that Symons is still in the womb of time; & that I've a month of self-respect still left me anyhow. And that's about all.

How Rudyard has scooped 'em, has he not! I saw Leonard advt today in the *Athenaeum*. It looks noble. I wish, of course — *enfin*! It's a triumph, & it is deserved.

Yes: I think the Cog. is possible. But I want to know, before saying go on, *what* he is to play.

W.H.P. wrote me a 'word of cordial congratulations' on my *National*.

E.A.Y.,
H.

---

[1] For some time Fitzroy Bell had been working on moving the *N.O.* to London as a means of ensuring its survival. Whibley had been asked by WEH to sort out rooms at the new office at 1 Great College Street, Westminster, and also to look for a house for his family.

[2] George Augustus Moore (1852-1933), Anglo-Irish novelist and playwright.

[3] Clement King Shorter (1857-1926), journalist. He was editor of the *Illustrated London News*, 1891-97, founding editor of the *Sketch*, 1893-97 and the *Sphere* 1900-26.

Of course the first thing to do is to see the rooms & how they are lighted.

H.

To R. Murray Gilchrist,[1] 22 July 1892
ALS: Morgan

1 Great College St., Westminster, S.W.[2]

Dear Mr. Gilchrist,

I had not intended to use 'The Basililk'[3] so soon, but I ran short of stuff this week & had no choice. You will find that I have ventured upon some further corrections — I hope you will think them improvements — here & there. They are mostly verbal, & I meant you to see the proof; but of course there was no time.

I am not sure that I can do anything with Miss Swarthmoor[4] now; but will you send me the Magazine?[5] I should like to see the sort of thing it is ere I decide. In any case, I should ask you to revise with some care.

Thank you, meanwhile, for two very striking stories.

Yours Very Faithfully,
W.E.H.

[1] Robert Murray Gilchrist (1868-1917), novelist and writer about the Peak District of England.
[2] WEH was in residence by 11 July 1892 (WEH to the Principal, St Andrews University, 11 July 1892, St Andrews University).
[3] Gilchrist's short story 'The Basilisk' appeared in the *National Observer*, 23 July 1892. It was included in *The Dedalus Book of Decadence: Moral Ruin*, ed. B. Stableford (1990).
[4] Gilchrist's epistolary story 'The Writings Of Miss Swarthmoor' appeared in the *National Observer*, 17 September 1892.
[5] This has not been identified.

To Mrs Fanny Douglas,[1] 14 October 1892
ALS: Morgan

11 Howard Place, Edinburgh

Dear Mrs. Douglas,

On reflection, I seem to see no possibilities in 'The Handkerchief'.[2] But if you give me 'The Shoe' (which might include the 'Stocking' & the 'Garter', perhaps)[3]

[1] I have been unable to establish her dates. She was a co-author of *The Gentlewoman's Book of Gardening* (1892) with Edith L. Chamberlain and sole author of *The Gentlewoman's Book of Dress* (1895). Both books appeared in the Victoria Library for Gentlewoman series.
[2] Not accepted by WEH. Mrs Douglas had previously published 'Evolution in Dress: The Petticoat', *National Observer*, 20 August 1892.
[3] 'Evolution in Dress: Shoes and Hose', *National Observer*, 29 October 1892.

& 'Underclothing',[4] I shall be charmed to take them on. The last should be quite possible.

Very Sincerely Yours,
W.E.H.

Be as daring as you can, & leave the rest to me.

[4] 'Evolution in Dress: Underwear', *National Observer*, 12 November 1892.

To W. C. Brownell, Friday 15 October 1892
ALS: Princeton

1 Great College Street, Westminster, S.W.

My dear Brownell,

I missed the first, but will set it. The second I have to read. After the third I'll write.

I am sending, through Mr. Bangs, a long affair in verse for the magazine[1] — per chance. 'Tis an attempt to show how I loved in the old *Arabian Nights*: How the book was part of life & how life was coloured & heightened by the book. I hope it may please.

Yours Always,
W.E.H.

[1] WEH's 'Arabian Nights' Entertainments' appeared in *Scribner's Magazine*, July 1893. This long poem recalled the young WEH's magical view of Gloucester. Scribners were pleased with the poem:

> 'We shall be very glad,' the editor wrote W. E. Henley in 1892, 'to take for the Magazine the poem 'Arabian Nights' Entertainments' which you were kind enough to send to us through Mr. Bangs. — It is seldom that we are able to print a poem of this length; but this has attracted us so much that we are unwilling to let the opportunity pass — even though the length may possibly delay publication for a few numbers, with the disposition of the Magazine's space unavoidably made for a little time ahead.'

(Roger Burlingame, *Of Making Many Books: A Hundred Years of Reading, Writing and Publishing*, New York, 1946, 250).

To Robert Fitzroy Bell, 6 November 1892
ALS: Yale

[Ashburton Lodge, 29 Ashburton Road,] Addiscombe[1]
My dear F.B.,

I wrote to the Marquees[2] on Friday. Also to George Wyndham.[3] I will duly let you know the result. I look for nothing immediate from the first. From the second, though, I should hear something about Arthur:[4] especially as I know from a third person that he was mighty keen to get the said Arthur to write.[5]

To be very frank: I think you are despairing much too soon. London is practically untried. If we were to die, it had been much wiser & better to have died in (& of) Edinburgh. But to come to London for the fag ends of a couple of seasons — one dead & one very hard to get alive — & *then* to expire — ! No: you mustn't think of it! What, rather, you shd. think of spending a certain time with us: taking your proper share in the direction of the journal & representing us in society — where we are unrepresented. Do that for six months & then, if you will, we'll talk of death. But not till then. Seriously, I believe that this is what you ought to — & must — do: you are out of touch with us already. You complain with the Edinburgh accent: the twang of Parliament House is all about your speech; a little while, & we shall have you swearing by the *Saturday Review*!

Thus, you are unjust to Parsons,[6] I think. I know that Hodgson[7] has asked him to write — & repeat himself — for the *N.R.* I know that when I was asked to name a person to send down to meet Cecil Rhodes & introduce him for the new *P.M.G.*, it was on the strength of his Imperialist & S. African work. I know, too, that, the points on which he has been strongest — the points on which he only has thought it well to dilate — that is the administrative quality of Toryism & the fact that Toryism, as we understand it, is a reforming influence, are precisely the points on which, a good while after us, all the Tory points are agreed, & on which the Marquees will probably go back to office. Why, then, take on Traill? And, if corrections you want, why not supply them yourself? You might do so well enough; but since we parted, I've had but one suggestion — & that not worth a dam — from you.

---

[1] The Henleys moved here in late September or early October 1892.
[2] Robert Arthur Talbot Gascoyne Cecil, 3rd Marquis of Salisbury (1830-1903), statesman and three times Conservative Prime Minister. WEH was seeking to obtain backing, both financial and literary, for the *National Observer*.
[3] George Wyndham (1863-1913), journalist and politician, was private secretary to Arthur James Balfour, 1887-89, and Chief Secretary for Ireland, 1900-05. Although both he and WEH came from vastly different social backgrounds they formed a lasting friendship. He was one of the financial backers of the *N.O.* and had been contributing to the *S.O.* since 1890; see J. W. Mackail and Guy Wyndham, eds, *Life and Letters of George Wyndham*, 2 vols [1924], *1*, 45.
[4] Balfour.
[5] There is no evidence that Balfour wrote for the *N.O.*
[6] Harold George Parsons.
[7] William Earl Hodgson (?1860-1910), journalist and writer. Parsons did not write for the *National Review*.

In respect of R.L.S.: please remember that Samoa is not exactly in the four-mile radius, & that there is barely time, as yet, to have answered my letter.[8] As for Barrie, I fear he's hopeless: but I will try him again *when I see him*; which I should do soon. R.K. I have asked to send, & no doubt he will send when he's ready: you know him well enough to know that wild horses wouldn't move him before. As for Gilbert Parker,[9] he has just concluded a very good engagement with the *Illustrated News* & is off to New York to negotiate another with the *Century*: solely, I hear, on the strength of his *N.O.* stories.[10] Now, if these be good enough to make other editors offer terms for their like the which are far beyond our means, why shouldn't they be just as generally acceptable *chez nous* as they are hoped to be elsewhere? As for Lowry,[11] you may have your will of *him*. But I do not believe those others would be a bit more attractive; & I *do* know they would cost a very great deal more money. The saving of which has always been a fad of mine: that is as regards the journal. But, if you please, I'll think the matter over, & see what seems best to be done; & then we will advise.

For the rest, we seem to be thriving in a way & to be fast becoming an influence. I hear from the Librarian of the Commons,[12] for example, that the *N.O.* is the journal most read & most run upon in the House. I hear from here & there that remote book stalls sell out early in the week. I can tell you (under purvey) that when the *P.M.G.* changed hands, it was to *me* that the new proprietor came for his staff; that I put in Marriott Watson as Assistant Editor; & that presently, when the time comes, I hope to have three or four other men in, & to find the journal working — co-operating — with us even more cordially than Low[13] & the *St. James's* have done. When the House is sitting, I hope to make Great College St. a house of call for Young Toryism; & and I believe I shall do so without much difficulty. All which, whether it tend or not to immediate prosperity, is at least good cause for the future.

It would be better, I think — in the meantime — to face it out with A.J.B., & tell him all you have to say, instead of writing it. Still, if you write, this will do as well as anything else. What I asked Wyndham to ask of him was this: Why does

[8] WEH had written to RLS asking for a story for the *N.O.* RLS replied that he would 'bear your wants in mind' (*Stevenson Letters*, 8, 13). No story was written.
[9] (Horatio) Gilbert (George) Parker (1862-1932), born in Canada, traveller, writer and MP. Knighted 1902, baronet 1915. His main works were Canadian historical novels. He dedicated his novel *Mrs Falchion* (1894) to 'William Ernest Henley / with admiration and regard'.
[10] Gilbert Parker contributed twelve short stories in the *N.O.* between 10 October 1891 and 5 November 1892.
[11] Henry Dawson Lowry (1869-1906). After leaving Oxford with a degree in chemistry he turned to journalism and novel writing. He was on the staff of the *P.M.G.* 1895 and the weekly *Black and White,* 1895-98. He edited the *Ludgate Magazine* from 1897.
[12] Ralph Charles Walpole (1844-1928) was Librarian from 1 April 1887 to 28 January 1908. His uncle Spencer Horatio Walpole (1806-98) was Home Secretary, 1852, 1858 and 1866.
[13] Sidney James Mark Low (1857-1932), writer and journalist, editor of the *St James's Gazette* 1888-97. He trained as a barrister but devoted his career to journalism. After leaving the *St James's Gazette* he became leader writer on the *Standard*, becoming literary editor in 1904. Knighted in 1918.

he (a professional Handelian) like Wagner? But as Wagnerism is more or less mutton — is muttonizing fast at any rate — perhaps Bimetallism[14] would suit our purpose better. I leave the thing to you. All I ask is that you do not fail to see him, & to do your best to screw some thing out of him.

Joseph Thomson[15] has written about Morocco. I will try & land Goschen.[16] Also Chaplin on Agriculture,[17] of which subject I want to make a speciality. Grahame's articles have been very widely read, I believe. Also, he threatens to bring old Lord Stanley[18] to see me; an infliction which, for the journal's sake, I suppose I must endure. I had rather you received & looked wise at him than I: for you are a future Under Secretary (at least), & that is your game in life. But as you are not on the spot, I must e'en do what I may.

Know you aught of the Souls?[19] And do you see that Margot Tennant is to (nominally) edit their new magazine? Happy Office Boy! Happy Publisher! Happy Foreman Printer!

Ever Yours,
W.E.H.

[14] The equality of gold and silver as the basis of a monetary system.

[15] Joseph Thomson, 'Morocco', *National Observer*, 12 November 1892. Joseph Thomson (1858-94), geologist, traveller and African explorer. He found fame as the first white explorer to cross the warlike country of the Masi people in Africa. Thomson's Gazelle is named after him.

[16] George Joachim Goschen (1831-1907), 1st Viscount, statesman. Chancellor of the Exchequer in Salisbury's government 1886 and founder of the Unionist Party.

[17] [?Henry Chaplin], 'The Agricultural Union', *National Observer*, 17 December 1892. Henry Chaplin (1840-1923), Conservative politician. President of the Board of Agriculture, 1889-92.

[18] Henry Edward John, 3rd Baron Stanley of Alderley (1827-1903), diplomat and writer.

[19] A select group of aristocrats bound together by wealth, intelligence and social standing; see Angela Lambert, *Unquiet Souls* (New York: 1984). Emma Alice Margaret Tennant (1864-1945), married Herbert Henry Asquith (1852-1928), statesman, later Earl of Oxford and Asquith, in 1894.

To Coventry Patmore, 11 November 1892
Text: Published in Champneys, *2*, 272.

1 Great College Street, Westminster

My dear Patmore,

I should have answered your first letter,[1] but there are days when I can do

[1] WEH's letter is in reply to Patmore's of 8 November 1892:

> Shall I offend you or make you despise my stupidity if I object that there is almost always one article in the *National Observer* which it is at once unwise in the interests of the Paper, and more than dubious in those of good taste and fair morals, to admit?
>
> I need not name the articles. You know, I think, that I am not prudish: I do not call the supreme good of humanity evil, as it is the nature of prudes to do; but it is for the sake of the supreme good that I desire to protest against its profanation by being made the jest, and, far worse, the means of gross pleasure to the multitude (Champneys, *2*, 272).

nothing at all, and on them when I can do anything, I have necessity to do too much.

I am sorry indeed that the *N.O.* is no longer to be read *chez vous*. But perhaps I could have looked for nothing else; I confess however, that the offence does not appear to me so offensive as all that. It is a romance — impossible, unreal — fantastical all: a failure, as I believe, but the failure of a very clever man; an error of taste, but the error of an exquisite artist *à ses heures*. I feel as though I myself, and not he, had written and were responsible for the effect. Which, as I have said, I am the first to regret,

What you say of my own verses doth both please and interest me. I am sure you have excellent grounds for saying what you say; but to defend or rather to explain my position would to write a volume about myself; which cannot as you know be done by letter. Someday we may meet and talk it out. Till then ...!

Every sincerely yours,
W.E.H.

I hope some day, to hear that a sobered and abashed *N.O.* is still tolerated at Lymington. Indeed to be plain, I am rather sorry for Lymington this week. For Greenwood (once more with us) is in his best form, & Blank & Dash & Three Stars & the others are 'equal to themselves!!'

However —!

Patmore was criticising H. B. Marriott Watson's short story 'The Pretty Woman' which appeared in the *N.O.* of 5 November 1892. The narrator's fiancée imitated the low *décolleté* of a Lady and when asked to refrain by the narrator reacts by wearing a garland of roses in place of the dress top.

To Charles Baxter, 15 November 1892
ALS: Yale

1 Great College Street, Westminster, S.W.

My dear Charles,

Very good: but all the same, write to Tree,[1] & say that the agreement having expired, you are prepared to consider the terms on which to conclude a new one.

The truth is, that the old agreement was absurd — is the decision, indeed, of every one to whom I have confessed it. Of course it was none of my making: as you remember, we had words about H.B.T, & I ended up by chucking the whole thing as you heard. When I tell you (in confidence, of course) that Barrie got £100

---

[1] Tree was manager of the Theatre Royal, Haymarket, London, from 1887-97. He had been given absolute London performance rights for two years from 9 October 1890 for *Beau Austin* and *Macaire*. He played the title role in the first performance of *Beau Austin* at the Theatre Royal on 3 November 1890. Neither play was a success.

from Irving for the privilege of first reading & six months in which to make up his mind — (he did that in two) — you will admit that Tree's two years lain upon *Macaire* & the *Beau* for nothing all is a little steep.

Of course you despise the plays — most justly, no doubt; but that needn't prevent you bargaining as though you believed in them. Of course, too, I'm not Jim Barrie; but neither is Jim Barrie R.L.S. plus me. At all events you are our agent, & it's your duty to your clients, & not allow yourself to be *bribed* to *act against their interests by suppers at swell hotels* & the privilege of going behind the scenes in pursuit of the *degraded creatures* who call themselves *actresses*.

Also, there will be a boom presently — a boom in Henley-&-Stevenson. So at it you go; & please remember all the while that at it you are that H.B.T. is something of a Jew, & has a wonderful eye for Number One.

E.A.Y,

H.

To Robert Fitzroy Bell, 23 January 1893
ALS: Yale

11 Howard Place, Edinburgh

My dear F.B.,

There is no question of unfriendliness. It is only that you do not shine in your letters. Which, indeed, have often made me wonder why & how you continued to be so good & courteous a gentleman in life & fact who could no nothing of the sort on paper.

What annoys & puzzles & enrages me is this enormous increase in the cost of production. In Edinburgh, I understood that we were losing at the rate of £40 per week; & here in London it is £70. How the devil does it come? I cannot understand.

I hear that W.H.P. is on his last legs — that, in fact, ... but no! I oughtn't to repeat what, after all, was told me in confidence: If he would but make up his mind to go, & go quickly, poor devil, your combination might come off next week.

It is an awful nuisance to have to face the action on Thursday.[1] Of course I'll see the lawyers; &, if I'm wanted, of course I'll go to the Court. But it *is* a nuisance, isn't it? I've been trying hard to recover Wallace from the past; & the more I think, the surer I am that he is mistaken. Not that that makes any difference to the point at issue. Only it is a comfort to know that he is mistaken.

I give my Baxter up. He is really too steep for words. And if he has bungled

---

[1] This was a libel case brought by Dr Abraham Wallace who was attacked in the *National Observer* of 16 April 1892 in a review of his wife's *In the Service of Love*. Dr Wallace was referred to as 'that objectionable and foolish person'. He was awarded £100 damages ('Law Report. Feb. 1. Wallace v. Douglas', *The Times*, 2 February 1893).

this business with the rest, it will be long ere I forgive him. Do please write by return & tell me the facts of the case; I want to know them, whether we get the Samoan's *MS* or not.[2]

Tell me what you think, too, of the current number: & especially of 'To Bow Bridge'.[3] To me it looks as if we had our hand on another coming man. At all events, here is some thing done well that has not — so far as I know — been done before.

Steuart[4] & Marriott are more in the office with Cust;[5] & I rather think that Vernon & Sanders[6] will go there too— Vernon as musical critic *en permanence*; Sanders as a bi-weeklyest [*sic*]. Charles[7] could get as much work from the same journal as he would care to do; while Wilfrid[8] has joined the *Westminster Gazette*. In fact, they're all provided for but Dunn[9] & me: which is a proud thought in some ways, & in others is far from it.

I met Anstey 'tother night, & quoted his own words to him till his countenance shone with joy & pride. He is to come to Westminster, & be taken to the sing-song next door. All the same, I fear there's nothing to be got out of him for the *N.O.*

The *Standard* is very well disposed to us, I am told; & will do us a good turn the first occasion possible. I shall do my very best to make one. There appears, for the rest, to be hope from G.W. & hope from Lord Stanley (who, by the way, is Egeria's[10] dearest enemy); but what is wanted most of all is patience & time. As I said, if we fail we make the most auspicious smash that ever was made in journalism: & that I've no sort of drive to do. If I had any money I wouldn't hesitate to buy you all out, & I believe that Dunn would put his shirt on the thing.

---

[2] RLS's story 'The Isle of Voices' was first offered to the *Graphic* which did not have space immediately. Baxter offered it to Bell by on 24 January 1893. It was published in four weekly instalments in the *N.O.* between 4 and 25 February 1893.

[3] Arthur Morrison, 'To Bow Bridge', *National Observer*, 21 January 1893. This was the first of a series of stories of Morrison's to be published in the *N.O.* Arthur Morrison (1863-1945) worked at the People's Palace in London's East End from 1887 to 1890. He then became a journalist and wrote for WEH, later working for *Macmillan's Magazine*. His experiences of the East End were used in his stories and his novels, particularly *Tales of Mean Streets* (1894), *A Child of the Jago* (1896) and *The Hole in the Wall* (1902). He was also the creator of the fictional detective Martin Hewitt, one of the numerous, but better, imitations of Conan Doyle's Sherlock Holmes. A collector of Japanese art, he and WEH became good friends.

[4] Probably the novelist and journalist John Alexander Steuart (1861-1932). He edited the *Publishers' Circular*, 1896-1900, and published a biography of RLS in 1924.

[5] Henry John Cockayne Cust (1861-1917), journalist, MP and man about town. He was editor of the *Pall Mall Gazette*, 1892-96, and a member of 'The Souls'.

[6] Vernon Blackburn (1867-1907), journalist. Music critic for the *Pall Mall Gazette* and sub-editor on the Catholic weekly the *Tablet*. The journalist and writer Lloyd Charles Sanders (1857-1927) wrote for the *National Observer*.

[7] Whibley.

[8] The journalist Wilfrid Pollock.

[9] James Nicol Dunn (1856-1919), journalist. Managing editor of the *Scots Observer* and the *National Observer*, editor of *Black and White* 1895-97, editor of the *Morning Post* 1905-1910 and editor of the *Star*, Johannesburg, 1911-14.

[10] Egeria was a female advisor but the reference here has not been identified.

That, of course, is but an expression of opinion & commercially = zero. But it may help you to understand why we are not exhilarated by your letters, & why, not being at all disposed to quarrel, I take no notice of them in writing.

And I must to home-cleaning & make the best I can of the fortnightly fashions.

Ever Yours,
W.E.H.

To Robert T. Hamilton Bruce, 13 February 1893
ALS: Yale

1 Great College Street, Westminster, S.W.

My dear Bruce,

Please post me the adventures of Fanny Hill.[1] Long an ornament of your drawing-room table, they are very much in request: particularly for purposes not wholly unconnected with *Slang*.

The Lord he knoweth how things will go; but anyhow we'll die in the blaze.

Methuen has asked me for a Lyrical Anthology;[2] so now for your Palgrave[3] revised, depleted, corrected, perfect!

I hear this morning [the] St. Andrews degree is an accomplished fact.[4] Such is life, all things come round to him that doth not wait for them.

Ever Yours, Dear Bruce,
W.E.H.

I expect the Châtelaine & the Emperor will be moving northwards in about a month. What are your *plans*? And please be definite as you can about the *Merry Muses*?[5]

---

[1] *Memoirs of a Woman of Pleasure*, commonly known as *Fanny Hill*, written by John Cleland (1709-89) and published 1748-49. It was suppressed as pornographic and declared illegal. It was not legally available in England until 1970.
[2] This was *English Lyrics: Chaucer to Poe, 1340-1809*, Selected and arranged by William Ernest Henley. It was published by Methuen in 1897.
[3] Palgrave's *Golden Treasury of Best Songs and Lyrical Poems in the English Language* (1861) was the pre-eminent anthology of the period and is still one of the most popular today. Francis Turner Palgrave (1824-97), poet and Professor of Poetry at Oxford, 1885-95.
[4] WEH received the degree of LL.D. from St Andrews University *in absentia* on 6 April 1893.
[5] *The Merry Muses of Caledonia*, a collection of bawdy Scottish songs, some attributed to Robert Burns, was printed *c.* 1800. WEH intended to publish an edition but did not do so. An edition was printed by the Burns Federation in 1911. The latest edition edited by James Barke and Sydney Smith Goodsir was published in Edinburgh 1959; revised London 1965.

To Arthur Morrison, 28 April 1893
ALS: Rochester

1 Great College Street, Westminster, S.W.

Dear A. M.,

I think a very great deal indeed of the last;[1] & so does everybody else — Whibley, Marriott Watson, & the rest — who has spoken of it. Decidedly that book of yours is going to be a *book*.

My great regret now is that I did not delete the initial paragraph. Which is more than useless; for it gives all that follows away.

Send me another at your leisure. Which will, I hope, be soon.[2]

Always Yours Sincerely,
W.E.H.

My brother left his drawings here the other night.

---

[1] 'Without Visible Means', *National Observer*, 22 April 1893. This was one of the stories that was published in his *Tales of Mean Streets*.
[2] Morrison's next story was 'In Business' published in the *National Observer*, 3 June 1893.

To Charles Baxter, 17 October 1893
ALS: Yale

Seaforth, Levenhall, Musselburgh, N.B.

My dear Charles,

I do hope to see you to-morrow (Wednesday).

Might I ask you to bring or send me Dunbar. *Poems*, 1836,[1] & the volume, or part, of Murray,[2] containing the verb 'to couple'? I am pressed for time as regards both (the Dunbar must be that particular edition) or I would wait till next week, when I could see them *in situ*.

E.A.Y.
H.

---

[1] WEH means the 1834 edition. William Dunbar (?1465-?1530), Scottish poet.
[2] *A New English Dictionary on Historical Principles*. Edited by J. A. H. Murray and others, 11 vols (Oxford, 1884-1933). James Augustus Henry Murray (1837-1915), schoolmaster, and first editor of what was later to be called the *Oxford English Dictionary*. Knighted 1908.

To Charles Baxter, 1 January 1894
ALS: Yale

Ashburton Lodge, Addiscombe, Surrey

My dear Charles,

Bless you for your good letter. It should have crossed one of mine. But I had a very bad belly ache, & missed the post.

'93 was a devil to us all. To you, dear Charles, a worse one than to any.[1] I hope with all my soul that '94 may & will make amends. At any rate to you.

It's good news that you are to be in town. We give Dunn a send-off on Saturday week.[2] It was arranged that the chairs of R.L.S. & Rudyard should be vacant. Then I suggested that you should come as R.L.S's *alter ego*, & fill his room. Can you manage to do that? Do it if you possibly can. It will please us all. And you must still further please us by lodging here. You say 'in 8 or ten days': it should be easy so to arrange the journey as to take this in.

We are asking all the old *Observers*: together with the new *Pall-Malls* — as Harry Cust & Iwan Muller.[3] Also George Wyndham & R.T.H.B.

I am greatly tickled by what you have to say about the *Ass*;[4] & have sent it all on the C.W. I am very glad I sent: 'tis my New Year's Gift, & it has come off better than I could have hoped. Also, bless you for your devotion to Ed. 2.[5] A 4*th* of the other book was issued with it;[6] so perhaps I ought to think better of '93 than I can & do.

The journal has been once more in the pangs of death & sepulchre.[7] I am so heartily sick of it all — especially of Bell's incompetence — that it was with something like despair I heard the news of another three months' life. 'Tis all too long & too exasperating to write. You shall hear it with your ears. Enough to say that the mismanagement in '93 was so colossal that it floored a practical buyer, who was in a position to make things hum. However — !

I shall take my name off the books of the Savile. I haven't been there for a whole year; & I can spend the £5/5/- to better purpose elsewhere. My debts oppress me horribly; & here is Bell proposing to reduce our wages all round! However — (as I said before) — — !

Did I tell you — (no, I didn't) — that last week they stole my beautiful coat,

---

[1] Baxter's wife, Grace, died on 24 March 1893.

[2] Dunn was leaving his position as business manager of the *N.O.* and becoming news editor of the *Pall Mall Gazette*. The send off would have been at the regular haunt of the *N.O.*, Solferino's Restaurant, Rupert Street, London.

[3] Ernest Bruce Iwan-Müller (1853-1910), journalist and writer, editor of the *Manchester Courier*, May 1884-June 1893, assistant editor of the *P.M.G.* June 1893-February 1896. He joined the *Daily Telegraph* after leaving the *P.M.G.*

[4] *Athenaeum.*

[5] The second edition of *The Song of the Sword and Other Verses* was retitled *London Voluntaries and Other Verses* (1893).

[6] *A Book of Verses.*

[7] Despite the move to London the journal was losing money and Bell was trying to find a buyer.

my ulster? Well, they did. Walked up stairs in a fog, & bound it together with Vernon Blackburn's new blue Ulster — from hooks outside my Westminster parlour door! And there was I with all that amount to M. & A. unpaid, & nothing possible but another order! I think I resented this last attention of '93 more vehemently than all the rest of them.

Have you any news of the Cannibal Islanders?[8] And what is this they tell me of 'A Backwoods Childhood' in *Annie Swan's New Magazine*?[9] God bless you, meanwhile; from all of us.

E.A.Y.,

H.

The Emperor hath a slight cold, but is otherwise well. So too are Mollie[10] & the Châtelaine. I found the other day a copy of *Kidnapped*, with Eddie's name in poor Gracie's hand in it. How it got among my books ...! Mollie will bring it back.

[8] The Stevensons.
[9] Fanny Stevenson's chapter of autobiography 'A Backwoods Childhood,' *Woman at Home*, January 1894. Annie Smith Swan, afterwards Burnett-Smith (1860-1943), novelist.
[10] Anna's sister.

To Robert Fitzroy Bell, 29 January 1894
ALS: Yale

Ashburton Lodge, Addiscombe, Surrey

My dear Bell,
    It is a case of tubercular meningitis.[1] The brain I gave her had in it the seed of death; & now we are waiting the end. I pray it come quickly.[2]
    Will you send me a cheque for my January salary? Make it payable to a London bank, so that I can get it cashed. I do not want to write cheques & we shall need much money.
    Do not write. We know all you would say. But life is ended, & words — words — words ————.

H.

The earlier symptoms of meningitis & of gastric catarrh are, it appears, identical.

[1] This is the first mention of Margaret's fatal illness in any letter, although she had what was thought to be gastric catarrh in November of the previous year (WEH to Charles Whibley, 28 November 1893, Pierpont Morgan).
[2] She died on 11 February 1894 aged nearly five and a half.

To Rudyard Kipling, [February 1894]
ALS: Sussex

Gt. College St., Westminster, S.W.

Dear Ruddy,

Our little one is dead. Something is left of her which still breathes. But really she died last week — of tubercular meningitis; & the best of life & the best in life died with her. What is left of her most royal & radiant self can scarce survive the week; &, for the moment, that thought is the sole comfort we have.

I had hoped you — 'Dada's Boy', *She* called you — would have known & wondered & delighted in her; as Barrie & Charles & Vernon & Parker & the rest have done. I had hoped that your girl[1] & she would have lived to be staunch & lifelong friends, as ourselves. I had hoped .... many things. But the end is this. And next week my wife & I begin the world anew.

She is very wonderful & beautiful — my wife. But I know — I know!

Don't write to me yet. I know all you will feel & would say; & presently — but not now.

Ever Yours,
W.E.H.

'My dada's a king.'

[*Added by WEH at the top of the letter*] I hear that the *N.O.* goes from us next week, & that the man Frank Harris is the new editor.[2]

[1] Josephine Kipling died at the same age on 6 March 1899.
[2] This was not so and WEH refuted it in a letter to *The Times*, 19 February 1894. Frank Harris (1856-1931), Irish writer and journalist, edited the *Evening News*, 1882-86, the *Fortnightly Review*, 1886-94, and the *Saturday Review*, 1894-98. While WEH and Anna were coping with Margaret's illness and subsequent death, Bell was doing his best to sell the *N.O.* WEH felt that all, except Charles Whibley, were against him, even his great friend Hamilton Bruce.

To Robert Fitzroy Bell, 1 February 1894
ALS: Yale

Ashburton Lodge, Addiscombe, Surrey

The effusion is very gradual as yet, & she is still conscious. She sleeps a great deal, & is out of pain. Indeed she is lapsing very placidly, & she will last some days longer.

Very many thanks for the remittance. In my misery I could not realize that the agony would be so long & slow. That is why I was in that necessary hurry.

May I count on the use of the office downstairs till June?[1] You see, this is her

[1] Great College Street.

house & not ours; & now she is gone, we cannot stay. It would break our hearts, you know; if they are not broken already. So I shall take my wife to Westminster, & thence we can move hither & thither as we will. This house, we shall strip at once, & try to let it. Well, if we can; not so well if we cannot. But leave it we must & will. And Westminster will be of the greatest use: especially if I can remove my work downstairs.

I found a place wherein to lay her to-day: West Wickham Churchyard, a beautiful tranquil spot, deep in sunny lanes, set round with noble trees, & overlooking a great rolling Champaign. It is practically a matter of influence: the disposition of the ground resting with one Sir John Lennard of Wickham Hall.[2] So I'm asking Harry Cust to look round for a possible backer among his friends.

To the end she remains the sweetest of God's creatures.

Ever Yours,
W.E.H.

Please show this to Bruce & Blaikie & Charles. I can*not* write to them.

---

[2] Sir John Farnaby Lennard, Bt (1816-99), of Wickham Court, Beckenham, Kent. Harry Cust, who owned a house at Cockayne Hatley, Bedfordshire, arranged for her burial in the churchyard of St John the Baptist, Cockayne Hatley. She was buried on 15 February 1894.

To Edward John Henley, 3 February 1894
ALS: Berg

Ashburton Lodge, Addiscombe, Surrey

Dear Ed,

There is nothing to say. It is horrible, but it must be faced & borne. That's all.

She had a quiet night last night, & is no worse to-day than she was two days ago. No weaker, even, than she would have been had she been afflicted with fever. She remains the sweetest of God's creatures.

We are to bury her at Hatley, in Harry Cust's own churchyard. He is giving us a piece of ground there in perpetuity. 'Tis a very lovely place — an old-world garden indeed; & there under trees & among the flowers she loved we shall lay her to rest.

Tell Will[1] that we have decided to strip the house, & store the furniture. We hope he'll take the job in hand: it will save Anna so much trouble! Indeed, she will not need to see the house again, once she leaves it for the funeral, but can go straight to Westminster.

---

[1] I have not been able to identify him.

Will you pay these bills for me? One is pretty heavy, but it has been owing for some time, & just now I want to write no cheques. We will settle by & by.

We suppose that Will will be with you over Sunday. If he isn't, send this on to him. If he is, please ask him to hold himself in readiness to come when I telegraph.

Anna & Mollie are both wonderful. With all our love.

Your Brother,

W.E.H.

To Robert Fitzroy Bell, 12 March 1894
ALS: Yale

[1 Great College Street, Westminster, S.W.]

My dear F.B.,

It is really intolerable — for the heart is going out of us all, & how the devil I continue to whip the team into a semblance of inspiration, is more than I can tell you. But of course it must be endured. Only —! For all our sakes you must do your best to contract the agony; for agony we feel & know it to be.

I don't think I'd waste any postage stamps on the new builders. There have been too many of them as it is. I would rather say, as I said before, that if you want the journal to have a chance of life, you should close with Harris. He is a ruffian, of course; but he has plenty of energy, heaps of impudence, mountains of self-confidence; & there's no doubt that he would do his own proprieting with gusto & to considerable purpose. I understand from you that terms were agreed upon long since: Dunn told me the other day that, according to Gray,[1] things were so far advanced that a couple of days might do the trick. This morning it's a question of terms. I don't understand it all & I like it even less.

It's all very well to talk about Spain but I've neither the money nor the energy, neither the humour nor the will. I don't like writing text for pictures; &, frankly, that is what I'm asked to do. It means, too, in this instance any amount of padding: which is abhorrent to me. But putting all that aside, I can resolve on nothing — not even where to go & live — until this business of the journal's settled. Which also is a reason why it should be settled soon.

Books are very scarce indeed, & I've the greatest difficulty in eking out the reviews. That is why I stretched out over *Jamie B.*[2] You may judge of the scorn & rage that filled my heart when I beheld the result of your study of the works of Smith![3] I took Crockett's new book for my own hand:[4] being minded to drop the jacket of Master R.L.S., for his impudence in likening C. to J.M.B. A *bêtise*

---

[1] Bell's solicitor.

[2] Barrie's 'Wrecked on an Island', *National Observer*, 17 February 1894.

[3] Bell's unsigned review of the *Question of the Day*, by Goldwin Smith, *National Observer*, 10 March 1894.

[4] WEH's unsigned review of S. R. Crockett's *The Raiders*, *National Observer*, 17 March 1894.

contained in a letter to a friend & now converted into a publisher's advt. which meets you at every turn.[5]

The enclosed is interesting. I've half a mind to take on Jerome K. as another 'Modern Man'.[6]

My wife is low — low! I cannot get her interested in anything. She has written to nobody as yet; but I know she means to write to Mrs. Bell. For whom, *du reste*, she has a little keepsake. But of this anon.

Ever Yours,
W.E.H.

There are no books at all to-day. As for copy, I've three stories & more than enough middle for the week's issue. The Indian copy has gone back: there was more than 25 columns of it. No doubt I could get it again.

[5] WEH, in his review of *The Raiders*, had complained of Unwin's quoting a private letter from RLS to Crockett praising Crockett's *The Stickit Minister* and comparing Crockett and Barrie in advertisements. An extract of the letter had been published in the *Scotsman* on 8 November 1893 and Unwin had quoted from it. Samuel Rutherford Crockett (1860-1914), prolific Scottish writer. After graduating from Edinburgh University he trained for the ministry and was ordained in 1886 as a Free Church minister. He later resigned in order to write full-time. *The Stickit Minister* (1893), a collection of stories, is probably his best work.
[6] Jerome K(lapla) Jerome (1859-1927), writer and journalist. Author of *Three Men in a Boat* (1889). Co-founder and editor of the monthly *Idler Magazine* and *To-Day*. WEH did not use him as a 'Modern Man'.

To H. G. Wells,[1] 29 March 1894
TLS: Illinois

3 James Street Mansions, Buckingham Gate, S.W.[2]
Dear Mr. Wells,

We propose to wake THE NATIONAL OBSERVER on Thursday, April 5th, at the Restaurant Solferino, Rupert Street, at 7.30, when the old staff will be united for the last time. We hope that you will make a point of being present.

Yours truly,
W. E. HENLEY,
CHARLES WHIBLEY.

PLEASE ANSWER.
MORNING DRESS.

[1] Wells had some early time-travelling papers published in the *Science Schools Journal* and he was asked by WEH for a contribution to the *National Observer*. WEH published two of Wells's papers, 'Time Travelling: Possibility or Paradox' on 17 March 1894 and 'The Time Machine', on 24 March 1894. Wells and WEH formed a long and close friendship.
[2] The Henleys were lent this flat by Mrs Christina Rogerson (WEH to Hamilton Bruce, 16 March 1894, Yale). They moved there on 22 March 1894.

To Robert Louis Stevenson, 22 May 1894
ALS: Houghton. Part published in *Stevenson Letters*, 8, 327-9

9 The Terrace, Barnes, S.W.[1]
Dear Lewis,
I know not if C.B. has told you the news. In any case, I think I ought to tell you that, having lost my life — (of which I can say nothing) — I have lost my work also, & am now excessively at large. On 24*th* March the *N.O.* passed into the keeping of a new hand.[2] I produced him his first number — that of the 31*st* — by way of friendship & general magnanimity; & since then he has had things all his own way. I suppose you have seen the results he has achieved? I have, & I am moved to wonder if the last five years have been at all: so utterly has he abolished the traces of what they saw done.

Worse still (perhaps) I am still squabbling with my late proprietor as to the compensation I should receive.[3] He does not seem to be so generously inspired as one might have believed him to be; &, at present, it looks as if I must hale him to the Courts. I have suggested compromise, & volunteered to have the matter referred. But he doesn't hear with that particular ear. As for myself, I spent so much upon the journal — time, money, character, energy — that I feel litigious when I think of him: an experience wholly new to me, for which — however — I am in no wise grateful.

The Tudors are paying, & paying well; & I have engaged to general-edit for Methuen a series of *English Classics*.[4] The idea is to reprint, in a form so comely the book will be delightful *quâ* book & so cheap that anybody who buys at all may buy[5] — a number of the masterpieces of English literature in every several

---

[1] The Henleys had moved here on 3 May 1894 (WEH to Baxter, 3 May 1894, Yale).
[2] The new editor of the *National Observer* was the lawyer and journalist James Edmund Vincent (1857-1909). He edited the *N.O.* until 1897. Vincent had joined *The Times* in 1886 and edited *Country Life*, 1897-1901. He was Chancellor of the diocese of Bangor, North Wales, from 1890 until his death. It has been assumed that the politician Edgar Vincent (1857-1941), later Viscount D'Abernon, had became proprietor and editor of the *National Observer* though there appears to be no evidence for this. The 1895 edition of *Sell's Dictionary of the World's Press* states that 'Mr. Vincent became proprietor as well as editor of the *National Observer* in March, 1894' (p. 71). It also refers to James Vincent as becoming editor (p. 131). Wells notes that Edgar Vincent was at the wake for the *N.O.* on 5 April 1894. H. G. Wells, *Experiment in Autobiography*, 2 vols (1934), 515.
[3] WEH and Bell were in dispute about the amount that WEH was owed. Despite the threat of legal action by both sides the matter was resolved and WEH received £350 instead of the £375 that he was seeking.
[4] The English Classics consisted of six titles according to the British Library Catalogue. However, only the following five titles have been identified: J. Morier's *The Adventures of Hajji Baba of Isphan*, introduced by E. G. Browne, 2 vols (1895); *The Comedies of William Congreve*, introduced by G. S. Street, 2 vols (1895); Sterne's *The Life and Opinions of Tristram Shandy, Gentleman*, introduced by Charles Whibley, 2 vols (1894); Izaak Walton's *The Lives of Doctor John Donne, Sir Henry Wotton, Mr. Richard Hooker, Mr. George Herbert and Doctor Robert Sanderson*, introduced by Vernon Blackburn (1895); and Dr Johnson's *The Lives of the Most Eminent English Poets*, introduced by J. H. Millar, 3 vols (1896).
[5] 3/6 a volume.

department: biography, travel, poetry, drama, fiction, & the rest. *Tristram Shandy* (2 vols) is printed off, & we follow it up with Congreve (the comedies only), Walton's *Lives*, *Haji Baba*, Burns (or Herrick or Keats), the *Journal* to *Stella*, *Amelia*,[6] & so on sticking to no period, but so arranging matters that, if we succeed, we shall in the end have taken in whatever is best worth reading in English. Hereby hangs a tale. Each book is furnished with an *Introduction* — biographies-critical — about 7000 or eight thousand words long, the work of a competent hand. Would you care to take on *The Pilgrim's Progress*?[7] I can't offer you much for the job: indeed, from the payee's point of view, it were beneath your notice. But the work would be a sort of little change for you, & in helping the series you would help me.

Tree's latest was to cut down *Macaire* to what he called a merry little farce (or words to that effect), which would play about three-quarters of an hour. This work of art — a parade for himself & Lionel Brough[8] — he proposed that we should sign. I need scarce say how I declined the proposal! I don't think, for the rest, that he can be doing very well. He hasn't had a success since *The Dancing Girl*,[9] but has gone plunging steadily from half-failure to half-failure: so that it is a matter for wonder that he keeps his doors open. But, for that matter, nobody pays now unless he writes farce or makes a piece for Arthur Roberts.[10] The public seems dead-sick of the serious drama, & will take no stock in it. Jones occasionally works off something that it likes: for instance, he has just knocked it with a play in which he utterly butchers & bedevils that scene which gave us the idea of *The King of Clubs*.[11] But he does it only now & then: the others not at all. So they've just revived *The Two Orphans* at the Adelphi;[12] & upon my word I don't think they could have done better.

If you haven't already heard it already, you will like to hear, I know, that Meredith is getting £1200 for the serial rights of *Lord Ormont & his Aminta*.[13] That is what it is to write for a magazine which is owned by a millionaire & edited by a leash of amateurs.[14] Also, he (G.M.) is writing a novel for *Scribner's* 'against time':[15] so that for once in his life he has a real chance of being fairly

---

[6] *Letters Written by the Late Jonathan Swift ... and Several of His Friends from the Year 1703 to 1740*, 4 vols (1766-68).

[7] RLS declined to write the introduction to Bunyan's *Pilgrim's Progress* owing to pressure of work.

[8] The Welsh actor Lionel Brough (1836-1909), who is best remembered for starting the selling of newspapers on the streets. He worked for the *Morning Star* and the *Daily Telegraph* before finally going on the stage.

[9] H. A. Jones's play at the Haymarket Theatre, London, from 15 January 1891 to 2 May 1891.

[10] The comedian and actor Arthur Roberts (1852-1933). He published his autobiography *Adventures of Arthur Roberts* in 1927.

[11] Jones's *The Masqueraders*. RLS and WEH's play was not written.

[12] John Oxenford's play at the Adelphi Theatre, London, from 12 May 1894 to 19 June 1894.

[13] Serialised in the *Pall Mall Magazine*, December 1893 to July 1894.

[14] The *Pall Mall Magazine* was founded in 1893 by the American financier William Waldorf Astor (1848-1919). Astor bought the *Pall Mall Gazette* in 1892. He was created first Viscount Astor in 1917.

[15] 'The Amazing Marriage', *Scribner's Magazine*, January 1895 to December 1895.

comprehensible on a first reading.

I hear that people in the U.S.A. are beginning to take my verses seriously: indeed, if all the tales be true, I shouldn't wonder if I got something of a boom there. Meanwhile, for *The Song of the Sword & Views and Reviews*, my rights last year were worth exactly £3/19/3! How does that strike a bloated contemporary like yourself? I think I've more verses in me — a new *In Memoriam*, perhaps — but they won't come yet. Nothing will. I am perfectly stagnant. The double reaction has been too much for me; & since I slated you & Crockett in my last *N.O.*, I have written but one poor article — a column in the *P.M.G.*, a journal I wish you saw.

We found Addiscombe intolerable: to live there had been madness & death. So, though the house is still on my hands, we set our faces other whither, & landed here. It is a quaint, pretty, & spacious house: with French windows, & a verandah, & an ivy tod in the railings thereof which must be at least a hundred & fifty years old. In the back is a gravelled yard with a two-stall stable; & in the front across the road is Father Thames — a perpetual miracle, a never-ending ever changing wonder. The back parts are probably Elizabethan: they have pointed gables, & the windows run in grooves, & are many-paned. The front is latish Georgian. Altogether a pleasant place — (& only £50 per ann!!!) — wherein our things look better than they have ever looked before. Only — we wonder what the devil *we* are doing in it: as, perhaps, we should wonder anywhere else, all the world over, until the end.

I hear extraordinary things about Marcel Schwob:[16] he seems to have read everything there is to read in every language; also, he has a special interest in thieves & highwaymen & slang (by the way, I would like you to read Captain Charles Johnson in the earlier texts; which are noble. But you *must* have the folio); also he is absolutely familiar with Meredith & R.L.S. What do you think of him?[17] Rudyard, too — I saw him 'tother day, & he is more like a natural force than anything I ever encountered. His head is buzzing with ideas: as hives with bees. I hear about you now & then from Barrie; but he is very much in the country, & we see nothing like so much of him as we want to.

I have written more than I had thought of writing in the beginning: but I imagine you won't mind that. Another stage is ended; another half turned over; & it seemed natural, somehow to go back to the stage & leaf beyond, & gossip & babble as of old. I don't think it has done me any harm. Far from it. And you?

Always Sincerely Yours,
W.E.H.[18]

---

[16] Marcel Schwob (1867-1905), French scholar, writer and medievalist.

[17] RLS thought that Schwob was a 'shadowy figure; very clever though' (*Stevenson Letters*, 8, 330).

[18] RLS wrote to Baxter (*Stevenson Letters*, 8, 332) that he thought the letter 'in very good taste and rather touching' but Fanny 'thought it was a letter preparatory to the asking of money' and RLS realised that could be so. Despite this and his distaste should WEH ask for money RLS authorised Baxter to pay WEH '(when necessary) five pounds a month'. He added that 'if I

P.S. I want to keep the older hacks 'off' *English Classics*, & to share introductions as much as possible among younger men. Not Le Galliennes, but the men who can *write*.

[*Added by WEH at the top of the letter*] I hear golden words — from Rudyard, among others — about the thing you published in *To-Day*.[19] I am glad indeed to hear (from C.B.) that it is to be a book, & not — as I had a certain reason to fear might be the case — a poor 'unlocked joy'.

gave him more, it would lead to his starting a gig and a Pomeranian dog'. This latter was quoted by Graham Balfour in his biography of RLS without WEH's name and the amount, and it is this that partly lead to WEH's attack in the *Pall Mall Magazine*.
[19] RLS and Lloyd Osbourne's *The Ebb-Tide* was published in thirteen weekly parts from 11 November 1893 to 3 February 1894.

To Robert Fitzroy Bell, 4 September 1894
ALS: Yale

9 The Terrace, Barnes, S.W.

My dear Bell,
    I didn't answer your last, for the simple reason that I was anxious *not* to see you just then. Do you understand? Or shall I say any more? Now, I want only to say that, if *you* will, I should like to go on as before.
    Please, therefore, to write & tell us how & where you both are. For ourselves, we have been up wonderfully: though I've done no work as yet, & my wife has often looked & been exceedingly unlike herself. No doubt, I shall do something soon; but I was tired to death when Vincent came in, & something had broken in me just before.
                        Ever Sincerely Yours,
                        W.E.H.

She would have been six years old to-day.

To H. G. Wells, 28 September 1894
ALS: Illinois. Part published in MacKenzie, 106

9 The Terrace, Barnes, S.W.

Dear Wells,
    Yesterday I had — a rare occurrence with me — a sempiternal headache. Today I've read — read every word; & with uncommon excitement. In your place I should go on? Rather! It may profit you little — though I'm not so confident, by a long way, about that as I was. But it is so full of invention, & the invention is so wonderful, so moving even — as I have found — that it must

certainly make you a reputation.

If you still doubt, go to Heinemann,[1] & say I asked you to consult him as to the vendibility of this thing in a finished state. If you like, I'll write to him; or, better still, I'll ask Charles Whibley to speak.

I will post the *MS.* to-morrow. At present, I've nothing to add, excepting that I don't much like the end — save, always an anticlimax.

Always Sincerely Yours,

W.E.H.

If I had the *P.M.B.*,[2] I should certainly stick you for the voyage.

[1] William Heinemann (1863-1920), founder of the publishing firm, published Wells's *The Time Machine* in June 1895.
[2] The *Pall Mall Budget*, a weekly edition of the best of the *Pall Mall Gazette*. Wells had various stories published in the *P.M.B.* during 1894.

To Charles Whibley, 1 October 1894
ALS: Morgan

9 The Terrace, Barnes, S.W.

Dear Boy,

By this time you will have seen the *Shandy*,[1] which cutteth a brave figure — surely? than it ever cut before. Your introduction reads exceeding well. Altogether. I am pleased. Why those bloody booksellers should prefer Dent & Saintsbury[2] before Constable & you remains a dark & hellish mystery.

Stedman[3] writes that about 650 of the *Prose* has been subscribed between London & the country: with 250 for America. Which seems to show that we judged too harshly of Nutt's conduct on the *Lyra*. I hope things will mend all round; or it may be that we shall not be asked for Vols. II & III.[4] — which would vex me to the soul. For indeed, I am really content with the thing, alike in design & in effect.

Do you see that Lady Granby has lost her eldest boy, the heir to the Dukedom?[5] At Cockayne too! My heart is sore for her.

[1] Whibley's edition of *The Life and Times of Tristram Shandy, Gentleman.*
[2] Saintsbury's edition of *The Works of Laurence Sterne* in 6 volumes was published by Dent in September and October 1894.
[3] The publisher Algernon Methuen Marshall Stedman (1856-1924), changed his name to Methuen on founding the publishing firm of Methuen and Co. in June 1889. He published a pamphlet *Peace or War in South Africa* in 1901 which was expanded as *The Tragedy of South Africa* in 1905. He was created a Baronet in 1916. WEH and Whibley's *A Book of English Prose, Character and Incident, 1387-1649* (1894) was published by Methuen.
[4] Of English Classics.
[5] Violet Granby (*née* Lindsay) (1856-1936), later Duchess of Rutland, would have met WEH through her lover Harry Cust. Her son, Lord Haddon, died aged nine on 28 September and

Have you heard aught of Onslow Ford?[6] And how far off is the end of the Heliodorus? In the ded. I sketched for the *Celestine*[7] (it is printed off) 'Forerunner' is better that 'Ancestor', don't you think? I wonder if Iwan will really & truly pull off that leader on the *Prose*! If he do, I'll bet O'Connor[8] rots it for weeks; so I hope & trust he will.

Steadman advertizes us (in *The Standard*) under the cheap editions of *Dodo* & *Barabbas*.[9] I wonder why.

My love to Lionardo.[10] I hear he's turned Society Butterfly, & is called the Agreeable Rattle of Hind Head. Is it true?

E.A.Y.

W.E.H.

Do you know Captain Alexander Smith's new book[11] about thieves? It is a find, in some ways. Make haste, & you'll be able to see it here.

WEH wrote a verse 'Two Days' to the memory of his daughter and Lord Haddon.
[6] Edward Onslow Ford (1852-1901), artist and sculptor, completed the Shelley memorial at University College, Oxford, and the Queen Victoria Memorial in Manchester. He designed the headstone for Margaret's grave at Cockayne Hatley. The headstone was in white marble with three bronze reliefs and it was later incorporated into a large stone memorial for WEH whose ashes were interred there in 1903. WEH's wife Anna was buried there in 1925.
[7] *Celestina or the Tragicke-Comedy of Calisto and Melibea. Englished from the Spanish of Fernando de Rojas by James Mabbe. Anno 1613.* Introduction by James Fitzmaurice-Kelly. *Tudor Translations*, 6 (1894).
[8] Thomas Power O'Connor (1848-1929), Irish journalist and politician. He founded the *Star* (1887), the *Sun* (1893) and *T. P.'s Weekly* (1902).
[9] *A Book of English Prose* and Whibley's *Tristram Shandy* were advertised immediately below E. F. Benson's *Dodo: a Detail of the Day* and Marie Corelli's *Barabbas: a Dream of the World's Tragedy* in the *Standard*, 1 October.
[10] Leonard Whibley.
[11] This may be his *'Thieves' New Canting Dictionary of the Words, Proverbs, Terms, and Phrases used in the Language of Thieves* (1719). Captain Alexander Smith flourished 1714-26.

To Charles Whibley, Monday [5 November 1894]
ALS: Morgan. Part published in Connell, 290.

9 The Terrace, Barnes, S.W.

Dear Boy,

I wanted to write, for indeed there's something to say. But, the cold leaving me at last, I took neuralgia of the brow & eyes & couldn't raise a pen.

(1) All right about the Presentation Copy. Your reasons are irresistible.

(2) *Frank Harris* has bought the *Saturday*, & G.S.[1] & the rest are suddenly on the town Harris first bombarded me with telegrams, & then drove down. He wants me to write for him *at a salary* & — so far as I can judge — at his

[1] George Saintsbury.

dictation. Cust & Ivan think I should hold him on & off; but I can't see that anything is to be served by that, I purpose to answer him with an unmitigable No. Tell me if you think I'm right; & if you are writing to them (Cust & Ivan) tell them so too. It's worth noting that Selwyn Image[2] is retained; also Herbert Horne;[3] also Arthur Symons & B. Shaw! What I should do in such a gallery I know not. Harris says 'Take charge of the poetry' — *i.e.* the reviewing of A.S & W.W. & Le G![4]

(3) Heinemann[5] came on Saturday afternoon. He is quite in earnest, & is even sanguine. *Only* — ! He wants money —£1000 to £1200; & I know not how to find it. I never could, as you know; & I never shall. He (W.H.) suggests that Blaikie might, & Bell; so I'll write to B. to-day. Bruce might possibly risk a hundred or two; but I don't like to ask him — especially as he's of a mind to pull *Slang* out of the rut, & set it going once more.

(4) It's said that Traill reviewed the *Shandy* in the *N.O.*[6] I hope for journalism's sake he is not responsible for the enclosure also.

(5) Try to write to me tomorrow at the Log House, Hindhead, Haslemere.[7]

E.A.Y.
W.E.H.

Harris named no terms.... Do you think I might try Leonard & Herbert in re the *N.R.*?

---

[2] Selwyn Image (1849-1930), stained glass designer, poet and book collector. He collaborated with Herbert Horne on the *Century Guild Hobby Horse*; see below.

[3] Herbert Percy Horne (1864-1916), architect and typographer. He was editor of the *Century Hobby Horse*, a journal of the Century Guild, one of the numerous art and craft/aesthetic organisations. Slade Professor of Fine Arts, Oxford University, 1910-16.

[4] Arthur Symons. William Watson (1858-1935), a poet in the style of Tennyson, knighted 1917, and Richard Le Gallienne.

[5] William Heinemann, together with George Wyndham, Iwan-Müller, Harry Cust and the barrister Sir Herbert Stephen (1857-1932), was attempting to acquire the *New Review* with a view to WEH becoming editor. The monthly *New Review* had been founded in June 1889 by its first editor Archibald (Thomas Newcomen) Grove (1855-1920). It ran general articles, literary essays and some poetry but it was struggling by mid-1894. Grove had trained as a barrister becoming MP for West Ham North from 1892 to 1895. He ceased to be editor in 1894.

[6] Whibley's edition of *Tristram Shandy* was reviewed in the *National Observer* of 27 October 1894.

[7] The home of Robert Davies Roberts (1851-1911), Fellow of Clare College, Cambridge, 1884-90. Secretary for Lecturers of Local Examinations and Lecturers Syndicate, Cambridge, 1894-1902.

To William Heinemann, 12 November 1894
ALS: Harvard

9 The Terrace, Barnes, S.W.
My dear Mr. Heinemann,
   Yours of the 10th reached me (at Hindhead) at mid-day to-day. I rejoice in your discovery.
   I have several promises: from good men, too.[1] But before we can go further, I want a sort of statement of the case from you. Will you make one out? What is wanted is the maximum & minimum of revenue by circulation; the ditto ditto of revenue in advertisements; the loss per number; the cost per number; & so forth. And the sooner I have it the sooner we can get to work.
   I shall not be disappointed if Baxter begins by saying no.

Always Sincerely Yours,
W.E.H.

[*Added by WEH at the top of the letter*] Who in the world is guilty of that outrageous attack on C.W. in the current *Saturday*?[2]

[1] For the *New Review*.
[2] A review of Whibley's *Tristram Shandy* in the *Saturday Review*, 10 November 1894.

To H. G. Wells, 26 November 1894
ALS: Illinois

9 The Terrace, Barnes, S.W.
My dear Wells,
   I hope you put in some work on the *MS*.[1] For I know that one reason why it wasn't a success elsewhere was that it was — not a picture but — a sketch. I thought you were going to do so, & that, when you had, you'd let me know: that I might write to Heinemann, & advise him of the advent of your work. As it is, I haven't written to Heinemann, & I tremble to think what judgement may have been passed upon what I esteem to be a quiet excellent & curious thing.
   We leave this to-morrow (Tuesday) for Barnes. Don't risk a cold by coming down unless you can do so with a fifty-to-one chance in your favour. But keep me posted all the same.
   Your Cook was really excellent:[2] I read him at least twice.

Always Sincerely Yours,
W.E.H.

[1] *The Time Machine*.
[2] Wells's short story 'A misunderstood artist', *Pall Mall Gazette*, 29 October 1894.

PS.

If this scheme of mine comes off, Heinemann is in it — up to the collar!

To Charles Whibley, Monday morning [17 December 1894]
ALS: Morgan. Part published in Connell, 292.

[London]

Dear Boy,

You will have heard by this time of the death of R.L.S.[1] It has upset us not a little; for though there had been differences, he was, save for my wife, the oldest friend, as he had been the dearest, I had on earth.

All this, however, is nought to the purpose here: which is to say that, if I can, I must get an obituary notice, & so may have to hold over your *Thieves.*[2] I won't if I can help it; but it looks as I must.

Will Marcel write of him for February, I wonder?[3] You might sound him for me.

I don't want an eulogy: but a straightforward criticism from the point of view of the French man of letters.

I shall not write of him anywhere: at least not yet. I've refused both Cust & Low already.

Read the enclosed from George W.[4] I am sure you will do us the little service he asks.

Poor Charles Baxter! It will be the worst blow he's had since Gracie died; & I fear for him much.[5]

E.A.Y.

[H.]

How would it be to bracket Marcel with Paul Bourget?[6] The points of view & the contrast would be worth having.

Write to me soon.

---

[1] RLS had died in Samoa of a brain haemorrhage on 3 December 1894. The news reached England on the morning of 17 December.
[2] Whibley's 'Two Thieves' was published in the *New Review* for March 1895.
[3] Schwob's 'R.L.S.' was published in the *New Review* for February1895. It was reprinted in his *Spicilège* (Paris, 1896)
[4] Wyndham's letter of 14 December asking questions about his edition of *North's Plutarch* in the *Tudor Translations*.
[5] Baxter had been drinking heavily.
[6] Charles Joseph Paul Bourget (1852-1935), French novelist and critic. He was not published by WEH in the *New Review*.

To James Nicol Dunn, [after 17 December 1894]
ALS: Virginia

9 The Terrace, Barnes, S.W.
Dear Mr. Dunn,
I believe we publish on the 29*th*, but this bad news from Samoa may keep us a little later, as Archer is trying to write me some sort of valediction.[1] He knew R.L.S.; & R.L.S. liked him well.

Apart from that: I have (1) 'The Woodman',[2] an original & moving allegory of life, by R.L.S., dated 'Vailima', & not impossibly the verse last written by his hand which we have seen. It is in octosyllabics, & is a hundred & forty-four lines long.

(2) Sir Charles Dilke on the Naval League:[3] the first of a series of twelve on the *real* question of the present day.

(3) Frederick Greenwood on the *rapprochement* between England & Russia:[4] written with special knowledge & on original lines.

(4) 'A Walking-Skirt' — some very graceful *vers de sociéte*; by George Wyndham, M.P.

(5) 'The Problem of Purity' by W. S. Lilly:[5] which is an eye-opener.

6) The Armenian Question; by 'A Diplomatist' — as to which consult the author.

(7) A note on the new Ibsen play; by Mr. G. Warrington Steevens:[6] as to which also, please consult the author.

(8) An article on the relations between France & England by Emile Ollivier:[7] which I purpose to publish in its original tongue.

(9) 'India: Impressions', by C. F. Keary[8] — the first batch — about which you know.

(10) 'An Eulogy of Charles the Second', by G. S. Street:[9] designed & written to the confusion of all Whig dogs — past, present & to come.

(11) 'The Next House', by George Fleming:[10] one of a set of *Little Stories*

---

[1] WEH had telegraphed Archer to write a memorial for the *New Review* (Charles Archer, *William Archer: Life, Work and Friendships,* 1931, 212). Archer's 'In Memoriam: R.L.S.' was in the *New Review*, January 1895.

[2] RLS's poem 'The Woodman'.

[3] Charles Dilke's 'The Navy'.

[4] Frederick Greenwood's 'The Talk of New Alliances'.

[5] W. S. Lilly's 'The Problem of Purity'. William Samuel Lilly (1840-1919), barrister and writer.

[6] G. W. Steevens's 'The New Ibsen'.

[7] Emile Ollivier's 'Les Sentiments de la France pour l'Angleterre'. Emile Ollivier (1825-1913), French statesman.

[8] C. F. Keary's 'India: Impressions (chaps. i-iii)'. Charles Francis Keary (1848-1917), novelist and writer on history and philosophy, who worked at the British Museum.

[9] George Slythe Street (1867-1936), writer.

[10] The writer Julia Constance Fletcher (1858-1938), daughter of an American clergyman. She wrote novels and from 1902 to 1910 she reviewed for the *Times Literary Supplement*.

About Women, which Mr. Heinemann has in hand for the coming spring: 'the best thing I've ever written,' she says.

(12) And chapters I-III of 'The Time Machine', by H. G. Wells, the most original & striking romance of forecast I ever read.

Perhaps I shan't get all these in, but I hope I shall.

Ever Yours,
W.E.H.

What has become of the suggested interviews for the *Budget*?[11] And how am I to thank you for your proffered help? I don't know, & I won't try.

If more light is needed, why not come to supper to-morrow night? Enclosed is one of the R.L.S. *MSS.* for Colvin.

[11] 'The Editor and his contributors. An interview with Mr. W. E. Henley', *Pall Mall Budget*, 27 December 1894, reprinted from the *Pall Mall Gazette*, 21 December 1894.

To William Archer, 21 December 1894
ALS: BL. Part published in Archer, 214 and Williamson, 263

9 The Terrace, Barnes, S.W.

Dear Archer,

My mind misgave me so last night & to-day that I went to town expressly to withdraw the obituary. When I got there, I found that Heinemann had anticipated me; so there you are.

I believe — now — that *nobody's* dead;[1] but that the thing is a daring & devilish plant: the same in kind, but far worse in degree, than those reports of serious illness which used to come suddenly, every now & again, from overseas. If I had kept my head, I should have saved you a bucketing, at least. But a general delusion is hard to understand; & so you had your pains, as I now hope & believe, in vain.

If the thing's true, your work will not, of course, be lost. And if it's not, then none, I believe, will so rejoice & be so exceeding glad as yourself.

In either case, you have made me your debtor by yet another good stroke at a

[1] There had been conflicting reports in the press as to whether RLS was dead or not. Confirmation came in a telegram of Sunday 23 December. In a later but undated letter to Archer WEH writes:

> I was wrong; & I ask your pardon. After these Frisco telegrams I abandon hope...Today I have felt it worse than ever before. I had hitherto hoped & believed that we had but to meet for the wrong to be made right. And now that's impossible; & there is nothing for us but, as I wrote of it to him, langsyne, for us to: 'Lie in the Peace of the Great Release/ As once in the grass together' (BL, quoted in Charles Archer, 214-15)

pinch; I thank you with all my heart.

To speak of the article itself: it is something too much, perhaps, of an eulogy. But I see no harm in that — (considering the circumstances, I don't see how it could have been aught else) — & I did not mean to suggest a single modification whether of opinion or of phrase. What I did purpose was to call the article R.L.S.', & to preface it with the last sentence of 'Aes Triplex';² & there, I take it, I should have had you with me to the hilt.

And now, dear Archer, hope & believe with me; & you shall see that you have done neither in vain.

Yours Always,
W.E.H

² The last two sentences of RLS's essay 'Aes Triplex' were quoted: 'In the hot-fit of life, a-tiptoe on the highest point of being, he passes at a bound on to the other side. The noise of the mallet and chisel is scarcely quenched, the trumpets are hardly done blowing, when trailing with him the clouds glory, this happy-starred, full-bloodied spirit shoots into the spiritual land.'

To Charles Whibley, 3 January 1895
ALS: Morgan. Part published in Connell, 294.

9 The Terrace, Barnes, S.W.

Dear Boy,

Glad you approve. The thing seems to have gone well & well enough. In six months, if we go so far as we've begun, Knowles will be running novels and & Courtney¹ printing variants on Sherlock Holmes! So buck up and, & be d—d to you!

By all means, write that explanation of policy; but also, by all means, send me back *Two Thieves*, corrected for press. If you don't, I'll print as it is; & the Common Fool may have his will of you in print.

What in God's name has become of *Heliodorus*?² Not a rumour has reached me since you swore the proofs had gone home again. I begin to think you must be Van Der Decken³ come alive again, & this wretched book a new version of the Flying Dutchman. Meanwhile, the North goes merrily on;⁴ & George's work is like to turn out excellent. I think he has answered the questions he

¹ William Leonard Courtney (1850-1928), editor of the *Fortnightly Review* from 1894 until his death.
² Whibley's introduction to *An Aethiopian History Written in Greek by Heliodorus. Englished by Thomas Underdowne. Anno 1587. Tudor Translations*, 5 (1895).
³ The main character in Wagner's opera *The Flying Dutchman*.
⁴ George Wyndham's introduction to volumes 7-12 of the *Tudor Translations, Plutarch's Lives of the Noble Grecians and Romans. Englished by Sir Thomas North. Anno 1579* (1895-96).

asked me to put to you. But there's no reason why you shouldn't write to him, if so disposed.

Bourget has not vouchsafed me the honour of a hanswer. So Marcel will probably face the music alone.

Colvin has written: to commend the Archer; to confess that at one time he thought that I had 'acted no true friend's part' by R.L.S.; & to suggest that the estrangement should cease. I have answered that the estrangement was one-sided first & last, but I didn't see how the effect of it could be reversed; & that I thought we'd better go on as we'd being going on ever since it pleased him to put me out of his life & to withdraw himself from mine.

The quality of the stuff I get poured in from without is simply appalling. I think I never realized till now how offensive to most people the *N.O.* must have seemed.

E.A.Y.,
W.E.H.

In the *Bookman*: Barrie writes Scots doggerel;[5] Archer is in the part of Chief Mourner,[6] & Ian Maclaren,[7] with a funeral sermon & a quote from the Grammarian's Funeral'. Eh [   ]!

[5] Barrie's poem 'Robert Louis Stevenson: Scotland's Lament', *Bookman*, January 1895.
[6] I have failed to find any article by Archer in the *Bookman* for either January or February.
[7] The Scottish Presbyterian minister and writer John Watson (1850-1907), whose poem 'In Memoriam' was published in the *Bookman* for January 1895. He wrote novels under the name Ian Maclaren. 'The Grammarian's Funeral' was written by Robert Browning in 1855.

To Alice Meynell, 8 January 1895
ALS: Texas

9 The Terrace, Barnes, S.W.

Dear Mrs. Meynell,

Do you care to discuss the art of the late Christina Rossetti in the February *N.R.* ? If you do, I shall be glad to keep a place for you.[1]

I know that you have written about this thing in the *P.M.G.* But I think you may like to do something finer, rarer, choicer than you have yet done - about 2,500 words — at most. And I could give you a week for it at least.

Very Sincerely Yours,
W.E.H.

[1] She had died on 29 December and Alice Meynell wrote in the *PMG* on 4 January. She wrote in the *New Review*, February 1895.

To H. G. Wells, 25 January 1895
ALS: Illinois

9 The Terrace, Barnes, S.W.
My dear Wells,
You do me much honour.[1] And I shall be pleased indeed to see my name in the front of so singular & original a piece of work.

But, I should warn you, ere it be too late: I am no Mascotte but the reverse. I bring bad luck, I fear: So that of all Stevenson's books (for example) the least solid, as far as I know, is *Virginibus Puerisque*. Now, I want *The Time Machine* to travel far; & — well, I need say no more than 'It is yet time!',[2] as I might at the Adelphi.

Ever Sincerely Yours,
W.E.H.

[1] Wells had dedicated *The Time Machine* 'To William Ernest Henley'. The complete story was published by WEH in the *New Review* between January and May 1895.
[2] Possibly a quotation from the play *Julian* (1823) by Mary Russell Mitford (1787-1855). She is remembered for her *Our Village* (1832).

To Macmillan and Co., 31 January 1895
ALS: BL

9 The Terrace, Barnes, S.W.
Dear Sirs,
(1) I have pleasure in sending you, registered, by this same post, what is practically the *MS.* of the London anthology:[1] that is to say, a list of the passages — some eighty in number — which I have selected for illustration; together with sufficient information as to the books wherein they occur to enable you to get the whole thing set, however roughly, for distribution among the several artists, with as little delay as possible.

(2) As you will see, the whole thing — title included — is 'under revision'. For my own convenience's sake I have strung the numbers together chronologically; but it is possible, of course — it may even be desirable — that they may be rearranged to suit the illustrations. I should note that the

[1] WEH had been asked by Macmillans (7 December 1894, BL) to select an anthology of verse about London to be illustrated by members of the Society of Illustrators. WEH replied (9 December 1894, BL) that he would but asked for the terms to be increased to £50 which they accepted. *A London Garland* was published in late 1895. Among the artists were Whistler, and Aubrey Beardsley who was closely identified with the *Yellow Book*. WEH contributed three poems, 'Nocturn', 'In Westminster' and 'Fog'.

chronological order ceases — (for various reasons) — with James Thomson,[2] the last among the dead; & that, for the present at least, the living are placed pretty much at random. No doubt, they will suffer some changing of place in the end.

(3) The rough notes — as to the character of the drawing which each number may suggest — are not a part of the book. They are simply for the guidance of the Committee in its work of apportioning the illustrations of the book; and, this being the case, I should be glad to have them set in a special type. Also, I think that, before you proceed to set up the material of the anthology, it will save time, & possibly trouble, if you set this *MS.*, as it reaches you, & send me half-a-dozen sets of proofs, for myself & the Committee: to the end that the Society may know what it is about, & that the work of revision — if revision there must be — go on *pari passu* with the work of getting the material ready for distribution.

(4) You will observe that, in the case of certain numbers — (those, for instance, by Tennyson, Rossetti, Matthew Arnold, James Thomson;[3] with all the living writers) — there will have to be applications to publishers for permission to print. I assume that this work will devolve upon you; & in every instance I have added the publisher's name to the passage, or poem, selected for illustration. I do not suppose that there will be any difficulty in the matter; but if there be, and I came render you assistance, I shall, of course, be very glad to do so.

(5) Most of the books from which I've quoted are in my hands; & such of them as you cannot readily come at are much at your service. In many cases I have referred, for your convenience's sake, to publications of your own: to *Poems of Places*,[4] for example, & to Palgrave's *Golden Treasury*. In others, as I have said, I can place the texts themselves in your hands.

(6) I shall be obliged by your acknowledgement of the receipt of the *MS.*

Very Faithfully Yours,
W. E. Henley

Messrs. Macmillan & Co.

---

[2] James Thomson ('B.V.') (1834-82). He is best remembered for 'The City of Dreadful Night' (1874), a long poem of desolation.
[3] The poet and playwright James Thomson (1700-48). He rose to prominence with the publication of the poem *The Seasons* as a complete edition in 1730.
[4] *Poems of Places*, ed. W. H. Longfellow, 2 vols (1877).

To Robert T. Hamilton Bruce, 23 February 1895
ALS: Yale

9 The Terrace, Barnes, S.W.

My dear Bruce,
A hurried line: to say that I never now seem able to do anything except on account of *The New Review*.

Also, that I have squared the Jacks,[1] & that whereas they thought of *beginning* with an illustrated *Burns*, & going on to the unpictured & cheap, they have now decided to begin with a *Burns unillustrated*, & to ring in the pictured afterwards. It is a great victory; but I put you on your honour, not to mention it to a living soul. Especially W.H., R.S.A.[2]

I hope that Henderson & I may draw on you for any books we cannot get elsewhere. We purpose to make the Second Edinburgh Edition the basis for the text as far as it goes;[3] but all sorts of eds. will have to be compared, & manuscripts —manuscripts! I am rather pleased than otherwise to find that most of the texts since Currie are shockingly corrupt:[4] 'especially Chamber's'![5] We purpose to render unto to Robert that which is his & to Currie & Co. that which is theirs. And I fancy Robert will be the gainer. At any rate, there will be a clean text; & that, I am given to understand, is what you get nowhere — not even in Scott Douglas.[6]

If you will help, you might let me know *what* editions you have. Also, please send me your facsimile of the Kilmarnock edition[7] & the type-written *Merry Muses: registered*: as a beginning, & as soon as may be. Also, a list of such song books as we may count on.

When you are in Glasgow, you might see the Shaggy *One*,[8] & hear him talk at large. I've arranged that he is to add the *Bell Scott MS.* (that precious pisspot!) to his store of broken crockery; but he's got to work for it! Find out *how much* he really knows about the whereabouts of *MSS.*, & if he really can get access to them. Of course, Henderson will see him; but I imagine Henderson won't make much out of him ('tis a real stickit minister;[9] & the shyest creature in the world); at all events, unless we know of something of him before hand. Let it be part of your share in the conspiracy, if you will, to tell us what there is to tell.

---

[1] In a letter to Hamilton Bruce WEH states that: 'An Edinburgh house has (this between ourselves) — commissioned me — a Saxon! A pockpudden! [contemptuous term for an Englishman] An Englisher! — to prepare a final edition of Burrns!' (2 December 1894, Yale). The edition was co-edited with the Scottish writer Thomas Finlayson Henderson (1844-1923). See *The Poetry of Robert Burns*. Centenary Edition, 4 vols, ed. W. E. Henley and T. F. Henderson (T. C. and E. C. Jack: Edinburgh, 1896-97).

[2] William B. Hole (1846-1917), painter and illustrator and member of the Royal Scottish Academy, supplied the illustrations to the Jacks' editions. The illustrated edition published by Caxton (n.d.) contains only one illustration by Hole.

[3] Robert Burns, *Poems chiefly in the Scottish Dialect* (Edinburgh, 1787).

[4] James Currie, ed, *The Works of Robert Burns*, 4 vols (1815).

[5] Robert Chambers, ed, *The Life and Works of Robert Burns*, 4 vols (Edinburgh, 1851-52).

[6] William Scott Douglas, ed, *The Works of Robert Burns*, 6 vols (Edinburgh, 1877-79).

[7] Robert Burns, *Poems chiefly in the Scottish Dialect* (Kilmarnock, 1786).

[8] Presumably Craibe Angus.

[9] A stuck or failed probationer minister who did not achieve ordination.

The poor Châtelaine has succumbed to a touch of influenza. I hope & believe it's nothing; but I've sent her to bed. I see Walter Blaikie to-morrow.

Yours Ever, Dear Bruce,
W.E.H.

I hope you like our Number Three.[10]

[10] The March *New Review*.

To H. G. Wells, 1 April 1895
ALS: Illinois. Part published in Mackenzie, 107.

9 The Terrace, Barnes, S.W.

My dear Wells,
    Our printers led me a merry dance last month which ended in the clapping on, against my will, of an extra chapter. Consequently, this last instalment is a little short: it runs in fact to less than nine pages.[1]
    Have you any more ideas? I should be glad to have a little more for my last; & it may be that you would not be sorry neither. Of course, it would be tommy-rot to write in for the sake of lengthening out; but I confess that, as it seems to me, at this point — with all the time before you — you might very well give your fancy play, &, at the same time, oblige you editor. The Traveller's stoppings might, for instance, begin some period earlier than they do, & he might even tell us about the last man & his friends, & the ultimate degeneracy of which they are the proof & the sign. Or — but you are a better hand at it than I! I will add (1) that I honestly believe that to amplify in some such way will be to magnify the effect of the story; & (2) that I can give you a clear week for the work.
    I should like to say that the story has been a good thing for the magazine & — I believe — has gone some way towards placing its author as a man of letters.
    Let me hear from you soon; as I am going away for a few days to get rid, if I can, of a ruining cold.

Yours Always Sincerely,
W.E. H.

What news of the other one?[2]

[1] Chapters ix-xii of the *Time Machine* in the *New Review* for April.
[2] Probably Wells's *The Island of Doctor Moreau* (1896).

To Charles Whibley, 13 April 1895
ALS: Morgan. Part published in Connell, 298-9.

9 The Terrace, Barnes, S.W.

My dear Charles,

I am up & about, but a hell of a lamester. There's an ulcer on the stump. And as big as a sixpence yet; & it is obvious that, much the worse as we are from wear, we shall be in luck if we succeed in getting away before the beginning of next month.

I am distressed to hear of your own poor case. It matters little about Mr. Pureney.[1] He will hold over well enough! But for yourself, it's another affair. Why don't you come over here for a few days' rest & change?

George Wyndham went to Florence yesterday. He returns by way of Paris, & proposes to look you up. Mind you turn on Marcel & Stéphane.[2] He is much pleased with himself over his Plutarch; & he's every right to be. It is really admirable: intelligent, thorough, right, & for the most part, so far as I know *new*. Did I tell you I mean to turn it on to you for the *N.R.*?[3] Anyhow, I do. It is one way of giving you a copy; for one thing. And you can make a little money by it besides.

We are troubled about the little headstone. Ford sent down his man some weeks ago; but Brickwell hadn't swallowed all his scruples, & wouldn't let him touch the work. Now Brickwell's all right; but Ford's man is not available till the 10*th* of May or so, when the *Strathnairn* will be done.[4] It's a nuisance, isn't it? Meanwhile, Ford will take on the enclosure, of course; so it will be all right in the end. But I wish — & so do we all — the thing were in its place.

Did you see R.L.S. his will? If you did, you'll know it won't be quite so bad as we feared it would. If you didn't, know that one fourth of the patrimony is divided between Bob & his two sisters; & that the other three-fourths with all the personalty, go to the robbers.[5] I haven't seen Bob; but I should think he felt corked enough. And that reminds me: so far as I know, the *Velasquez*[6] he's to do is, as I told you, a piece of showmany designed to set forth the merits of certain pictures, of which Bell & Co.[7] possess *clichés*, etched & otherwise produced. Shall I write & ask him to come & see me, & talk it out with him? Let me know

---

[1] Whibley's 'Thomas Pureney: Prisoner Ordinary' was published in the *New Review* for May 1895.
[2] The French symbolist poet Stéphane Mallarmé (1842-98). WEH had published his 'Vers et Musique en France' in the *National Observer*, 26 March 1892. Mallarmé did not write in the *New Review*.
[3] Whibley's review was published in the *New Review* for June 1895.
[4] Ford was finishing his bronze equestrian statue of Field Marshall Lord Strathnairn (1801-85) which was erected in Knightsbridge and unveiled in June 1895.
[5] Fanny and her children.
[6] Bob's *The Art of Velasquez* (1895).
[7] Bob Stevenson's publisher George Bell.

by return; & be sure I'll do anything I can. As for Heinemann I don't believe he need worrit about the matter; & I'll tell him so as soon's I see him.

Yes: the Bugger at Bay[8] was on the whole a pleasing sight. The air is alive with rumours, of course; but I believe no new arrests will be made, & that morality will be satisfied if Oscar gets two years; as of course he will. Why he didn't stay at Monte Carlo, once he got there, God alone knows. Seeing that he was cognizant of all these arseoles out of place, & that, despite his cognizance, he returned to face the music, & play the Roman fool to Carson's Destiny,[9] I can only conjecture that, what between personal & professional vanity, he was stark mad. Be this as it may, he is mad no more. Holloway & Bow St. have taken his hair out of curl in more senses than one. And I am pretty sure that he's having a damn bad time.

Yes: Bobbie it was who drove down with the dressing-case.[10] I hear that he is ill; & am very glad to hear it. By the way, when Catamite Atkins[11] — (we have Expert Moore: why not the other thing?)[12] — returned to the embraces of his spouse from that horrible Moulin Rouge, he found him, says the *Sun*, in talk 'with a person called Schwabe'. Is this Marcel? And if Marcel it be, is not he precious glad that I wouldn't let him call on Oscar when he was within the confines of this isle?

One cheerful feature of this situation is: that Bob[13] is scandalized beyond expression by the ingratitude of Oscar's pathics.

By the way, when you meet G.W. remember (1) that Alfred Douglas's mother is a cousin of his,[14] & that, for her sake, he is anxious to do his best for that egregious young jackass.

The ingenious Z has knocked 'em.[15] A better advert, no journal ever had. You

---

[8] Oscar Wilde had been arrested on a charge of committing indecent acts after having lost a libel action against the 8th Marquess of Queensberry (1844-1900). The jury disagreed at the first trial and after a second he was sentenced to two years. The phrase 'Bugger at Bay' was coined by Charles Baxter (WEH to Hamilton Bruce, 13 April 1895, Yale). The reference is to Sir Edwin Landseer's famous painting *The Stag at Bay*.

[9] Edward Henry Carson (1854-1935), barrister and politician, who defended Queensberry. Knighted 1900, created baron 1921.

[10] Ross had taken Wilde's suitcase to Bow Street police station after Wilde's arrest but had been refused entry.

[11] Frederick Atkins, one of Wilde's young men, had been introduced to Wilde by a Maurice Schwabe.

[12] The Irish novelist, George Moore, supported Sir William Eden in court in his quarrel with Whistler over a portrait of Lady Eden.

[13] Robert Ross.

[14] Sybil Montgomery (1845-1935), Marchioness of Queensberry, mother of Lord Alfred Bruce Douglas (1870-1945), known as Bosie, poet and intimate friend of Oscar Wilde. He was editor of the *Academy*, 1907-10.

[15] Z, 'Two Demagogues: a Parallel and a Moral [Randolph Church and Joseph Chamberlain],' *New Review*, April 1895. This article is attributed to the statesman George Nathaniel Curzon (1856-1925), Viceroy of India, 1898-1905, Marquess of Kedleston 1921, Foreign Secretary 1918-1924.

have seen that J.C. is 'incensed'?[16] Why shouldn't he be? The funny thing is, that nobody has come forth in his defence. Millar,[17] too, has convicted the critics of being persons of four letters in a style & to a point which have made them mad. Indeed, I wish I'd held over your Nordeau.[18] It has been more or less quoted; but the other things were actualities in a sense to which it wouldn't pretend. So that on the whole it hasn't done as it ought. Still, the *N.O.* effect has been complete; & I expect to hear that our circulation is going steadily down.

Fitzroy Bell is for Paris. He asks me if you still believe him to be a common brute. *Do* you?

E.A.Y.

H.

[16] Joseph Chamberlain.
[17] J. H. Millar, 'The Literature of the Kailyard', *New Review*, April 1895.
[18] Whibley's 'The True Degenerate', *New Review*, April 1895. Max Simon Nordeau (1845-1923), Hungarian doctor and sociologist.

To Mrs. Thomas Stevenson,[1] 25 June 1895
ALS: Yale

9 The Terrace, Barnes, S.W.

My dear Mrs. Stevenson,

Please do not think us ingrates. We shall value the gift all life long, & take care that it passes into the right hands at the end.

For the rest, I can say nothing. Words are but words; & though Lewis ceased long since to be the Lewis I had known, I never did anything but love him, while I believed all through that we should meet some day, & be once more as we were of old. That much — & that you are continually in our thoughts — that & no more.

The vases have not yet come. Perhaps they never will. Life seems to have gone out with her, & the call to be up & doing again comes fainter & fainter as we go on. The end must be as it may; but nothing can ever make us what we were when she was ours.

[1] Stevenson's mother Margaret Isabella, *née* Balfour (1829-97). After the death of her husband Thomas she had accompanied RLS and Fanny to America, travelled with them in the South Seas, and lived at Vailima, Samoa. After RLS's death she returned to Edinburgh to live with her sister.

My wife will write to you soon. She finds it as hard to write on her part as I have found it hard on mine.

Yours ever sincerely,
W. E. Henley

We had to leave town, & go to Deal (I had six weeks of bed), or we should have called on you.[2]

---

[2] This was not the first time WEH had failed to call on RLS's mother. In December 1891 RLS wrote bitterly to Baxter that WEH 'has not been to see my mother' and 'that I am done with him for time and for eternity' (*Stevenson Letters*, 7, 52).

.

To Charles Whibley, 9 August 1895
ALS: Morgan. Part published in Connell, 305.

9 The Terrace, Barnes, S.W.
Dear Boy,
I was glad indeed to get your letter. We couldn't make out what had come of you; & yesterday I wrote to Low[1] to ask him if he knew.

For ourselves, this business of the Chair[2] has kept us pretty lively. For a moment, I thought I'd a chance; but, though I recognized long since, I'd none, others have been less sage, & are of writing letters & attaching signatures there has been no end. Mrs. Oliphant has done her damnedest all over the shop; so has Barrie, & Blaikie, & Bell, & George W.; Meredith has signed, & Hardy. But just now the betting at the Savile, is 6 to 1 on the Saint, & no takers. I hear from Bruce that Simon Laurie[3] says that both I & the Saint are too old; & my own opinion has been, since long, that the thing is a foregone conclusion for Walter Raleigh.[4] But the Saint & his partizans are cocksure; & if I'm to be beaten by him, I shall have something *not* nice to say to the men who ran me agin my will.

Heinemann dines to-night; to settle about a new Byron.[5] The *Burns* comes on

---

[1] Sidney Low.
[2] In a letter to Bell (19 May 1895, Yale) WEH thanked him, Bruce and Walter Blaikie, for their suggestion that he apply for the Chair of Rhetoric and English Literature at Edinburgh, lately vacated by David Masson. Although rather reluctant, he made a formal application, which no longer exists. George Saintsbury was appointed in September.
[3] Simon Somerville Laurie (1829-90), Scottish educationalist and writer on philosophy.
[4] Walter Alexander Raleigh (1861-1922), Professor of English Literature at Liverpool University, 1889-1900, and Professor of English Literature at Oxford from 1904 until his death. Knighted 1911.
[5] In a letter to the poet Wilfrid Scawen Blunt WEH writes: 'I have undertaken to prepare a new edition — in ten volumes — of Byron, verse & prose. Can you help me in the matter?' (19

apace: a good book it will be. Did I tell you that over fifty of his letters (I mean R.B.'s), unpublished — even virgin! — had been put into my hands to do with as I will? That will make 'em sit up, won't it? Also, I've finished the draft of my *English Lyrics*; & a very good book it is.

Kelly[6] has gone up no end: (1) the *Quixote*, Spanish text — revised, corrected, cleaned, Cervantistified — for Nutt; (2) *Spanish Literature* in the series edited by Gosse; & (3) *Spanish Literature* in two vols. octavo, for Heinemann.

Tree is a mere *farceur*. I told him I was averse from cuts, but would consider anything he had to say; & he straightaway vanished into space. I think he wanted the thing as a stop-gap for *Trilby*;[7] but I had made it clear, that wasn't the sort of hairpin *I* was; so he broke at another point.

C.B. has been going strong: so strong that they say he is to be removed from the control of R.L.S. his business. I've not seen him; but I heard — from E. G. Saunders[8] — that, after unparalleled achievements in the Lapping line[9] — he had suddenly knocked off. Walter Blaikie, however, who came here largely on his account had to depart without seeing him; & I am not inclined to put my faith to any story of reform that isn't backed by Zeb. *He* says he can effect a cure; but C.B. doesn't appear to want him to have the chance. Meanwhile, he (C.B.) has rooms in Staple Inn: where he has laid down a Persian rug for which he paid £55, & receives that dreadful Gaukroger woman.[10] Also, he has gone in with Saunders, who has a wonderful colour-printing patent in hand, & that may be the saving of him. The Literary Agent business appears to have chucked him.

I will do my utmost to take in the new *Parallel*.[11] Send it straight to Gilmer,[12] & tell him — from me — to rush it through Harrison's[13] hands as fast as ever he

September 1895, West Sussex Record Office, Chichester). However, only the first volume was published and the venture failed as there were copyright problems but more importantly, a new edition was being prepared by R. E. Prothero to be published by John Murray. WEH's volume was *The Works of Lord Byron, I. The Letters 1804-1813* (1897). Wilfrid Scawen Blunt (1840-1922), poet, diplomat, traveller and seeker of independence for other countries from British rule.
[6] James Fitzmaurice-Kelly (1857-1923), scholar. Professor of Spanish Language and Literature, Liverpool University, 1909-16, Professor of Spanish Language and Literature, King's College, London, 1916-20. He was writing the introduction to *The History of Don Quixote of the Mancha. Translated from the Spanish of Miguel de Cervantes by Thomas Shelton. Annis 1612, 1620* as vols 13-16 of the *Tudor Translations* (1896). His *A History of Spanish Literature* was published by Heinemann (1898) in the series Short Histories of the Literature of the World, edited by Gosse.
[7] George Du Maurier's novel *Trilby* had been adapted for the stage with Tree playing the part of Svengali. George [Louis Palmella Busson] Du Maurier (1834-96), novelist and illustrator for *Punch*.
[8] I have been unable to identify him.
[9] Baxter's drinking had become a serious problem and was affecting his duties as RLS's executor. He was also working with Blaikie on the Edinburgh Edition of RLS's works.
[10] Baxter married Marie Louise Gaukroger in October 1895.
[11] Probably Whibley's article 'Two cracksmen: Deacon Brodie and Charles Peace', *New Review*, October 1895.
[12] John William Gilmer (1865-1933) was assistant editor of the *New Review* from 17 January 1895 until the final issue in December 1897.
[13] Harrison and Sons, 45-7 St Martin's Lane, London EC.

can. Then we'll see.

Neither of us is very much: though the break up of the drought & the cooler weather have not been wholly in vain. The truth is — but why go back on it? You know, & — *suffit!*

I've seen nobody but Vernon & Chrisse[14] (now) for weeks; so I've no more news.

E.A.Y.

H.

Who, a'God's name, is Romain Coolus?[15] He looks like a ponce. Is he one?

[14] Christina Steevens.

[15] The writer René (or René-Max) Weil (1868-1952), French novelist, playwright and critic. He wrote under the name Romain Coolus.

To H. G. Wells, 5 September 1895
ALS: Illinois

9 The Terrace, Barnes, S.W.

My dear Wells,

You are an 'igstrawn'y & ascentric' young man; & *The Wonderful Visit*[1] (albeit a little sloppy here & there; albeit, too, as you say too quickly done) is very good reading indeed. I laughed over it all the time: especially at the Tramp; & the Curate (going to bed); & the Tinker. And it isn't everything that gets me like that. There is brains in the book; brains to any extent. Brains; & character; & humour. And what more is wanted, says you? Well, frankly; I don't know. I know it should have been better than it is; & that's all. And I am moved to suspect that the real fault is the one you've named: that the thing has been too quickly done. I believe it will succeed, even as it is. In fact, the people you tried it on in vain must have been beyond the run of mankind. But I can't help feeling that it might, & ought to, have been very much stronger, more moving, more direct & elemental, than it is.

For heaven's sake, take care of yourself. You have an unique talent; and — you've finished three books,[2] at least, within the year, & are up to the elbows in a fourth! It is magnificent, of course; but it can't be literature. I am waiting with the greatest interest, the keenest curiosity, to see what comes of the Nationalist

[1] Published 1895.

[2] It is not clear whether WEH is referring to published books or to completed manuscripts. The following three books were published in 1895: *Select Conversations with an Uncle, The Time Machine* and *The Wonderful Visit.* The fourth book being written may have been *The Stolen Bacillus and Other Incidents* which was published in November 1895.

visitation: the idea is so strong, & you are working it out with so much gusto, that I have great hopes of it. When it's off your hands, you must take a rest, & slum. I believe in your imagination; & I don't want to see it foundered. I believe in your future; & I don't want to see it commonplaced. And you really frighten me: you work so easily, & up to a certain level all you do is so equal in excellence. But you can do better — far better; & to begin with, you must begin by taking yourself more seriously. Understand: I like the *Visit*. And in writing thus to you, I am playing (my favourite part) the Elderly Ass. All the same ——— !

Yours Ever Sincerely,
W.E.H.

To Alfred Nutt, 5 September 1895
ALS: Yale

9 The Terrace, Barnes, S.W.

Dear A. N.,
    All right. We will meet this week, as you say.
    Meanwhile, why a selection? Why not the whole thing? Four *Tudors* will take the lot, & take it easily & well. And I want exceedingly to make it one number of the series: which it will help to strengthen & establish not less than the North has done.
    Meanwhile, too, why '96? We are due with Fenton & Holland first[1] — (to say nothing of Shelton) — & I want to take charge of the book myself. Now, what between Byron & Burns, I've precious little time for anything — some journalism. And this is a piece of work that needs both labour & reading.
    We are leaving Barnes — or rather, we are meditating flight — for the simple reason that the place does not agree with us. It is enervating & demoralizing to an extent! To write a letter needs a strong effort of the will; & as for verses, or an article — — — ! Nothing could be lovelier than the forenoons & the sunsets. But they don't produce a revenue, & we get feebler & more fatuous every day.
    I suppose you saw Raleigh in the *Fortnightly*?[2] An excellent article! What has become of that scoundrel York Powell?[3] And where are the *Classical* & the

---

[1] *Certain Tragical Discourses of Bandello. Translated by Geffraie Fenton. 1567.* Introduction by Robert Langton Douglas. *Tudor Translations,* 19-20 (1898); *Suetonius. History of Twelve Caesars. Translated into English by Philemon Holland. Anno 1606.* Introduction by Charles Whibley. *Tudor Translations,* 21-22 (1899).
[2] Walter Raleigh's review of *Plutarch's Lives* in the *Fortnightly Review,* September 1895.
[3] Powell reviewed *Plutarch's Lives* in the *Academy,* 1 February 1896. Frederick York Powell (1850-1904), historian and Icelandic scholar. He was Regius Professor of Modern History, Oxford University from 1894 until his death.

Review of History?[4] The *M. Guardian* was the most superior thing I ever read:[5] I thought at first it must have been God the Father himself. But it hadn't any brains; & he'd hardly write for a penny Radical; if he did 'twas in the absence of the Ghost. In any case they do not catch me any more.

Yours Ever,
W.E.H.

Edinburgh be d—d!

[4] It was not reviewed in the *Classical Review*. There was a short review in the *English Historical Review*, January 1896.
[5] 'Books of the Week', *Manchester Guardian*, 6 August 1895.

To Charles Whibley, 18 September 1895
ALS: Morgan

9 The Terrace, Barnes, S.W.

My dear Boy,
    I succeeded in screwing £20 out of Steadman: on account of the first from *English Classics*. His argument was: he promised thus much, through you, in the event of the series succeeding! Which is absurd. Thus far I've had from him £25, on account of *English Prose*; £50, *do. English Lyrics*; & £20, *do. English Classics*. Not a magnificent amount, I think: considering the status of the grateful recipient! Jack (of Edinburgh) is paying £450 for his new *Burns* & Heinemann £500 for his new *Byron*; and there is more work in the *English Lyrics* than in either.
    (2) I will think about the *Scotland*. On the whole, I am against the idea. Especially for [   ]:[1] who should have come to *me* for the series. Did you know, by the way, the Saint is doing one — *Epochs of European Literature*[2] — for Blackwood? Gosse, Hannay, Traill, all the *Saturday* gang — are of the party; & W.H.P. is down for the Romantic Renaissance.[3]
    (3) I shall be rather sick if I clash with Mowbray Morris[4] next month. What price Captain Hind?[5] I could manage one in December. By the way, you'll get your Constable in time for your book, anyhow, as W.B. is going to make me a present of the book.

[1] WEH's handwriting is illegible and neither the book nor the publisher has been identified.
[2] *Periods of European Literature*, ed. George Saintsbury, 12 vols (Edinburgh and London, 1897).
[3] Pollock did not contribute to the series.
[4] Mowbray Walter Morris (1849-1911) was editor of *Macmillan's Magazine*. Whibley had two articles published in October, his 'Moll Cutpurse' in *Macmillan's Magazine* and his 'Two Cracksmen' in the *New Review*.
[5] The highwayman Captain Hind (1618-51) was one of the characters in Whibley's *A Book of Scoundrels* (1897).

(4) Bruce is still at Nunwick: a letter thence arrived with yours. I've writ to say he is expected *chez vous* on his return journey.

(5) *Where* is Marcel? I don't believe there's no such a person any more.

(6) No news of the Chair: except that, if it fell to me, I shall decline it.

(7) We've found a good house at Woodside Park;[6] & are now engaged in trying to make the people get rid of it. If they will, all right. If they won't, —— —— !

(8) What of James Mc N.?

E.A.Y.,
H.

⁶ North-west London.

To William Heinemann, 22 September 1895
ALS: Harvard

9 The Terrace, Barnes, S.W.

Dear Heinemann,

Why such hurry? I don't want to start the prose till I have learned how far we can depend upon the Lovelaces,[1] & if there is any to be had. And as for verse, I haven't yet decided — not by any means! — on the order in which I should like it to appear. In any case, I think it would be a mistake to start with the *Childe*.

I am working out a chronological scheme whose effect would be to give the modern reader — what he's never had — a view of Byron as he appeared to his contemporaries. As Moore[2] arranged him you start with Childe Harold: that is, you have Cantos 1 & 2 (1811), all right then you go straight to Canto 3 (1816), though there have been any numbers of *Laras* & *Corsairs* in between; & from Canto 3 you go on to Canto 4, written when he was eight & twenty — after *Manfred*, too! — & representing this part of his genius in its perfection. Which seems to me absurd. What has the writer of Canto IV to do with the boy of two & twenty who is responsible for Cantos 1 & 2? It is surely a mistake to think of Childe Harold as an organic whole under such [?cricks.] as these? For myself, I am rapidly getting convinced that the true Byron is one which should show him flashing from satire to story & from story to meditation, & thence to drama & lyric, & so to satire again: even as he appeared to his own public.

At any rate, the idea is worth considering & I should like to talk it over & out.

¹ Ralph, 2nd Earl of Lovelace (1839-1906), had inherited papers from Byron's wife Annabella.
² Thomas Moore, *The Works of Lord Byron: with his Letters and Journals, and his Life*, 17 vols [ed. John Wright] (1832-33). The Irish poet, writer, and friend of Byron, Thomas Moore (1779-1852), published many editions of *Byron*.

Not to-morrow, I fear; as I must go to Woodside Park. But thereafter whenever you will.

Sincerely Yours Always,
W.E.H.

To Lord Windsor,[1] 26 September 1895
ALS: Morgan

9 The Terrace, Barnes, S.W.

Dear Lord Windsor,

It *is* slight: slighter than I had thought it would be. Worse than that, it contains an original idea; & that idea is, I think, too good to publish in so 'occasional' a shape. Why — (since you ask me to be critical) — not suppress the purely bibliothecal part of the address, & rewrite, at greater length, & with all manner of illustrations, the theory that fiction is an essential in human happiness & a necessary of human life? If you would care to do this, I shall be delighted to help in any way I might, & to publish the results in the *N.R.*[2]

There are so many points whereon to dilate — from Homer: which is, after all, only the novel plus music — down to R.L.S., & 'Annie M. Swann', & the nameless rabble which scribble romantic rubbish for the penny press, that to-night I will do no more than put the question. Why not indeed?

I wish I'd heard with you that 'Te Deum' of Purcell's.[3] You must have had a rare good time while it was on.

I am glad to know you like *Wisdom*.[4] It is a work which only an imaginative man could do, & none but an imaginative man can appreciate.

I hope you will care for our October part.

Yours Very Sincerely,
W.E.H.

---

[1] Lord Robert George Windsor Clive (1857-1923), succeeded as Baron Windsor in 1869. In 1883 he married Alberta ('Gay') Paget, who was a member of the 'Souls'. He was created Earl of Plymouth in 1905. WEH would have met him through George Wyndham. WEH dedicated his *View and Reviews: II Art* to him.
[2] Nothing by Lord Windsor was published in the *N.R.*
[3] Henry Purcell (1659-95).
[4] Arthur Schopenhaur's *Wisdom of Life* (1890).

To Lord Windsor, 18 October 1895
ALS: Morgan

9 The Terrace, Barnes, S.W.

Dear Lord Windsor,

I hope the article grows apace. I *may* be able to suggest a point or two, when I see it. Meanwhile, I would ask you to note that it is really of very little consequence whether the stuff provided be good or bad, *so long as it's fiction.* The truth is there is no such thing as a Public: or rather what is called *the* Public consists of many smaller publics. It's a sort of faggot, & the withe that keeps its sticks together is a taste for novel-reading. And what is agreeable to one component is infinitely tedious to another. The shop-girl, for instance, doats on *Bow Bells*,[1] but would perish with *Middlemarch*; the errand boy rejoices in *Starlight Bess* (No.2 given away with Number 1) but would find nothing but tedium in *Dick Ryder*;[2] the Sporting Bart. is at home with Surtees & Hawley Smart,[3] but I doubt if he cares for Whyte Melville;[4] & so on all through Society. And it is especially to be noted that good work is never popular in the sense of commanding the largest number of readers *at a time*. Miss Annie Swann, for instance, has at least five times as big a public as Jim Barrie, both in Scotland & this side of the Cheviots. Most striking, most suggestive, in this connexion is the case of R.L.S. He wrote *Treasure Island, The Black Arrow,* & *Kidnapped* for a rag called *Young Folks' Paper*. None of the three was a success; but the two first were steadily (& devilishly) imitated in the same paper, which lived for years on the rubbish thus produced. Stevenson's true public would have found it unreadable. Not so *this* public — a Board School public, one may call it. It's taste was all for hog wash; & it wouldn't be happy till it got it. No: you can insist that the stuff provided be mainly non-poisonous (& even so, you can never be sure that the born maniac will not poison himself with it); but you cannot insist on literary quality, for, if you do, you disgust at once the *non-* (or even *anti-*) literary publics; which is as much as to say, that you deprive two-thirds of the enormous mob of persons who can read of the only reading which they can tackle & enjoy.

For the rest, the *A*ge knows what it wants, & *gets it*. The Jacobin gang read *Justine*[5] & the curious filth of Retif: the serious Nonconformist of a few years back read *Middlemarch* & *Deronda*; the gents in the bazaars delight to batten

---

[1] *Bow Bells: a Weekly Magazine of General Literature and Art, for Family Reading*, 12 November 1887, then as *Bow Bells Weekly*, 6 January 1888-15 March 1897.
[2] Dick Ryder was the highwayman hero of Marriott Watson's *Galloping Dick* (1896), part of which had appeared in the *New Review*. He wrote two sequels.
[3] Robert Smith Surtees (1805-64), sporting journalist and pre-eminent fox-hunting novelist, best remembered for his comic character Mr Jorrocks. [Henry] Hawley Smart (1833-93), sporting journalist, racing and fox-hunting novelist.
[4] George Henry Whyte-Melville (1821-78), soldier and later a well-known hunting novelist.
[5] Jacobins, a French radical political club formed in 1789. *Justine ou les Malheurs de la Vertu* (1791), a sexual novel by Comte Donatien Alphonse Sade, known as the Marquis de Sade (1740-1814), French novelist.

their fancies on the originals of Burton's translation;[6] I like Dickens & Dumas & Cervantes & Sir Walter. And so on, & so on! There are scores of mansions in the House of Fiction; &, if you come to counting noses, the most popular are those at which the sign changes year by year, & the author of *Anonyma* is succeeded, almost ere he's had time to drink himself to death, by the author of *The Twenty Captains*,[7] a *Midshipman Jack*,[8] a *Mary's Wrong*, a *Lord Bertie's Wooing*, or any thing you like to name.

I fear this is an [   ] scrawl; but this is an aspect of the question which does *not* present itself to men like Roberts & Co.[9] And it is an aspect which has got — as I think you'll own — to be considered.

I have asked the trustees of my late friend John O'Neill[10] to send you a prospectus of the proposal to publish the second volume of his *Night of the Gods*. As to the *idée recue* of the book I cannot speak; being no folk-lorist. But the book itself is certainly the most amazing farrago of ideas, & slang, & odd, out-of-the-way reading in all manner of lingoes which has appeared since Burton's *Anatomy*;[11] & I hope you may care with us, that it should be completed.

Yours Very Sincerely,
W.E.H.

[6] Sir Richard Francis Burton (1821-90), explorer, linguist, author of travel books and translator of Arabian erotic literature, including *The Arabian Nights*.
[7] A novel by William Stephens Hayward.
[8] A novel by Charles Ledyard Norton (1837-1909).
[9] This may be a reference to the Royal Literary Fund and its secretary Arthur Llewellyn Roberts (1855-1919). It was founded in 1790 as the Literary Fund Society to aid authors and their dependants. It received its Royal Charter in 1845.
[10] John O'Neill (?1837-95), student of Japanese and Accountant General in Cyprus. His *Night of the Gods: Cosmic and Cosmogonic Mythology and Symbolism* was published in 2 vols, 1893-95.
[11] Robert Burton, *The Anatomy of Melancholy: what it is* (Oxford, 1621). Robert Burton (1577-1640), cleric.

To Lord Windsor, 14 November 1895
ALS: Morgan

9 The Terrace, Barnes, S.W.

Dear Lord Windsor,

I hope you will be as good as your word. I don't think it will be for our January issue, though. It has to be out so early next month that I must start upon it the moment the December number's out of hand. And I should like you to hurry.

I am very glad to hear that your *Tudors* are complete. The last Plutarchs, making the series twelve volumes strong, are very nearly off the machine; & I am putting in hand the next number, which is Fenton's selections from Bandello. As for other things to have — since I may tell you of anything I know — those *English Classics* of mine are very good books indeed. The ordinary issue is quite cheap — 3/6 a volume — & certainly comely. The Jap. edition is much costlier & — as usual with Jap. editions — less well printed than I could wish. But the Jap. edition has the prettier page, having a larger margin than the other. Ever so little more white paper in that other, & the Jap. would be out of it. But there it is!

I was pleased indeed to hear that the fracture has been successfully set, & that we may look for nothing now but good news.

Always Sincerely Yours,
W. E. Henley

George Wyndham, by the way, is writing an Introduction to Shakespeare's *Poems* for the *English Classics*.[1] I fear it will be the last of the series.

---

[1] *The Poems of Shakespeare*, edited with an introduction and notes by G. Wyndham (1898). It was not included in the *English Classics*.

To the Royal Literary Fund, 2 December 1895
ALS: RLF

9 The Terrace, Barnes, S.W.

Dear Sir,

I have pleasure in stating that I consider Mrs. John O'Neill the worthiest possible subject for the attention of your Committee.

For her late husband & his work I had a very strong regard. He was a constant contributor to *The Scots* — (& *The National*) — *Observer* during the five years of my editorship; & I can honestly say, as many besides might do, that I never read an article of his without learning something & without bringing away some such odd expressive turn of phrase as stamps the man of letters. I am no folk-lorist, & I know nothing of the scientific value of *The Night of the Gods* — the monumental book on which, as you are aware, he was engaged at the moment of his untimely & unexpected death. What I can say of it is this: there has been collected no such *corpus* of curious & recondite lore since Burton published his *Anatomy*. It is the same, in a greater or less degree, with most of that he wrote. Much of it is journalism; but it is all scholarly, & it is all the work of a *writer* — it is all, I mean, an approximation to literature. I was so sensible of this that, as soon as I took on *The New Review* (at the end of '94), I made haste to secure an article by John O'Neill.[1] I got one — the last of his I was ever to use; & I think now, as I thought then, that he probably was the only living Englishman who could have

---

[1] John O'Neill, 'The last conquest of China', *New Review*, February 1895.

been at once so learned in fact & so popular (in the good sense) in style.

It is with very great regret that I hear that his widow is straitened in her means: — that, in fact, she has not been able to realize his estate unaided, & has nothing but a very small pension on which to depend for the rest of her life. As I said, I think her the worthiest possible subject for the interest of your Committee; & I shall be sincerely pleased to know that interest has been bestowed upon her.[2]

Very Faithfully Yours,
W. E. Henley

The Secretary,
Royal Literary Fund.

[2] O'Neill's widow Henrietta was granted £100.

To John W. Gilmer, 1 January 1896
ALS: Yale

9 The Terrace, Barnes, S.W.

Dear Gilmer,

I am glad you didn't come this afternoon as, if you had, you'd have found me prostrate with colic. I've had a bad turn on for days, & can get nothing done.

However, there's a lot ready for the printers, & a lot to go back. And will you tell Sydney S.[1] that the 22nd suits Stephen[2] well enough; so we'd best make it that day: if so be, that is, that it suits the others — Cust, Ivan & Co — as well; which is for you to discuss.

It is a nuisance to miss the Wreath: especially through as an ape as Alfred Austin.[3] All the same, 'My head is bloody but unbowed'.[4]

Yours ever sincerely,
W.E.H.

Please tell Pawling he hasn't answered my question about a *Man of Straw*.[5]

[1] Sydney Southgate Pawling (1862-1923), a partner in the firm of William Heinemann. He was a nephew of Charles Mudie (of the Circulating Library) and joined Heinemann in 1893 as literary advisor and business partner.
[2] Herbert Stephen.
[3] WEH's friends had been canvassing for him to become Poet Laureate but Alfred Austin (1835-1913) was appointed. Of private means he edited the *National Review*, a Conservative monthly from 1887 to 1895. A prolific writer of poetry he was much parodied and his appointment was unpopular in view of the stature of some of the other contenders, such as Alice Meynell (suggested by Coventry Patmore), Kipling and William Watson.
[4] WEH's 'Invictus'.
[5] A novel by Edwin William Pugh (1874-1930) published by Heinemann in 1896.

To Robert Fitzroy Bell, 8 January 1896
ALS: Yale

9 The Terrace, Barnes, S.W.

My dear F. B.,

You can guess why you've gone so long unanswered. This morning's news —
& especially the effect of that dunghill message from Berlin[1] have done me good.
The new Flying Squadron is noble;[2] &, after all, if we've failed,[3] it's as only
Englishmen can. So I feel more cheerful knowing the Nation in line at last — (for
the first time I can remember) — & confident that, if there's got to be any
fighting, it will be well & cheerfully done.

There is little news, except that our First Volume (of Burns) is passed for press
so that I can never dare to cross the Marches any more! I wonder what you'll
think of it? Walter B. is cock-a-hoop & so are the Jacks. The Library Ed. should
be your mark. The other is — well! I don't like the illustrations, as you know; &
Hole's have not converted me. Far from it!

We have Furse's picture with us now:[4] a most beautiful suggestion rather than
a portrait, though it has lovely points as portraiture. We do not look at it much, as
yet. But I am sure that thus far it has done us good — both of us. I wonder if you
saw a quatorzain I printed late last year in the *N.R.?*[5] It falls somehow into line
with this thing of Furse's: that's why I mentioned it. Barrie's little memory (in the
current *Scribner's*) is very pretty,[6] but disappointingly slight.

Our cordial good wishes to both of you for '96.

Yours Ever Sincerely,
W.E.H.

I should have liked you to see my *London Garland*. But it costs a guinea, & they
only gave me *one copy*.

---

[1] A report from Berlin in *The Times* of 8 January stating that neither German settlers nor German
troops would intervene in the Transvaal.

[2] A naval flying squadron of six ships was to be commissioned ready to sail to any danger spot at
short notice.

[3] WEH is referring to the Jameson Raid of January 1896. Dr Leander Starr Jameson (1853-1917)
was a close friend and supporter of Cecil Rhodes in his belief for a British Africa. The population
of the Transvaal were dissatisfied with the South African Republic and were preparing to rise
against it in Johannesburg. Jameson had formed a force in support should the need arise. He acted
rather rashly in an attempt to precipitate the rising and was captured by the Boers. He was returned
to the British who sentenced him to ten months in prison in England. He was released due to
illness after eight months. His fortunes changed and he became Prime Minister of the Cape Colony
from 1904 to 1908. He was created a Baronet in 1911.

[4] Charles Furse had produced a posthumous portrait of Margaret based on a photograph.

[5] WEH's poem 'Two Days'.

[6] The character of Reddy in Barrie's *Sentimental Tommy* was based on Margaret Emma Henley.
The first chapter was published in *Scribner's Magazine*, January 1896.

To Alice Meynell, 19 January 1896
ALS: Texas

9 The Terrace, Barnes, S.W.

My dear Mrs. Meynell,

We read your last Autolycus[1] with singular pleasure. We know your point of view so well; & we can recall (as we do) with pride the fact that the Golden Child was always that & nothing more. I could wish, though, that you had credited Charles Dickens with his share in the change. I cannot make out my argument now; but, shortly, it is this. My mother was not a Dickens child; & she suffered horribly. I was; & I enjoyed my life. And in the third generation, the Child can scarce, we love to think, have had a half-hour's pain, nor have reached, had she remained with us, a single bitter memory. Of course, the world has gone on getting civilized, & in this matter there is more decivilization than one cares to think. But that it took the forking road from Barbarism (or barbarity) is largely, very largely, due — as I know — to the man who gave us Paul Dombey, Pip & D.C. And I wish you had been able to say it.

Some day we may talk this over. Meanwhile, I want to thank you for making the point you made last Friday.

My wife has tried to write to you these many days. But we have both been down with a cold: the worst I can recall. I think, though, after to-morrow when she goes to Muswell Hill to look at a house, she will be able to redeem her credit.

Always Sincerely Yours,
W.E.H.

Are you never going to honour us of *The New Review* again?[2]

---

[1] 'The Wares of Autolycus. That Pretty Person', *Pall Mall Gazette*, 17 January 1896. A short essay in which Alice Meynell regrets the hasty abandonment of childhood. Alice Meynell contributed a weekly article in the series *The Wares of Autolycus* every Friday from 2 June 1893 until 25 March 1896 and then every Wednesday until 28 December 1898.
[2] Alice Meynell did not write again for the *New Review*.

To Harold Frederic,[1] 1 May 1896
ALS: Fales

Stanley Lodge, Muswell Hill, N.[2]

Dear Frederic,

I read your article with a pleased surprize.[3] I hadn't the slightest notion it was coming; nor till I got half-way through did I guess whose it must be. I think there might be some pretty effects in the way of counter checking to be got out of your remarks on our politics; but I am none the less glad to have it — especially as it comes from you.

I am glad, too — very glad indeed — to know that *Illumination*[4] is a great success — & deserves to be. I am bogged in Byron for the moment, & dare not take it up. But I shall be free a few days hence I hope: & then I promise myself some fun.

I *do* hope that Uncle Dudley is going to make his mark in his new clothes. I haven't seen the dear old thing as yet.

But he is on his way.

Yours Always Sincerely,
W.E.H.

[1] Harold Frederic (1856-98), American novelist and London correspondent of the *New York Times*.
[2] The Henleys had moved here by 3 April 1896 (WEH to Alice Meynell, [4 April 1896], Texas).
[3] 'Henley's Art as Editor', *New York Times*, 5 April 1896. In this article Frederic gave a *résumé* of Henley's journalistic career and praised Henley as the 'only English writer of the first class who holds a magazine editorship.' In commenting on Henley's staff, which included H. G. Wells, J. M. Barrie and Marriott Watson, he refers to Whibley as 'the most Henleyesque figure of them all'.
[4] Frederic's best known novel *The Damnation of Theron Ware* (1896), published in England as *Illumination* (1896), describes the downfall and revival of a Methodist minister.

To James McNeil Whistler, 20 May 1896
ALS: Glasgow

Stanley Lodge, Muswell Hill, N.

My dear Whistler,

I fear to trespass on your seclusion. Yet I must do so with a word. *We* also have been tried. But the worst, I think, is yet to come for one or other of us in that which has befallen you. And that has made us think of you, often & tenderly, with peculiar sympathy during these many sorrowful months.[1]

We cannot say 'Be comforted'; for there are afflictions for which there is no comfort, & this of yours is chief of them. We can but assure you that we shall not

[1] Whistler's wife, Trixie, had died of cancer on 10 May 1896. They were married in 1887.

cease from regarding you, & that we rejoice to think that you have in your hands a means of solace in that art in which your achievement has placed you first among living men.

Yours Ever Sincerely,
W. E. Henley

To William Rothenstein,[1] 5 June 1896
ALS: Harvard

Stanley Lodge, Muswell Hill, N.

Dear Mr. Rothenstein,
    I am dismayed to come across a letter from you which is a month old, & has not, I fear, been answered. It got slipped into a book, & has lain there, forgotten (I am ashamed to say) until to-day.
    The truth is, I never paid that visit to London, after all. I have a great deal of heavy work on hand, & I had to fall-to, to make up for much lost time.
    If the occasion be still with you, & you care to come here, I shall — I scarce need say — be happy to sit for you.[2]

Very Sincerely Yours,
W. E. Henley

---

[1] William Rothenstein (1872-1945), artist and portrait painter, knighted 1931.
[2] Rothenstein was drawing portraits of well-known people for his *English Portraits* (1898). When he had completed WEH's portrait he asked Wilde to write the notes for it. Wilde's pen picture of WEH was clever but unflattering:

> He founded a school and has survived all his disciples. He has always thought too much about himself, which is wise; and written too much about others, which is foolish. His prose is the beautiful prose of a poet, and his poetry the beautiful poetry of a prose-writer. His personality is insistent. To converse with him is a physical no less than an intellectual recreation. He is never forgotten by his enemies, and often forgiven by his friends. He has added several new words to the language, and his style is an open secret. He has fought a good fight and has had to face every difficulty except popularity. (*Men and Memories: Recollections of William Rothenstein 1872-1900*, (1931), *1*, 312)

Wilde's work was rejected and Max Beerbohm wrote instead. (Henry) Max(imilian) Beerbohm · (1872-1956), writer, critic and caricaturist, and half-brother of Herbert Beerbohm Tree.

To William Roberts,[1] **16 June 1896**
ALS: Hayward

The New Review, 21 Bedford Street, Covent Garden, London, W.C.
Dear Sir,
   I am in a little difficulty about 'Romney as an Investment',[2] which I read only yesterday. What I had hoped to find was some account of the means by which a sixth-rate painter[3] — (for I can in no wise fathom your opinion of Romney) — has been forced into a position as regards the market-price of his work scarce, if at all, inferior to Sir Joshua's own,[4] & vastly superior to that of incomparably better men. What I found was (1) a criticism on Romney, which I couldn't possibly publish, & (2) a list of prices which, admirably thorough as it seems to be, gets us 'no forwarder' than we were, & which, if I may say so, in its present condition, scarce material for a critical review.
   This is my difficulty; & I will confess that I don't see how it is to be over come. I could get over the first part — the eulogy — easily enough, by substituting plain facts for opinions. What bothers me is the second: the long list of prices, with no account of the conditions & circumstances under which the pounds & shillings of the beginning have evolved into thousands of the end. I cannot believe that this is an effect of honest marketing; & I am not alone — far from it — in that capacity. Nor can I think that it is wholly the outcome of a craze for Eighteenth Century English work. Still less can I agree with you that it is a true gauge to the recognition of Romney's merits as a painter. To myself, as to many others, it is largely the work of a combination of dealers; & that is the view which I had hoped to find compounded in your article.
   I am extremely sorry to have to write thus; for the thing has been long indeed in hand, & your patience has been exemplary. I shall be glad indeed to hear that you can suggest a way-out of what seems to me a blind-alley.

Sincerely Yours,
W. E. Henley

W. Roberts Esq.

---

[1] William Roberts (1862-1940), writer on books and bookselling and author of *The Earlier History of English Bookselling* (1889).
[2] An article rejected by WEH but subsequently published in *Temple Bar*, September 1896.
[3] George Romney (1734-1802), portrait painter. WEH in his *Views and Reviews: Art* writes that Romney has 'charm' but 'there is scarce any sense in which he can be said to have been an artist' (124).
[4] Sir Joshua Reynolds (1723-92), the most successful English portrait painter of his period. Founding President of the Royal Academy, 1768-90. WEH writes that Reynolds 'whatever his place in the art of Britain, is a far more brilliant and conspicuous figure in the art of the world than any Englishman before or since his time' (*Views and Reviews*, 120).

To Lord Rosebery,[1] 14 July 1896
ALS: NLS

Stanley Lodge, Muswell Hill, N.
The Right Hon. The Earl of Rosebery, K.G., etc

My dear Sir,
    I telegraphed to you this morning (1) that Vols. I & II were sent off yesterday, to Berkeley Square; & (2) that you would find whatever is known about the *J.B.*[2] in the Notes to it in Vol. II. In case the parcel should have lingered by the way, I will note that the *J.B.* was published in 1799 as a chap-book or tract, by Stuart & Meikle of Glasgow. It had been in being full fourteen years ere it got into print.
    I am pretty certain that Burns did not refer to his obscenities, when he spoke with Maria Riddell[3] at Brow, so much as to the crowd of 'pitaphs'& 'pigrams' which he produced, & which, as I think, have done him more harm with posterity than all his work besides. He had, I believe, a peculiar gift, an exceptional & remarkable talent, for what is called bawdy, & I would not for anything destroy his achievement in it. Indeed, I think *The Merry Muses* not by any means the least precious part of his legacy to the world: for the reason that, not only does it show him at his best (in a sense) as editor & lyrist, but also that it brings us clearer than any book I know to the Scotland whence he sprang, to the models he used, & — in several cases, at least — to the originals he made his own. And I purpose, once this edition of mine is out of the way, to reprint that very remarkable volume in such a form & in such numbers — (250 copies, say) — as will make a second disappearance impossible. This, however, is by the way. My point is that Burns, while a man of genius, was also a peasant, & was, moreover, the mouthpiece of a society which talked & sang habitual of things which are nowadays unmentionable & that to make him anything else — to make him, for instance, the sort of tame, blithering sentimental Scot who in those days would write Whig leaders for a Glasgow daily, nor ever presume upon his sex — (which *he* would have called by another name) — to the profit of any but his lawful spouse, is to make of him a thing he had scorned to be, & to render it impossible for any but those who really want to distinguish between truth & lies, to realize the man, or the man's work, or the Scotland to which he was born, & whose living voice he was.
    There's a humorous side to the question too. Isn't it rather fun, for instance, to reflect that *the Man's a Man for A 'That*[4] — ('the Marseillaise of humanity') —

[1]Archibald Philip Primrose, (1847-1929), 5th Earl of Rosebery, statesman and writer. Prime Minister, March 1894-June 1895. WEH had written to Lord Rosebery for permission to see his Burns manuscript collection. A correspondence developed over the years and from time to time Rosebery supplied WEH and Anna with birds from his estates.
[2] 'The Jolly Beggars'.
[3] Mrs Walter Riddell.
[4] 'Is there for honest poverty'.

was suggested by, & modelled on — even to the use of certain mannerisms — a song no living man could sing aloud? That the same is true — literally — of 'Green Grow the Rashes', and 'John Anderson, My Jo', & 'Duncan Gray' & 'Comin' Through the Rye', & a score besides? *I* think it is; & I think, too, that the literary interest which attaches to this part of Burns's work is tenfold stronger that that of at least the half of his published work. This is as much as to say that I heartily applaud your resolve to burn nothing in Burns's hand o'write. It is hard — some times — to know when he was copying another & when he was expressing himself. Some times he was doing both. And very often to burn would be to burn not only R.B. but a bit of Old Scotland.

Forgive this long scrawl. The gist of it is, really, that I am glad, & proud to have the means of unearthing that pleasant pasquil on the Lady of Lincluden.[5]

Very Sincerely Yours,
W. E. Henley

[5] Burns's satire 'On Grizzel Grimme' [Mrs Grizzel Young of Lincluden]. Lord Rosebery gave permission for its publication.

To Lord Windsor, 4 October 1896

Stanley Lodge, Muswell Hill, N.

Dear Lord Windsor,

Have you any suggestions, or have you landed any Royal or Noble contributors? I haven't worried you hitherto, though G.W. said I was to do so: partly because the *N. Review* has done pretty well, I think, in the material course of things; & partly because I've been so deep in Burns & Byron, I haven't had the heart or the time for anything else. But the year is running out; & when Mr. Ramsey has done with the Pretorians,[1] & Mr. Crawshay has told us of the Germans in Africa,[2] we shall have nothing to watch the world withal. Unless G.W. brings home a new S. Africa.[3]

Talking of Byron: I have the very greatest difficulty in getting hold of books. I've been hunting *Pugilistica*[4] for months, & a thing called *Byroniana: The*

[1] G. G. Ramsey, 'The case of the Pretoria prisoners (Part I)', *New Review*, October 1896. George Gilbert Ramsey (1839-1921), scholar.
[2] The unsigned 'German policy in Central Africa', *New Review*, February 1897. Richard Crawshay has not been identified but according to the *Wellesley Index to Victorian Periodicals*, vol. 5, was a contributor to the *Geographical Journal*, 1894, 1902 and 1903.
[3] George Wyndham was very interested in the political unrest in South Africa and left for that country on 15 August 1896 returning before the end of November 1896 (J. W. Mackail and Guy Wyndham, *Life and Letters of George Wyndham*, *1*, 60).
[4] H. D. Miles, *Pugilistica: Being one Hundred and Forty-Four Years of the History of British Boxing ... From 1719... to ...1863*, 3 vols (1880-81).

Opinions of Lord B. on Men, etc (1834) for more than that.[5] *Pugilistica* I think I've run to ground; but of the other — *rien de rien*! Have you got it in your library? If you have —! But indeed I should be glad to borrow anything — books, pamphlets, squibs,[6] memoirs, *crim. con.*,[7] trials, *anything* — I could get. The curious thing is, there is so little to be got! I've tried Haig & Belvoir[8] & neither has given me *anything*. And I'm groping after what is to be got about a brute like Yarmouth[9] — who in life was called 'Red Herrings', & in death is remembered as the original of Disraeli's Lord Eskdale & Thackeray's Marquis of Steyne[10] — almost in despair.

Everything else is 'in a concatenation according'. It's all too near to be history, & too far not to be more or less forgot. And there I am. If you *could* come to my rescue, I am sure you would. But there it is! I believe nobody can. And my Regency————!

Yours Ever Sincerely,

W.E.H.

[5] *Byroniana. The Opinions of Lord Byron on Men, Manners and Things: with the Parish Clerk's Album kept at His Burial Place, Hucknall Torkard* (1834).
[6] Personal satires.
[7] Criminal conversation, i.e. adultery.
[8] Haig Hall, Wigan, home of James Ludovic Lindsay (1847-1913), 26th Earl of Crawford and Balcarres. Belvoir Castle, Leicestershire, was the home of Henry John Brinsley Manners (1852-1925), Marquess of Granby and later 8th Duke of Rutland.
[9] Francis-Charles Seymour-Conway (1777-1842), Earl of Yarmouth and 3rd Marquis of Hertford.
[10] Lord Monmouth, a character in Disraeli's novel *Coningsby* (1844) was based on Yarmouth and Lord Steyne was a character in Thackeray's *Vanity Fair*.

To Lord Windsor, 16 October 1896
ALS: Morgan

Stanley Lodge, Muswell Hill, N.

Dear Lord Windsor,

I hope you will be able to find me something. A file of some rascally old print, say — *The Satirist, The Scrounge*,[1] anything of that sort, even the *John Bull*.[2] Fashion-books, pamphlets, scoundrelisms anything rank with the time! 'Twas an age of libellous & clandestine publications. I have found at the B.M. the (so called) *Confessions* of Lord Yarmouth's valet[3] (Lord Yarmouth gave Thackeray

[1] *The Satirist, or Monthly Meteor* (1808-14); *The Scrounge; or Monthly Expositor of Imposture and Folly* (1811-15).
[2] *The John Bull Magazine and Literary Recorder* (1824).
[3] Nicholas Suisse, *The Confessions of Nicholas Suisse, Late Valet to the Marquis of Hertford* (1842).

the Marquis of Steyne & Disraeli the Earl of Whathisname in *Coningsby*) & it's practically a bawdy book. Such stuff is worthless in forty-nine ways; but in the fiftieth it's useful enough. This by way of note. I want to recreate the Regency; & I care not what material I put into the pot.

I am glad indeed to know that you have read the *Jago* with the eye of faith. The rest is still more striking than that you have seen. And I've reason to believe that there will be a dead set against the book the moment it makes its appearance. So we must do what we can to put the Sentimentalists to shame. It's a pity that we should have to do so; but we English find it so very much easier to be moral & wrong than to be artistic & right that, I suppose, there's no help for it.

I wish I knew where Balcarres is. He has sent me trophies of his gun; & I know not where to write to him.

There are two excellent articles in the November issue: a second Ramsey,[4] much better than the first; & E. G. Browne[5] — Persian Browne — on Cyprus, the latter (between ourselves) a quasi-official paper, which was rescued from the *Chronicle*, & passed on to us. Do you know Walter of *The Times*?[6] I don't; & G.W., who does, is in S. Africa; so I fear they'll go unremarked.

Always Sincerely Yours,
W.E.H.

---

[4] G. G. Ramsey, 'The case of the Pretoria prisoners (Part II, concl.)', *New Review*, November 1896.
[5] Edward G. Browne, 'England's duty to Cyprus', *New Review*, November 1896. Edward Granville Browne (1862-1926), traveller and Persian scholar. He was the Sir Thomas Adams Professor of Arabic at Cambridge, 1902-26.
[6] Arthur Fraser Walter (1846-1910), chief proprietor of *The Times* and subsequently first Chairman of The Times Publishing Co. Ltd in 1908.

To Lord Windsor, 25 October 1896
ALS: Morgan

Stanley Lodge, Muswell Hill, N.

Dear Lord Windsor,

Very many thanks. All the books you mention — even Huish[1] — will be welcome. If you could add to them Windham's *Diaries*, & Crabb Robinson[2] — books one wants to have by one, but one doesn't particularly want to own — I

---

[1] Robert Huish (1777-1850), biographical writer.
[2] Mrs H. Baring, ed., *The Diary of the Right Hon. William Windham 1784 to 1810* (1866). William Windham (1750-1810), statesman. T. Sadler, ed., *Diary, Reminiscences, and Correspondence of H. C. Robinson ...* , 3 vols (1869). Henry Crabb Robinson (1775-1867), barrister for *The Times*, and its special correspondent in Germany, Spain and Portugal.

should be still more deeply obliged.

Have you seen Charles Whibley's *Book of Scoundrels*? Authority in these matters there is none; but I hear that George Meredith is a *fervent*, & is calling out that it is literature all over the shop. It is pleasant to know that he's doing so — to me at least; for the book is nothing if not ironical, & irony is the thing which Meredith has always tried to do, & has so seldom done that to me his books have very much the effect of a long row of 'set pieces' in the fire works line, which have been rained on, & then lighted, & then ———

I am trying to get far enough away from the Wicked Lord B. — & the lewd, drunken, ruffianly, crim.-conning Age that was his to write something for the *N.R.* about this delicious new book of Barrie's.[3] I hope I shall manage it. Morrison is to be out next week;[4] & I hear that a dead set at it is expected: I suppose from the Toynbee Hall[5] & Socialist clique. They may rot it; but they won't kill it, & they couldn't write it — could they?

I hear, too, that G.W. is on his way home. But he comes too late for Walter & the November *N.R.*[6]

Always Sincerely Yours,
W.E.H.

[3] *Sentimental Tommy: the Story of his Boyhood* (1896). WEH did not write of it.
[4] *A Child of the Jago.*
[5] Toynbee Hall was an educational institution established in 1883 in the East End of London. It was named after the economist and socialist Arnold Toynbee (1852-83). After graduating from Oxford Toynbee became a tutor at Balliol and later Bursar and his influence was extensive in the four year period before his early death.
[6] This was a reference to Walter Raleigh's 'The Human Bacillus', *New Review*, November 1896. The article gives a philosophical view of man's place in society and his right to survive. Raleigh asks by what right we inflict ourselves on others 'waging war on all creatures we cannot enslave'.

To Robert Fitzroy Bell, 13 December 1896
ALS: Yale

Stanley Lodge, Muswell Hill, N.

My dear F.B.,

No end of thanks for your letter. My absence pained me;[1] yet I felt, somehow, in view of those lean last years, that really it was for the best: — that to swagger round as a pal of the R.L.S. who had discontinued my society, & told me, plainly to go to hell, & trouble him no more, was not the right & proper thing for me to do. So that — well, *I couldn't* anyhow! And there's an end! But I needn't say that

[1] A meeting had been held in Edinburgh under the chairmanship of Lord Rosebery on 10 December 1896 to discuss the possibility of a memorial to RLS.

I rejoice & am exceedingly glad to know the meeting a success — (the good Colvin telegraphed from King's Cross) — & that my remarks were read with the others, & pleasantly received.[2]

You might, I think, have sent me a *Scotsman report*. I saw only the ever-damnable, & thrice-despicable *Times*,[3] which put its pile on the Peer, & squeezed James Matthew into half-a-dozen lines (It hasn't, by the way, reviewed *Tommie* yet!). If I were young & energetic I'd start an Anti-*Times* Association. Indeed I'm not sure that I won't as it is.

Thus far the journals are civil enough to *Byron I*. But did Colvin tell you of my disappointment? Of the coalition (Murray-Heinemann) that might have given me the *Final Byron*, even as I've got the (more or less) *Final Burns*, but didn't come off after all? After *that*, what are reviews — or good or bad or indifferent?

I read *Margaret Ogilive* to-day;[4] & I appreciate, as I couldn't before, what the writer meant when he told me on his return from the House of death what certain verses of mine[5] had been to him during his sojourn therein, & why he asked me to give him a copy of them in my own handwriting. As for these miserable Scots who are writing of it, I'd have them up to the triangles (first) & bar them from Crockett & Maclaren (their natural food) for the term of their natural lives.

Yours ever,
W.E.H.

[*Added by WEH at the top of the letter*] Our worst day of the year — it used to be her best — is coming on us fast. Spare a thought on it. I fear that Tommie will go unnoticed after all.

---

[2] The meeting was reported in the *Scotsman*, 11 December 1896.
[3] 'Rosebery in Edinburgh', *The Times*, 11 December 1896.
[4] Barrie's biographical account of his mother published in 1896.
[5] WEH's 'Invictus'. In his Rectorial Address delivered at St Andrews University, 3 May 1922, Barrie quotes 'Invictus' and adds that: 'If you want an example of courage try Henley' (*Courage*, [1922], 29-30).

To Robert Fitzroy Bell, 30 December 1896
ALS: Yale

Stanley Lodge, Muswell Hill, N.

My dear F.B.,

What a splendid present! I have 'almost forgot the taste' of Burgundy, & as for Krug (extra sec) — — ! Well, well! It was good of you to remember us, & we are grateful.

I wish, now, I'd come to the meeting. That d—d thing is growing, growing; & I mean to have it out as soon as I can lay hands on a competent surgeon. It gives me no trouble — these fatty cysts are mere eyesores; but I hate it none the less, &

so does my wife.[1]

On the whole I wish he hadn't published *Margaret Ogilvie*. It is a matter too private for the great, goggle-eyed, slavering general — don't you think? But it's a wonderful bit of work, of its kind, & if he could have done it in lyric verse — — ! But he couldn't, & there's an end of that. And it's done in prose, & published, & there's an end of that. But I'm sure he has done himself an ill turn with many good men. This, of course, between ourselves.

The Byron seems to fizz — if one believes the reviews. Have you done your dooty by the Notes, I wonder? They appear to amuse their readers. They most certainly amused the writer: who, by the way, is by this time convinced that he, too, *In Arcadia vixit* — backed Jem Belcher[2] to his shirt, & lost what was left of him at Waiter's,[3] & kicked Brummell,[4] & heard T.M. sing *Bendemeer's Stream* (was it at Lady Holland's — I forget!),[5] & wrote (& published) a poem called *The Childhood of Cain: a Mystery*,[6] & — But this is not an autobiography. A trip, though: — I foresee in some volume yet to come a Note — a Henley Note — on 'the genial delights of Crim Con.' which, with others, will rank me not far below Buckle,[7] & a good deal higher than Robert Chambers.[8]

I am, meanwhile, trying to gird my loins for the essay on Robbie[9] — Robbie, ye ken! And I wish to Heaven I'd done so before I took on this 'dear, d—d distracting' Regency. Lang & I exchange polite letters about the relative criminality of Robbie & 'the Wicked Lord B'. But I don't seem to get much forwarder. And I find myself hawking after every 'Molesey Hurst'[10] & Waiter's & the sublime Harriette Wilson. I never was, I never could have been, a Scots peasant, with an eye for *anything* in pettycoats! And, as for the Regency, if you'll believe me, my dear boy, there was a time when 'Red Herrings'[11] (as we used to call him) & a little woman whom he adored were more mixed up with me than — — ! But, as I said, this isn't an autobiography. And all I wanted to say is, That I

[1] WEH's cyst was removed before 19 January 1897 (19 January 1897, Pierpont Morgan, quoted by Connell, 316).
[2] Jem Belcher, a prize fighter of the period.
[3] A fashionable club of the period.
[4] George Bryan Brummell (1778-1840), known as Beau Brummell, was a leader in fashion and a friend of the Prince Regent, later George IV.
[5] Thomas Moore wrote a song called *Bendemeer's Stream*. Lady Elizabeth Holland (1770-1845), wife of the 3rd Lord Holland.
[6] *Cain, a mystery* (1821).
[7] Possibly a reference to Henry Thomas Buckle (1821-62), whose major work was the *History of Civilisation in England*, 2 vols (1857, 1861).
[8] Probably a reference to Robert Chambers (1802-71), publisher and editor of Burns's *Works*.
[9] WEH's 'Life: Genius: Achievement,' in *Burns*, 4. It was reprinted as *Burns: Life, Genius Achievement* (Edinburgh, 1898).
[10] Molesey, or Moulsey, Hurst, a meadow near Hampton Court, was the scene of a prize-fight between Jem Belcher and Tom Cribb; Harriette Wilson, a famous courtesan of the period; Waiter's Club, Piccadilly, London.
[11] The 3rd Marquis of Hertford.

hope I shall do Robbie justice, & that I shall forget him, as though he'd never been, as soon as he flickers (poor [   ], futile ghost of a Great Man) out of my purview.

And so, — for I have babbled too long — God have you in his keeping & the best of all possible good wishes, from us both to both you, for '97.

Yours Ever,
W.E.H.

Is one R. T. Hamilton Bruce in Edinburgh? *R.S.V.P.*

To Clement K. Shorter, 11 March 1897
ALS: BL

[The Chummery,] South View, Crowborough, Sussex[1]
My dear Sir,

I've been — not unwell but — severely, even seriously, ill; & I am down here to refit. It isn't probable that I shall be in London by the 23rd; but even if I were, I should feel obliged, owing to the condition of my inside, to decline your very courteous invitation. That invitation, under ordinary circumstances, it would have given me great pleasure to accept. For, since Leslie Stephen sent me Omar (when I lay in the Edinburgh Infirmary),[2] Omar has been something of an influence with me; & I should rejoice to do honour to the man who made him acceptable & intelligible to us Westerns — who is, in fact, very much more Omar to us than Omar himself.

I've to thank you for a very cordial notice of my first Byron — in *The Star* (was it?).[3] I thought much of the comparison in your last paragraph: of Byron & Napoleon. I agree with you: that the King is returning from evil, & that other King has returned. If he lay by the way, it shall be, I promise you, no fault of mine.

But I was laid by the heels at the next moment when I ought to have been stripped for the start, & toeing the mark. And I've lost a good seven weeks. And, *enfin* — !

Very Sincerely Yours,
W. E. Henley

Clement K. Shorter Esq.

---

[1] The Henleys arrived here on 24 February (WEH to Whibley, 21 February 1897, Pierpont Morgan).
[2] *The Rubaiyat of Omar Khayyam, the Astronomer-Poet of Persia*, translated by Edward FitzGerald (1859). Edward FitzGerald (1809-83), writer and translator. Shorter wrote the introduction to a 1905 edition.
[3] Shorter's 'Mr. Henley's *Byron*', the *Star*, 13 February 1897.

To William Archer, 22 [23] April 1897
ALS: BL

Stanley Lodge, Muswell Hill, N.

My dear Archer,

Henderson sends me a long column from to-day's *D.C.*,[1] which he insists is yours. I don't know, after what you told me, in the beginning, that he's right; but it reads like you, & if it be yours indeed, then let me thank you for it, to begin with, & go on to compliment you for the most sensible Scot (Henderson excepted) I've ever met.

I am really obliged to you for putting your foot, for all it's worth, on the silly complaint that we want to belittle the Bard. And you get as near as next to nothing to the facts of the case in your statement of what Burns did. But I think you scarce realize the immense advantage to him the corpus of folk-song was on which he worked. Did you ever try to write a song? If you ever have, you'll know what a suggestion's worth. Given the 'lyrical idea', & you are right. It takes time & trouble; but you're right. R.B. had his lyrical ideas ready made; & more R.B. had the sentiment, the feeling, the tone, the style, even the type — all ready to his hand I think, & so does Henderson, that he owes as much to the old Innominators as the old Innominators owe to him. And as a person who has written songs I never open his book without wishing I had, or possibly have, 'arf his complaint'.

I have been miserably ill; & I'm two months behind everything. Even now I am not myself & my *Burns* Essay is done with effort & at a snail's pace. And this is why I've never asked you for Genest.[2] When the Burns is done, you'll hear from me; for I must fall in to Byron II with all possible insistence. Till then — — — !

Don't the old *Deacon-Admiral-Beau* stuff look monstrous fine in the *Edinburgh* edition type?[3] My feelings, when I gaze, are pretty much those of a dustman in a duke's robes. But I don't wholly dislike myself, even so.

Yours Ever Sincerely,
W.E.H.

[1] A review of vol. 3 of *The Poetry of Burns*, *Daily Chronicle*, 23 April 1897.
[2] John Genest (1764-1839), cleric and author of *Some Aspects of the English Stage, from the Restoration in 1666 to 1830* (Bath, 1882).
[3] The plays were published in vol. 22 of the Edinburgh Edition of RLS's *Works* in April 1897.

To Lord Rosebery, 19 May 1897
ALS: NLS

Stanley Lodge, Muswell Hill, N.

Dear Lord Rosebery,

I have at last got off my *Essay*, so that the *Centenary Burns* is as good as done: though the *Essay* is still to pass through the press. Now I purpose to put through *The Merry Muses* with all possible speed; & before I begin the work, I want, if I may, to talk with you, &, if I may, persuade you to show me that volume of Glenriddell Collections. The *M.M.*, as it stands, consists of 95 numbers, some by R.B., some tickled by R.B., some folksong pure & simple. What, as an editor, I wish to see is how many of them are included in your collection. For, in truth, this is, not a reprint of a bawdy book but, a private publication which (a) is of the greatest possible interest to the true student of Burns, & (b) is the most striking collection of folk-bawd which, so far as I know, exists in literature.

I am clear of my Burns, for the moment, &, being very tired indeed, I haven't yet gone back to my Byron. If you care to see me, I will come to you in Berkeley Square any day you please. I've not been outside my own gate for at least two months: not, in fact, since I re-entered it after convalescing from a bad, bad illness in the early part of the year. Such has been my devotion to the Ploughing Poet! But if you can give me a quiet half-hour —— —— !

May I say that I've read your Centenary speeches[1] with profit & with pleasure, both. I could wish that you hadn't kind of bracketed Shakespeare & the Bard. But then, of course, I'm an Englishman. But I'm grateful no end to you for declining to have any white washing, & for looking the facts of those last years at Dumfries full in the face.[2] The bourgeois, the genteel, the barley-sugar Burns of the latest apotheosis is impossible. I have tried to show him as he was: the peasant of genius, killed by his environment & his temperament — a Mirabeau[3] without a chance, in fact: a Mirabeau without a chance. 'Great is his strength', you say, but 'great' (why not 'greater'?) in his weakness'. That, as I think, is very nearly the last word. *Mirabeau-paysan*: what chance is there for such a creature? My Dumfries chapter is *nothing*. For pity's sake I cannot write it. The whole thing goes by default. Given the winter & bawding, the man couldn't have been other. As *you* see. And ......

---

[1] *Addresses Delivered at the Opening of the Burns Exhibition, Glasgow, 15th July, 1896, and at the Public Meeting in Commemoration of the Centenary of the Poet's Death held in St. Andrew's Halls, Glasgow, 21st July, 1896, by ... the Earl of Rosebery ... and Others* (Glasgow, 1896). The centenary speeches were reported in *The Times* of 22 July 1896.

[2] WEH sums up Burns's final years at Dumfries as 'a story of decadence'.

[3] Honoré Gabriel Victor Riqueti, Comte de Mirabeau (1749-91), French orator and rake.

This, I assure you, is written to the 'serious Burns student': not to the owner of the Glenriddell Collections.

Very Sincerely Yours,
W.E.H.

To William Heinemann, 2 August 1897
ALS: Houghton

Stanley Lodge, Muswell Hill. N.

Dear Gabriel John,[1]
Here is all the W.B. I have.[2] The rest went back (per J. W. Gilmer) for insertions. Please understand that I must have a set of corrected pages; ere I start my introduction. Or I promise nothing.

I have been horribly seedy; & I am by no means myself yet — tho' better in every way than I was. The Brighton air should do me good, & pull me up, & make me Byronize. Anyhow, I'm taking down many books, & feel that Vol. V, though it's a hell of a job, will probably get done ere I depart the shadow of the Pavillion. But, for Heaven's sake don't put money on the event. I have been devilish ill — ill as I never was before. And it has shaken me damnably. When I work, I am better than ever. But the difficulty is to work.

My address is 29 Sussex Square. This to the end (I hope) of August. Come by all means. We shall be delighted to see you. As (I hope) you know.

I haven't seen the August *N.R.* What has become of me that I — the Editor — shouldn't?

And now, a word: please turn on Rudyard, if you can, *at once*. If he won't, for his old Editor & (you) his present friend, then he is a common brute. But I think he will; for I don't regard him in that light at all. Anyhow turn, you, him on. I'd write myself; but he has ignored my existence since he returned; & I can't.

Yours Ever,
W.E.H.

---

[1] A reference to Ibsen's play *John Gabriel Borkman* translated by William Archer and published by Heinemann in 1897.
[2] Henley and Wyndham were preparing an edition of Blunt's poetry published as *The Poetry of Wilfrid Blunt* (1898). In a later letter to Heinemann WEH enclosed the Introduction, 'A poor thing but it has cost me three nights' (24 May 1898, Harvard).

To Lord Rosebery, 29 September 1897
ALS: NLS

Stanley Lodge, Muswell Hill, N.

Dear Lord Rosebery,

I want to include you in the portrait-gallery which is now running in *The New Review*. Would you presently give Mr. Nicholson a sitting?[1] It's nothing formal, nothing terrible: just a few moments of talk, & (as he works from all the documents he can lay hands on) the thing, so far as the sitter is concerned, is done.

Our next (October) is Rudyard Kipling;[2] & after him Cecil Rhodes. Then I should like to place Lord Rosebery.

Burns IV is out at last. I hope that, if you do me the honour to read my 'Essay', you won't disagree with me all over the shop (so to speak): that, in fact, you'll make allowances for my Southern blood breeding. I have seen two or three Scots reviews; &, really, they are quite respectful. I had looked for the shortest shrift & the longest rope ever known in Scotia's fair domain. And I've not yet got over the shock.

Very Sincerely Yours,
W. E. Henley

[1] Lord Rosebery did not sit for Nicholson. William Newzam Prior Nicholson (1872-1949), painter and engraver, knighted in 1936. WEH later wrote the verses for Nicholson's *London Types* (1898).
[2] Nicholson's 'Portrait of Rudyard Kipling' appeared in the *New Review*, October 1897 and his 'Portrait of Cecil Rhodes' in the November issue. In all Nicholson produced seven portraits for the *New Review*, the first being his well-known portrait of Queen Victoria in the June issue.

To Robert T. Hamilton Bruce, 9 October 1897
ALS: Yale

Stanley Lodge, Muswell Hill, N.

My dear Bruce,

I asked Henderson to send you that number of the *British Weekly*.[1] I haven't read the rubbish, but I gather that it's the nastiest, thus far, that has got into print.

[1] Robertson Nicoll's unsigned 'The Correspondence of Claudius Clear: Mr. Henley on Burns the Rake', *British Weekly*, 30 September 1897. In his review Robertson remarks that he first came across Henley as a reviewer in the *Academy*. 'He was good-natured, but dull.' In a scathing attack on WEH as a critic he states that WEH's claim to attention was his 'deliberate intention to give pain' and that he was a 'literary swash-buckler'. He therefore dismisses WEH as a critic before attacking his *Essay* on Burns. WEH is also attacked for editing Burns because he is not a Scotsman. The journalist and writer William Robertson Nicoll (1851-1923) wrote the Claudius Clear column in the *British Weekly* for many years. He was editor of the *British Weekly* from 1886 until his death. In 1891 he founded the *Bookman*. He was knighted in 1909.

To tell you the truth, I don't believe there will be any storm at all. The *Scotsman*,[2] for example, is civil: compares me to (1) Carlyle, & (2) Meissonier.[3] This last made me shudder; but it was the most magnificent compliment (come to think of it) the *Scotsman* could pay me. As for the *British Weekly*, 'tis the work of one Robertson Nicoll, who has, it seems, conspired with the Wallace[4] wight to ruin the Centenary & sell the wight Wallace's edition — his reissue of Chambers, that is. What the wretch wants — & what the wretch won't get — is recognition from me in print. My work is done, & they may undo it if they can. Beyond that I cannot & will not go.

No: I don't think there will be any storm at all. I fancy that Robertson Nicoll — (by the way, he is running Annie Swan for all he's worth) — & Wallace will do their worst. And their pals in the Scots press will do theirs: so that many estimable folk in Scotland will remain for years under the impression that my Burns is a kind of vocal Phallus — as it were a Singing Prick. But, as I've said, my work is *done*; & in ten years time all these audacities of mine will be sheer commonplace. Commonplace so common that none will be at pains to unearth them.

I must tell you of a delightful development: yesterday morning the postman delivered a big envelope, with an address couched in terms so insolent as the writer — a Glasgow gent — could make. It contained, no word but, *a small assortment of toy obscenities*. If I've reached so far home as *that*, I think I may well sing *Nunc Dimittis*.

The English prints are mostly heart & soul with me. But here's the rub: the English public doesn't give a d—n for Burns. I don't blame it: it has so much besides! Even the Wallace admits that Burns is not exactly Shakespeare: though he finds a 'tender beauty' in the first six lines of *The Jolly Beggars*. Even old Grosart,[5] though he believes in Mary Campbell's[6] maidenhead & is prepared to differ here & there & everywhere, admits that my Burns is a man. So, old chap, on the whole, I think *we'll do*. You builded better than (I think) you knew when,

---

[2] *Scotsman*, 27 September 1897.

[3] 'To seek a comparison from the art of painting, the work is like a picture by Meissonier, so accurate in detail, so much in little space, pathetic and serene. Every word of it is well felt and well written' (*Scotsman*, 27 September 1897). The French painter and sculptor Jean Louis Ernest Meissonier (1815-91) was greatly collectable during his lifetime. In his *Views and Reviews: Art* WEH dismisses him with: 'His merits are obvious: so obvious that no millionaire can go wrong with him.'

[4] William Wallace (1843-1921), barrister and editor of the *Glasgow Herald*, 1906-09. William Wallace, ed. *The Life and Works of Robert Burns*, ed. Robert Chambers, 4 vols, (Edinburgh, 1896).

[5] Alexander Balloch Grosart (1827-99), Presbyterian minister and Elizabethan scholar.

[6] One of Burns's mistresses. She and Burns were going to elope but she suddenly died. After that she was to become a person of outstanding memory to many Scots. WEH tried to show her as he thought she was, a peasant girl ready to elope with Burns. He was affected by the attacks on his view of Mary Campbell that he and Henderson replied with 'The cult of Mary Campbell' in the *New Review*, June 1897.

long years syne, in the smokingroom at George Square, you told me that your Burns was the last of old Scotland. Anyhow, that's the view of him that has got to stand. And it has taken Henderson & me three years to build the beggar his Pyramides.

I hear that those letters which we couldn't get are merely documents in so far as Dumfries is concerned. They will *never*, so I'm told, get into print. The shock to puir auld Scotia would be too great.

If you come to London *sans* seeing us, then we shall hold you false, man sworn, middering, rot — in fact a Common Burnsite. So beware!

Yours Ever, dear Bruce,
W.E.H.

To William Archer, 21 November 1897
ALS: BL

Stanley Lodge, Muswell Hill, N.

My dear Archer,

Glad that Valentine[1] approves. Tell him to be sure to get the right kind of pallor — a seaman-beggar's tan with the livid quality that comes of Rum & hard living. The corkscrew curls quite natty, too, & the brass wrist-buckle bright & worn with an air.

Gaunt *should* be old fashioned. Kit a generation later by all means. If Gaunt wears shoe-buckles, let them be of iron. Pew's should be of brass — very smart; but his crab-shells as *avachis* & degraded as you please.

As for the Prologue:[2] here it is. If you like it — well. Get it put into type, & print it on your programmes. I am not yet pleased with it (I should think not); but I may better it in places, if you give me a proof . And, if Miss Robins[3] finds some verses too full of syllables, I can easily prove to her that none is, — if she will give me the chance. For the rest, do as you like. Exactly. Like it (that is) or lump it. And, if you can suggest improvement, buck & fear not.

---

[1] The actor Sydney Valentine (1865-1919) played Pew in a production of WEH and RLS's *Admiral Guinea* at the Avenue Theatre, London, 29 November 1897.

[2] Two printed copies of WEH's *Prologue to Admiral Guinea*, amended by WEH and Archer are in the British Library.

[3] The American actress Elizabeth Robins (1862-1952) and William Archer had formed a new theatre company called the New Century Theatre and *Admiral Guinea* was their second production with Elizabeth Robins reading the *Prologue*, though apparently not with much enthusiasm.

Whether *The World* be wise or not, I am sure, dear Archer, that you've done your best & kindest, & that your great reward would be the recognition of the *Admiral* as an evening billster.

Yours Ever,

W.E.H.

Have you the *Lyrics*? If you haven't, let me know.

To Charles Baxter, 22 November 1897
ALS: Glasgow Mitchell

Stanley Lodge, Muswell Hill, N.

My dear Charles,

(1) The only copy of *The M.M.*, Ed. 1 — the only one of any interest — is with Bruce. It is unique in that it is annotated by Scott-Douglas — who knew his Burns down to the ground, & had access to *MSS.* which the prudery of modern owners has withheld from *us*. What *I* have is a careful transcript: made for reference & press.

(2) This I will send, of course. But before I send it, I should like to talk the thing over with you.

(3) As for the prospectus: I can't write it till I can recover a certain lamentable (but rather thorough) account of the thing in *The Burns Chronicle* by David M'Naught[1] (David the Son of Nothing). The story of *The M.M.* is obscure. But the book is accepted (with groans & tears & upheavings of the bowels of compassion) by Good Burnsites. And even Henderson was moved to write (in *The Centenary Burns*) that it is 'probably almost certainly', Robert's work. It consists of ninety-five numbers: some acknowledged Robert, some old with retouches by Robert, some old with never a touch of Robert; & is of the very highest interest both as a note on the quality of Robert's mind & a reflection of the mind of the Scots Peasant reacting against the tyranny of the Kirk. It is, in fact, the most remarkable book of bawd I ever saw. Lewis would have wallowed in it; & everybody who reads it will do the same. I will gladly preface & annotate it, & *sign my work*: partly (a) because I would rather die than let so remarkable a book get lost; &, partly, (*b*) because I want to give your sainted step-brother-in-law another 'sweet morsel' to chew for the rest of his days.

(4) How near it came to being utterly lost you'll realize when I tell you that (*a*) Burns's copy is the only one I've ever seen of the *Princeps*; & (*b*) it has been often reprinted, & in every reprint has lost a lot of its original virtue; so that the

---

[1] D. M'Naught, 'The Merry Muses of Caledonia', *Annual Burns Chronicle and Club Directory*, February 1894. WEH is mistaken about the Christian name, it is Duncan MacNaught, the editor of the *Chronicle*.

last (which I haven't seen), is probably a common bawdy book, with nothing distinctive in it. This so true that we (Henderson & I) were attacked with the utmost fury for our references to the book by a wretched bugger who'd only seen the late (say the second) Edition, & was eager to believe, for Robert's sake, that there could be no other.

(5) Them's my sentiments. Now let us meet & talk. Business.

E.A.Y.
W.E.H.

[*Added by WEH at top of the letter*] I hope you read & liked the *Essay*. I confess *I* like it. And I read it yesterday for commas for a reprint (at a shilling) to be issued on the Bard's birthday. Not a word to recall.

H.

4. The Final Years: 1898-1903

With his resignation from the editorship of the *New Review*[1] Henley entered upon a period of his life when he no longer wielded the editorial pen nor controlled the literary fortunes of his young writers. His *Poems* was published in January 1898 and was well received. Henley then began to concentrate on a variety of literary projects but he was constantly hampered by ill-health.

He worked with the painter William Nicholson on *London Types* (1898) and collaborated on a selection of Wilfrid Blunt's poetry with George Wyndham (1898). He was on the move again, this time to the seaside resort of Worthing on the Sussex coast. Here he wrote a monthly article for the *Pall Mall Magazine*, which included his 'assassin' article on Stevenson in December 1901. The Boer War fired him to write patriotic verse which appeared in the *Sphere* and was also published as *For England's Sake* (1901). He published his lyrical *Hawthorn and Lavender* (1901) and started on an edition of Shakespeare which was completed by Walter Raleigh. He also worked on editions of *Smollett* (1899-1901), *Fielding* (1903) and *Hazlitt* (1902-04). In 1902 the Henleys made what was to be their final move, this time to Woking in Surrey. An accident while boarding a train left him severely shaken and contributed to his further poor health. His last published literary work was his *A Song of Speed* (1903) in praise of the motor car. He died on 11 July 1903.

---

[1] The *New Review* had ceased publication in December 1897 with the following announcement:

> With the present number Mr. W. E. Henley resigns his editorship of *The New Review*. This step is forced upon him by uncertain health and the necessities of his own literary work. In consequence of his retirement it is not intended to continue the publication of *The New Review* in its present form An entire break will be made with the past. Shape, price, style, mode of publication — all will be changed

To C. Lewis Hind,[1] 11 January 1897 [1898]
ALS: Huntington
Private

Stanley Lodge, Muswell Hill, N.

Dear Hind,

Your letter gave us both great pleasure.[2] Good news is always good news; & it does not always travel fast. So that we found your idea of a special messenger one of peculiar happiness.

You do me honour — truly — in selecting any work of mine for distinction; and, on the whole, I am glad that the work you have selected for distinction is the Burns Essay. Yet I am half-disposed to wonder why it wasn't *English Lyrics*. For, to be perfectly honest, I do think the book quite the best bit of work I ever did.

It is a good thing, though, that you have distinguished the *Burns Essay*: good for me & good, I take it, for Burns. The thing has been grossly misrepresented; & your award will set people — even Scots people — reading it for its own sake; so that what I believe to be the real Burns — what, at any rate, is demonstrably nearer the real Burns than anything else I've seen — will begin to take shape in people's minds. And in this way Burns & letters & humanity itself will profit.

Yours Sincerely Always,
W. E. Henley

---

[1] Charles Lewis Hind (1862-1927), journalist, sub-editor of the *Art Journal* (1887-92), editor of the *Pall Mall Budget* (1893-95) and the *Academy* (1896-1903).
[2] In January 1898 the *Academy* awarded prizes for the best two books of 1897. WEH received the second prize of fifty guineas for his *Burns Essay* and the actor, poet and playwright Stephen Phillips (1864-1915), one hundred guineas for his *Poems* (1897.

To Wilfrid Scawen Blunt, 21 January 1898
ALS: Meynell

Stanley Lodge, Muswell Hill, N.

Dear Blunt,

G.W. has conveyed your views to me. They are natural enough, I own. And I hasten to confess that the sole culprit is myself. Since my illness last year, my health has been wretched, & my working hours have been so few, that I am a good eight months behind my second Byron.[1] Heinemann has just as much reason to complain of me as you have, as you see; yet to keep myself free for his work I've refused more commissions than I care to say. There is the matter

---

[1] WEH's 'second Byron' was, in fact, volume 5, *Verse Volume 1*. Although announced as due to appear in April 1898 it was never published.

in a nutshell.

I hoped to have the selection ready for the Autumn season. I will certainly have it ready for the Spring. I wish I hadn't to excuse myself; but I must, & on these grounds.

I fear this place does not agree with me, & that I shall never be better till I get away from it. However, Byron II is nearing the end at last, & when it is out of hand, I can take you on — as I meant to do years ago & I will. And, on the whole, I think you'll find you haven't lost by waiting.

Yours Very Sincerely,
W. E. Henley

To Charles Whibley, 28 January 1898
ALS: Morgan. Part published in Connell, 333-4.

Stanley Lodge, Muswell Hill, N.

Dear Boy,

I haven't written (1) because I've fallen into a lethargy, & (2) because I'd nothing to say. Yesterday, I got, however, a letter from Bill Blackwood, who wants you to write for *Maga*. Why not, in effect? Write to W. B., 45 George St., & propound your notions. He wants me to write for *Maga*; & I wish I could.[1] But I seem [un]fit to write for anything.

A sheet of Wednesday's *Scotsman* sent herewith.[2] It should make you smile. That blackguard half-breed, Story,[3] takes the cake, of course. Nothing more

---

[1] In a letter to Blackwood WEH writes that he 'might take on Dickens' (WEH to William Blackwood, 25 January 1898, NLS). However, although he was advertised as the author of a Dickens in Blackwood's *Modern English Writers* series, no such book was completed.

[2] *Scotsman*, 26 January 1898. A leader commenting on the various Burns Night celebrations made reference to Henley's 'now notorious Centenary Biography' and continued that:

> He [Burns] should at least have justice. It will probably be the sentence of posterity, if posterity indeed concern itself with the matter — it is certainly the judgment of contemporary Scotsmen — that Mr Henley has dealt sparingly in generosity and even in justice in his estimate of Burns; that his essay, brilliant as it is as a literary exercise, is an essential failure in so far as it attempts to penetrate to the heart of the man, or to give the 'form and impress' of his time, class, and surroundings; that it approaches Burns in a mistaken spirit and attitude, and that it contains, and even when one accepts the writer's point of view, needless causes of offence... . If wrong has been done, the pity should be, not for Burns, but for his critic, who will be the real sufferer.

[3] Robert Herbert Story (1835-1907), cleric. Principal of Glasgow University, 1898-1901 and Chaplain-in-Ordinary to Queen Victoria, 1886-1901. In his address to the Rosebery Club he remarked:

offensive was ever uttered. Think of the Dear Thing being brought out of her grave for the edification of a parcel of half-drunk Common Burnsites! The desecration is unpardonable. Of course it was done by a cleric.

Provost Glover (of Dumfries) is less fully reported (worthy man) than he deserved. Said he: — 'It is the laborious verbiage of an acclimatized Cockney cuckoo, hatched in Gloucester — (laughter) — & now perchance perched upon the dizzy heights of Muswell Hill, from which, if inclined, he might take a periodical flight of libidinously sportive imagination, & wing his way to the pleasantries of St. John's Wood. The nightly *battus* there might tempt his Muse, & in a spirit of enquiry amidst the gay garments of much negotiable virtue', etc, etc. Hadn't they a beano? Now, *hadn't* they? Meanwhile, the *Essay* sells, & sells, & sells. Nothing, in fact, is wanted but Arthur's official announcement to me the best abused person in England.

Please note that (1) 'Common Burnsite' & 'Bare-legged Beatrice' have come to stay, & (2) that none of these gents has a word for 'bonnie Jean'[4] & very few a word for Highland Mary.

We have taken to breakfasting at noon, & starting the working day at two o'clock. I am hideously sterile & lethargical: perhaps an effect of this monstrous winter (I've worn no waistcoat for days). I hope so; if it be not, I'm dished. I weary of annotating *English Bards*.[5] It must be done, but I'll make short work of *Harold* I & II. Ted is on his way home — too ill, I fear, to do much more. He arrives on Monday — is it? Anyhow, he arrives. Saw Bruce tother night, but we'd so much to say that nothing at all got said. Tell Marcel, I want to write, but can't yet energize a reply to his last. Give him my love, & tell me how he goes. There's no more news of the Civil List.[6]

Without desiring to intrude on the sacred domain of a man's private life, he might say that Mr. Henley had been in many ways extremely unfortunate, and that at the time he was probably just beginning his work on Burns, he was smitten to the ground with the sorest affliction that could try a man of his temperament and character — the death of a daughter to whom he clung with profound tenacity and affection.

[4] Burns's wife Jean Armour.
[5] For his *Byron*.
[6] WEH had resigned from the *New Review* in December 1897 due to ill-health and pressure of literary work. Moves had been made to obtain for WEH a Civil List pension. George Wyndham and Rudyard Kipling were independently putting WEH forward for the pension (Treasury file T1/9250/7195, Public Records Office, Kew). Among those supporting the award were Barrie, Conan Doyle, Hardy, Henry James, and Yeats. Kipling had written to Wyndham on 17 December 1897 stating that: 'I don't think many folk realize how hard up W.E.H. must be sometimes. ... He does very big work and gets no particular sort of prices. Moreover, all his life he has been supporting other people — sometimes of his own family and sometimes outside it' (Kipling to George Wyndham, *The Letters of Rudyard Kipling*, ed. T. Pinney, 2, 326-37). On 29 April 1898 WEH, 'In recognition of his literary merits and of his inadequate means of support', was awarded a Civil List pension of £225.

Anna has had a touch of the grippe, & just now is out for the first time these ten days. I do hope you elude the brute.

Yours Ever Affectionately,
H.

To William Blackwood, 29 January 1898
ALS: NLS

Stanley Lodge, Muswell Hill, N.

My dear Blackwood,

(1) Many thanks indeed. I hope to take on your *C.D.* It would give me very great pleasure to set him in what I conceive to be his proper place — as well as a very great honour. But health's not what it was, & such time as mine must be given, this good while yet, to the wicked Lord B-r-n. So you mustn't be too sanguine.

(2) As to R.L.S., I feel sure that, as a publisher, you are wise & right; & I am pleased to find you falling in with my suggestion that a good youngster is better, far better, than an exhausted hack. Write, then, to Leslie Cope Cornford,[1] c/o Lieutenant Hill, R.N, Cheyney House, Sheerness. (He is just now getting up & taking on the Navy — on Rudyard K's advice.). If you give him the man, I shall look after the book, of course; & so, I doubt not, will others. So you'll certainly get a novel & living thing.

(3) Have you yet a man for Thackeray? If you haven't, I believe I can give you the very best in the world.[2] At all events, I can give you the man *I'd* pick, if I were on the judgement seat. Let me know; &, if I may further obtrude myself, let me know about your *George Eliot.*[3] I don't believe in the withered hack. But I do believe in good work; & I think — I am sure, indeed — I know where to get it.

(4) I've writ to Whibley,[4] & I doubt not that he'll write to you. Fitzmaurice-Kelly, of whom, I think, Hepburn Millar spoke to you, appears to me to have read everything & certainly writes with any amount of brio & gest & style. He

---

[1] Leslie Cope Cornford (1867-1927), trained as an architect but later became a novelist. From 1906 he was on the staff of the *Standard*. He was naval and military correspondent of the *Morning Post*, 1914-18. Cornford produced *Robert Louis Stevenson* for Blackwood's Modern English writers series (Edinburgh, 1899). WEH's help is acknowledged in the Preface.

[2] In a later letter to Blackwood (4 February 1898, NLS) WEH suggested Charles Francis Keary. However, Charles Whibley wrote the *Thackeray* (Edinburgh and London, 1903).

[3] Sidney Lee was to have written *George Eliot*. The book, though advertised in the *Modern English Writers* series, was not published. Sidney Lee, born Solomon Lazarus Levi (1859-1926), Shakespearean scholar and editor of the *Dictionary of National Biography* from 1891. He was knighted in 1911.

[4] 28 January 1898 (Pierpont Morgan).

is busied just now on (a) a monumental reprint of the princeps of *D. Quixote*,[5] in the style of the *Cambridge Shakespeare*[6] & (b) a short history of *Spanish Literature*; so that probably he won't attack you for some little time. When he does, though, cherish him; for he's worth it.

(5) As for Colvin's R.L.S.:[7] if I'm alive, I'll certainly take it on for you. But God alone knows, when it will be ready. You shall have due notice of it — if I'm alive. And that's all I can say.

(6) I wish that poor dead woman hadn't committed *Maga* to such a frightfully reactionary view of the *Centenary Burns*.[8] For a real bit of Ebony on the book would just now, I feel, have done much, especially for Burns. However, it's past praying for now.

Yours Ever Sincerely,
W.E.H.

PS.
Reading this over. I am amazed by my own impudence in suggesting this name & that. But I can't help it. The truth is *I should have been a Scot*: & then — who'd have noted it.

[5] *Don Quixote de la Manche. Primera edición del texto restitudio, con notas y una introducción por J. Fitzmaurice-Kelly y Juan Ormsby*, 2 vols (1898, 1899).
[6] *The Works of William Shakespeare*, ed. W. G. Clark and J. Glover, 9 vols (Cambridge and London, 1863-1866), known as the Cambridge edition.
[7] Colvin was writing the authorised biography of RLS but after disagreements with Fanny and Lloyd Osbourne over the delay he relinquished the task and edited RLS letters.
[8] Margaret Oliphant's review in *Blackwood's*, April 1897.

To Robert Fitzroy Bell, 6 May 1898
ALS: Yale

Stanley Lodge, Muswell Hill, N.

My dear F.B.,
We shall be pleased indeed to see you! To-day I feel almost alive; &, though I've work on hand which I can never do in time, I don't feel like prussic acid when I think of it. Which is a point gained. As to our coming to London: well! if we must, we must. But of course you'll come to us — won't you?

I wish I could see you for an hour any where, for I want to talk to you as Primrose Leaguer.[1]

I don't know if you remember certain articles on Imperialism by one C. de

[1] The Primrose League was founded in 1883 by Lord Randolph Churchill and others in memory of Disraeli to further Conservative aims.

Thierry in the late *N.R.*[2] Anyhow, I've revised them very carefully, the attacks on Joe have been suppressed,[3] the eulogies on H.M. & the Great Earl[4] remain, the thing is timely, apt & useful. I am to preface it with a few words.[5] And I thought of suggesting to the writer that he would do well to dedicate it to the Primrose League.[6] Would the P.L. respond? The bookling (Duckworth) is published at 1/6 (I think) more for honour & glory than Oof, & would distribute brilliantly & well.

Tell me your thought. If you like I can show you the sheets. Meanwhile, I am keenly interested in the matter, & have spent as much time & pencil on it as on at least three numbers of the late, unique, the never-to-be-forgotten *N.O.*

Our love to you both.

Yours Ever,
W.E.H.

[2] C. de Thierry [Mrs J. (Weston) Campbell], 'Imperialism', September and October 1897.
[3] Joseph Chamberlain.
[4] Queen Victoria and Disraeli.
[5] Introduction, *Imperialism*, by C. de Thierry (1898).
[6] 'To / The Primrose League / in admiration of / its principles, its aims / and its effects. / C. De T.'

To William Heinemann, 13 May 1898
ALS: Harvard
Private.

Stanley Lodge, Muswell Hill, N.

My dear Heinemann,

Many thanks indeed. And now for something else. I am in a difficulty, & I want your advice, &, if it may be so, your help. Felix Semon[1] has sentenced my brother, E.J.H., to the Adirondacks; he must get there as soon as ever he can; & he wants to raise £200 or so to that end. If he could borrow privily, his wife — who has an admirable engagement, (American) which starts in August, would engage to give a loan upon her salary (it begins at £50 a week & goes on to £60) of £50 per month so that the whole thing would be cleared off by Xmas next, interest & all. The syndicate, in whose engagement she is, is of the highest character (I forget almost, but I think she calls it 'the Boston'), but, for obvious reasons, she doesn't want to anticipate her salary. The questions are (1) Is such a

[1] Sir Felix Semon (1849-1921), physician. Teddy Henley was told to visit the Adirondack Mountains in New York State for his health. In a later letter WEH asked Heinemann for a loan of £200 (16 May 1898, Harvard). However, WEH did receive at least £50 from Heinemann (WEH to Heinemann, 19 May 1898, Harvard).

security as she can give marketable? And (2) can you, as my friend (&
practically, the only man of business I know, excepting S.S.P.) tell me where the
market, if it exists, is to be found.

Again, this failing, it has occurred to me that Mrs. E.J.,[2] whose life is a perfect
one, might emulate C.W., & invest & borrow on the investment. Will you tell me
if that be so? She is a good honest creature (though an American), &, though a
vagabond, she bears an excellent name in her profession. Do think the thing out,
& tell me all you can. I'm anxious to help, & I don't know where to begin. That's
the fact. And I come to you as an infant bleating in the night.

I got Murray II. It's not ill done, & it has many more letters in it than
Heinemann I. Prothero pays me in his Introduction as handsome a compliment as
one man could inflict upon another.[3] Look it up, & rejoice on it. I've lots to say,
but I won't say it here. All I will say is that we are not beaten yet.

If you'd rather talk than write about this business of E.J.H.'s come any day
you please. Breakfast, 12. noon; supper 8.0 p.m.

Yours Ever,
W.E.H.

---

[2] Baxter in a letter to RLS (23 May 1891, Yale) wrote: 'our respectable friend...Ted has
married another lady, never having been legally married to the Padley.' There is nothing to
suggest any illegality in his marriage to Kate Grace Padley and no reference has been found, so
far, to a second marriage.
[3] WEH meant vol. 1 which was published in May 1898. The second volume was not published
until November 1898.

> No one can regret more sincerely than myself — no one has cause to regret — the
> circumstances which placed this wealth of new material in my hands rather than in
> those of the true poet and brilliant critic, who, to enthusiasm for Byron, and wide
> acquaintance with the literature and social life of the day, adds the rarer gift of giving
> life and significance to bygone events or trivial details by unconsciously interesting his
> readers in his own living personality.

(Prothero, R. E., ed., *The Works of Lord Byron 1*, vi). Rowland Edmund Prothero (1851-
1937), politician and writer. The two editions were being published simultaneously but due to
copyright problems WEH did not publish beyond volume one. There was talk of collaboration
between Heinemann and John Murray but nothing came of it.

To John Murray,[1] 12 August 1898
ALS: Murray

Stanley Lodge, Muswell Hill, N.

Dear Mr. Murray,

Mr. Heinemann has told me of your very generous & kindly action in the matter of a certain article.[2] And I hasten to thank you.

As for the article itself, there is much in it which — frankly — I deserve. I could scarce have believed that bad health, bad eyesight, or bad handwriting, & a bad reader would among these have contrived to make me look so criminally careless. However, I've had my lesson; & I hope it will do me good.

As soon as I am really myself again,[3] I purpose to call on you in Albemarle St (I want to see the famous screen). But it won't be for some time yet.

Yours very sincerely,
W. E. Henley

[1] John Murray (1851-1928) became head of the firm in 1892. He edited *Byron's Correspondence* (1922). Created K.C.V.O. in 1926.
[2] Walter Sichel's 'The Two Byrons', *Fortnightly Review*, August 1898. In his review of the two editions of Byron Sichel states that 'Prothero's range of supplementary knowledge is infinitely wider' than WEH's.

Heinemann's undertaking, on the other hand cannot pretend to compete with Mr. Murray's in material. In all regards we have been woefully disappointed . . . . notes appended by him are slipshod and incorrect, sometimes pretentious and misleading, usually of at least second impression, and seldom scholarlike or solid . . . the general slovenliness of the whole, attest the forced manner in which the volume seems to have been rushed through to the press. . . .

In closing we beg Mr. Henley not to take any of our strictures amiss. They are dictated neither by captiousness nor disrespect. We honour Mr. Henley's capacities so much and had looked forward so eagerly to his editorship of *The Byron Letters*, that the disappointment has been proportioned to the anticipation. If we are wrong, he will set us right. But if we are not, we can only wish that he had approached this enterprise with a little more care, a little more research, a keener penetration, and a deeper sense of responsibility.

[3] WEH had had an operation in late May or early June of this year for piles. In a letter to Whibley WEH remarks that: 'There is nothing for it but an operation. So next week, if I can work it off, I purpose to submit my rectum to the knife (or whatever it is) of H. P. Dean' (25 May 1898, Pierpont Morgan).

To H. G. Wells, 2 October 1898
ALS: Illinois

Steine Villa, Seaford, Sussex[1]

My dear John Wellington,[2]

This from the (no longer) groping hand.

We shall leave this region soon. Our house maid has eloped with a local builder under peculiar agonizing circumstances. What will become of it all I know not (but can guess). Meanwhile, we must also church it. In what direction? *Chi Lo sa*? Meanwhile, communicate no more till you hear you safely may.

Meanwhile, what's the matter? Why is the 'ome un-'omely?[3]

I went out yesterday, & have been coughing ever since. Also bronchial-tubing. I — the Presence — no less! And if the Presence lives up to his bronchial tubes, then, by God, you have a spectacle which can never be enjoyed by *me*.

I am getting mighty sick of it — Presence though I be. However — — — !

Yours Always,
W.E.H.

This life is mysterious. For instance; Why should we have come to Seaford to find a local builder who wanted our housemaid? Why should we have had a housemaid whom nothing would satisfy but a local builder? And housemaids, are they all — but no! The question is too vast, too spacious, too — *enfin*! And the Local Builder; in the Abstract, in the Concrete, subjective & objective; has relations to Housemaids (a) in general & (b) in Particular; his — — 'O Christ!' (says Whitman) 'this is mastering me'.[4] Make it a novel, & Pinkerize it.[5] As for me, I will speak no more.

---

[1] The Henleys were on holiday from before 16 September (WEH to Whibley, 16 September 1898, Pierpont Morgan).
[2] A joke reference to the character in Gilbert and Sullivan's opera *The Sorcerer* (1877): 'Oh! my name is John Wellington Wells/ I'm a dealer in magic and spells.'
[3] Wells had moved to Beach Cottage, Sandgate, Kent, late September/early October 1898.
[4] 'O Christ! My fit is mastering me!' from Walt Whitman's 'Song of Myself' (verse 37, line 1) in his *Leaves of Grass* (1855).
[5] The literary agent James Brand Pinker (1863-1922), who included Wells and Conrad among his clients.

To William Blackwood, 10 October 1898
ALS: NLS

5 West View, Seaford, Sussex[1]

My dear Blackwood,

A horrible cold — in head & chest — has made a wreck of me; or I should have writ to you days ago. I am still no good; but we have found new quarters, & there I hope to improve apace.

Hepburn Millar has done his 'Kipling' excellent well.[2] He should have had ten pages more. But within the limits imposed on him he is first-rate.

I like the 'Autobiography'.[3] But I want to see the second instalment ere I declare myself.

To finish with *Maga* (for the moment): Next week an old friend MacLaren Cobban publishes his *Angel of the Covenant* — an historical romance of Montrose.[4] It is a capital piece of work, covering the same ground, more or less, as *John Splendid*.[5] A man named Alexander Stuart — a good writer & a good fellow — is anxious to compare the two novelists, Munro & Cobban, in *Maga*;[6] he has broached the matter to your London agent, who seems (they tell me) not considering to take the thing on. If *you*, on your side, will agree, I shall be personally obliged. As I've no doubt whatever that *Maga* would profit, I don't scruple to make the suggestion.

I have seen & talked with L.C.C.[7] Something will come of the interview, no doubt (I've been trying to get to Brighton to be near the fountain head). *What* — exactly what — remains to be seen. Meanwhile, I note that Eve Simpson is publishing a book about R.L.S. in Edinburgh (Hodder & Stoughton).[8] This should be useful. Couldn't we get advance sheets?

Yours Ever Sincerely,
W.E.H.

---

[1] The Henleys had moved here by 8 October 1898 (WEH to Whibley, 8 October 1898, Pierpont Morgan).
[2] 'The works of Mr. Kipling', *Blackwood's Magazine*, October 1898.
[3] Hannah Lynch's unsigned 'Autobiography of a child (chaps I-IV)', *Blackwood's Magazine*, October 1898. Hannah Lynch (1862-1904), Irish nationalist novelist.
[4] Cobban's *The Angel of the Covenant* (1898).
[5] Neil Munro, *John Splendid: a Tale of a Poor Gentleman and the Little Wars of Lorn* (Edinburgh and London, 1898). Neil Munro (1864-1930), Glasgow journalist who wrote historical novels of his native Scotland and published poetry in journals, especially *Blackwood's*. Today he is mainly known for his *Para Handy* stories of a Highland coastal trading boat. He edited the *Glasgow Evening News*, 1918-24.
[6] Stuart's 'Montrose and Argyll in fiction', *Blackwood's Magazine*, January 1899. Alexander Stuart (1859-1909), novelist.
[7] Cornford was at Ovingdean Grange, near Brighton.
[8] Eve Blantyre Simpson, *Robert Louis Stevenson's Edinburgh Days* (1898). Evelyn Blantyre Simpson (1856-1920), writer and sister of Sir Walter Grindlay Simpson.

To Lord Windsor, 13 October 1898
ALS: Morgan

5 West View, Seaford, Sussex.
My dear Lord Windsor,
I should have writ before; but I've been having the vilest of times. We got to Seaford a month syne; & for some days all went well. Then I caught cold; then I began to cough; then I started to run down, & ran — ran — ran. Till I was about as good a man as when you called on me in Southampton Row.[1] Then we left that house — which, we found, was putid with dry rot — & came to this one which at any rate is clean, & where I am already beginning to pick up a little. If we can, we shall presently remove to Brighton; & there — for the cough has rather frightened us — there, it may be, we shall winter.

It's horrid bad luck, is it not? Especially as I had begun, & more than begun, to be sure of a useful autumn. But there it is, & I can but make the best of it.

All manner of thanks for the birds. My wife; who is allotted to such matters, joins with me in the strongest terms.

Have you read *The Day's Work*?[2] There is some of Rudyard's best in it. And does Lady Windsor sing? Because, if she do, I'd like to ask her acceptance of a certain album; five songs of mine set by Francis Korbay,[3] whom she may know (he teaches singing at the R.A.M.);[4] & set, so far as I can see, quite admirably.

George Wyndham writes that he is *not* to go to the F.O. And the news depresses & angers me no end. Of one thing I am glad & for one thing truly thankful: I am not a politician *anyhow*.

Forgive this blast of egoism, & believe me,

Yours Ever Sincerely,
W. E. Henley

---

[1] The Henleys were at Russell Mansions, 144 Southampton Row, for a short period (WEH to William Blackwood, 20 June 1898, NLS). The flat belonged to Christina Steevens.
[2] Rudyard Kipling, *The Day's Work* (1898).
[3] Francis Korbay, *Five Songs from 'A Book of Verses' by W. E. Henley* (1898). The poems were: 'Bring her again, O western wind'; 'Thick is the darkness ...'; 'While the west is paling ...'; 'The full sea rolls and thunders ...'; and 'Out of the night that covers me,'. Francis Alexander Korbay (1846-1913), composer.
[4] The Royal Academy of Music, London.

To H. G. Wells, 28 October 1898
ALS: Illinois

5 West View, Seaford, Sussex
My dear Wells,
Thank you for your letter. I wish you had seen him, the astonishing creature that he was.[1] Even in London, all voiceless & pulled down, he created an impression which sets men wondering that he *can* be dead — so instant was his magnetism, so abounding his temperament. I shall always believe that no English-speaking actor since Edmund Kean[2] had so high a gift as he.

I am a bit better this last day or two, & we shall go hence — unless I back down again — early next week. To Muswell Hill, of course; *en route*, I hope for Brighton.

Have you seen *The Day's Work*?[3] Some of it is really magnificent. See me on it in to-morrow's *Outlook*: my first deliverance since the end of May.

Yours Ever,
W.E.H.

[1] Edward John Henley had died of tuberculosis of the throat at Lake Placid, New York, on 16 October 1898. He seems to have been a gifted actor but wasted his talents.
[2] Edmund Kean (1787/90-1833), famous Shakespearean tragic actor.
[3] WEH reviewed it in the *Outlook*, 29 October 1898. This was the weekly journal which replaced the *New Review* in 1898; it lasted until 1928.

To Lord Windsor, 28 October 1898
ALS: Morgan

5 West View, Seaford, Sussex
My dear Lord Windsor,
We haven't succeeded in lodging ourselves at Brighton. But we are in treaty for a house; & it may be that we shall succeed in pulling it off. Meanwhile, we go back, early next week, to Muswell Hill.

No: I haven't read *John Splendid* yet. It waits me at home, & I shall to read it soon. It is a success, I hear. But I must read it ere I can join. I know Munro only as a writer of short stories thus far; & he is sometimes excellent indeed. Do you remember a certain 'Jus primae noctis' in *The New Review*?[1] If you missed it, 'twould pay you, I think, to look it up. To my mind it is a little *chef d'oeurve*.

As to Rudyard, he annoys me. I've spun some words about him in this week's *Outlook*; but they seem to me insignificant & vain. I want to call the critics up, & give them three dozen apiece for daring to differ from so notable a performance.

[1] Neil Munro's short story 'Jus primae noctis', *New Review*, June 1897.

There's some rubbish in the book, of course; but not to recognize 'The Ship that Found Herself' & 'The Brushwood Boy' for things unique in literature seems to me criminal. How I long for the old *National Observer* when I read such turpitudes! In its day the wretches went in dread of their skins. Now....!

I hope that Lady Windsor duly received the songs. The first ('Bring her again, etc') has been set a round score of times, at least — notably by an American,[2] whose name I forget. But this one seems the best, so far. The others, two, are still better, or so it seems to me — greedy of music with a personal, vibrant note in it. Pray let me hear if they have hit.

Since you wrote, George Wyndham has taken the W.O.,[3] & is swelling round with the Sirdar[4] — no less! He writes, too, in excellent spirits. I think, for my part, that he must do well wherever he goes; & I am content in the thought. But, all the same, it ought to have been the F.O.

Yours Always Sincerely,
W.E.H.

[2] Mrs H. H. A. Beach, 'The Western Wind,' *Songs, op. 11* (Boston, 1889). Amy Marcy Beach, *née* Cheny (1867-1944), the first serious American woman composer.
[3] Wyndham had been appointed Under-Secretary for War.
[4] Horatio Herbert Kitchener (1850-1916), 1st Earl Kitchener. As a Major General he was appointed Sirdar or Commander-in-Chief of the Egyptian army in 1892. After a successful campaign in the Sudan he returned to London on 27 October. He served in South Africa during the Boer War.

To H. G. Wells, 24 February 1899
ALS: Illinois

9 Park Crescent, Worthing[1]

Dear Sir,
Your esteemed favour to hand, & a portrait of Mrs. W. E. Henley will be forwarded to your address in the course of the next two days. Meanwhile, permit me to direct your attention to the fact that a copy of a work[2] recently published by me was forwarded for your consideration yesterday, by self & partner, from the distant post office. That work is not, I should add, designed for perusal by the Young; but may be confidently recommended to the mind of riper Years. I trust that it will meet with your approval, I am,

Dear Sir,
Your Obedient Servant,
W. E. Addlehead

[1] The Henleys had moved here on 19 January (WEH to H. G. Wells, 18 January 1899, Illinois).
[2] *Slang*, 4.

To Charles Whibley, 13 March 1899
ALS: Morgan

St. George's Lodge, Chesswood Road, Worthing[1]

Dear Boy,

(1)We go for Urquhart Motteux in 3 vols.[2] So send me dates of (a) Sir Thomas his birth & death[3] & (2) the publication of Bks. 1 & 2. As soon as ever you can.(2) You are pledged to give us your copy by the end of July. And we pay you £50: half on delivery, half on return of proof.

(3) And there you are.

E.A.Y.,
W.E.H.

---

[1] The Henleys had moved here by 4 March 1899 (WEH to Fisher Unwin, 4 March 1899, NYPL).
[2] *Rabelais. Garganta and Pantagruel. Translated into English by Sir Thomas Urquhart and Peter Le Motteux. Annis 1653-1694.* Introduction by Charles Whibley. *Tudor Translations*, 24-26 (1900).
[3] Sir Thomas Urquhart (1611-60).

To Elizabeth Pennell,[1] 8 May 1899
ALS: Congress

St. George's Lodge, Chesswood Road, Worthing

My dear Elizabeth R.,

It seems aeons since we met & talked. Is there never a chance of you wheeling down to us some Saturday? 'Tis an easy day's ride, through pretty country, & Worthing itself, between downs & scars, is, I think, the leafiest place I ever saw. Already this little angle of ours is a delight & a refreshment to the eye, & a few days hence it will be all chestnut bloom, & white & purple lilac, & golden chain. And we get a good twelve hours' bright sunshine day in day out. And blackbird & thrush are at it all the time: as if the world would never grow old, & such things as winter & death had never been.

Meanwhile, we have had bad luck. Matilda, our maid, whom you remember at Croydon,[2] has been sick, well nigh unto death, of typhoid (caught, as we

---

[1] The American writer Elizabeth Robins (1856-1936), who had married the illustrator and lithographer Joseph Pennell (1857-1926), settled in London in 1884. They collaborated on *The Life of James McNeil Whistler* (1908). WEH had met her through Charles Whibley. An account of her friendship with WEH is in her *Nights: Rome, Venice, in the Æsthetic Eighties. London, Paris, in the Fighting Nineties* (1916).
[2] Ashburton Lodge, 29 Ashburton Road, Addiscombe.

believe, in Croydon). The fever has run its course, but she declines, thus far, to get better, & persists — poor wretch! — in indulging in abnormal temperatures. Of course, we've a nurse; but it's pretty bad, all the same.

As for my dear Bruce's death,[3] I will not speak of it. I think I scarce realize it yet — all that he meant to me & all that it means.

How are you both? Do write & give me a little news! And London ... I've a longing to see St. James's Park at Whitsuntide — under the slant rays of a westering sun. How I wish you could see the sunset as I write!

Yours Ever Affectionately,
W.E.H.

[3] Bruce had died on 24 April 1899.

To Bernard Capes,[1] 2 August 1899
ALS: Fales

St. George's Lodge, Chesswood Road, Worthing

Dear Mr. Capes,

Forgive me, please! It was a mare's nest. I thought of the M'Clure-Harper combination;[2] but it appears that you are already of the band.

All the same, I want you to know the new English agent — Leslie Cope Cornford. He is (I think I may say) a pupil of mine; & he's a very good fellow as well as a real man of letters. This without prejudice to A. P. Watt,[3] whose 10 p/c. remains inviolate.

I woke up 'tother morning, about 3 o'clock; & for about a minute & a half the 'Eddy on the Floor'[4] gave me as good a hit of creeps as I can remember to have had. Of course, I'll go through those proofs.[5] Also, I mean to look at the *Lake*[6] again, & see what — if anything — is wrong. I mean, with the style. Of course, if you write carefully — if you write with a care for the *mot propre*, the swing of the sentence, the life of the phrase — the Average Jackass, whose ideal of writing is mere ink-slinging, is sure to call you affected. That's

[1] Bernard Edward Joseph Capes (1854-1918), novelist. He was editor of the *Theatre* from January to October 1890 and co-editor from November 1890 to May 1892.
[2] The American publisher S(amuel) S(ydney) McClure (1857-1949) ran a literary syndicate and published *McClure's Magazine*.
[3] Alexander Pollock Watt (1834-1914) was one of the first literary agents.
[4] Capes's ghost story 'The Eddy on the Floor' in his *At a Winter's Fire* (1899). It has been included in many anthologies the latest being *Victorian Ghost Stories: an Oxford Anthology*, edited by Michael Cox and R. A. Gilbert (Oxford, 1991).
[5] The proofs of Capes's latest novel *Our Lady of Darkness: a Novel* (Edinburgh and London, 1899), an adventure story set during the French Revolution. It was published in September.
[6] Capes's adventure story *The Lake of Wine* (1898).

nothing. I want to read to see if you are with Meredith (who is impossible, *à la fin des fins*) or with R.L.S. When (if ever I manage to do what I want to do) I'll ask you to waste a morning on me. And we'll see.

Yours Always Sincerely,
W. E. H.

How I wish you had been on tap in the days of my hold upon the *New Review*.

To Lloyd Osbourne, 9 September 1899
Copy: NLS[1]

St. George's Lodge, Chesswood Road, Worthing.
Dear Osbourne,
I have no explanations to give, and I am surprised that at this date you should ask for any.[2]
At the time of your first visit to England, after Lewis's death, I declined any further intercourse with your family. I am at a loss to understand why you break in upon me here & now.

Yours very truly,
W. E. Henley

[1] Probably by Graham Balfour (1858-1929), RLS's cousin and biographer.
[2] According to Williamson (267-8) Lloyd came to Worthing to visit WEH but WEH refused to see him and sent his brother Anthony Henley to turn him back at the station.

To Austin Dobson, 6 October 1899
ALS: London

St. George's Lodge, Chesswood Road, Worthing
Dear Dobbie,
Where can I see a copy of Smollett on Habakkuk Hilding?[1] If you can help me, I shall bless you.

[1] *A Faithful Narrative of the Base and Inhuman Arts that were Lately Practised upon the Brain of Habbakkuk Hilding, Justice, Dealer, and Chapman, who now lies in His House in Covent-Garden, in a Deplorable State of Lunacy; a Dreadful Monument of False Friendship and Delusion. By Drawcausir Alexander, Fencing-master and Philomath* (1752). This was a pamphlet attacking the novelist and playwright Henry Fielding (1707-54) for plagiarism, among other things, probably written by Smollett. WEH was writing an introduction to an edition of Smollett published in 12 vols (Westminster, 1899-1901). Tobias George Smollett (1721-71), physician, novelist, poet and political writer.

The summer has been a trying one, & has made me monstrous fat. However, it gave me some verses;[2] the first for many moons. I know not if they be good or bad. But you'll soon be able to judge for yourself.

This is the leafiest, pleasantest place. I would we'd known of it years ago.

How are you? And what are you doing? And the good Cosmo? My love to you both, anyhow.

> Yours Ever,
> W.E.H.

[2] These verses were published as 'Hawthorn and Lavender: Songs and Madrigals' in the *North American Review* for November 1899, June 1901, and September 1901. They were subsequently republished in book form as *Hawthorn and Lavender with Other Verses* in October 1901.

To H. G. Wells, 8 December 1899
ALS: Illinois

> St. George's Lodge, Chesswood Road, Worthing

Mr. H. G. Wells,

Dear Sir,

Our leading literary journal having described you as 'unutterably dull',[1] I write these few lines, hoping you are well as it leaves me at present, to inform you that there must be an end to our acquaintance.

As, however, I do not wish to part company in an unfriendly spirit, I take the present opportunity (1) to ask you how you are, & (2) to intimate to you that, if you wish to keep yourself abreast of the intellectual movement of the epoch — (as distinguished from its mere *announcement*, by propagation of *pseudo-scientific stories*) — you will find, in the *North American Review* for November certain verses which I believe will make you rather wish you expressed yourself in anything but — (what seems to you but is *not*) prose.[2]

> I am, Dear Sir,
> Yours Faithfully,
> W. E. Henley

[1] In a review of Wells's *Tales of Space and Time* in the *Athenaeum*, 2 December 1899, the reviewer wrote: 'The usual grocer or chemist or bank-clerk sees extraordinary visions, and has unusual experiences, and we have another glimpse of the world as represented in *When the Sleeper Awakes*, which we feel convinced Mr. Wells has elaborated after a wearisome contemplation of the Great Wheel; but all his conceptions seem to us unutterably dull.'

[2] In a letter to WEH (4 February 1900, *The Correspondence of H. G. Wells*, ed. David C. Smith, 1998, *1*, 351) Wells writes: 'You say things I feel & understand & you say them better than I could imagine them said....This of yours is organic. It is life, surging.'

To Charles Whibley, 15 December 1899
ALS: Morgan. Part published in Connell, 345-46.

St. George's Lodge, [Chesswood Road,] Worthing

Dear Boy,
No: the end of the year is the end of the year. There is plenty of vitality in the first 3 weeks of January; & you will find yourself advertized for 'early in February'.[1] So play up.

We want no Marlborough. A Clive or two would do us. A few Baden Powells[2] mightn't be so bad. What we want above all is a War office: with a competent chief. What we want is an army of mounted infantry & field artillery, with (as I said) a few Baden Powells 'up'. We shall do the thing in our own way & at our own time, of course. But we shall pay our own price for it. That is plain.

E.A.Y.
W.E.H.

'Clemmy' is an excellent, an admirable suggestion. But I don't want to ask for his beastly book unless I am certain of a result.[3]

---

[1] Whibley's *Rabelais*.
[2] Robert Stephenson Smyth Baden Powell (1857-1941), a successful soldier against the Boers. He later founded the Boy Scout movement. Created a Baron in 1929.
[3] Possibly the second edition of Clement Shorter's *Victorian Literature: Sixty Years of Books and Bookmen* (1899).

To Charles Whibley, 11 March 1900
ALS: Morgan. Part published in Connell, 349.

St. George's Lodge, Chesswood Road, Worthing

Dear Boy,
The Rabs. goes out on Monday. If there be any point you'd like brought out (any point in your *Introduction*, I mean), write a line to James Fitzmaurice-Kelly, 14 Palace Gardens Mansion, W., who has it for the *Post*

Nutt writes that my copy was special, & that you & R.A.M.[1] came off only yesterday.

I've doctored Motteux his advertizement, & decided to print his translation of the *Pro[g]nostication* & the *Letters*.[2] I am sure you'll agree with me.

---

[1] Bob Stevenson.
[2] *The Fifth Book of The Works of Francis Rabelais, M. D. ... containing Heroic Deeds and Sayings of the Great Pantagruel to which is added the Pantagruelian Prognostication,*

Skeat[3] says, Will you write to him (St. James's Place, S.W.)?

I am posting my ditty to Marlowe to-night.[4] I think of bringing out a sheaflet (7 numbers in all; *England, my England* among 'em) in a neat *plaquette* within the next few days.[5] So look out for me, & keep me at least a paragraph.

The more I think things out, the more am I convinced that Kruger & Steyn[6] are mad. Also, that the common (or garden) Boer is a common maniac. Did you see, by the way, the *Pall Mall* for Saturday, with its true story of the pro-Boer 'M.A.Oxon',[7] who is a form-master at Cheltenham? It licks even Kruger & Steyn. I've never read anything like it in my life.

I am sending *Rabelais* to H.C.[8]

E.A.Y.
W.E.H.

Tell me what you think of my idea of a *plaquette*.[9]

Rabelais's Letters and Several Other Pieces by that Author. (1694). Translated by Peter Anthony Motteux (1660-1718).
[3] Walter William Skeat (1835-1912), scholar of Old and Middle English. Professor of Anglo-Saxon at Cambridge from 1878 until his death.
[4] Thomas Marlowe (1868-1935), managing editor of the *Daily Mail*, 1899-1926.
[5] WEH's *For England's Sake: Verses and Songs in Time of War* (1900). The booklet consisted of twelve poems.
[6] Marthinus Theunis Steyn (1857-1916), President of the Orange Free State, 1896-1902. Stephanus Johannus Paulus Kruger (1825-1904), President of the Transvaal, or South African Republic, 1883-1900, and leader of the Boers.
[7] A report in the *Pall Mall Gazette*, 10 March 1900, on correspondence in the *Gloucestershire Echo* concerning a schoolmaster at Cheltenham College who gave three hundred lines as a punishment to a boy who stamped his feet at the news of the relief of Ladysmith from the Boers.
[8] Harry Cust.
[9] A thin booklet.

To William Blackwood, 30 March 1900
ALS: NLS

St. George's Lodge, Chesswood Road, Worthing

My dear Blackwood,

Very many thanks for yours. I look forward to *Maga's* pronouncement on Smollett.[1] I am pretty sure that the retort will be better reading than the provocation.

---

[1] *The Works of Tobias Smollett* was reviewed in *Blackwood's Magazine* for May 1900. The reviewer remarked: 'What he [WEH] did for Burns he has done on a smaller scale for Smollett', and 'we thank Mr. Henley for the final edition of a great English classic'.

I think, & think again of titles for G.W.S. Vol. I.[2] As thus: —

>Miscellaneous
>Things Seen
>.Impressions of Men, Cities, & Books
>A Journalist's Leavings

& so on. These, if you like, might be adapted thus: —

>Things Seen
>being
>Impressions of Men, Cities, & Books

or thus: —

>Men, Cities & Books
>Impressions (or Things Seen)

or thus: — but no! I'll try no more now. In a day or two I'll send you a couple of suggestions for title-pages complete.

I don't yet know (being sore ber-sted) how long the introduction will be. Probably it will run to 20-25 pp. Certainly no more. It should be with you — I fear to promise having so much on hand, & so little working time; but it should be with you about the middle of next month.

Meanwhile, you have the body of the book.

>Yours Always Sincerely,
>W.E.H.

What price

>Pulvis et Umbra
>Men & Cities & Books?

[2] Steevens was the *Daily Mail*'s correspondent in South Africa and he died of typhoid at Ladysmith on 15 January 1900. Blackwood published an edition of his works in seven vols (1900–02) which his widow dedicated to WEH. Steevens's tombstone at the municipal · cemetery in Ladysmith bears the four-line verse that WEH wrote for the book.

To Clement K. Shorter, 5 April 1900
ALS: Brotherton

St. George's Lodge, Chesswood Road, Worthing

My dear Sir,

Do you care for yet another — next week? It is called 'The Last Post',[1] & pretty well completes the little cycle of lyrics — of a kind — on which I've had no choice but to busy myself of late.

'Tis in two stanzas: of eighteen lines apiece. Don't, please, mind saying no, if you'd rather not have it; as I mean to make a *plaquette* of it & the rest, & put it before the public very soon.

Yours Very Truly,
W. E. Henley

Clement K. Shorter Esq.

---

[1] WEH's war poem 'The Last Post' was published in the *Sphere* for 21 April 1900. He published two others in the *Sphere*, 'A Song of Empire', 17 February 1900 and 'The Levy of Shields', 24 March. All three were included in his *For England's Sake*.

To H. B. Marriott Watson, 18 April 1900
Text: Payen-Payne, 45-6. Published in Connell, 350.

St. George's Lodge, Chesswood Road, Worthing

My dear Marriott,

You builded better than you knew. I learn from Cobban, that all things ended for him this morning; and I am glad in the knowledge.[1] There could have been no worse thing in life than for that brilliant and far-soaring spirit to have passed through all the gradual humiliations of dissolution. And, as I say, I am glad that the end came thus mercifully and soon.

I don't know that I can be of any use; but if you think that I can, you have but to take me on, and tell me what to do. I rather fear that any demand for a pension might fail; but I see no reason why we should not ask for a grant. Indeed, I have already laid myself out (so to speak) in that direction. Meanwhile, I know nothing but what you, and Cobban can tell me. So please, dear Marriott, tell me all you can.

Who is to tell of him in the Press?[2] By God, it makes me sick to think of the

---

[1] Bob Stevenson had died on 18 April 1900 following a stroke.
[2] WEH wrote of him in the *Pall Mall Magazine* for July 1900. In this article he acknowledges Bob Stevenson as the creator of 'art criticism in England' and finds him a greater man than RLS. WEH revised the article as 'A Critic of Art' in his *Views and Reviews: Art*.

hundreds of appreciations there were of his cousin, and the few, the very few, that can come of him.

Your affectionate,
H.

To Charles Whibley, 22 April 1900
ALS: Morgan. Published in Connell, 350

St. George's Lodge, Chesswood Road, Worthing

My dear Boy,
Yes: it's a sickening business. I haven't written to Louisa, for the simple reason that I could find nothing to say. When a man has been so dear & near as Bob was to me, the best is silence. I shall try to say a few words about him in my next *P.M.M.* But God knows how it will come out. It will be better, I hope, than Colvin on (Raleigh) 'the relict of R.L.S.',[1] anyhow. I hope that you also will write, & in *Maga*.[2] If you do, do not — I ask it as a favour — forget that you owe the writing Bob to *me*, & that, as I believe, none else could have brought him into being.
Come as soon as ever you can. And the sooner you send your copy the better for us all. It is woefully late; but once I get it I shall cease grieving.

E.A.Y.
W.E.H.

[Added by WEH at the top of the letter] Louisa declines to let us ask for anything from the C. List.[3]

[1] Colvin's obituary notice on Bob Stevenson in the *Pall Mall Gazette*, 20 April 1900.
[2] Whibley wrote of Bob (without mentioning WEH): 'He was always a profound philosopher: he laughed at most things, and understood them all...Now he would dazzle you with the fireworks of paradox, now he would speak with the daring of Rabelais and a mercurial gaiety which was all his own.' ('Musing without Method', *Blackwood's Magazine*, June 1900, reprinted in his *Musings without Method*).
[3] She later changed her mind and was awarded '£100 per ann. On the Civil List, & £50 from the Royal Bounty' (WEH to Whibley, 6 March 1901, Pierpont Morgan, quoted by Connell, 359)

To H. G. Wells, 25 April 1900
ALS: Illinois

St. George's Lodge, Chesswood Road, Worthing

My dear H.G.,

I will say but this: your letter brings him nearer to me than I had ever dreamed that anything except his resurrection could.[1]

Will you not — must you not — ought you not to — cast so notable & so great an impression of him into permanent form?[2] To me your duty is clear.

It matters not when: this was no R.L.S., who after all, was but an ordinary human being: one of ourselves, with a style & a more insolent & commanding selfishness. This was the man the nearest God I've ever seen, or shall ever see. It is for you, surely, who have so keen & so large a vision of him to make this plain. Some day — soon. Not too soon. But soon enough.

I shall try to say a little in the *P.M.M.* of what I feel. Unhappily, he is no loss to me — as he is to you. I lost him years ago; & my great bereavement, which came after, made me indifferent to most things under the visiting moon; or I might have tried to get back upon the old familiar terms, & have taken up life again in the old affectionate way. It was not to be; & I can but faintly appreciate what I missed. However, It was inevitable. Yet I loved him till the end, & till the end, whether he knew it or not, I championed him. And I think that in his wise, scarce human way, he loved me.

Your picture of him is a joy — of a kind. I want you, if you will, to send one to Walter Raleigh, 63 Canning St., Liverpool; to whom, if I may, I wish to show your letter.

It is almost time — isn't it? — for a migration from Sandgate westwards? I'd like to tell you how I made him write: I mean, write for the press: & so become influential & self-supporting. But that's a story will keep.

Write & tell us a little about yourselves.

Yours, my dear H.G.,
W.E.H.

Have you heard of the post-mortem? Cobban wrote of it to me. But that again is for another day.

---

[1] Wells's letter concerning Bob Stevenson has not been found.
[2] Wells briefly described Bob in his *First and Last Things* (1908) and in his *Experiment in Autobiography* (1934) he writes that 'Bob's style of talk was grafted on to' the character of Ewart in his novel *Tono-Bungay* (1909).

To Graham Balfour, 20 June 1900
ALS: NLS

St. George's Lodge, Chesswood Road, Worthing

Dear Mr. Balfour,

No: I can't help you at all.[1] I remember vaguely some thing of the kind, but I am pretty certain it never came off. Lewis was always full of schemes & plans & fancies. You left him hot on one, &, the next time you saw him, you found, to your distress (having gone all the way with him) that he'd forgotten all about it. I take it that here is a case in point.

In any case, if the thing came to a head, I think that Baxter would have a note of it.

Perhaps Lewis's cousin, Katharine de Mattos, may recall those times better than I. She was at Skerryvore a great deal then — or I am much mistaken. Indeed I remember that she & Lewis were at one time engaged on a comic Zolaism — *Ce sacré Illingsworze*,[2] or words to that effect — the fun of which consisted largely, if not wholly, in the application of Zola's distemperate & exorbitantly lecherous view of art & life to Bournemouth. This was possibly an outcome of the design which Lewis mentions in his letter. At all events, you might possibly apply to the lady with advantage. I don't know her address; but c/o Mrs. Stevenson,[3] 41 Oxford Rd., Chiswick, would certainly find her.

Thank you very much for what you say about myself. I have long hoped to meet you. Perhaps — through Barrie, say, — I may presently get my wish. Meanwhile, I am sure you will be interested in what I've written about Bob — my dear old friend — in the July *P.M.M.* published to-day. If you read it, & like it, I hope you'll tell me.

Yours very sincerely,
W. E. Henley

[1] Balfour's official biography *The Life Of Robert Louis Stevenson* was published in two volumes in 1901.
[2] The comic letters mentioned in WEH's letter to RLS of 28 July 1886.
[3] Bob's widow.

To Sidney Lee, [August/early September 1900]
ALS: Bodley

St. George's Lodge, Chesswood Road, Worthing

Dear Mr. Lee,

I am sorry to have misrepresented you, & especially sorry (if I may so) to hear of it so late.[1] I will most certainly make you such amends as I may; but I cannot now say anything in print until the December issue of *The P.M.M.*, which appears about the middle of November.[2] Had I heard from you a week ago, I would have been a month earlier. As it is, there is nothing, I fear, for it but waiting.

I should tell you that I had already heard, from 'Thormanby'[3] (I do not know his real name) that you had been more catholic than Leslie Stephen. Unfortunately, his letter found me far away from home, so that I could not verify & *préciser* his statements.

I note that you 'harp & carp' at my use of the word 'Lewis'.[4] Of course you've every right — &, it may be, every provocation — to do so. I don't defend the use of it, whether humorous or not. I will but remark that neither Byron nor Keats would have objected, neither Wellington nor Palmerston;[5] & I'm quite content to be d—d in their presence.

Yours Very Truly,
W. E. Henley

---

[1] In a postscript to an article, 'Ex Libris. Old England', in the *Pall Mall Magazine* for September 1900 WEH had criticized the *DNB* for its poor treatment of sporting personalities. Lee, in a letter now lost, protested at this slight. WEH wrote the 'Ex Libris' column in the *P.M.M.* from July 1899 to February 1903.

[2] In the December issue of the *P.M.M.*, WEH made a reserved apology in a postscript to another article, his reservation being that 'in the matter of sport, the *D.N.B.* has not been altogether so well guided as it might have been' ('Ex Libris. Brown the Poet').

[3] Thormanby [W. W. Dixon], *Boxers and their Battles* (1900), one of the books discussed by WEH in the September *P.M.M.*

[4] In his article on Bob Stevenson WEH had referred to RLS as 'Lewis'.

[5] Henry John Temple, 3rd Viscount Palmerston (1784-1865), Prime Minister, 1855-58, and 1859-65.

To the Editor, *Cornhill Magazine*,[1] 8 October 1900
ALS: NLS

St. George's Lodge, Chesswood Road, Worthing

Dear Sir,
   I am obliged by your request. But for the moment I have nothing to offer you. My verse, being mainly lyrical, is a matter of moods; & of late these have been rare with me; & for the two or three lyrics I have on hand, I fear that none is worth your while.
   If anything comes to me, I shall not hesitate to accept your invitation. But I grow more & more scrupulous; & I fear that you will have to wait.[2]

Yours Very Truly,
W. E. Henley

The Editor,
The Cornhill Magazine,
Etc.

---

[1] Reginald John Smith (1857-1916), barrister and publisher. Editor of the *Cornhill Magazine*, January 1898-1916.
[2] WEH did not contribute any verse.

To John Stephen Farmer, 12 October 1900
ALS: Morgan

St. George's Lodge, Chesswood Road, Worthing

Dear Mr. Farmer,
   Yours is indeed the hardest of cases. I wish I could help further. But I've just lost half my income, & must fend for myself. All the same, I'll see if there is nothing to be done outside.[1]
   If my name & influence as a signatory be of the least use with the R.L.F.,[2] please do your best with them. I say this because there are those who found them useful.
   As for the fiver, when you can pay it, please do so. I haven't any doubt but that I'll be very glad to get it. But don't let it distress you — not for a moment.
   If the dictionary could be done, & done soon, I think you'd score heavily.

---

[1] Farmer was constantly lacking funds. With a previous letter WEH had sent £5 to Farmer (2 October 1900, Pierpont Morgan). Farmer had made a previous application on 27 June 1899 to the R.L.F. and received £75.
[2] WEH did not approach the R.L.F. on Farmer's behalf until 1903 (WEH to L. Roberts, 4 May. 1903, RLF archives).

So when *you* are ready, *I* am. You will tell me — won't you? And, as you are comparing, I had better do all the revision I can in *MS*.

Yours Very Sincerely,
W.E.H.

To Lord Windsor, 16 October 1900
ALS: Morgan

St. George's Lodge, Chesswood Road, Worthing
My dear Lord Windsor,
    I have been ailing of late: ailing in mind & body. Or I'd have writ before.
    You are right in surmizing that I am not desperately interested in Ruskin.[1] The fact is, I never 'took' him: I knew naught of him at the proper age & stage; & when I began to know him I was under other influences. But I read you with respect: I thought your plea for him neither ill-considered nor excessive. I recognize the fact, that he made us all attempt to feel, & that some are very much the happier for his passing. At the same time I realize — I can't help realizing — that he was all wrong: that he did more for the 'literary' picture & more for the 'painter-poet', than any man that lived; & I am strongly inclined to hold that those who got good out of him, got it in his despite, & simply because they were built that way'. He persuaded people to feel — more often than not, very much more often than not, on false pretences. But he persuaded them to feel — or to think they felt; & among them were certain, better gifted than himself in the matter of feeling & perception, whom he set going. That I take to be his sole merit as an art critic. For the rest, he did his best to bedevil painting, pretty much as Wagner has done *his* best — but at first hand — to bedevil music: by teaching his public to look at it for a thousand anti-pictorial qualities, & to despise in it — Constable, Rubens, Corot, Van Dyck, Claude, Gaspar Poussin, Jan Steen[2] — such essential qualities as it has. *Et puis voilà!* You have learned of him, & there you are: you consider him dispassionately, but on the whole with kindness. I've spent a number of years in fighting him & in damning his evangel, & here I am. And 'so', as Touchstone says, 'we measured swords & parted'.[3] He has given me much trouble & is responsible for much foul work & for some fortunes got on false pretences — with consequences on the other side that proceed from these results. But, honestly, I can say that I'm glad he was, & that I wish there were more like him. If we had but one on the right side, for example!
    But a truce to Ruskinism — *pro & anti*. I wonder if you are interested enough

---

[1] Ruskin had died on 20 January 1900.
[2] Claude Lorraine (1600-82), French landscape painter; Gaspard Dughet (1615-75), French landscape painter, adopted the surname of his brother-in-law Nicholas Poussin. Jan Steen (c.1626-79), Dutch painter.
[3] *As You Like It*, V. iv. 85.

in slang to help a man who is compiling a big book on it who is just now at dead low water. His name is John S. Farmer; & for some years past he has been engaged, with my assistance, on a book called *Slang & its Analogues*, of which four volumes have already appeared, & of which the remaining two are fairly on their way to completion. It is not a work for Drawing room tables; for slang is of its essence obscene. But it is, of its kind, the best there is; & I believe that Murray, of *the* Dictionary, has just used & quoted it, & has said that, so far as it goes, it's all right. Meanwhile, Farmer has published other things, & has just now broken down completely. An application to the Literary Fund for immediate relief was supported by Furnivall, Gollancz,[4] & Sidney Lee; but at the last meeting there wasn't a quorum & so it was postponed till some time in November. I've done what I could — which isn't much; & now it occurs to me to come to you. If you could help him with a gift, so that he could tide over the next few weeks — (he has, I needn't say, a wife & family) — *Slang & its Analogues* would be nearer, perceptibly nearer, completion than it is. If you aren't interested in the subject — which, to be sure, is very lewd, base & astonishing, & goes to my head like Milton's English — then forgive me my suggestion & let us say no more about it.[5]

We have beaten them royally, but I'd have liked a few gains more. Anyhow they're eaten up, & we can work out our policy in S. Africa in peace.[6]

Ever Yours Sincerely,
W.E.H.

[4] Israel Gollancz (1864-1930), Shakespearean scholar, Professor of English at King's College, London, 1905-30, and a founder member of the British Academy in 1901 and its first Secretary.
[5] In a letter to WEH Farmer thanks his unknown benefactor (Lord Windsor) for £10 (17 November 1900, Pierpont Morgan). He also writes that he had received a grant from the RLF though he did not stipulate the amount (£75).
[6] The Transvaal had been annexed by the British on 1 September 1900 and it was assumed that the end of the war was imminent.

To R. Murray Gilchrist, 3 January 1901
ALS: Morgan

St. George's Lodge, Chesswood Road, Worthing

My dear Mr. Gilchrist,

I owe you a letter since — how long? I had a rather not try to calculate. But I know it's an inconsumable time, for the thought of it has more than once been with me in the watches of the night.

I read *The Courtesy Dame*[1] — (this, after all, is what I wanted to say) —

[1] Published 1900.

with very great pleasure. It has character & atmosphere, & is excellently written. You are going steadily up & up; & 'tis not without a sense of pride that I watch your ascending. I remember how I backed you long ago, & I rejoice to know that I was justified in you, as in so many more.

As for me, I am a kind of walking imposture. I look well, but have wretched health. I talk bravely, & do nothing. I cannot hope nor believe that the New Century has much in the way of work in hand for me. But I both hope & believe that he looks for much to you. And I do not think he will look in vain.

With every good wishes.

> Yours always truly,
> W.E.H.

PS.
I had hoped to say something of the *Dame* in print. But I 'got left'.

To John Stephen Farmer, 15 February 1901
ALS: Morgan

> *St. George's Lodge, Chesswood Road, Worthing*

Dear Mr. Farmer,

(1) A line to say that I posted *N* slips in a registered parcel to-day. (2) I've just had occasion to consult the *Century*[1] under '*N*'. I find that many of our quotes are taken from it. I am sure the source of these should be acknowledged in our page.

(3) I came on a phrase unknown: 'Night-liner' = a night-walking cab. I think that whether English or American, we should take it in.

(4) What price '*Non-est-inventus*' (= Absent)?

> Yours Very Truly,
> W.E.H.

---

[1] *The Century Dictionary of the English Language*, 6 vols, ed. W. D. Whitney (1890-91).

To Grant Richards,[1] 5 March 1901
ALS: Fales

St. George's Lodge, Chesswood Road, Worthing

Dear Mr. Richards,

I've been miserably seedy for some dozen days. But I can now look forward to a better time.

I daren't open Wareing's parcel till to-day.[2] But I think his work is excellent. I know it's all I wanted.

I've given him the names of two more Shakespeares — both cheap — which I think we should have in hand.

The Furness *Variorum*[3] is excellent — as far as it goes. But it don't go more than a third of the way.

As to the Prospectus: I must do a play before I know anything about it.

Haven't you raised a new poet? If you have, I wish you'd send me his book.

Yours Very Truly,
W. E. Henley

[1] (Thomas Franklin) Grant Richards (1872-1948), author and founder of the publishing firm of Grant Richards.
[2] Alfred J. Wareing (1876-1942), actor and theatre manager. Founder of Glasgow repertory theatre 1909, and Librarian of the Shakespeare Memorial Library, Stratford-on-Avon, 1931-33. He assisted WEH on his edition of *The Works of Shakespeare*, The Edinburgh Folio, 10 vols (1901-04). The task was not completed at his death and Walter Raleigh completed the edition. Grant Richards in his *Author Hunting* (1934, 44) refers to WEH's 'Edinburgh Shakespeare — a folio that was a failure in everything but appearance'.
[3] Horace Howard Furness, *A New Variorum Edition of Shakespeare*, vols 1-15 (Philadelphia, 1871-1907).

To Lord Windsor, 5 May 1901
ALS: Morgan

St. George's Lodge, Chesswood Road, Worthing

My dear Lord Windsor,

The Dante Society has asked the Cavaliere Agsto Sindici[1] to lecture on the dialect of the Campagna Romana: the dialect & the legend: & to illustrate the lecture with some of the sonnets in which, writing in the very speech of the Campagna — which he has been studying since Solferino — he has embodied some of the legends of the Campagna. Heinemann, whose father-in-law the Cavaliere is, asks me to preside.[2] I would gladly do so but (a) I know nothing

[1] Augusto Sindici (1839-1921), Italian poet.
[2] Heinemann had married Donna Magda Stuart Sindici in 1889 but they were later divorced.

of procedure in such matters, & (b), what's an hundred times more important, I know nothing of Italian; except that I read Dante & Boccaccio long years ago. So I have declined the honour; & I write to beg you, as one of the very few Englishmen who know anything at all about it, to take the place which, had I been able to fill it, I should very gladly have taken. In your stead.

The lecture — *causerie* — call it what you will — is down for (I think) the 22*nd* May.[3] It should be extremely interesting. Heinemann, who came down to me yesterday, purposes to call on you to-morrow — or whenever he may; & he will tell you more than I can. In any case, I hope I wrong nobody if I say that I hope to learn that you are interested.

I learn that Willeby[4] has gone to St. Fagan's I hope he'll pick up a few tunes there, & set them to my verses. They are not the worst I've done. But one's ever dissatisfied.

Yours Ever Sincerely,
W. E. Henley

The Sindici — Sindici — appears to be a distinguished, a really distinguished poet. It seems that in Italy one can be so: in dialect. I read the other day, for instance, of one Belli,[5] who ran the life of Rome into sonnets in the Roman tongue. And of course there's Meli[6] in Sicilian, & several gents in Venetian. And this speech of the Campagna seems to be the most wonderful of all: as near Latin, I take it, as can be. And yet Italian. 'Tis an odd business: here's Leopardi,[7] writing Roman-Tuscan, & Belli writing Roman, & Baffo[8] writing Venetian, & the Cavaliere Sindici writing Campagnesca; yet all are classic, all are formalists, all are Italian. A sonnet in pure Yorks, a Cardiff (St. Fagan's) English, or my own native Gloucestershire, or what is left of the lingo of Burns — what would it be worth? 'Tis, in truth, a most curious business.

---

[3] No report of the Dante Society appears in *The Times* for May 1901. The A.G.M. was held on 5 June 1901 at the Pferiffer Hall, Harley Street, London

[4] Charles Arthur Henry Willeby (1870/71-1955), composer. He set some of WEH's poems to music.

[5] Guiseppo Gioacchino Belli (1791-1863), Italian poet, well-known for over two thousand poems in the Roman dialect.

[6] Giovanni Meli (1740-1815), Sicilian physician and poet.

[7] Giacomo Leopardi (1798-1837), major Italian poet.

[8] Franceschina Baffo, sixteenth-century Venetian poet.

To H. G. Wells, 21 May 1901
ALS: Illinois

                    St. George's Lodge, [Chesswood Road,] Worthing
My dear H.G.,

I sympathise — deeply — ; & I hope you gave Lloyd Sanders beans.[1] There were so many — too many — omissions! But we'll have it all over again presently; on a bigger scale. And then — you'll see.

On the whole, I thought Lloyd did his work excellently — so far as he did it at all. There's lots of me which he knew nothing about; & he was silent as to these; while, on the other hand he ignored some things that were well within his purview. But his article, I really think, is the first to put me on my feet for what I am — or, rather, for what I was. And he had but three days to do it in. And he did not consult (as he weeps to me) the faithful Dunn. 'Tis pity. But even so, the Historic Figure (if I may say so), begins to take on shape & substance; & I am content.

Have you seen, or heard of, Nicholson's portrait?[2] Painted by subscription? And now on view at the F. A. Society's rooms in Bond St? He purposes to make a wood-cut of it; & again I am content. A most genial work; & an excellent bit of painting.[3] If you haven't seen it already, you must come presently, & see it here.

Did my Missus write to yours? She said she did; but God He knows the truth of things — He, & only He. Anyhow, my Missus is away North — to Glasgow, Annan, East Linton. If I could move, I should be a gay widower. But I can't; so I'm not. And there you are!

---

[1] Lloyd Sanders' article (with a photograph) on WEH in *Literature*, 11 May 1901. Sanders wrote of some of the writers published by WEH but omitted to name Wells.

[2] A portrait of WEH entitled *Man of Letters* (now in the Tate Gallery) on view at The Fine Arts Society, Bond Street, London. The painting was later on show at the Third Exhibition of the International Society of Sculptors, Painters and Gravers at 191 Piccadilly from 7 October to 10 December 1901. Wells saw the portrait in October and wrote to WEH that: 'I have seen the Wonderful, the Glorious, the Incredible, the Dazzling, the Simply and Altogether True, the Final and Only Possible Portrait of yourself' (*Correspondence of H. G. Wells, 1*, 382).

[3] This is in strong contrast to his views of a woodcut of the portrait later in the year [reproduced in M. Steen. *William Nicholson* (1943)]·

'Tis an enormous disappointment. The grace, the wit, the gaiety, the personality of the picture have departed with the colour (especially!) & the size; & its defects are exaggerated to an extent which makes the reproduction impossible.

To come to details? I shall name but one. Note the extraordinary monotony — the abnormal want of *moulding* — in the right side of the face. From tip to bottom, the surface is the same. It is hard to tell flesh from hair, & there's no feature left. 'Tis all one dabb of sameness. That the painter should think it good enough surprizes me not a little, & distresses me more. Probably he's tired of his work. But that's no excuse for such a show on his sitter, & none for such an affront to his patrons' (WEH to Sydney Pawling, 6 September 1901, University of Virginia).

I happened on a *Strand*⁴ the other day; & found you, as ever, intent on blood & wounds: — 'Confusion, honour, murder, guts, & death'.⁵ Have you a set of proofs you can lend me? If you have, pass 'em along, Sir! Pass 'em along!

You too, by God's help, & in God's name, are going to be jolly happy. At least, I hope so. And if I hope aright, I can wish you no better than to go in the same old idiotic, triumphing way —

Yours Ever, my dear,
W.E.H.

⁴ Wells's 'The First Men in the Moon' in the *Strand Magazine*, December 1900-August 1901.
⁵ 'Vengeance! plague! death! confusion.' *Lear*, II. iv. 91.

To William Paton Ker,¹ 23 May 1901
ALS: London

St. George's Lodge, Chesswood Road, Worthing

My dear Ker,

Rags? But such rags! I was just wandering how to approach you (on my bended knees, of course), when these 40 pages came in. For God's sake, go on, go on. Rags or not, these are what's wanted. At the printing office. Just now.

Your Second Volume should reach you soon. A real monument, Ker — a monument! Over 500 pp.; yet lovely to look upon, & weighing less in hand than Billy Heinemann's latest novel.

I — what am I doing? I don't know. I've been writing verses. Lyrics. Novels in metre. Rot. *I'll* never do anything worth remembering. Not me. Also, I am supposed to be editing a Shakespeare. Now, Ker, lay your hand, your good right hand, upon your heart, & answer me candidly: — Is there anybody in the world who is less fitted to edit Shakespeare than I am? If there be, produce him; & we'll do the trick together.

You must come, & eat with me, soon. My wife's away. But I dare say we can vittle you all right. Meanwhile:

Rags — & rags, — & rags again.

Yours Ever,
W.E.H.

¹ William Paton Ker (1855-1923), scholar and author. Professor of English Literature, University College, Cardiff 1883-89 and Professor of English Language, University College, London, 1889-1922. He was writing the introduction to *The Chronicle of Froissart. Translated by Sir John Bouchier, Lord Bervers. 1523-1525. Tudor Translations*, 27-32 (1901).

It reminds me of the excellent Elizabeth Bellwood:[2] —
    Rags & bones was all that was left
    Of the man that struck O'Hara!

I don't know why. 'Rags', I take it ... The human mind!

[2] Bessie Bellwood, stage name of Elizabeth Ann Katherine Mahoney (1847-96), ballad singer and music hall artist. The lines quoted by WEH come from the chorus of 'The Man That Struck O'Hara' written by J. F. Mitchell, composed and sung by Walter Munroe. The lines should read: 'Rags and bones were all we left / of the man that struck O'Hara.'

To Sydney Southgate Pawling, 26 August 1901
ALS: Virginia

St. George's Lodge, Chesswood Road, Worthing
Dear Sydney,
    They're all right.[1] There's a heat about them, a force, an authority of sincerity, which brings 'em home. Home to me, anyhow. As to the Public, I say nothing — knowing even less. But therein you're an expert, ain't you?
    I'm up to the eye-brows — worse luck — in Iwan's *M.S.*[2] 'Tis a curious work. Very interesting; not well-written; very long. But I think it should do. I've done some 200 pp. word by word, & I haven't come on Milner yet.[3] I hope to get through the pile this week. After which I must fight for my own hand: having more to do than I know how to do, & being bent on a holiday of sorts next month, or early October ... However, I doubt not I'll [   ] through with it.
    The good thing is that my book of verses is out of hand at last. I am reprinting *London Types* in it, & I've dedicated them to an S.S.P.[4] I wonder if he'll resent the impertinence? If he do, there's still time.

Yours Ever,
W.E.H.

PS.
MS. to-morrow. Please note that all this about Iwan's book is strictly *private & confidential.*

[1] *Hawthorn and Lavender.*
[2] E. B. Iwan-Müller, *Lord Milner in South Africa* (1902).
[3] Lord Alfred Milner (1854-1925), statesman. Governor of the Transvaal, May 1897-January 1901, High Commissioner for South Africa, 1897-1905.
[4] WEH's *Hawthorn and Lavender* was dedicated 'To S.S.P.'

To A. R. Waller,[1] 18 September 1901
ALS: BL

St. George's Lodge, Chesswood Road, Worthing

Dear Sir,

I have your address from Mr. Dent.[2] I heard from him this morning that he had asked you to call *at once*. It will give me very great pleasure to make your acquaintance, but for the next few days I am so full that, if you come, we could get no talk. So I telegraphed for your whereabouts; & now I write. I ought to have done so long ago; but I've had much to do, & I've had illness in the house, & been wretchedly ill myself; so I didn't. Please forgive me.

Dent, in writing sent me your Prospectus. 'Tis the first I've seen of it. It tells me that there is much of Hazlitt which I haven't read. I hasten to add that, having no mind for metaphysics — or should I say philosophy? — there is much of *that* which I never read. The *Political Essays* (1819),[3] however, are new to me, &, I take it, are worth reading: so I've writ to Bain[4] for the book. Heaven send he have it!

Could you lend me (1) the *Principal Picture-Galleries:*[5] & (2) the *English Stage*.[6] I have both some where. But I *cannot* lay hands on them. If you can help me to them, I will keep them but for a few days, till the end of the month, by which time I hope that my *petit boniment* [small quack's show] will have got itself done.

Yours Very Truly,
W. E. Henley

A. R. Waller Esq.

PS. I have your address from a telegram. I hope that telegram has not misled me.

---

[1] Alfred Rayney Waller (1867-1922), literary editor and journalist. He was co-editing *The Collected Works of William Hazlitt* (1902-04) for which WEH was writing the introduction.
[2] Joseph Malaby Dent (1849-1926), founder of the publishing firm. He started the successful *Everyman's Library* in 1904.
[3] Hazlitt's *Political Essays, with Sketches of Public Characters* (1819).
[4] The Haymarket bookseller.
[5] Hazlitt's *Sketches of the Principal Picture-Galleries in England. With a Criticism on 'Marriage à la Mode'* (1824).
[6] Hazlitt's *A View of the English Stage: or, a Series of Dramatic Criticisms* (1818).

To Lord Milner, [?November 1901]
ALS: New College

19 Albert Mansions, Battersea, S.W.[1]

Dear Lord Milner,

Iwan-Müller thinks that I may be pardoned for sending you a copy of my new book of verses, & for writing to you to say that I've sent it. It goes with this & I hope (I blush as I write it down; like Sterne's Reporting Angel)[2] — I hope that you'll find bits in it that are not wholly & utterly devoid from literature. Very soon I hope to send you — (but this will be per favour of the Colonial Office) — Vols. 3 & 4 of your *Froissart.*[3] They are an unconceivable time on the way; but each one is 500 pp. solid; & they can't be rushed. If they could have been, they would have been: for you.

Of course I am a beggar; & to this extent. If you receive, from Pagan, Burmah, the papers of a certain Ernest Dawson,[4] who asks for civil employment, I beg you to consider them with a careful & kindly eye. Dawson was one of Lumsden's Horse; was at least once under fire (& wrote of the experience with a modesty & an intelligence that pleased me); got entail twice; & was invalided home — to Woking. There I met him. He is one of those big, blond, sweet-tempered capable Englishmen who never lose heart, nor are ever angry enough on a great just issue; but who end by having their own way (which is England's) with whomever they are set to rule. I read that that is the sort of man you want: the administratory Englishman trained in India. So, violent as it may seem, I do not hesitate to recommend him, 'for all I'm worth', to your notice.

It is absurd in me who have never met you (but I have talked of you, & at you, & about you for hours) to write thus to you: as if I had known you for years. But I must & tell you that the weather here is damnable; that Iwan is magnificent all the time; that George Wyndham teams with ideas, & has (I think) Ireland in the hollow of his left hand,[5] or, (if you'd rather) in his least important waistcoat pocket. As for me, I edit Shakespeare, & may not write of politics. But I think that the Empire is (if I may say so) going strong, & that the Adversary has never a leg to stand on: except such very wooden ones as are

---

[1] 'We've taken a small flat at 19 Albert Mansions, Battersea, & shall move in for a space as soon as we can get the rooms (three & a kitchen) furnished' (WEH to Charles Whibley, 8 October 1901, Pierpont Morgan).
[2] The Recording Angel in Laurence Sterne's *The Life and Opinions of Tristram Shandy, Gentleman,* (1759-67). Either WEH is mistaken over 'Reporting Angel' or he is making a joke.
[3] Dedicated to Milner.
[4] Ernest Dawson (1863-1949), late Captain, Lumsden's Horse. Dawson had transferred from the Upper Burma Volunteer Rifles in Mandalay, where he had served as a Second Lieutenant, to Lumsden's Horse which served in South Africa from 25 March 1900 to December 1900. He had worked in the Burmese Civil Service. He wrote *Some Notes on the War in South Africa, with Reference to Indian Volunteers* (Simla, India 1901).
[5] George Wyndham was Chief Secretary for Ireland from 9 November 1901 to 5 March 1905.

provided by the pro-Boer press. As to which, the last gossip is that the *Daily News* has once more changed editors,[6] etc., & is henceforth (so says Iwan) to be run on the principles of the Sermon on the Mount. Meanwhile, what I want is a new law against traitors & high treason. And if I die without seeing it: without the knowledge that Mr. Blank Dash was yesterday whipped at the cart's tail from (say) Fleet St. to (say) Duke St.; & that Mr. So-&-So stood to-day in the pillory, & lost an eye, & most of his front teeth in the experience; & that Mr. Three-Stars is to-morrow morning at 8 a.m. precisely to lose his head on Tower Hill: if, I say, I don't live to see these methods applied to the very pestilent set of whom I wot, then shall I die a disappointed man.

Forgive my hobbling, & believe me, with ever-increasing admiration & gratitude,

Yours Very Sincerely,

W. E. Henley

---

[6] E. T. Cook (1857-1919), editor from 1896, resigned in January 19012 and R. C. Lehmann took charge until A. G. Gardiner (1865-1946) became editor in February 1902.

To Clement K. Shorter, 19 November 1901
ALS: Quayle

19, Albert Mansions, Battersea, S.W.

Dear Mr. Shorter,

Very many thanks. I see no reason why, if you can endure my politics, we should not come to terms.[1]

Those you offer are not those on which I am 'running the show' just now. But I don't suppose there need be any difficulty over them.

The chief of difficulties is the politics. I don't think I shall ever be more violent than I am to-day. But I must have leave to say what I think needs saying; or there can be no deal.

---

[1] The *Sphere* was publishing 'An Impression of the Week'. WEH was asked to contribute an occasional page, his first being 23 November 1901. WEH contributed seven articles in this series in the *Sphere*, the final one being on 29 March 1902. In his first article WEH dealt with the England cricket tour in Australia, and the Boer War. His violence in politics was directed against the Boers and the British waste of money, as he saw it, spent on concentration camps for Boer women and their families while their husbands and sons were killing British troops. Although critical of the slow progress of the war he believed that the Boers would be defeated.

We are here for some days yet. Perhaps you could come some afternoon, & talk it over.

Yours Very Sincerely,
W.E.H.

To Charles Whibley, 27 November 1901
ALS: Morgan. Part published in Connell, 364.

19 Albert Mansions, Battersea, S.W.

Dear Boy,
    After all — we couldn't get away, *we couldn't*, to-day; & I'd have given no end to know where you were.
    However, bar accidents (*D.V.*, in fact), we go to-morrow,[1] & do not return till there's a prospect of less fog.
    'Tis a great pity that we are so far apart at this moment. But, of course, it can't be helped. There is so much to talk about, though, & (even) so much to do, that it's a pity.
    I've heard nothing of Cust. What he wants, what's his game, what he's up to — all this, so far as I'm concerned, is so much bog. Does he mean to do the Machiavel?[2] I know not. Do you? *If* you do, for God's sake, let me know. And, if you could convey to him the impression that he's shaping more like the Abstract Shit than anyone I've known since R.L.S. — perhaps you may help *him*. I don't expect it will much help *me*. But it might: so take it on. All the same, it will end in Faith: I know it will end in Faith.
    This is writ in fury, Dear Charles; but it is written, also, over a grave[3]: a grave which is ours (thank God!) as well as yours. And the memory soothes & tranquillizes & brightens even as though the *excellent* little creature were there — there with her gaiety, & her strength & her fragility. I cannot tell you how much this passing has affected us. But then we don't need — do we?

E.A.Y.
W.E.H.

---

[1] WEH and Anna were returning to Worthing.
[2] Cust wrote the introduction to Machiavelli's *The Art of War* and *Florentine History. Tudor Translations*, 39-40 (1905).
[3] His daughter Margaret's grave.

To Charles Whibley, 1 December 1901
ALS: Morgan. Part published in Connell, 369.

St. George's Lodge, Chesswood Road, Worthing

Dear Boy,

Ever so many thanks for yours. I cannot write; for the last 24 hours have been a kind of fever-dream: a filthy internal fill, which will not keep its place: and I'm exhausted.

But I must thank you for what you say in *Maga* about me & Hazlitt both;[1] & I must thank you for what you write about me & R.L.S.[2] Of course, I'm not going to queer my pitch by repeating it: you may be sure of *that*. Meanwhile, did you see Colvin in last night's *P.M.M.*?[3] 'O la, Dickey!' The *World* is uncommon nasty[4] (the cutting came to me in an anonymous letter); & our good old George R. Sims is more than sprightly in this morning's *Ref.*[5]

---

[1] Whibley's review of *Hazlitt* in *Blackwood's Magazine*, December 1901. Reprinted in his *Musings without Method* (1902).

[2] Presumably in a letter to WEH. In his monthly article in the *Pall Mall Magazine*, December 1901, WEH had reviewed Graham Balfour's *The Life of Robert Louis Stevenson*. He attacked the public image of RLS, the 'Seraph in Chocolate, this barley-sugar effigy of a real man' as represented by Balfour. WEH wanted to destroy what he saw as the myth and sentiment that had developed since RLS's death and restore, as he saw him, to his rightful position as a man. It was also an attack on Fanny and his anger at RLS's reference in a letter to Baxter (*Stevenson Letters, 8*, 332) to WEH 'starting a gig and a Pomeranian dog' should WEH receive more money from RLS. WEH made much of his own role in RLS's life. His attack draw heavy criticism from the literary world. Many had been aware of a quarrel between the two but not its cause and WEH's own reputation suffered as a result of his outburst of apparent jealousy and he was seen as an embittered man forever in the shadow of his old friend. However, there was support from many of his friends.

[3] Colvin's letter in the *Pall Mall Gazette* (not *P.M.M.*), 30 November 1901, in which he writes that his friendship with RLS was longer than WEH's and that he has no wish to enter into the debate.

[4] 'What the World says,' *World*, 27 November 1901. The writer agrees that RLS's genius has been over estimated but the fact

> affords poor excuse for Mr. Henley's war-dance upon the grave of the friend whose memory he has hitherto been supposed to cherish with peculiar reverence and affection. Humour has never been Mr. Henley's strong point, or he might have been spared the absurdity of gibbeting the remains of his friend and co-worker as those of a vain and selfish egotist in an article which presents perhaps as ludicrous an exhibition of splenetic vanity and aggressive self-love and self-assertion as has ever been afforded by a considerable man of letters.

[5] A letter entitled 'Stevenson's valet on his master and signed 'as above', in the *Referee*, 1 December 1901. It is written in a jocular vein: 'Mr. Stevensons [*sic*] was always a good and generous master to me but I am one who puts duty to the 'Public' before gratitude and have no more hesitation in showing him 'up in his habits as he lived' than Quassiamodo in pushing his kind Patron off his pedastle.'

If you *could* take on *H. & L.* in the 4th page of *The D.M.,* I should take it kindly of you.[6] But don't worrit about it in any case whatever.

E.A.Y.,

W.E.H.

[6] It was reviewed in the *Daily Mail*, 4 April 1902.

To Lord Rosebery, 2 December 1901
ALS: NLS

St. George's Lodge, Chesswood Road, Worthing

Dear Lord Rosebery,

Many thanks for the birds. At this home (which will soon be ours no more) such visitors are ever welcome.

I suppose that some faint rumour of the riot over a note on R.L.S., which I contributed to the current *Pall Mall Magazine*, has reached your ears? If it have, please accept my assurances that I withdraw no word, & that at the proper time, if it ever come, I shall be prepared with more.[1]

Of course I've taken no more notice of these brawlers over R.L.S. than I took of those that brawled over Robert Burns. I believe that I am right in the last case as I was in the first.

Yours Very Sincerely,

W. E. Henley

[1] WEH did not write again about RLS although he gave an interview to the *Sun*, 25 November 1901. He is quoted in this interview as saying:

'I have kept silent for five years against the ill-natured attacks and every kind of innuendo, and I can do this for another five years. This is not the first time that I have fought in a forlorn hope.' The interviewer then asked: 'But in respect to the charges of resentment and disloyalty. Won't you refute them?'

'So much bosh,' said Mr. Henley. 'These gentlemen have not apparently taken the trouble to read my article carefully or in the right spirit, or it would be impossible for them to take such a view of my motives. Some day I may deal with the whole subject in my own way. Until then I can afford to remain and will remain, absolute.'

To Clement K. Shorter, 8 December 1901
ALS: Berg
Private

St. George's Lodge, Chesswood Road, Worthing

Dear Mr. Shorter,

Yours of the 6*th* to hand this morning. So I couldn't telegraph a 'Yes'; nor could I take your lead, as the best part of my 'Impressions' was writ last night.[1]

I fear there's a lot of politics in it. But that this is so is less my fault than yours. I told you, in the beginning, I wanted to talk politics & you said, practically: — 'All right! Fire away'. Hence the politicality of these presents. However, pass this, & I'll do my best to be better next time.

As for my 'critics' (as you pleasantly & obligingly style them); I have nothing to say either *to* them or *about* them. In fact, I don't see where they come in. I have put certain facts on record; and they have hammered me for putting those facts on record. But they haven't trounced my statements, nor have they disproved — they have not even attempted to disprove — my case. So I leave them alone. *When* I take them on — if ever I take them on — I shall want more 'room & verge' than I can get in *The Sphere*. Meanwhile, your readers must long for me, & batten on the stuff supplied by the other side.

Let me thank you — heartily — for what seemed to me the very common-sensible view of the whole proceedings which you sketched in your last number.[2] That, at all events, is the spirit in which, whatever the issue, the controversy should have been, but was not, taken by the *Bandar Log*,[3] the Monkey-House, which calls itself the London Press. It has a fine opinion of itself, that London Press; but I had the Scots Press on me, three or four years ago, in the matter of Burns; & there isn't a pin to choose between the metropolitan & the provincial. Also, in both cases I believe the effect will be the same.

This, with the stuff, is posted (at 8.10; at our G.P.O.) in time for delivery to-morrow (Monday) morning. If I get a proof to-morrow (Monday) night, I can post it so as to reach you by second delivery on Tuesday.

Yours Very Truly,
W.E.H.

---

[1] In his article on 14 December 1901, WEH writes: 'My impression of last week is something blurred, something informal and confused.' He remarks on the successful tour of the Prince of Wales round the Empire and of his speech at the Guildhall. WEH refers to a report in a Brighton paper of a certain Mr Lehmann who spoke at a pro-Boer meeting which ended in uproar despite his praise of British troops.

[2] Shorter's 'A Literary Letter', *Sphere*, 7 December 1901. Shorter in a general essay on RLS notes the 'extravagant laudation' of RLS which 'has brought its nemesis'. He states, in passing, that WEH is not one of those critics who finds that Stevenson is not such a considerable writer 'once he is dead'.

[3] The Bandar Log were the despised Monkey-People in Kipling's 'Kaa's Hunting', one of the stories in his *Jungle Book* (1894).

To Clement K. Shorter, 14 January 1902
ALS: Brotherton

St. George's Lodge, Chesswood Road, Worthing

Dear Mr. Shorter,

Many thanks for yours. I will do my best next Monday. I fear, however, that I am scarce the man you want. I like the work (or I should not do it at the price) & because it keeps me in touch with affairs & the outside world. But it seems to me that politics are the only matter worth writing about just now, & that not to write about them when one has a chance of writing is to range oneself among the flannelled fools & the muddied oafs at once.[1]

However, I'll do my best on Monday; & there after as may be. We come to town next week, & perhaps we may meet, & settle matters once & for all.

Yours Very Sincerely,
W. E. Henley

[1] Kipling, in his poem 'The Islanders' published in *The Times*, 4 January 1902, had attacked the English for their failure to understand the truth about the Boer War and their inaction in finishing it. He attacked the very essence of the English — their love of cricket and football. In a letter to Clement Shorter (9 January 1902, Leeds University) WEH writes: 'For once, I think, the Youth has gone wide of the mark.' Despite this view WEH defends the poem: 'I am an ardent Kiplingite' ('Mr. Kipling and the "Muddied Oafs"', *Sphere*, 25 January 1902). He feels that Kipling had shamed the public in their indifference to the war but that the poem would not have any effect on the war, though he foresees a more efficient army in about ten years time. He was glad that the poem was published but that Kipling was wrong in his hard condemnation of the public. WEH also attacks Alfred Austin's letter (signed A.A.) in *The Times* of 7 January, saying that if he is the Poet Laureate, it is not his job to write against Kipling but to write verse. Kipling referred to 'flannelled fools at the wicket or muddied oafs at the goals' in his poem.

To John Stephen Farmer, 22 January 1902
ALS: Morgan

St. George's Lodge, Chesswood Road, Worthing

Dear Mr. Farmer,

(1) Very many thanks. But it's far beyond a rascal poet like me.

(2) I am sending (a) a box, containing 21 vols. of plays, & Burton's *Anatomy* (3 vols); & (b) a parcel containing Mill's *Pugilistica* (3 vols), an odd but precious volume of *The Fancy, Ireland Sixty Years Since*,[1] which has a whole chapter about slang songs, *etcetera* — among the same a lot of old Tudor proofs, which are worth looking at, & may be cut up. Of these the Plays are of no great importance: the others are, so please deal with 'em at your convenience, & have

[1] [Right Hon. J. E. Walsh], *Sketches of Ireland Sixty Years Ago* (Dublin 1847).

'em ready against the time when we can shelve 'em once again.

(3) I haven't included any Pope:[2] I took a look at the prose, & found nothing but good English. I wish we could somehow land the *Miscellanies*[3] — Swift, Pope, & Arbuthnot; also more of Swift. With these & Brown & Ward[4] we ought to defy chance.

We are thinking of going to Battersea on Saturday (19 Albert Mansions); but I fear we shan't get off till Monday. However ———!

(5) I've several slips from Stockwell this morning, & will work them off as soon as ever I can. To-morrow, in any case, I'll post you divers quots for Please, Pleasure, Punk, among others; so don't close till you get 'em.

Yours Very Truly,
W.E.H.

[2] His best known works are *Essay on Criticism* (1711), *The Rape of the Lock* (1712) and *An Essay on Man* (1733-34). With Swift and John Arbuthnot (1667-1735) he was a member of the Scriblerus Club designed to attack, through satire, the shortcomings of the period.
[3] *Miscellanies in Prose and Verse*, ed. J. Swift, A. Pope, J. Arbuthnot and J. Gay, 4 vols (1727). John Arbuthnot (1667-1735), writer and Court physician to Queen Anne.
[4] Thomas Brown (1663-1704), satirist. He is best remembered for the epigram:

> I do not love thee, Dr. Fell,
> The reason why I cannot tell;
> But this I know, and know full well,
> I do not love thee, Dr. Fell.

Dr John Fell, the Dean of Christ Church, Oxford, had threatened to expel Brown. Edward 'Ned' Ward (1667-1731), innkeeper and writer on London life. His best known works were *The London-Spy* (1698-1709) and *Hudibras Revisited* (1705).

To Arthur Morrison, 25 March 1902
ALS: Rochester

Heather Brae, Maybury Hill, Woking[1]

Dear Arthur,

How would you translate into living slang the dead Elizabethan 'silly-cheat'? 'Tis Autolycus, in *The Winter's Tale*.[2] He hates the highway, he does: his revenue is 'the silly-cheat'. At first I thought it was a kind of reference to a confidence-trick. But I looked into it; & found that 'silly' don't mean 'stoopid', & does mean 'helpless, feeble, wretched' (cheat, of course = lay, trick, fake).

[1] Written on 19 Albert Mansions notepaper. The Henleys had been looking for a house in the Woking area for some time and moved there on 26 March.
[2] *The Winter's Tale*, IV. iii. 28. WEH probably needed the information for his edition of Shakespeare.

Well, how to put that? Autolycus constantly examples his confession by falling down & wishing he'd never been born, & swearing he was murdered & robbed; & so cops the Clown.[3] Well, now, Arthur Morrison, how to put into words?

I didn't answer your last, because I really didn't see that I could help you any way. My dear boy, you've done a good thing[4] — a blamed good thing; & there's an end on't. All *I* can do, to look on, & applaud.

But I'll look at the letter again; & if I can find anything in it that needs reply, I'll take it on. Meanwhile, it's packed & inaccessible.

We go to Woking to-morrow morn. We'll be there, I think, about a fortnight when we come back to Battersea. And so we shall go dodging back & forth, I take it till early summer. Is it to be there or here? Like the cabman in Pickwick: 'All I asts is vhere?'

Yours Always,
W.E.H.

[3] A character in the play.
[4] *The Hole in the Wall.*

To Charles Whibley, 7 April 1902
ALS: Morgan. Published in Connell, 371.

Heather Brae, Maybury Hill, Woking

Dear Boy,

I got badly thrown on my way hither, on Coombe & Malden station.[1] By one extraordinary piece of luck (or turn of favour) I saved my life. But I was horribly shaken, & I've had to be in cotton-wool (so to speak) all the time. I am still a bit groggy, at times, so I shall not be at Battersea so soon as I'd hoped.

I'd have writ before; but 'tis enough that these things happen. To write about them afterwards is difficult. So please, forgive.

E.A.Y.
W.E.H.

[1] On 26 March. The accident was not reported in the local press. Williamson states that WEH was 'dragged some way along the platform' as he attempted to board the train. In a letter to A. Hass, 13 May 1902 (Payen-Payne), WEH writes: 'A fool-guard started his train before I could board it. ... I got off with a severe shaking and a shock to the system which made me useless and worse for five weeks.'

To Frederick George Kitton,[1] **8 May 1902**
ALS: Morgan

Heather Brae, Maybury Hill, Woking

Dear Sir,

I am glad to hear that the unexpected has (as usual) come off; & I will take on *Chuzzlewit*[2] with very great pleasure. My terms are £7 per thousand words.

All the same, I am sorry to lose the two books — the *Uncommercial* & *American Notes* — of which I wrote: there is so much of all but the very best Dickens in the first; while the second is matter for a very curious & entertaining Introduction, which (for the rest) I have at my finger ends, & *which wants writing*. If, then, it were possible, I would gladly take on these as well.

If you *have* a book to give away, I should like to put it in the way of Mr. Leslie Cope Cornford (1 Madeira Estate, Black Rock, Brighton), who is an ardent Dickensite, & has written a very competent & illuminating little book on Stevenson. His interest (he's primarily a novelist) is in story & character; but if you don't give me the *Uncommercial* (for instance), I am sure that he would introduce it beautifully: with a real feeling (that is) for the excellent & remarkable work which it sets forth.[3]

Yours Very Truly,
W. E. Henley

PS.

Cornford's *Stevenson* was done for Blackwood: in the series for which I'm down for a Dickens.

---

[1] Frederick George Kitton (1865-1903), writer, artist, and editor of more than one edition of Dickens.
[2] WEH had been asked to contribute to Kitton's new edition of *The Complete Works of Charles Dickens*, 15 vols (1903-08). He contributed the introduction to vol. 9, *Reprinted Pieces*, but he died before his introduction was typeset. The *Uncommercial Traveller* (a collection of articles from *Household Words*) and *American Notes* were not included in this edition.
[3] Cornford did not contribute.

To H. G. Wells, 23 May 1902
ALS: Illinois

19 Albert Mansions, Battersea, S.W.

Dear H.G.,

I gather from your esteemed favour (1) that you are developing a bow-window; (2) that Philip is getting articulate;[1] & (3) that you are writing a book.[2] 1 & 2 are in the lie of things — the natural order. But what price the book? I want to know about *that*.

As for me: I am a common humbug. *I'm* all right. Given a good surgeon, & the question is What can't you do? On Friday, 9*th* May, I took a lot of chloroform, etc; & on Sunday 18*th* May I came on to these cupboards, a better man than I've been for months.[3] I'll tell you all about it when we meet. 'Which God send soon.'

Our address at Woking: at which we purpose to be found in the first days of June; is Heather Brae, Maybury Hill. Come; & see; & *envy*.

Yours Ever,
W.E.H.

[1] George Philip Wells was born on 17 July 1901.
[2] Probably Wells's *The Sea Lady* which was published in August 1902.
[3] The nature of the operation has not been discovered.

To Austin Dobson, 13 June 1902
ALS: London

Heather Brae, Maybury Hill, Woking

My dear A.D.,

I am very glad to have the *C.G.J.*[1] if it were only for the matter under the head-line *Covent Garden*. Be sure that I'll cherish the volume, & return it to you safe & sound, as soon as ever I've broke the back of my Introduction.[2]

Of your *Journal of a V. to L.*[3] I'll only say that I think Croscup is very lucky in winning you to let him print it in the edition of his. I would, with all my heart, that he could persuade you to annotate the plays & all like this![4] It ought to be done & it will never be done unless you do it.

[1] *The Covent Garden Journal*. By Sir Alexander Drawcansir [Henry Fielding], a twice-weekly paper, 4 January 1752-11 November 1752.
[2] *The Works of Henry Fielding*, 16 vols, with an essay by WEH, published by Croscup and Sterling (New York, 1902) and Heinemann (1903). The edition was of 385 copies per publisher to subscribers only.
[3] An edition of Fielding's *Journal of a Voyage to Lisbon* was published by Dobson in 1891.
[4] Dobson did not annotate the plays.

I wired (*excusez de peu!*) to you for the *Miscellanies*.[5] I can't get 'em out of the L.L.[6]

It has rained, rained, rained all day; & I feel at least two hundred years old. Well, well——

Yours Ever,
W.E.H.

[5] WEH received the book, which was needed for his work on *Slang*, by 16 June 1902 (WEH to Austin Dobson, 16 June 1902, London University).
[6] The London Library.

To John Stephen Farmer, 16 June 1902
ALS: Morgan

Heather Brae, Maybury Hill, Woking

Dear Mr. Farmer,

Many thanks for both of yours. In reply: — (a) I've no slips yet from Stockwell. Who seems to have gone mad with forgetfulness.

(b) I like your idea of reprinting the *travesties*; but I don't see why you should include *Hudibras*[1] among 'em. It isn't a *travestie* for one thing: I mean, it isn't a burlesque of any piece of literature. Cotton, Radcliffe, Bridges[2] — these are all right; but Butler's out of it. Moreover, he has been so often reprinted, & can be had for so little, that reprinting is scarce worth your while. On the other hand, if your game to burlesque verse, what price Henry Fielding with the *Covent Garden Tragedy* & *Tom Thumb the Great*?[3] To my mind the best burlesque in the language, if we ignore Byron & that marvellous *Vision of Judgement*.[4]

(c) I think it should be impressed on Stockwell that *I* can't always keep my dates: especially when *he* doesn't keep his. There are times when I've nought to do, & the slips would be most welcome; & again there are times when every moment I bestow upon the slips is stolen from other & more profitable work. If he would keep his promise, I'd keep mine — anyhow. Can nothing be done to make him play up?

[1] A satirical poem by Samuel Butler published in three parts in 1663, 1664 and 1678.
[2] Charles Cotton (1630-87), poet and translator, published his *Scarronnides*, a burlesque of the *Aeneid*, in 1664. Mrs Ann Radcliffe, *née* Ward (1764-1823), a leading writer of the Gothic novel. Her most successful novel was *The Mysteries of Udolpho* (1794). Thomas Bridges (*fl.* 1759-75), playwright and satirical writer. He published a parody of Homer in 1762 and a burlesque of Milton's *Paradise Lost* in 1765.
[3] Fielding's farce *Tom Thumb, a Tragedy* (1730) was published in a different version as *The Tragedy of Tragedies, or, The Life and Death of Tom Thumb the Great* in 1731.
[4] Byron's satirical poem published in 1822.

(d) I suppose that there's nothing for it but to face the music, & give the 3 extra sheets &, as that is the case, the sooner the music's faced the better.

Yours Very Truly,

W.E.H.

I *do* hope the burlesques will come off; & the *Merry Songs* also.[5]

Much thanks for the Tom Brown. When you next go to the B.M., could you find me the date?

---

[5] Farmer was desperately in need of finance and had published in 1895-97 his *Merry Songs and Ballads* in five volumes. He included some poems from the *Merry Muses* taken from WEH's transcripts. He advertised a manuscript issue of fifty holograph copies taken from the original text of the *Merry Muses*. One such copy is known.

To John Stephen Farmer, 7 August 1902
ALS: Morgan

Heather Brae, Maybury Hill, Woking

Dear Mr. Farmer,

Please, don't give way. It's not true that I dislike your system. What *is* true is that I think you run it too far. Also, it brings you dangerously near the question of origins which question, you remember, should in no case be mooted in our work. For the rest, I see no reason why, with due heed to selection in the matter of quotes, terseness in the matter of definition; & a right-down understanding of what is & what is not slang, we should need any more than one extra part. If you please to talk it out with me, come when you will. Meanwhile, them's my sentiments.

As to 'The Rosy': Dickens may, or may not be, as uncertain as you say he is. This phrase, however, was invented — or rather was made slang by him; in *The Old Curiosity Shop*; & the 1861 perversion (= blood) is simply a reference to 'claret' in the old pugilistical sense.

All right about G. & the holidays.

Yours Always Truly,

W.E.H.

To Sydney Southgate Pawling, 26 September 1902
ALS: RLF

Heather Brae, Maybury Hill, Woking

My dear Pawling,

It's a good thing that, for men of Pugh's parts in Pugh's case,[1] there is such a charity as the Literary Fund. I knew him — I still know him — as a writer of extraordinary promise & of performance scarce less extraordinary; &, as you know, I gave him every chance I could. His was an unique experience, & he wrote of it with an unique pen. Lower-middle-class London (if I may say so) has had, to my thinking, very few more faithful &, at the same time, more masterly & brilliant exponents than the author of *A Man of Straw*. I cannot tell why he has not succeeded: I can but suppose that the cause of his failure, or break-down, or whatever we like to call it, is that bad health, whose ills you did so much to palliate in the beginnings of your connexion with him. Be this as it may, the fact is, that he has broken down, & that this uncommon talent is in danger of extinction. Clearly, he is a case for the Literary Fund; & I think that we should press his claim upon it as hard as ever we can.

There is so much that is exceptional in the poor boy's case: the grinding poverty from which you rescued him, & in which he observed his material, & continued to practice, as it were at death's door, his art; the quality & the completeness of his results, as soon as he had fairly recovered from his origins; the fine courage & the good apprehensive spirit which were essential in him for so long. (Indeed, they are few I know, of whom I could write as I can of him.) What, I take it, he now wants is rest: rest, & the where withal to make another book. If I can help him, with you, to a grant from the Fund I shall be better pleased than I can say. A mind & a pen like Pugh's are rare; & I say this knowing (as you know I know) something about it.

I've nothing else to say; but if I can advance Pugh's interests by writing to the Committee, or interviewing Presidents or anything of that sort, here I am.

Yours Ever Sincerely,
W.E.H.

---

[1] The novelist William Edwin Pugh had applied to the R.L.F. on 23 September 1902 and received £75. His earlier stories of the slum life of the London cockney were now no longer in vogue and he had fallen on hard times.

To Arthur Morrison, 9 November 1902
ALS: Rochester

Heather Brae, Maybury Hill, Woking

My dear Arthur M.,

I fancy 'Badalia H.'[1] is ahead of you in point of time. But what of that? She's a poor thing, anyhow; & the fool that would call *Mean Streets* an imitation is fool enough to say anything. Why vex your soul about him?

Meanwhile, I rejoice in *The Hole in the Wall*. It's excellent good work; & 'tis good news to see it's in its Third Edition.

You must send me your *Painters in Japan*,[2] anon. I'd love to read. And I do not see the review.

I've no news: except that I've been for three short spins in Harmsworth's best motor, & *am infatuated*.[3] Also, I'm better — far better — than I was. Also, I've lots of little tinkering jobs on hand, & never seem to get any of 'em done; so that when it will be Battersea again is more than I know.

Yours Ever,
W.E.H.

---

[1] Rudyard Kipling's 'The Record of Badalia Herodsfoot' was one of the stories in his *Many Inventions* (1893).

[2] Morrison's *The Painters of Japan* was published in the *Monthly Review*, July 1902-December 1902 (less October). It was later published in two volumes in 1911.

[3] The result of this was a poem 'A Song of Speed. To Alfred Harmsworth', *World's Work*, April 1903. It was subsequently published in booklet form as *A Song of Speed* (1903). Alfred Charles William Harmsworth (1865-1922), journalist and newspaper magnate and proprietor. He founded the *Daily Mail* in 1896 and was chief proprietor of *The Times* from 1908 until his death. He was created 1st Viscount Northcliffe in 1917. He was a friend of the Henleys and after WEH's death he paid Anna's rent at Park Mansions, Battersea, for nineteen years (R. Pound and G. Harmsworth, *Northcliffe*, 1959, 262).

To H. G. Wells, 17 November 1902
ALS: Illinois

Heather Brae, Maybury Hill, Woking

My dear H.G.,

How are you & yours? Especially George Philip? You might let us know: big & glorious & resplendent as you are, you might let us know. I think you might. Yes; H.G.; I *almost* think, you might. You don't agree? Ah, well! Probably (being a successful author: a man who might buy a motor-car, if he cared to do anything so like everybody else), you're right. Let me, *please*, apologize for addressing you with that insufferable familiarity. Dear Mr. Wells (then), do not be angered, nor suffer a simple wrinkle to distain the marble of your millionairish brow. Suffer me to start again, & to start in a vein which better becomes (if I may be allowed an opinion in the matter) our respective stations.

Honoured Sir,

And Patron (if I may venture to so express myself), I take the liberty to introduce to your notice a Cove, one Ernest Dawson, fresh from South Africa (*viâ* Burma, where the poor bloke holds an appointment), & delighted to think, & to hold, & to believe that, through my humble intermediary, he may be permitted to gaze upon that Celebrated Author of *The Time Machine*, & even, if that Celebrated Author be moved to condescend to his great but simple need, on an Author, Celebrated indeed, but not so Celebrated as the Celebrated H. G. Wells: I mean the Celebrated Joseph Conrad.[1] He is a good Cove (though I say it that shouldn't); so treat him as a good Cove should be treated by a Celebrated Author. Also, he is a large, quiet, human kind of Cove; so if I may, honoured Mr. Wells, express myself in terms of a familiarity which, in my grovelling state, I am far from feeling, do the best for him you can, & be d—d to you.

I've a Stomach; & a Liver; & there are times when I'm almost mad with either one or the other. But neither is perennial. Have you nothing to tell me of Pugh? Our love to you both.

E.A.,
W.E.H.

[1] After twenty years as a seaman Conrad settled on a literary career in England in 1894 and his experiences at sea run through many of his novels. WEH published *The Nigger of the 'Narcissus'* in the *New Review* from August to December 1897. From the start of his writing career in England Conrad had set out to establish his place in letters by being published by Henley. On hearing that the *Nigger* was to appear in the *New Review* Conrad wrote: 'Now I have conquered Henley, I ain't 'fraid of the divvle himself' (Conrad to Edward Garnett, 7 December 1896, in *The Collected Letters of Joseph Conrad*, eds F. R. Karl and L. Davies, Cambridge, 1983-86, vol. 1).

To Lord Windsor, 30 November 1902
ALS: Morgan

Heather Brae, Maybury Hill, Woking

My dear Lord,

As that powerful thinker, the Governor of North Carolina, observed to that mighty Intellect, the Governor of South Carolina: — 'It's a long time between drinks'.[1] And I wonder why. Worthing was accessible enough: even to Birds.

[1] This is a reference to a traditional story which RLS used in *The Wrong Box* (ch. VIII) where one of the characters remarked: ' "Do you know … what the Governor of South Carolina said to the Governor of North Carolina?" "It's a long time between drinks", observed that powerful

Woking is not accessible at all: especially, it seems to Birds. And what I'd like to know is whether or not it's any fault of mine.

I've had vile times since I saw & talked with you. Times are so vile that I've kept no Jovian eye on portrait-painters, & even Rodin has fallen out of my field of vision. If this were not so, I should have writ to you weeks ago to ask you, as C.C. of W.,[2] for a place in one or other of the Parks in which Rodin could set up an exhibition of his *Oeuvre*, as he did in Paris,[3] & has since done in Prague.[4] It is possible, it is even probable, that others have stirred in this matter before me. If that be so, I will merely urge you (if I may say so) to incline most favourably to the pleading of *Your Petitioners.*[5] And if it be not, I will, if you will tell me so, proceed to badger you in the good old official way.

Meanwhile, what (I ask it again) — *what* have we done that no Birds have come to us from Hewell, & none from Shropshire neither?

Yours Ever Sincerely,
W. E. Henley

thinker.' The conversation was also used by Kipling in his *The Light that Failed* (ch. 8).
[2] Lord Windsor was Chief Commissioner of Works.
[3] June 1900.
[4] Prague, May 1902.
[5] A London exhibition was not held.

To Charles Whibley, 21 December 1902
ALS: Morgan

Heather Brae, Maybury Hill, Woking

My dear Charles,

You are for the *Fielding* (16 vols.). Thus much I am assured. But as for the - when: I can say nothing. It beats me. All I know is, they forced my hand on the Terminal,[1] so as to make me deliver it in August, & they are still footling with the proofs. A fortnight more, & I could have done my best work.

You say no word to me about the date of the *Thackeray.*[2] Why?

E.A.Y.
W.E.H.

[1] WEH's Introduction.
[2] Whibley's book.

To J. A. Hammerton,[1] **[?late 1902]**
ALS: Morgan

Heather Brae, Maybury Hill, Woking

Dear Sir,

By all means, use the 'Apparition',[2] if you think it fills the bill. As for the prose,[3] please send me the stuff you wish to quote, & I will pass it in judgement. I can say nothing about it until I have it before me.

Yours Faithfully,
W. E. Henley

J. A. Hammerton

---

[1] John Alexander Hammerton (1871-1949), writer, journalist, compiler and editor of *Stevensoniana: an Anecdotal Life and Appreciation of Robert Louis Stevenson* (Edinburgh 1903). Knighted 1932.

[2] The poem describing the young RLS was used.

[3] This was WEH's *Pall Mall Magazine* article on RLS. He gave permission for its use. In his introduction to the revised edition of *Stevensoniana* (1907), Hammerton, commenting on a criticism he had received for printing even part of the article, quoted a letter from WEH:

> As for the *P.M.M.* I want to make a distinction. You may take all you wish of it, till you come to the last paragraph. You excerpt a few lines from this: but I bar. *Take the whole paragraph, please*; or end on 'rare fellows in their day.' You see, it cost me a lot to write that paragraph. I should not have written it, had I not felt the occasion very instant. Had I known what I know now, I should pretty certainly have dotted i's and crossed t's. I say no more. Only I say that that paragraph is what I mean, and what I want to leave.

To H. G. Wells, [?January 1903]
ALS: Illinois

Heather Brae, Maybury Hill, Woking

My dear H.G.,

I've read, by accident, your remarks on the teaching of English in the current *Fortnightly*,[1] God prosper you! And may I live to rejoice in your prosperity!

But I've my doubts. Do they want it? *Voyons un peu.* Henley & Whibley's *Prose* was designed in three vols, would have included all manner of master-bits, in character & narrative, between John of Trevisa[2] & Charles Dickens; would have been, as I believe, the best guide to English ever conceivable done.

---

[1] Wells's 'Mankind in the Making. IV: The Beginnings of the Mind and Language', *Fortnightly Review*, January 1903.

[2] John de Trevisa (c.1340-1401), English prose translator.

Why isn't it, you says? Because that rotten pro-Boerizer Methuen,[3] calmly stept in & bucked the scheme. It wasn't in a line with the wretched, piddling school books on his list, you see; & Charles & I owe money on it to this day; besides being disconsidered for an arbitrary & (to all appearances) given futile determination of limits, we offered to buy it of the bugger. And would he sell it? Not *him*! So there it stinks & rots; & if God only condemns him to rot & stink in the same way, I'll be a Deist right away.

Again, you ask for a lyric anthology. Have you seen mine? If you haven't, ask the same Methuen to spring you a copy. I owe him money on that, too. Yet I believe it will realize your ideal of what a lyric anthology should be. Does he sell it? Not a bloody bit of it. He has a very large 'school connection'; &, as I said, I owe him money on it. As many as nine copies were sold in these Islands last year, & one Colonial (God! how I'd like to meet him!) went a mucker on it. Into that book I put myself, H.G.: myself & five & twenty years of such scholarship as I've achieved. And that bloody Pro-Boer has rendered it of none avail. That book has every thing in it that a school-book should have: it ranges between Chaucer & Poe, it takes in the Bible, I think there's no good lyric in English but is contained in it; & every year the Pro-Boer tells me I owe him money on it. And he'll no more sell this one than he'll sell the other. The other — the *Prose* — he cut up inhumanly in delivering; this one he has only aborted. The result's the same. That old jackass Palgrave's *Golden Treasury* is a property. This, an hundred times the better book, is a [   ]. *Et puis voilà.*

Write (if you haven't it already) to Nutt, & ask him to send you *Lyra Heroica*. That has got into schools,[4] & the youth of England is being trained on it. I hope George Philip will bless me for it presently; whatever his parent think of it. At any rate, if you don't know it, look at it, & we'll talk when we meet.

The 22*nd* Jan. is our Silver Wedding day; & we hope to spend it at 31 Park Mansions, Battersea Park, S.W. If you're at that Inn of yours, & don't look in on us, that day, so shall you be Eternally damned, [   ], harried, & bemauled, even as the Pro-Boerizer of whom I've written.

Yours Ever,
W.E.H.

---

[3] Methuen's *Peace or War in South Africa* was favourable to the Boers and on page 2 a quotation from the *Guardian* describes Methuen as 'Pro-Boer'.
[4] The last school edition was in 1912.

To Charles Baxter, 18 January 1903
ALS: British Columbia

Heather Brae, Maybury Hill, Woking

My dear Charles,

On Thursday, the 22*nd*, we celebrate (furtively & shyly, as becomes our modest place in the World of Letters) our Silver Wedding Day. So far as I know, the tryst is Café Verrey, 1 p.m.; but human life is full of accidents, & there may be rubs; in which case 31 Park Mansions, Battersea Park, S.W., is the general *rendez-vous*. And there you are. And now, hark back over five-&-twenty years, & recall the Church[1] & the old sun, & the swept-up snow; & St. David's St., & the excellent advice you gave us at the fire-side, before we started for Tron.[2] I think there was a fiver in it. Or was it more? I know not. Anyhow I remember the advice. Mr. Micawber could have done no better;[3] & I wish, with all my heart, we'd been able to abide by it.

This, however, is by the way. The main thing is, Thursday is our Silver Wedding day; & that, whatever has come & gone meanwhile, we cannot let it go by, without a word to our oldest friend nor a reminder to him of that day, a quarter-century ago, when he looked so well, talked so well, did so well, that it seemed that any shadow of dissention, parting, unkindness, was impossible.

Your Ever Affectionate,
(Always)
W.E.H.
A.J.H.

[1] Baxter was one of the two official witnesses of the marriage on 22 January 1878, the other being Anne Jenkin. Baxter replied from Paris on 21 January that he was unable to attend and that 'how well I remember that morning' (Pierpont Morgan).
[2] On their honeymoon?
[3] Mr Wilkins Micawber's famous remark in *David Copperfield*: 'Annual income twenty pounds, annual expenditure nineteen nineteen six, result happiness. Annual income twenty pounds, annual expenditure twenty pounds ought and six, result misery' (ch. 12).

To Charles Whibley, 8 March 1903
ALS: Morgan

31 Park Mansions, Battersea, S.W.

What is wrong, Charles? Have you also got appendicitis? Or what?

And where is your bloody *Thackeray*? And will you kindly return those *occupying* slips? And will you please state whether or not you acknowledge yourself for the biggest *quacker* in the world?

I hear that H.C. is *de retour*. Also that he reminds the *Spectator* of Richard Le Gallienne.[1] Well, well!

E.A.
W.E.H.

PS. Look out for Raleigh's *Wordsworth*: published to-morrow. A fierce brilliant attempt to make something out of nothing.

[1] I have not found any reference to Harry Cust in the *Spectator*.

To John Alexander Todd,[1] 25 March 1903
ALS: Duke

19 Albert Mansions, Battersea, S.W.

Dear Mr. Todd,
    This is to ask you, please, to send Tybalt,[2] on Thursday next (the 27th) to his new home, by the train for Guildford, which leaves Worthing at 11.50 a.m. At Guildford his Mistress will meet him, & cycle with him thence to Woking. His address there is 'Heather Brae, Maybury Hill'; & if you send your account to it, I doubt not it will be duly honoured.
    I think this Shoreham-Horsham-Guildford route's the best for him. We've talked it over a great deal, his Mistress & I; & we think it's the best. Please pay his fare , then, to Guildford; &, if necessary, tip the Guard; & tell him to let the beast have plenty of water. And I shall be forever obliged to you.
    He's a ruffian, of course. But he's very dear to us. And I thank you very heartily for the care you've had of him, & the pains you've taken with him. I look to see him outlast us both. If you can give me any tips to that end, please do so.

Yours Very Truly,
W. E. Henley

[1] John Alexander Todd (b. 1871) M.R.C.V.S, the Worthing Veterinary and Canine infirmary, Chapel Road, Worthing. He graduated from the Glasgow Veterinary College on 18 July 1896 and then practised in Brighton before moving to Worthing. While in Worthing he was Veterinary-Lieutenant to the Sussex Imperial Yeomanry. He later moved to West Kirby, Cheshire. He is last mentioned in the *Register of Veterinary Surgeons* for 1917 and I have been unable to find any other information.
[2] WEH's Irish Terrier had been in kennels for about a month (WEH to Todd, 22 February 1903, Duke University).

PS.

We go to Woking to-morrow (Wednesday) morning. His Majesty's Post is rot. Send us a telegram, please, to say that some form of Irish Terrier will exist in Worthing for some time. I am rather inclined to believe that, when the end comes, Woking & Worthing will in the matter go arm in arm.

To George Wyndham, 31 March 1903
ALS: Morgan

31 Park Mansions, Battersea Park, S.W.

My dear George,

Make it Thursday or Friday if you can. For we must to Woking on the 8th or 9th; or, if we overstay that limit, remain here till the holiday's over. Which I don't want to do; in as much as I must forthwith buckle to work in earnest.

If it ain't be so, you must give me Saturday or Sunday, very soon. Saturday night at Sutton Court;[1] Sunday on the Mercedes, with the Young Napoleon; & lunch [ ] at Maybury.

Did Arthur read the *Song*? I wonder! If there be no 'reviewing' this quarter I shall eliminate the ambitions from my final programme.

I am sorry that there's nothing done as yet for that other party you wot of. It would have been better bestowed than in nine-tenths of the cases we know.[2] Ten times better, at least.

I've read the *Song* again. I shudder here & there. But it's all right. I feel that the trick is done, & that it won't be better done in that way in my time, anyhow. I've had some good letters; but the Glorious Press has either funked or burked it.

Iwan told me that on the night of the speech you covered yourself with glory:[3] 'personal. political, & ministerial'. I for my part, don't see how such a statement: one so bristling with figures, technicalities, difficulties: *could* have been better made, 'simple & dignified': so wrote C. Whibley to me. And what better could you have? They used to wallow before the Old Rotter's Budgets; but not one of them could compare with the desperate, the almost uncanny lucidity of this one. I rejoice, George dear, & am exceedingly glad that you are *not* an orator: I mean in the bad sense of the word; that is, that you are not 3/4ths historian & 1/8th a man of affairs. And I am sure that, if I live long enough, I shall see you do bigger things & talk on bigger things than this.

---

[1] Sutton Place, near Guilford, Surrey, was the home of Alfred Harmsworth.
[2] James MacLaren Cobban had applied to the Royal Literary Fund, his sponsors being WEH and Iwan-Müller. He was granted £50 on 6 April 1903.
[3] Wyndham introduced the Irish Land Purchase Bill on 25 March in the House of Commons. *The Times*, 26 March 1903, reported that 'Mr. Wyndham's speech yesterday fully deserves the praise for lucidity of statement and for generosity of spirit which it was received in all quarters of the House of Commons.' It became law, with amendments, on 14 August of the same year.

Meanwhile, be happy in the thought of a renewed, a rejuvenated Ireland; & stay where you are, till your work is as good as done.

It's a good enough government, if they would but see it. But they can't, or won't. They won't see Arthur, or you, & Arnold Forster, & Chamberlain, & Selborne, & Onslow,[4] & Windsor. They can see nothing but Brodrick,[5] & George Hamilton.[6] I hear that Harry is Caving,[7] also Gilbert Parker. *What* do they want? And, if they want anything, why don't they join the opposition at once? True politics is an extraordinary game: 'a most astronrary & assontic' business.

Send me a telegram to-morrow, if possible, to say if it shall be here or *là-bas*.

Yours ever affectionate,
W.E.H.

[4] William Waldegrave Palmer (1859-1942), as 2nd Earl of Selborne was Under-Secretary for the Colonies, 1895-1900; William Hillier Onslow (1853-1911), as 4th Earl of Onslow was Under-Secretary for the Colonies, 1900-03.
[5] (William) St John (Freemantle) Brodrick (1856-1942) was Secretary of State for War, 1900-03.
[6] George Francis Hamilton (1845-1927), Secretary of State for India, 1895-1903.
[7] Political slang for a small group within a political party who disagree with the main body.

To Arthur Llewellyn Roberts, 4 May 1903
ALS: RLF

Heather Brae, Maybury Hill, Woking

Dear Sir,

Mr. J. S. Farmer, with whom I have collaborated, these some years past, on a *Dictionary of Slang & it's Analogues*, tells me that he has applied to your Fund for a grant in aid, & asks me to support his application.[1] I have very great pleasure in acceding to his request.

It is a fact that during the last eighteen months he has worked so hard that the work in which I am particularly interested is some 800 to 900 pages longer than it was, & that all this compilation has been done in the teeth of all manner of difficulties, set-backs, troubles, disheartenings. It is a pleasure to me to reflect that, thanks to this solid effort on Mr. Farmer's part, we are appreciably nearer to the end of what I do not hesitate to say is out-&-away the best, the fullest, & the most scholarly & smart lexicon of its kind ever done in English, or, for that matter, in French either.

I can help the enterprize, & I have helped it, with counsel, corrections,

[1] Farmer applied on the 4 May 1903 and was awarded £50.

readily as I am able to command. But I cannot help it with money; & therefore I am especially happy in asking help for its author from your Fund, & on backing an appeal which has, I believe, the support of so excellent a scholar and so good & thorough-paced a man of letters as Dr. Furnivall.[2]

Yours Very Faithfully,
W. E. Henley

L. Roberts Esq.

[2] Furnivall, together with WEH and Henry Bradley, supported Farmer. Henry Bradley (1845-1923), writer and lexicographer. Senior editor of the *Oxford Dictionary*, 1915-23.

To Lord Windsor, 12 June 1903
ALS: Morgan

Heather Brae, Maybury Hill, Woking

My dear Lord,
This infernal *renouveau* has been too much for me; & I feel a hundred winters old. I can do nothing: not even write letters. And I'm a good six weeks behind all my engagements; so that I enter on the blasting summer which is (apparently) before us with health & spirits 'in a concatenation ascending'.

You said you were grateful to me for *Speed*? I can't believe it's I you mean. It must be somebody else of the same name. No palsied old wreck like *me* could ever have made any such verse as *that*. However, ...

I hope to see you when you get back to town. Either here or at Battersea. Alfred Harmsworth has been giving me the use of an excellent Panhard; & I've had some good spins on it. But the north-easters & the rains have fairly knocked it on the head; & I find myself biffed in that direction, as in all others.

However — — —

Yours Ever Sincerely,
W.E.H.[1]

[1] At his death on 11 July 1903 WEH left work outstanding but also debts of about £500. He had also had an advance of £200 for literary work. Wyndham and Lord Windsor cleared the debts and Barrie repaid the £200 advance. WEH was cremated at Brookwood Cemetery, Worthing, on 14 July. Among the many mourners were George Wyndham, Barrie, Wells, Kenneth Grahame, Charles Whibley and Lord Windsor. WEH's ashes were buried in his daughter's grave at Cockayne Hatley. A Memorial Fund was launched and on 11 July 1907 Rodin's copy of his bust of WEH was unveiled in the Crypt of St Paul's Cathedral by the Earl of Plymouth (Lord Windsor). In his address the Earl of Plymouth referred to the "two great traits in his character which we all recognise — courage and enthusiasm — a courage which enabled him, or rather impelled him, to make the most at all times of his brilliant talents that Providence had blessed him with.' WEH's enthusiasm was "an enthusiasm which acted like a sort of vivifying

cordial amongst his disciples, and it will not be said that the least of his enduring work was the power of obtaining the best results from others and of enabling them to make the best use of their talents.' Harry Cust best summed up WEH as a man: 'From myself, and I am not meet to be called a disciple, a debt is due. Henley can never be repaid or forgotten. I came to him a perfect stranger and I found in an hour a friend for life, a master of difficulty and emergency, a wise, if somewhat strenuous, mentor and counsellor' (*The Henley Memorial*, 1908).

Index of Recipients

Index